FRANCIS OF ASSISI

Pope Kenny
Toan Nguyen
of Europe

FRANCIS OF ASSISI

A New Biography

[AUGUSTINE THOMPSON, O.P.]

CORNELL UNIVERSITY PRESS

ITHACA AND LONDON

FRONTISPIECE ILLUSTRATION
Frater Franciscus, anonymous fresco, before 1228, Sacro Speco,
Monastero di San Benedetto, Subiaco, Italy.
Used with permission.

First published 2012 by Cornell University Press

Printed in the United States of America

Library of Congress Cataloging-in-Publication Data

Thompson, Augustine.
 Francis of Assisi: a new biography / Augustine Thompson.
  p. cm.
 Includes bibliographical references and index.
 ISBN 978-0-8014-5070-9 (cloth: alk. paper)
 1. Francis, of Assisi, Saint, 1182–1226. 2. Christian saints—
Italy—Assisi—Biography. I. Title.
 BX4700.F6T46 2012
 271'.302—dc23
 [B]   2011037724

Cloth printing 10 9 8 7 6 5 4 3

[CONTENTS]

PART II
Sources and Debates

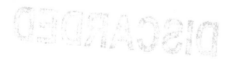

[INTRODUCTION]

THIS BOOK IS subtitled *A New Biography,* by which I mean not just a recent biography, but one that also presents a new portrait of the man known as Saint Francis of Assisi. We are fortunate to have a great mass of stories, anecdotes, reports, and writings about Francis dating from his own century, most of which scholars now consider in some or all respects "legendary." This life is the first sustained attempt in English to treat these medieval sources for Francis in a consistently, sometimes ruthlessly, critical manner. The goal is to reveal, as much as we can, the man behind the legends.

With one notable exception—the Italian Francis scholar Raoul Manselli—even academic writers on Francis seem to rely on the same set of stories mostly put together in the same way. Or, after Manselli, they do not go much beyond his reconstructions. Sometimes they even claim that it is impossible to find the man behind the legends. Popular writers, on the other hand, give different spins to Francis's life as a whole but usually repeat events in it as if their historical truth were obvious. Or, at best, they label them "legendary," without attempting to find the historical reality behind them.

In writing this book, I have asked a series of questions about the evidence we have for Francis. First, who wrote the text? Was it Francis, someone who knew him, or someone who just heard about him? Oddly, many popular biographies favor hearsay stories over Francis's own writings. Next, when was the document written? I have great doubts about whether we can trust reports composed over two generations after Francis's death, and for which we have no earlier evidence. This is especially the case with miracle stories, not because

I do not think miracles happen, but because Francis was a canonized saint, and for medieval people, adding more miracles to his "biography" was not fraud, but an act of homage and piety. The famous Wolf of Gubbio failed that test. On the other hand, Francis's life would be incomplete without the popular perception of miraculous power that surrounded his person after he became a "living saint" in his later years. Above all, I have been highly skeptical of any story in which Francis is made the mouthpiece for a party involved in some debate within his order years after his death, especially stories on the Franciscan practice of poverty.

This reading of the sources for Francis has resulted in a number of divergences from the usual story. The Francis I have come to know has proved a more complex and personally conflicted man than the saint of the legends. It is, I think, misleading to assimilate him to some stereotyped image of "holiness," especially one that suggests that a "saint" never has crises of faith, is never angry or depressed, never passes judgments, and never becomes frustrated with himself or others. Francis's very humanity makes him, I think, more impressive and challenging than a saint who embodied that (impossible) kind of holiness. I would also emphasize that my "Historical Francis" is no more the "real Francis" than the Francis of the legends and popular biographies. He is "historical" in that the picture I have painted is the result of historical method, not theological reflection or pious edification. That said, I do think that my Francis is closer to the man known by his thirteenth-century contemporaries than the figure we find in the modern biographies I have read. I do hope that my portrait reveals a Francis that will provide stimulus for new theological reflection and for richer Christian piety.

I came to Francis as something of an outsider. As a historian, I was new to the contentious and often bitter world of academic controversy over the Historical Francis. Especially for his modern followers, the Franciscan friars, nuns, sisters, and lay tertiaries, how one imagines Francis and his concerns has powerful, sometimes highly divisive, implications for living one's life today. I have no personal stake in those internal Franciscan debates. As Americans colloquially say, I don't have a dog in that fight.

But I must also be forthcoming. Although I write principally as a historian, I am also a Catholic Christian, a priest, and a member of the Order of Preachers, the Dominicans, who are often considered the twin of Francis's own Friars Minor. I admit that I never had much devotion to Saint Francis, and I always found it mildly amusing that we Dominicans refer to him as "Our Holy Father Francis," using the title "Father," which he went out of his way to avoid. As I have worked on this biography, my respect for Francis and for his vision has increased, and I hope that this book will speak to modern people, believers and unbelievers alike, and that the Francis I have come to know will have something to say to them today.

Some readers of this book will be scholars, perhaps Franciscans, who have spent years studying the Middle Ages, the Order of Friars Minor, or its founder. They will have questions about methods and sources; for those readers I have provided commentaries on each chapter in part 2 of this book, "Sources and Debates." These explain the decisions that lie behind my narrative. The section of "Sources and Debates" titled "On the 'Franciscan Question'" answers some questions that all readers might have about the scholarly debates, which are usually characterized as the "Search for the Historical Francis" and have now lasted over one hundred years. Specialists will want to read all these commentary sections systematically, probably along with the life. Other readers will want to look into these comments only occasionally, when they wonder about why I describe incidents of Francis's life the way I do. Readers who want to consult the commentary sections will find page references there that correspond to the text of the life.

If readers are in their fifties, as I am, they may have been introduced to Francis by Franco Zefferelli's film *Brother Sun, Sister Moon,* the last and perhaps greatest monument in a line of romantic interpretations going back over a hundred years. In this story, Francis was a free spirit, a wild religious genius, a kind of medieval hippie, misunderstood and then exploited by the "medieval Church." Or perhaps they know him as the man who spoke to animals, a nature mystic, an ecologist, a pacifist, a feminist, a "voice for our time." For others, he is the little plaster man on the birdbath, the most charming and nonthreatening of Catholic saints. Like Jesus, Francis belongs to everyone, and so everyone, or almost everyone, has his or her own Francis. And this is probably the way it has to be.

In years of teaching, I have often been astounded at how unhappy students can be when they encounter a different Francis from the one they expect. Oddly enough, the most painful moment usually comes when they discover that Saint Francis did not write the "Peace Prayer of Saint Francis"—a popular hymn best known by its opening words "Make me a channel of your peace," and sung to a tune written by the Anglican composer Sebastian Temple. Many are quite shocked to find that this song is not identical to Francis's "Canticle of Brother Sun," from which Zefferelli took the name of his movie. The "Peace Prayer" is modern and anonymous, originally written in French, and dates to about 1912, when it was published in a minor French spiritual magazine, *La Clochette.* Noble as its sentiments are, Francis would not have written such a piece, focused as it is on the self, with its constant repetition of the pronouns "I" and "me," the words "God" and "Jesus" never appearing once. There are a good number of other stories that will not appear here either, "Francis and the Wolf of Gubbio" being perhaps the most famous. Nor will Francis's supposed encounter with Saint Dominic—an omission that very much annoys a number of my Dominican brothers who have read my drafts or discussed this work with me. We all have our own "Francis."

In historical writing, I usually avoid suggesting what the past should mean for modern readers. But as many have asked me what I have learned from Francis, I will make some suggestions as to what he has taught me as a Catholic Christian. I am sure that he will teach each reader something different, so these reflections are purely my own. First, he taught me that the love of God is something that remakes the soul, and doing good for others follows from this; it is not merely doing good to others. Francis was more about being than doing. And the others whom the Christian serves are to be loved for themselves, no matter how unlovable, not because we can fix them by our good works. Second, rather than a call to accomplish any mission, program, or vision, a religious vocation is about a change in one's perception of God and creation. Above all, it has nothing to do with success, personal or corporate, which is something that always eluded Francis. Third, true freedom of spirit, indeed true Christian freedom, comes from obedience, not autonomy. And as Francis showed many times in his actions, obedience is not an abstraction but involves concrete submission to another's will. Freedom means becoming a "slave of all." Last—and I hope this subverts everything I have just written—there are no ready and clear roads to true Christian holiness.

[PART I]

The Life

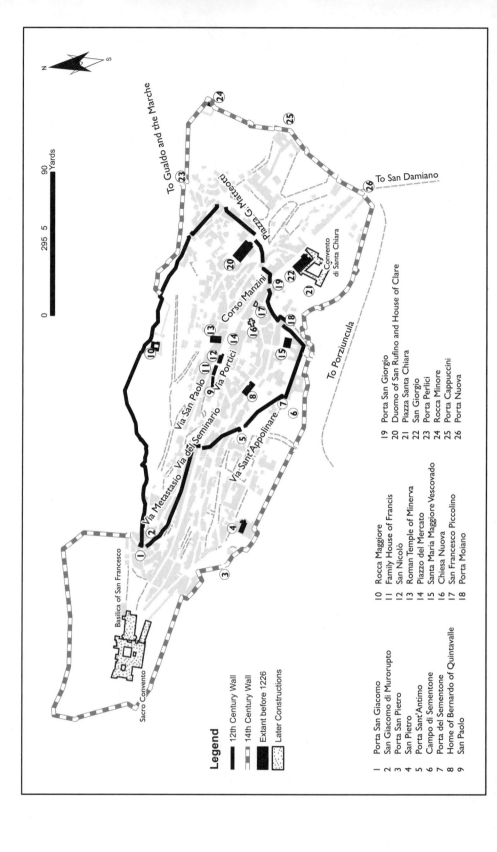

Legend

- ▬ 12th Century Wall
- ▦ 14th Century Wall
- ■ Extant before 1226
- ▦ Later Constructions

1. Porta San Giacomo
2. San Giacomo di Murorupto
3. Porta San Pietro
4. Porta Sant'Antimo
5. Campo di Sementone
6. Porta del Sementone
7. Home of Bernardo of Quintavalle
8. San Paolo
9. San Paolo

10. Rocca Maggiore
11. Family House of Francis
12. San Nicolò
13. Roman Temple of Minerva
14. Piazzo del Mercato
15. Santa Maria Maggiore Vescovado
16. Chiesa Nuova
17. San Francesco Piccolino
18. Porta Moiano

19. Porta San Giorgio
20. Duomo of San Rufino and House of Clare
21. Piazza Santa Chiara
22. San Giorgio
23. Porta Perlici
24. Rocca Minore
25. Porta Cappuccini
26. Porta Nuova

[1]

"WHEN I WAS IN MY SINS"

1181–1205

Francis's City, Home, and Family

TO KNOW A medieval Italian was to know his city, and the man we know as Saint Francis was from Assisi. Assisi lies on a series of terraces on the southwestern slope of a mountain rising nearly 900 feet above the plain in the Valle Umbra, just where the Topino River merges with the Chiascio. The modern city is circled by late medieval walls and covers an area nearly twice that of the early thirteenth-century city. The population of Assisi in Francis's time, between two thousand and three thousand, was about half that within its walls today. It was a city in Francis's day, but by the standards of the time a small city. All the citizens of the commune would have recognized each other on sight, if not by name. Below the city in the Middle Ages, circling the mountain, lay the Via Francigena. On this route, Assisi lay about halfway between two larger cities of the region, Perugia to the northwest and Foligno to the southeast. The Via was the route of commerce, linking the region southward to Rome and north- and westward to the cities of the Tuscany and Lombardy regions. A medieval visitor to Assisi would have entered the town at the southernmost corner of its walls, near what was then the Campo di Sementone. This field was used for military exercises and games. The Campo later gave its name to the Porta di Sementone in the current wall. Travelers entered the city through a gate on what is now Via Sant'Appolinare, near the monastery of that name.

Once inside the walls, it was only a walk of 100 yards to the church of Santa Maria Maggiore, the original cathedral and the palace of the bishop.

From the apse of Santa Maria Maggiore, the medieval wall ran almost directly east, crossing one of the principal medieval streets, now Corso Manzini, which passed out of the city through the Porta San Giorgio, where the Corso now enters Piazza Santa Chiara. Angling a bit north, the wall passed behind the duomo of San Rufino, ending at the north corner of the modern Piazza G. Matteotti. The wall then ran up the hill to Rocca Maggiore at the top. Down the hill, the walls formed a spur westward to Porta San Giacomo and then back toward the city along Via Metastasio. In the late 1100s, when Francis was born, this was a neighborhood of wealthy families—called "Murorupto" from the collapsed Roman walls.

The wall then turned sharply south, at the point where the modern Via San Francesco becomes the Via del Seminario. Here, one passed through the Portella di Panzo on the way to what is now Piazza del Comune, or, in the time of Francis, the Piazza del Mercato. In the 1100s, this piazza was surrounded by fortified towers belonging to powerful families. These were razed following the rise of the *popolo*. After 1212, this new popular government was resident in the palazzo built there on the ruins of the Roman temple of Minerva. In 1228, through expansion to the east, the piazza received its modern dimensions. A little over 150 yards east of this piazza lies the cathedral of San Rufino, reconstructed beginning in 1140 and finally completed through a subvention from the commune in 1210. The altar was not consecrated until 1228, by Gregory IX; the edifice itself was not consecrated until 1253, by Innocent IV. The city wall extended due south from Portella di Panzo to what is now Via Appolinare, just above the modern Porta di Sementone.

The high medieval city thus excluded the areas where today one finds the Sacro Convento and basilica of San Francesco, the church and monastery of Santa Chiara, the Roman amphitheater, and the monastery of San Pietro. Various churches lay outside the walls. That of San Giorgio, where Francis was educated, was outside the gate on what is now Corso Manzini. San Giorgio was demolished in 1259 to construct the church of Santa Chiara. Farther afield, a little over two miles south of the modern city, was the church of San Damiano. Out some two and a half miles to the southwest, during Francis's youth, lay the then-abandoned church of Santa Maria degli Angeli. It pertained to the Benedictine monastery of Subasio and would later play an important role in Francis's life. So, when Francis was born, Assisi was smaller, and the area around it was far less developed and urban than it is today. Even after the expansion of the walls in the later thirteenth and fourteenth centuries, much of the new "urban" area was vacant, without houses or other construction. Open fields extended across the plain to the river below, but even there, as in the area of Santa Maria degli Angeli, there were large tracts of woods.

In comparison to large cities like Florence and Rome, or even nearby Perugia and Foligno, Assisi was a small town of little military or economic importance. But it was not untouched by the political and economic changes of the late twelfth century. Previously subject, like the rest of northern and central Italy, to the overlordship of the German emperors, Assisi, along with other communes of the valley of Spoleto, attempted to throw off imperial control. As a result, it was besieged and taken by the imperial army under the command of Archbishop Christian of Mainz in 1174. On Christmas 1177, while resident in Assisi, the emperor Frederick Barbarossa appointed Conrad of Urslingen, already Duke of Spoleto, as Count of Assisi and Nocera.

As was typical of most Italian communes in the later 1100s, Assisi itself was plagued by political factions. A faction of the well-to-do, the *boni homines,* whose wealth lay principally in rural landholdings, fought other families, the *popolo,* whose wealth lay principally in urban commerce. We should be cautious about viewing this as a "class conflict." The "popular" faction was wealthy, and both groups had a stake in rural property as well as in commerce. In 1197, the rising of the *popolo* of Assisi provoked a civil war that resulted in the expulsion of the *boni* and their exile to Perugia by 1202. The towers of the exiled families, concentrated in the neighborhood around the cathedral and the region of the Murorupto, were leveled.

The opportunistic factions sought to form networks of alliances (to which later Italians gave the names "Ghibelline" and "Guelf") centered on the emperor or the pope. Assisi, constantly at war with "Guelf" Perugia, has been called "Ghibelline," but this probably meant little politically. After the establishment of the popular government, the commune began the long process of subjugating its *contado* (surrounding countryside), eliminating the strongholds of the rural nobility at Sassorosso and San Savino. Meanwhile, the city suffered further factionalism as the *minores* contested internal control with the *maiores.* This conflict would be resolved only by a comprehensive peace pact among the factions in 1210.

The family of Francis's father, Pietro di Bernardone, and his wife, Pica, whose house lay on Via San Paolo just off the busy commercial district on the west end of the Piazza del Mercato, away from the mountain and between the local parish church of San Nicolò di Piazza and the small Benedictine foundation of San Paolo, was allied with the popular faction. The family house was valuable real estate, in the center of the porticoed streets of the principal commercial zone, with a view onto the city's main piazza. When assessed for taxes, it was in the top third of the houses of the neighborhood. Francis's earliest biographer, Thomas of Celano, was of the opinion that the future saint was "very rich."

Francis came from well-established money by communal standards. This does not mean that his family was from the nobility, whether French or Italian, nor did the family have a surname. Bernardone was Pietro's patronymic, the name of his father, not a family name. Nor did the family belong to the *boni homines,* who fled Assisi during the civil wars at the turn of the century. Francis himself was very conscious that his parents could not socialize as equals with Assisi's older noble families.

Of the merchant Pietro himself, we know very little, but what we do know is suggestive. Later in life, when Francis wanted brothers to humiliate him about his ancestry, he had them call him a "worthless peasant day-laborer" (*rusticum, mercanarium, et inutilem*), to which he would reply: "Yes, that is what the son of Pietro di Bernardone needs to hear." The adult Pietro himself was neither worthless nor rustic, but rather a successful urban merchant, so this abuse hints at a humble background for Pietro. Perhaps Pietro's father, Bernardone, was one of those "useless peasant day-laborers" who were moving into the Italian cities in the 1100s. Historians have found no records of Pietro's family, and his only financial doings known involve not his mercantile business, but land investments in the country. Most likely, Pietro, like many country people of the period, came to town to seek his fortune; yet, unlike most, he did very well. He ended up with a prosperous business and a house on the piazza, even if he always maintained a certain sense of inferiority to the established classes. Pietro probably died before 1215. His son Francis never mentioned his death, at least not in any of his extant writings.

Comparatively extensive records in the Assisi archives paint a very different picture of Pietro's wife, Pica, Francis's mother. Her father was probably named Giovanni—her son Angelo later "remade" his deceased grandfather by naming his son "Giovannetto." He was probably of local origin and also of a mercantile family. Pica seems to have predeceased her husband, Pietro. She was dead by 1211, at which date her son Angelo "remade" her by naming his own son "Picone," a male version of her name. Pica probably had other children besides Angelo and Francis, but of them we know nothing. Oddly, Angelo himself never appeared in any record as Angelo di Pietro, but always as Angelo di Pica, under his matronymic. This may suggest that his father had died, or that he was Pica's child by an earlier marriage. We cannot be sure. Records suggest that the successful family business was itself founded on Pica's dowry. So Pietro, the man from the country, had made a very good match and, on his wife's resources, established a flourishing business.

We do not know how he did this, but one can imagine a story out of Horatio Alger. Perhaps the newly married Pietro had partnered with Pica's father in the cloth trade, learned commerce, and finally established a place of his own in the town. But this is speculation. In any case, the inheritance, of which Angelo later became the sole male heir, was ample. Along with movables, it included the city house and five tracts of land in the country. So, most likely, Angelo's consistent use of the matronymic "di Pica" shows, as it usually does in Italian names of the period, that his fortune came from his mother's, not his father's, side of the family.

Birth and Youth

As medieval sources tell us Francis's age at his death and at the time of his conversion, we can calculate that he was born in either 1181 or 1182, years that the chronicles tell us were a period of want, if not famine, in the valley of Spoleto. Beyond that we cannot go. We are on marginally surer ground if we place his baptism on Saturday, 28 March 1182. The practice then in use in Italian cities was to baptize all healthy children in Holy Week during the Easter Vigil on the afternoon of Holy Saturday. Francis's group of infants would include those born in 1181 after Easter and those born before Easter in 1182. Francis was plunged three times—in the name of the Father, and of the Son, and of the Holy Spirit—into the waters of the city font at the duomo of San Rufino, a few blocks from his home. The bishop presided for at least the first couple of baptisms and then stood aside so that he could confirm the neophytes. Some cities in Lombardy deferred the children's first communion until the following morning. In Assisi, Francis would have received his first communion, as a babe in arms, before the altar of the cathedral at the end of the vigil. Easter baptism of the city's children was the major civic festival in the Italian communes, and we can imagine Pica and Pietro proudly walking through the main piazza after the festivities, along with Francis's godparents, who would have carried the child in their arms. A splendid supper followed this, the baptism of a male child.

Pica's child, whom we know as Francis, Francesco in Italian, may have received the baptismal name of Giovanni, that is, John, as some of his early biographers claim. They also tell us that the birth occurred while his father was away in France. April was the time for business travel, since the roads north, closed in winter, were then open. These hagiographers overtly reconfigure Francis's family after that of John the Baptist, with Pica as the holy Elizabeth. Pietro is an anti-Zacharias, refusing to allow the future saint to be called "John." This hagiographic modeling of Francis's birth and naming on a scriptural model began a long process of remaking Francis according to biblical types. The role of biblical models makes it more likely that, from the beginning, he was "Francesco," that is, "Frenchy," a pet name suggested by his father's or maternal grandfather's commercial links with France. The name, while not common, was already in use well before his birth, and it was not a novelty, as is often claimed.

Of Francis's youth, we know even less. As a boy, he was probably sent to school at the hospital of San Giorgio, where he received an education that would allow him to follow in his father's profession as a merchant. Francis seems to have been a younger child, if not the youngest, the apple of his mother's eye. At school, he acquired a rudimentary knowledge of Latin, sufficient to write simple, if often ungrammatical, prose suitable for business records. For more formal writing and contract drafting, he would have hired a notary. At some point, Francis learned sufficient French to sing popular songs and carry on simple conversations, again with occasionally defective grammar. Francis became so comfortable speaking and singing in French that he did so "spontaneously" and with little reflection. His love of poetry may well have encouraged a love of French (or better, Provençal), the vernacular literary idiom of his age. Perhaps he polished his French during business travel with his father, or with family business contacts who visited Assisi. Beyond the identity of the languages he picked up, how he got them is mostly pure conjecture. In the course of learning the family business, he surely mastered the accounting techniques and practices of the period, a skill he learned on the job, not at school.

About the year 1195, as he was approaching the age of fourteen or so, Francis began to work as an apprentice in his father's business. He learned to sell cloth, keep financial records, and control inventory. It is likely that he even traveled to France with his father to make purchases of cloth. Gifted with a keen mind and an engaging and expansive personality, he quickly proved himself an able salesman. He made contacts and friends easily. Within a short time, he became a member of a *societas iuvenum,* a kind of fraternity or boys' club typical in the Italian cities of the period. Such groups were a kind of dining association, providing, along with recreation, networking opportunities for the sons of the wealthy and influential. Francis ran with a youth gang of the well-to-do.

He may not have had the aristocratic family background of some of his companions, but family wealth and his openhanded generosity made up for this. He became the leader of his *societas,* carrying his baton of office as they paraded through the streets of Assisi. He led them in singing and joking on their way to and from dinner at various watering holes. Francis lavished money and care on these dinners and parties, enough to earn him the reputation of a prodigal. And, to his parents' consternation, he often bolted from meals at home to join his friends for revelry. Although his parents tried to rein in some of his excesses and bad manners, seeing their son at the center of the Assisi "smart set" blunted their criticisms. It was easy to spoil such a charming and promising young man.

Francis's personality included a touch of vanity and narcissism. He added patches of old and faded cloth to the silk and fine wool of his cloaks, producing an outlandish, even clownlike, effect. He did not care what others thought of his violations of convention and cavalier attitude toward expenses, so long as they noticed him and made him the center of attention. On the other hand, there is no direct evidence that he was immoral, intemperate, or debauched. Francis's major flaws were of the spirit, not the body.

The young man's most endearing quality, after his generosity, was his naturally courteous manner. Later witnesses described his deportment as courtly, more refined than that typical of a merchant's son. Whether Francis was patterning himself on the knights of the romances, with which he was no doubt familiar, or aping the manners of his betters is difficult to say. He was extraordinarily sensitive. Once, while Francis was busy in the shop, a poor beggar dropped in, hoping for a handout. Francis uncharacteristically dismissed him with a brush-off and went back to work. The affair ate at him. He was courteous to rich men and nobles, but his good breeding had not extended to this beggar. Contrite, he swore to show civility to everyone regardless of class, even beggars asking for handouts in God's name, and ran after the man to make up for refusing him alms.

The story rings true. Francis was averse to ugliness, whether physical or social. Pain, suffering, and physical deformity incited a visceral horror in him. He later wrote of this period, when he was "in his sins," saying that nothing was more revolting to him than the combination of those traits found in lepers. He avoided such outcasts, whose physical deformities were generally considered the external expression of moral or spiritual ones, holding his nose and running away from them. There was a natural limit to his courtesy and good manners.

Military Adventures

The period of Francis's apprenticeship was a turbulent one in the history of Assisi. In March of 1198, the popular government destroyed the Rocca, symbol of imperial overlordship, and, during the next year, it demolished the towers of the urban nobility, now mostly exiled to Perugia. On 1 October 1201, the city formed an alliance with Foligno to the south, to which Bevagna, Spello, Nocera, and Fabriano all contributed. Assisi and its allies were now in a position of strength, and they moved against Perugia. Francis's family supported the Assisi government, and the twenty-two-year-old merchant served in the communal militia, at the side of the very youths he was accustomed to lead on nighttime rambles. He was wealthy enough to afford a horse and so served with the mounted troops rather than the foot soldiers.

The allied militias advanced toward the Ospedale di Collestrada, east of Ponte San Giovanni, where the Perugians had crossed the river. The result was a disastrous and bloody defeat for Assisi. Francis and his companions in arms were imprisoned at Perugia for a year or more. As was fitting for one outfitted with a horse, and so obviously from a rich background, Francis ended up imprisoned not with the ordinary soldiers, but with the aristocratic knights. Early biographers say that Francis did his best to keep spirits up, reconciling disputes among the prisoners and even befriending a bitter knight whom the other prisoners had been avoiding. Whether this flattering picture is historical is hard to say. But prison was hard on Francis, physically and mentally. By the time of his release, probably in late 1203, his health was severely damaged. The once extroverted and cheerful young man had turned in on himself. Perhaps he was ransomed home by his family precisely because of his declining health. Assisi's military situation then changed on 8 June 1204, when the city swore allegiance to the papacy in the person of Cardinal Leo di Brancalone. The interdict for attacking pro-papal Perugia, which had suspended all religious services in Assisi, was removed and peace restored.

Francis had seen companions and friends butchered in a bloody and savage battle; he had been held in prison under miserable and trying conditions. This was a long way from Assisi nightlife and from communal dreams of glorious victory over Perugia. His first biographer speaks of Francis as "worn down by a long illness" at this time. The crisis lasted about eighteen months, from late 1203 to the spring of 1205. The broken veteran began wandering listlessly about the house; he took no joy in the beauties of nature that had previously delighted him.

More disturbingly, Francis was now plagued by strange dreams, including one in which he saw his own house piled high with weapons of war. He had war-related flashbacks, which his earliest biographer says left him confused and unsure of himself. Medical or psychological diagnosis at such a remove is impossible, but descriptions of Francis's condition make it resemble symptoms commonly found in soldiers who have survived horrible experiences during war. If modern examples of such a condition are any indication, he probably also began to experience bouts of self-loathing and guilt.

Nevertheless, in spring 1205, probably around April, Francis broke out of his depression, throwing himself into preparations for a new military venture.

The papacy had been conducting a more or less fruitless war in southern Italy in support of the young emperor Frederick II's claim to the throne of Sicily. Following Assisi's reconciliation with the papacy, a local nobleman, whose name has not come down to us, gathered followers to go south and join this struggle. Although unsettled and listless, Francis forced himself into the military preparations necessary to join the militia. Perhaps he had decided to confront directly the demons of his Perugia misadventure. But the veteran's behavior remained erratic. On one occasion, after procuring his rig and finery as a horseman, Francis turned around and gave it all away to a poor knight. But, by summer, having acquired a new horse and hired a squire, he rode south to join the host.

Francis got as far as Spoleto, some thirty miles from Assisi, a day's journey on horseback. That night, before falling asleep, seemingly experiencing some anxiety about his intentions, he recounted them to a companion, perhaps to his squire. The upshot of the conversation was that he now realized that following a minor vassal rather than the lord in charge of the expedition was not a formula for glory. Later recounting turned this "lord" into God in heaven, but such a spiritual motivation for heading home seems far from Francis's unsettled state of mind. Whatever happened on the fateful night, Francis abandoned returning to the military life as the solution to his problems. With that option closed, he was now truly adrift. The next day he headed back to Assisi.

Francis had journeyed the eighteen or so miles to Foligno when he decided to put an end, once and for all, to his military endeavors. He sold his finery and arms, as well as his horse, and put on a cheaper set of clothes. He then walked on to Assisi, twelve miles distant, and arrived on the outskirts, surely tired, late that evening. Two miles outside of Assisi, off the main road in the valley, he came to the old run-down church of San Damiano. This church, first recorded as a Benedictine priory in 1030, had become dependent on the duomo of San Rufino and since had fallen into a state of squalid disrepair for lack of much of a congregation so far outside the walls of the city.

Nevertheless, Francis found the priest responsible for the place, Don Peter by name, and asked permission to stay the night. The priest agreed, but when Francis asked him to hold the money from the Foligno sale, the priest refused. Don Peter had no desire to incur the legal risks of being a depository for money that belonged to a local youth with a reputation for prodigality. So Francis entered the church for the night and left the cash on a window ledge. He then forgot about it entirely. The next day, he left to go back to his family, where he tried to pick up what remained of his old life.

Francis in Crisis

Shortly after his return to Assisi, Francis's old friends elected him to preside over one of their dinners and to pay for it in his usual generous way. Francis went along with their plans, but he was moody, neither laughing nor singing. Having feasted and enjoyed the moment, the group paraded through the streets as they had always done, but Francis fell behind, silent and self-absorbed, emotionally numb. When his friends realized that they had lost him, they retraced their steps and found him standing alone. This was a different Francis from the one they had known before his military service. As he had given up his plans of military glory, they asked him if he had other goals in mind, perhaps marriage. Francis answered them only in riddles, or with silence. The marriage question became a running joke among them. One thing was clear: the conviviality that had previously delighted him had lost its flavor.

Much to his father's dismay, Francis also lost interest in the business and stopped coming to work in the shop. His old employment, like his old pleasures, held no attraction for him. He withdrew ever more deeply into himself, often hiding in his bedroom. Later biographers label his growing self-hatred a gift of God-given humility to replace his earlier vanity and frivolity. His previous carefree life may well have tormented him, but what exact delinquencies he detected in himself we will probably never know. As noted above, after his narrow escape from battle and harsh imprisonment, Francis may have been suffering from the kind of self-loathing and guilt often found in those who have survived such traumas. Whatever the state of his soul, he chose the remedy of the age for expiating personal sin. He performed the traditional works of penance: almsgiving, prayer, and bodily mortification.

When out of the house, Francis gave alms to any beggar who asked. When money ran out, he literally gave the shirt off his back. He secretly purchased furnishings for poor churches and had them delivered anonymously to the priests serving them. It seems that these alms were an attempt to buy himself back into divine favor. Francis's conduct especially troubled his father. His son's previous prodigality carried with it an air of courtesy and good breeding, and his hard and successful work in the business had more than paid for it. Now Francis had ceased to work, and his actions seemed compulsive rather than spontaneous. Pietro rebuked his son for his behavior and ordered him to return to work. Francis disobeyed. When his father was gone, and he was alone with his mother at meals, he piled the table high with food. Then, over her protests, he took the surplus out and gave it away to beggars. His loving but uncomprehending mother had no choice but to indulge him in this odd behavior.

In a typically medieval fashion, Francis sought spiritual relief by going on pilgrimage to Rome to pray at the tomb of St. Peter. Perhaps the Apostle could help him. Francis approached the tomb and threw handfuls of money through the grille before the altar. As the coins clattered through the grate, onlookers were astonished, as much by the exhibitionism as by the size of the offering. Biographers tell us that, on leaving the church, he exchanged clothing with a beggar and, in fractured French, begged alms of every passerby. If news of Francis's behavior at St. Peter's ever got back to his father, his anxiety surely worsened. Francis seemed to be slipping from idiosyncrasy into madness.

On his return from Rome, Francis approached his bishop, Guido II of Assisi, for advice and counsel. The troubled veteran belonged to a notable family, and Guido listened to his problems patiently, if not willingly. Francis's quest for solitude and prayer now increased, and his self-mortification intensified. His earlier, large circle of friends had contracted to one close companion who could put up with his odd behavior. Sadly, there is no record of his patient friend's name. Francis wandered the forests with this friend, sometimes leaving him to stand outside a cave near Assisi while the troubled young man spent long periods in isolation. Francis was racked by demonic fears and perhaps hallucinations. He had always hated the ugly and deformed, and the sight of a hunchbacked woman of Assisi, real or imagined, convinced him that he was in danger of being smitten with a similar deformity. He again bitterly repented his sins and saw his own soul in the physical repulsiveness of the hunchback.

On occasion, returning from his refuge in the forest, the troubled penitent stopped to pray in the church of San Damiano. Before the altar he begged God to reveal his will. Two admittedly late manuscripts of *The Legend of the Three Companions* carry in the margin a prayer that, in its simplicity, probably reflects his words or at least their general sense. Although the text is Latin, not Italian, it may be Francis's oldest extant composition: "Most high glorious God, enlighten the darkness of my heart and give me true Faith, certain Hope, and perfect Charity; give me perception and knowledge, Lord, that I might carry out your holy and true command."

Francis, having found some relief in prayer at San Damiano, returned there more and more frequently. He gave the priest, Don Peter, money to pay for oil to light a lamp before the crucifix above the altar where he prayed. Contemplating Christ's Passion before the crucifix had a profound and visceral effect on Francis; he wept uncontrollably and, in his desire to unite himself to the naked and crucified Christ, he mortified his body with ever more savage penances. Soon Francis moved out of the family home and took up residence at San Damiano, where he became a freelance penitent or *conversus* attached to the church. Whether this was suggested to him by Don Peter or by Bishop Guido, or was a spontaneous act of his own, we do not know. When he made the move, he did it without consulting his parents, or even informing them.

Francis "Leaves the World"

Francis moved out of the family home and took up residence at San Damiano in late 1205, about six months after his return to Assisi. Over those six months, his parents had watched as their son's behavior went from moody and distracted to withdrawn and isolated and finally to bizarre and self-destructive. Now, suddenly, he simply disappeared. One can imagine Pietro and Pica's frustration changing to anxiety, and then to alarm. Pietro went about frantically, searching for information about his son. He finally located him at San Damiano, living in filth. Francis's biographer Thomas of Celano tells us that when Pietro "learned that Francis was living in that place in such a way, he was touched inwardly with sorrow of heart and deeply disturbed by the sudden turn of events." Later hagiographers usually paint Pietro in the darkest of colors, but this early passage probably reflects the man's true personality: a loving father deeply wounded by his son's agony, now struggling to find a way to help him. Pietro gathered a group of friends to help retrieve his son and bring him home.

Word reached Francis ahead of time. He hid from his father for over a month, probably with the connivance of Don Peter. A sympathetic member of the family household supplied him with food. When Francis finally came out of hiding and appeared in public on the streets of Assisi, he was so emaciated and unkempt that people threw mud at him. They called him insane and blamed his madness on his fasting and self-mortification. Horrified by the news, Pietro went to retrieve his vagabond son. He then took him home and locked him up, arguing and reasoning with him for several days in the hope of bringing him to his senses. Francis, however, was completely deaf to him. Eventually, Pietro had to leave town on business, and Pica, "moved by maternal instinct," as Thomas of Celano tells us, let her boy leave the house. Francis immediately ran back to San Damiano and returned to his former habits.

When Pietro returned from his business trip to find his son gone, he exploded with frustration at his wife. It was obvious that his every attempt to talk, or even beat, some sense into his son had failed. The business trip had given Pietro time to consider how to deal with the situation. His son was clearly out of his mind, perhaps irrevocably. Pietro had to protect his family and his business. Were his wife Pica to die, her dowry, on which the business was founded (and in which Pietro had, under civil law, only a life interest), would pass to Angelo and Francis. Angelo was a cooperative business partner, but Francis would probably lose, squander, or give away his portion, effectively crippling the family enterprise.

Pietro made one last attempt to reason with his son. He went to find him at San Damiano, where Francis came out to meet him. It was a painful encounter. Francis was in tears, making it impossible for Pietro to communicate with him. Understanding that the issue was at least in part financial, Francis offered his father the proceeds from the sale of the horse and arms in Foligno. Living at San Damiano as a penitent, he probably considered himself free of family affairs. He did not truly grasp what was at stake. The danger to the business lay in Francis's legal right to half of his mother's dowry, not in some relatively minor loss from the sale of a horse.

Unable to make Francis understand, Pietro took the purse and left. As Francis was of age, over twenty-five years old, Pietro was forced to go to law against his son. He went to the communal magistrates and began the process for excluding Francis from claims on the dowry. The grounds were probably mental incapacity. Perhaps he merely intended to have a custodian appointed to manage his son's affairs, something normal in cases of mental incapacity. Recognizing Pietro's rights and the gravity of the matter, the city sent a bailiff to summon Francis before the tribunal. When the bailiff arrived, Francis, showing unexpected legal savvy, invoked his status as an ecclesiastical person and refused to recognize the authority of the court. The judges, who had no other choice, remanded the case to Bishop Guido. As ecclesiastical judge, the bishop summoned Francis to reply to his father. This he freely did, Thomas of Celano tells us, saying that he would do so willingly "because the bishop is the father of souls."

It appears that Guido, who had already been advising Francis, now preferred to serve as mediator between son and father, rather than acting as a judge. In the presence of Francis's whole family, including Pica and Angelo, as would be fitting in an action on her dowry, the bishop urged Francis to renounce any claim on his family's resources and to depend on God alone. Without hesitation, Francis agreed to renounce his claim. Then, in a gesture that must have come easily to his somewhat exhibitionistic temperament, Francis withdrew into an adjoining room, removed the fine clothing typical of his family's station, and stripped down to the penitent's hair shirt he was wearing underneath. He came out and put his old garments at his father's feet. He then turned to those present and declared: "Until now I have called Pietro di Bernardone my father. But, because I have proposed to serve God, I return to him the money on account of which he was so upset, and also all the clothing which is his, wanting to say, from now on: 'Our Father who art in heaven,' and not 'My father, Pietro di Bernardone.'"

Those present broke out in tears at the pathos of the scene. The bishop then performed a gesture that mimicked the ritual by which one became a brother of penance. Usually in that ceremony the new brother was covered with an altar cloth from the shrine of the confraternity's patron saint. Bishop Guido covered Francis with his mantle. The silent Pietro picked up the clothes, turned, and went home with the rest of the family. We do not know if he ever spoke in peace with his son again.

Francis was now free to follow his own path, a path that led him away from family and city. The physical and spiritual freedom must have been an exhilarating experience. It was now the winter of 1206 and snowing. Francis wandered alone in the woods, singing songs to God in his bad French. Suddenly, two robbers overtook him and demanded that he identify himself. Hagiographers claim that he replied that he was the "Herald of the Great King." Finding that Francis had no money, the two toughs beat him, stripped him of his tunic and hair shirt, and left him for dead. Battered and suffering from the cold, Francis made his way to a nearby monastery, perhaps that of San Verecondio in Vallingegno, just south of Gubbio. The monks took him in for several days, allowing him to work as a menial domestic. In spite of the shelter and warmth of the kitchen, he could not shake the cold from his body, so, after a short time, he left the monastery and headed off to Gubbio, where he was taken in and clothed by an old acquaintance.

Frustrated, and suddenly unsure that this was the life God had chosen for him, he headed back to Assisi, where he had the experience that would change his life forever. Years later he would write in his Testament: "The Lord granted me, brother Francis, to begin doing penance this way: When I was in my sins, just to see lepers was very bitter for me. And the Lord himself took me among them, and I showed mercy to them. And on leaving them, what seemed bitter to me had turned for me into sweetness of body and soul. And afterwards I waited a little and left the world."

This encounter with lepers, not the act of stripping off his clothing before the bishop, would always be for Francis the core of his religious conversion. As near as we can tell, it happened on the outskirts of Assisi, perhaps at the leprosarium of San Rufino dell'Arce, which was on the way back from Gubbio. Or it could have been at San Lazzaro near Rivo Torto, or perhaps at San Salvatore delle Pareti, as reported by Bonaventure.

Wherever the leprosarium was, Francis lodged there with the residents and earned his keep caring for them. His experience with them had nothing to do with choices between wealth and poverty, knightly pride and humility, or even doing service instead of conducting business. It was a dramatic personal reorientation that brought forth spiritual fruit. As Francis showed mercy to these outcasts, he came to experience God's own gift of mercy to himself. As he cleaned the lepers' bodies, dressed their wounds, and treated them as human beings, not as refuse to be fled from in horror, his perceptions changed. What before was ugly and repulsive now caused him delight and joy, not only spiritually, but also viscerally and physically. Francis's aesthetic sense, so central to his personality, had been transformed, even inverted. The startled veteran sensed himself, by God's grace and no power of his own, remade into a different man. Just as suddenly, the sins that had been tormenting him seemed to melt away, and Francis experienced a kind of spiritual rebirth and healing. Not long after this encounter, later accounts tell us, perhaps in allegory, that Francis was walking down a road and met one of these same lepers. He embraced the man in his arms and kissed him. Francis's spiritual nightmare was over; he had found peace.

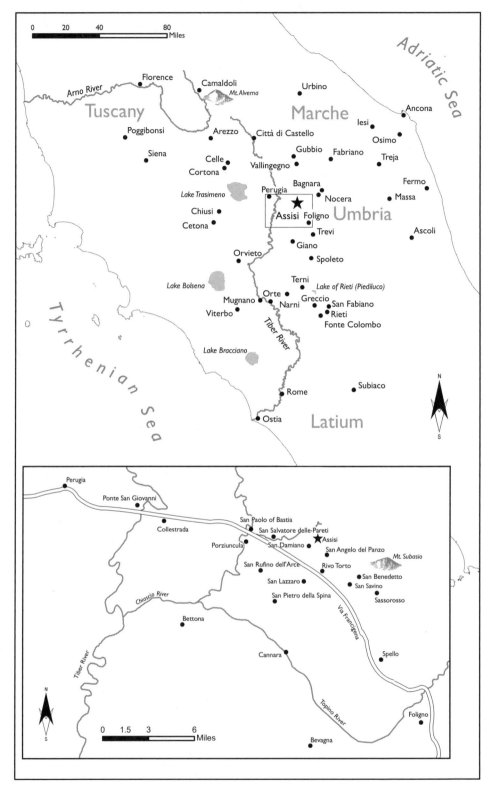

Central Italy and the environs of Assisi

[2]

THE PENITENT FROM ASSISI

1206–1209

Francis at San Damiano

F RANCIS CONTINUED TO live and work among the lepers, taking temporary refuge in churches, praying, working, and, at least at San Damiano, repairing the building. In the lonely and decayed church, Francis found a substitute for the home in Assisi that he had lost. There he became aware of such a powerful divine presence that the once-distant God became for him tangibly present. In medieval Italian piety, God manifested himself in concrete ways and particular places. Francis encountered at San Damiano the consoling presence of the Savior who had suffered and died for him. It was a presence that he grew to recognize in other churches as well. Of this he later wrote: "And the Lord granted me such faith in churches, that thus I would pray simply and say: We adore you, Lord Jesus Christ, in all your churches throughout the whole world, and we bless you, because by your Holy Cross you have redeemed the world." His prayer, like others written by his lay contemporaries, drew on the Church's liturgy for its words. Francis adopted the acclamation of Christ Crucified from the Liturgy of the Passion on Good Friday for his own use. Christ's work of redemption became real and present to him in a way that it had not been before. In the humble chapel of San Damiano, as in every Catholic church, the power of the Cross was available to save the world. Where he had previously prayed before the late twelfth-century painted Umbrian cross of San Damiano for the gifts of Faith, Hope, Charity, and the wisdom to know God's will, he now adored there the Lord who had led him to the lepers, changed his heart, and now seemed to be calling him to something more.

When Francis recorded this prayer and proclaimed his faith that Christ Crucified could be found in all the churches of the world, he added his reason for venerating the priests who served those churches: "I do this because, in this world, I see nothing corporally of the most high Son of God except his Most Holy Body and Most Holy Blood, which they receive and which they alone minister to others. And these Most Holy Mysteries I want above all things to honor, to have venerated, and to be placed in precious places." The Body that died on the Cross for his salvation became present every day on the altar, and this visible presence of the invisible God hallowed the poor, crumbling church in the Assisi *contado*. Francis returned often to the theme of the Eucharist in his writing, far more consistently than to that of poverty, which has attracted so much medieval and modern attention. As Christ's real presence in the Host made San Damiano a sacred spot, it gave Francis a multitude of spiritual fathers to replace his earthly father, Pietro di Bernardone. He wrote: "The Lord gave me, and gives me still, such faith in those priests, who live according to the rite of the Holy Roman Church, because of their orders that, were they to persecute me, I would still want to have recourse to them....And I do not want to consider any sin in them, because I discern the Son of God in them, and they are my lords." Changed internally by his ministry to the lepers, and beginning now to feel spiritually at home, Francis decided to adopt an external sign of his choice of penance. He took off his secular clothes and dressed in the plain subdued tunic typical of a brother of penance. In external appearance, he now wore the symbol of the ecclesiastical status he had earlier claimed before Bishop Guido.

Later writers describe Francis at this time as wearing the black tunic of a lay "hermit," with a leather belt and a staff. This is unlikely. Even more unlikely did Francis intend his attire as a uniform indicating membership in a particular religious order. While canonically recognized, brothers of penance were laymen, not religious, and they had in this period no standardized "habit." They wore ordinary clothing of a dark color. In any case, "hermit," as his biographers use it, did not mean someone who had withdrawn into isolation or absolute seclusion. The convert continued to live in the world, while attached to the church of San Damiano.

The man who had previously used his hands only in bookkeeping and in buying and selling turned them to physical labor in a distinctively medieval form of piety, church repair. As a brother of penance, he still could keep and manage money, and, whether from resources taken with him when he left his family or with money he made by manual labor, Francis bought the stones and other supplies that he needed to refurbish the building. Some of the stones came from Don Silvester, an elderly priest of Assisi, who took the opportunity to grossly overcharge him. Francis made no complaint and paid the asking price. He attended the Divine Office and Mass daily at San Damiano or other nearby churches. As was becoming common among lay penitents, he rose early for Matins, reciting Pater Nosters as the priests and clerics sang the long night office.

When his money ran out, as it occasionally did, he went into town seeking his needs from the people of Assisi. Later witnesses said he used to ask for building stones, saying: "Whoever gives me one stone, will get one reward; whoever gives me two, will get two rewards"—from God, it was understood. This solicitation came even less naturally to Francis than physical labor. Before the restoration was completed, Francis wanted a lamp to burn before the cross in San Damiano church. Such a light was the archetypal symbol of lay devotion to an image or relic in high medieval Italy. Out of cash, he went looking for money to pay for the oil to fill it. He came upon a group of men gambling. Perhaps it included some of his former friends. Unable to approach them directly for help, he put on a persona different from the Italian merchant of Assisi and asked for oil in his imperfect French. Switching languages was a psychological move that Francis used to distance himself as a penitent from his former, sinful self. He had already used it in Rome; he would continue to employ it for the rest of his life.

As a dependent of San Damiano, Francis could claim food and shelter from its priest, Don Peter, who also provided him with some of the delicacies and sweets that he had enjoyed while living the life of a rich young man in the world. As Francis later admitted, he ate them gladly and sometimes turned up his nose at dishes he found disagreeable. The outside observer, not knowing Francis's internal state, would have seen in him a rich boy playacting at conventional forms of piety. People on the street insulted and abused him. On occasion, he encountered his father, and Pietro, suffering deeply out of love for the child who was humiliating himself daily in public, scolded, berated, and even cursed him. Francis hired a down-and-outer named Alberto to go around with him and loudly pronounce a blessing every time his father abused him.

God Sends Francis Followers

Beyond living for the day, ministering to lepers, praying before the cross, and repairing San Damiano, Francis had no clear objective or set form of life. More than anything he resembled the sort of pious hanger-on that churches have attracted from time immemorial. After the encounter with the lepers in the summer of 1206, Francis continued his freelance solitary penitent's life for almost two years.

Divested of his fine clothing, Francis cut an unimposing and unlikely figure. He was short, slight, indeed gaunt. His most notable features were probably his dark hair and eyes, which contrasted with his fair skin, his small, angular features, and his white teeth. Although not a "portrait" in the modern sense, the fresco of "Brother Francis" in the Sacro Speco of Subiaco Benedictine monastery, painted within two years of Francis's death, if not while he was still alive, resembles the earliest descriptions. Very noticeable is the thin neck, straight nose, small mouth, and sparse beard. Francis presents a very similar face in what is likely the next oldest extant painting of him after his death, that by Margarito of Arezzo, painted about 1250. In an admittedly late legend, one of his followers called him "unattractive." Other than his odd behavior, there was little that would make him stand out in a crowd.

Francis does not seem to have expected anything much to change in his solitary, hermit style of life. When change did come it seems to have taken him by surprise. He later laconically wrote of what happened next: "The Lord gave me some brothers." One spring day in 1208, a young man from Assisi, perhaps an acquaintance, arrived at San Damiano looking for Francis. His name was Bernard of Quintavalle and, after speaking with Francis at some length, he decided to join him in his life of prayer, solitude, and penance. Bernard gave away his possessions in the piazza outside the church of San Giorgio, where Francis had studied as a boy, and went to live as a penitent with him. At virtually the same time, another man from Assisi, apparently named Peter, arrived and asked to join Francis. The two men came from very different backgrounds; Bernard was of comfortable status, and Peter was rather poor, so it is unlikely that they came together or knew each other previously. What the two men did share was that both had been inspired by Francis's decision to leave the world, seeing in him an authenticity that had escaped most citizens of Assisi.

Both men wanted the same thing: to imitate Francis in the practice of penance. Their arrival, however, was so unexpected that Francis was unsure how to proceed. It appears that Don Peter, the priest-caretaker of San Damiano, was no longer on the scene; perhaps he had left the building to the care of Francis. Bishop Guido seems to have been out of town. Years later, Francis himself described his situation in one short sentence: "There was no one to tell me what to do." So, on Wednesday, 16 April 1208, Francis and his two new companions went into town, to his family's parish church, San Nicolò di Piazza, at the bottom of the Piazza del Mercato, and found the parish priest.

Sadly, his name was never recorded, but Francis must have known him well and trusted him enough to confide in him.

The three men asked the priest to reveal the Lord's will for them by performing a *sortes biblicae,* the opening of the Bible at random to find a verse that would reveal God's will. Educated theologians considered this practice one step above superstition, and the canonists of the time debated whether it was even permissible. Nevertheless, it was a popular practice in lay piety, and the learned were generally willing to tolerate it.

Entering the church of San Nicolò, the three men prayed together with the priest and had him show them "the Gospel of our Lord Jesus Christ." As there was no complete Bible at hand, the priest used his altar missal. The actual missal they consulted can be seen today in the Walters Art Museum in Baltimore, Maryland. It is a simple manuscript, with a few decorated letters and only one full-page illumination, the Crucifixion, facing the Canon. It dates from the late 1100s or very early 1200s; damage, erasures, and additions show years of use. It was a fairly new book in 1208, and Francis had probably seen it many times at church when he attended Mass with his family.

As was customary in the practice of *sortes biblicae,* the priest would have opened the missal three times, explaining the meaning of each of the texts as he went along. Because none of the three penitents could read Latin very well, the priest translated as well as interpreted the texts for them. On the first opening, to folio 132^v, the priest found the Gospel of Wednesday in the week of the Fifth Sunday after Pentecost, Mark 10:17–21, which contains the verse "Go, sell what you have, and give to the poor, and you will have treasure in heaven; and come, follow me." As was customary, the priest then opened the missal a second time, now to folio 119^v, Thursday of the Octave of Pentecost, with its Gospel, Luke 9:1–6, and the passage "Take nothing for your journey, no staff, nor bag, nor bread, nor money; and do not have two tunics." Finally, for the third and final time, the book was opened, and, on folio 216^v, the Mass for 11 August, the Vigil of St. Lawrence, appeared with the Gospel Matthew 16:24–28. The priest's finger picked out the verse "If anyone would come after me, let him deny himself and take up his Cross and follow me."

Taken as a whole, the three passages called for a shockingly radical renunciation of the world: give all to the poor, take nothing on the journey, and embrace the Cross. They carefully committed the texts to memory. These texts would become the core of what Francis would call his "form of life." God himself had revealed them to Francis to show him what he was to do. Although not a single person present realized it, they had taken the first step in founding the Franciscan Order.

The Penitents Go to Rome

For perhaps as long as a year, Francis meditated on the "form of the Holy Gospel" that God had revealed at the church of San Nicolò. More and more, it seemed clear to him that the command to "give up everything" and "take up the Cross" demanded that he abandon his own will and subject himself to the will of God alone. But that choice carried within it the risk of delusion: the identification of one's own desires, possibly selfish or deluded, with divine commands. God had revealed to him the "form of Gospel," but he had also sent him followers. In this case, obedient Catholic that he was, Francis wanted Church approval for this project. That would ensure that his way of life was truly from God.

Francis also sought the freedom from self-will that could come only from subjecting oneself in obedience to the will of another. With his spiritual director Bishop Guido away on church business and Don Peter out of the picture, Francis decided that final approval of what he believed God had revealed to him would have to come from the priest of priests, the pope himself. Some have speculated that Francis might have first consulted theologians or canonists before reaching this decision, but there is nothing to suggest that this was the case. Nor is it clear that Francis thought of this approval in a legal sense as the foundation of a religious order. Most likely he was concerned only about its propriety as a form of life for himself and a couple of companions. Whatever the case, it was decided that the three men would travel as a group to Rome.

In advance of their departure, Francis took care to write down a very short summary of the passages from the Bible they had heard. Unfortunately, the written summary has not survived, so there is no way to examine it. No evidence suggests that he employed a notary or scribe, much less a theologian or canonist, to write it. More than likely, he used the rudimentary Latin he had learned in the shop, writing out the words of the three Gospels as best he could, perhaps adding what was necessary to fit the texts together into a coherent whole. He wanted this "form of life" to be in God's words more than his own. He may have added short elaborations of his own relating the biblical texts to the group's eremitical style of life and their service in leper hospitals. Modern writers have come to call this document the first Franciscan "Rule," but that suggests a more legally sophisticated document than this form of life was. It has been better called Francis's *praepositum*—his proposed form of life. Before they left, as a sign that his desire was to follow God's will and not his own, Francis had the group select someone other than himself to be the leader: someone to whom he could be subordinate and obedient. The decision was easy; they chose the one who had been with Francis the longest and came from the higher social background, Bernard of Quintavalle.

The three left the city and took the Via Francigena, the pilgrim road to Rome that passed by Assisi. Within a few days, they arrived at the residence of the papal court, the Lateran. There they unexpectedly ran into Bishop Guido, who was surprised, and not a little annoyed, that they were in town. Francis's earliest biographer describes the bishop's negative reaction as "strong." As a penitent and ecclesiastical person, Francis was answerable to his bishop. Guido had never discussed drawing up a way of life, much less a religious rule, with Francis. In fact, the bishop probably did not view Francis and his new companions as a special movement; they were merely another band of lay penitents. That they had gone and created what might be considered a rule for themselves and now wanted to consult the pope about it suggested that his own advice and direction were not sufficient. Francis was, in effect, going over his bishop's head.

Francis explained his intentions to the bishop. That he, rather than Bernard, did the explaining, indicates how quickly Bernard's role as leader was abandoned. In fact, Francis himself would speak for the group throughout the entire Roman visit. Francis now strove to convince his bishop of their authenticity. When at last Guido was persuaded that Francis was not trying to avoid his jurisdiction, and when he understood that the men's intention was simply to do God's will, he calmed down and agreed to help them get access to the Roman Curia. So the bishop now found himself responsible for the petition of the little group. The three were moderately literate, somewhat cultivated men, not beggars or paupers. The bishop might have wondered if men from that background might not eventually just give up the way of life that they were proposing for approval. The bishop's offer of support was a remarkable decision and says much for Francis's power of persuasion. The three men were, after all, an insignificant and marginal part of the Assisi religious scene. Now their bishop offered them access to the pope himself.

The bishop used his connections to get Francis and his followers an audience with an insider at the Curia, John of San Paolo Colonna, the cardinal bishop of Sabina. Colonna came from one of the most aristocratic of Roman families and had been a Benedictine abbot before being raised to the cardinalate. It is hard to believe that he fully understood what the former merchant had in mind to do. On the other hand, Cardinal Colonna was experienced with popular religious movements, having served as a go-between for Durandus of Huesca, the ex-Waldensian, and Pope Innocent III when Durandus was reconciled to the Church. He probably thought of Francis's little band in the same terms: laymen who wanted to live a common life, practice works of piety, and (perhaps) preach repentance. For Cardinal Colonna, as probably for Pope Innocent, Francis and his group probably seemed little more than a minor variant on the movements of "Apostolic Life," orthodox and heretical, that had proliferated during the twelfth century. Francis represented something much more radical, but at this early date this was not so evident.

The cardinal received Francis kindly, even if he was a bit patronizing. To no one's surprise except Francis's, he offered the group some typical paternal advice: join one of the traditional orders, or at least adopt a conventional style of monastic life. The cardinal viewed them primarily as contemplatives, a group of lay hermits. We might also hear the cardinal saying as he advised them: "And, please, leave the pope alone; he is a busy man." The cardinal probably imagined that he knew what the "penitents from Assisi" were: laymen playing at the monastic life. They seemed the kind of pious gyrovagues that the Church had been trying to regularize since the days of the Desert Fathers. Francis's "form of life" sounded suspiciously like one that Saint Benedict, the father of monks, had warned against. Francis and his friends stayed with the cardinal for several days, trying to make him understand their intention. Eventually he was convinced to help them. He most likely did so as a favor to his friend Bishop Guido.

The cardinal set up a meeting with Pope Innocent, at which he would act as the group's proctor or procurator, their legal representative. He may also have thought this project was the kind of thing the pope would willingly entertain. Innocent had made bold moves to reconcile heretical preaching groups and encourage lay evangelization. He had recently approved a northern Italian lay group (the Humiliati) that had run afoul of Church authorities, and two bands of former Waldensians (the Poor Catholics and the Reconciled Poor). Colonna probably argued that since Innocent was open to new movements and new ideas, this seemingly orthodox brotherhood should deserve at least a hearing.

If normal procedure was followed, Francis's project was raised during a routine consistory, probably by Cardinal Colonna as procurator, or, perhaps, by him and Bishop Guido together. The cardinal sketched the men's intentions: to live as penitents and follow literally a number of biblical counsels. To Innocent this would have sounded like any number of wayward evangelical lay preaching groups with which he had dealt. Still, this group came with impeccable credentials: a cardinal and a bishop to vouch for their orthodoxy. Doubtless he also heard about their good work among the lepers and their church repair projects. Francis was most likely not even present. Rather, the pope and his curia received Francis's petition from Cardinal Colonna, while the companions waited, perhaps impatiently, outside.

Within a few days, certainly not more than a week, Francis and his two companions received a summons to attend the papal curia with their procurator. The penitents stood quietly to the side, perhaps never even entering the room when the pope issued his decision. The ecclesiastics alone determined their case, probably speaking in Latin, which none of the men could have followed had they been present. In the end, Innocent approved the cardinal procurator's request. Then the pope had the little band approach him to receive his apostolic blessing. Francis knelt at the pope's feet and swore obedience, and after that, the other two brothers knelt before Francis and promised obedience to him. To a former Benedictine like Cardinal Colonna, it must have resembled his rite of religious profession.

According to Thomas of Celano, Pope Innocent addressed the little group and said something to this effect: "Go with the Lord, brothers, and, as the Lord will see fit to inspire you, preach penance to all. When the almighty Lord increases you in numbers and grace, come back to me with joy, and I will grant you more things than these and, with greater confidence, I will entrust you with greater things." This was not quite the commission that Francis was expecting. And it shows that Innocent saw the group in a somewhat different light than the cardinal. The pope thought of them as a group of lay preachers. Francis's *praepositum* had been approved implicitly, rather than explicitly, by this commission to preach penance. In sending them off to preach, Innocent did something other than merely approve their intention to give up all things, take up the Cross, and follow Christ. In style of life, he assimilated them to the various lay preaching groups he had been approving for some ten years. It was, for the brothers, a wholly unexpected development.

The verbal confirmation of their life was provisional; they would have to show their worth, attract new members, and then come back before he would do "greater things" for them. The approbation of the group was all in a morning's work for Innocent. We should not be surprised if, after a couple of weeks, the Assisi penitents had slipped from his memory forever. But perhaps not. A few years later, Innocent preached a sermon on John the Baptist in which his image of the Forerunner sounds remarkably like Francis. John refused to be a priest, gave up all his money and social position, and adopted a life of fasting and penance preaching. He determined to become *minus* (lesser) so that Christ could increase. Perhaps Innocent never forgot the obscure penitent from Assisi after all.

The brothers were now the responsibility of their procurator, Cardinal Colonna, and their brotherhood was to be profoundly changed by the commission to preach. Francis never conceived of himself as telling people, even his two followers, what to do. He praised penance but never told individuals that they needed it. He preached by actions more than words. Indeed, he never learned to "preach" in the conventional sense. Years later in Bologna, his hearers thought he sounded more like a government official urging action than a preacher. There is no evidence that either of his followers had ever spoken in public. The cardinal knew that such a group, should they begin to preach publicly, would immediately encounter suspicion from the clergy and scorn from the laity. What to do? He decided that the best course was to give them official public status. So he had them tonsured, the distinctive haircut that would mark them as clerics and as orthodox Catholics. It was about all the cardinal could do for them on his own.

It now fell to Francis to decide what would come of the pontiff's approval, what it meant that they had been tonsured, and how they could fulfill the commission to preach. The combination of events was somewhat unsettling. Nevertheless, Francis was amazed that the pope had given his approval so quickly and so easily. The night before the three left for Umbria, he reportedly had a dream. He saw a tall beautiful tree, and as he approached it to take cover under it, he saw himself grow to such a size that he could place his hand on the top of the tree and bend it down to where he was on the ground. The next day, he told the dream to Bernard and Peter. It seemed to Francis that it was a symbol of what had just happened. Innocent, the religious leader of the world, had condescended to hear his petition and had bowed to his request. Francis was now sure that his mission was not something of his own choosing, but was the will of the Church and of God.

Francis, Bernard, and Peter visited the tomb of the apostle Peter. They then took the road back to the valley of Spoleto. Walking up the Via Francigena, they began to discuss, even argue over, the "warnings and commands" that Pope Innocent had given them. The biblical "form of life" Innocent had approved gave them no clear directions for preaching. A commission for lay preaching was neither new nor unheard-of, just the opposite. Penance preaching had been commonly practiced by evangelical laymen since the early 1100s. Usually those who took up this work, like the followers of Bernard Prim or Durandus of Huesca, had benefited from study of the Gospels, often with the help of a priest or other teacher. The Assisi penitents had done nothing of the sort.

Francis was reduced to spiritual agony over how to combine the solitary aspects of penance and prayer with the public work of preaching. His initial conversion had taken the form of retreat into solitude and quiet manual labor. Preaching implied possession of a holiness and wisdom superior to that of the speaker's hearers. This was not how Francis understood himself. Distress over this interior conflict would plague Francis for the rest of his life. In any case, there is no convincing evidence that Francis and his followers went out to preach until several years after the visit to Rome. Papal commission to preach or not, Francis was determined that his movement would not be defined by penance preaching or any other kind of preaching.

About halfway back from Rome to Assisi, having come a distance of some fifty miles, the band camped near the papal city of Viterbo at the small town of Orte. If they had taken any food or other resources with them, these were now expended after two or three days on the road. They begged bread from a passing stranger and bedded down near an abandoned tomb. They spent some time there, far from their families, the papal court, and home. Physical deprivation mixed with spiritual confusion and brought further anxiety. It was probably with a mixture of relief and exaltation that they finally arrived at Assisi.

The Fraternity of Brothers

Francis made the decision to take up a more ordered and structured way of life after little or no planning, but he did it. About two miles outside Assisi, he and his companions came upon and occupied an abandoned shed near the bend in the crooked stream known as Rivo Torto. It was the fraternity's first *locus,* their first place of residence. The stay in this deserted and miserable place, later highly romanticized and idealized, lasted about three months, until the end of 1209. Having no rule of life but his own experiences and the Gospel that God had revealed to him, Francis first of all set the example of manual labor. Rivo Torto was close to the leprosarium of San Lazzaro, where the brothers had probably earlier worked and lodged. Subordination of himself to those who were the most despised and outcast of society had been Francis's first penance, and he continued to practice it.

Those who were unwilling to do this, Francis said, had no claim to membership in the brotherhood; there were to be no exceptions. His followers were to work at whatever craft or skill they had in order to obtain food and necessities. Later stories of this period idealize begging as the true expression of the brothers' poverty and even speak of Francis having to send the brothers to beg alone, because of the band's small size. When he looked back, Francis mentioned begging only as an alternative to manual labor, or when those who had hired the brothers refused them payment. There is little reason to believe it played a major role at Rivo Torto. They lived by day labor.

About this time or soon after, the group adopted a new form of dress. In literal conformity to the Gospel reading from Matthew, which said to "carry the Cross," they used a single tunic, making it cross-shaped, roughly cut in the form of a T. This was not so much a "habit" in the canonical sense as a modified peasant smock. There was no concern about the color or type of material.

Francis himself later described it as bound with a cord rather than a belt. The famous fresco of "Brother Francis" at Subiaco, the earliest image of the saint, shows the habit as a nondescript gray-brown color with an ample hood. Francis's cord is shown in a light color, almost white, and has three knots in it, all on one of the two hanging ends. The habit falls all the way to his ankles, which are bare, with no sign of any sandals. Predating the later controversies over the shape and poverty of the habit, this is probably a trustworthy representation of Francis's first followers' actual attire. Francis wore the tonsure, the result of Cardinal Colonna's initiative. But there is no evidence that laymen who later joined his group were tonsured in order to become clerics. They remained laymen, "lay brothers."

Francis, in his Testament, added that the brothers wore trousers under the habit. Among contemporary religious, the use of trousers signaled that the wearer was traveling on the road, not living in a monastery. From the beginning, then, Francis probably understood the following of Jesus as being "on the road," not attached to any particular place. Whether or not the trousers were an intentional statement about itinerancy, the life of the first followers was unstable and not yet linked to any one place, not even Rivo Torto. Nonetheless, the group's simple religious garb and increased association with one particular place of residence was the first step toward regularization of what was previously an ad hoc life of penance.

Francis soon, and unexpectedly, found that more men wanted to join his group. Within a short time, perhaps within a couple of weeks (the traditional date is 23 April 1209, which is probably a couple of weeks too early), another young man from Assisi, Giles, joined the brothers' community. He lived with them for a while, still wearing lay clothing, trying to make up his mind whether to stay or leave. One day, a poor man happened to come by asking for help. Francis turned to Giles and told him: "Give the poor brother your mantle." Without hesitating, the young man took it off his back and gave it to him. It was a transforming moment for Giles, who immediately adopted the little group's way of life. He would be present at Francis's death. Giles was the first "lay brother" of the new fraternity, joining the initial three, who had been tonsured as clerics.

Francis quickly learned the burden of responsibility involved in caring for his few subordinates, especially when conditions were hard. On one occasion at Rivo Torto, a brother woke in the middle of the night and cried out that he was dying of hunger. Francis, showing already the sensitivity that would make him a revered doctor of souls, had the whole community get up and eat with the brother so that he would not be shamed by having to eat alone. This also involved the entire group in resolving a difficulty that might merely have remained a private one between superior and subject. Francis used the event as an opportunity to counsel moderation in fasting and self-mortification. His first followers were prone to exaggerated and destructive mortification that had little to do with the Gospel texts that inspired their leader. Francis's natural feelings of compassion for suffering, the same trait that drew him to the lepers, found expression in the care of sick and confused brothers.

At least one other recruit joined the band in the shed at Rivo Torto, but this man proved far less suitable. He prayed little and would not work. Francis took to calling him "Brother Fly," because, unlike bees, who work for their keep, flies live off the work of others and waste it. Finally, Francis told him to leave, which he did, seemingly without any remorse. The community discovered the conflicts and difficulties of religious life at close quarters. Francis found himself cast in the role of an authority and superior. As there was hardly a place to sleep or sit inside the shed, Francis was reduced to writing the brothers' names with chalk on the beams of the hut over each one's sleeping place to prevent squabbles over space. It was cramped, drafty, and dirty, but at least it was a place to pray and sleep.

One incident allows us to date the stay at Rivo Torto with greater precision. When the emperor Otto IV and his entourage passed through the Valle Umbra on the nearby highway in September of 1209, Francis forbade the brothers to go out and gawk. But one brother, seemingly with Francis's permission, did go out to shout that all glory is passing, a jab that probably also masked a bit of anti-imperial, pro-communal Assisi pride.

Francis at the Porziuncula

Francis intended the residence at Rivo Torto to be temporary. The community needed not just more space to sleep, but also a church in which to sing the Divine Office. With the tonsure, they were now a group of clerics, not merely a gathering of lay penitents. Implicitly acknowledging his special relationship with Bishop Guido, Francis went first to him, explained their changed situation, and asked for a church of their own where a larger community of brothers could live. The bishop, probably with good reason, turned down the request. Francis then went to the cathedral chapter of San Rufino, perhaps hoping to get possession of his previous place of residence, San Damiano, since this church belonged to them rather than to the bishop. The canons, however, replied that they had no place to give him. Finally, Francis approached the Benedictine monastery on Monte Subasio. These monks owned a ruined chapel, Santa Maria degli Angeli, which lay a little over two and a half miles southwest of the city, beyond the leprosarium of San Salvatore delle Pareti, in the district known as the Porziuncula, "the Little Portion." As this building was not in use, the abbot offered to lease it to the group for a basket of fish a year, the kind of nominal rent typically used to prevent the occupants from getting ownership through the legal principle of prescription.

The brothers repaired the Santa Maria degli Angeli, and when it became usable in the spring of 1210, the community abandoned the shed at Rivo Torto, handing it over to a group of poor lepers, and took up residence in a group of wattle-and-daub cells of their own construction around the church. Now they possessed for themselves a place where they could bless Christ, the one who had died on the Cross to save the world, and sing the Office in honor of his Father in heaven.

As the weather improved, Francis himself became an ever more visible presence around Assisi. He wandered about the town and district, visiting shrines and churches. The squalor of some of these places, the result of meager resources or even total abandonment, offended both his religious and his aesthetic sensibilities. He began to carry a broom with him to sweep out the refuse. Unasked, he washed the dirty altar linen and decorated the altars. When people asked him about this (one can imagine the reactions of the resident priests), he linked penance for sin with care for sacred places. He wanted to ensure that the worship of God and the performance of the sacraments had only the finest equipment and preparation.

Whether because of a lack of welcome from local clergy or the progress of his cleanup campaign, Francis drifted farther and farther from Assisi. He attracted attention, and not all of it was negative. New recruits began to arrive. Among the most important was the priest who had once sold building stones to Francis at a steep price, but who had since undergone a change of heart, elderly Don Silvester. The group, which now included at least four clerics, finally had a member who was in orders. He could sing Mass, something without which the brothers' new church would have been incomplete. More importantly, he could teach brothers with sufficient literacy to sing the Office. This should not surprise us as all thirteenth-century clergy, both monastic and secular, were obliged to sing the Office daily. Silvester's arrival also meant that he brought his liturgical books and ritual instruments. The brothers were no longer dependent on local churches for their religious needs, at least while they were around Assisi.

Over the next few months, probably much to Francis's surprise, even more men arrived to join the little group. Early writers give names to some of them—Sabbatino, Masseo, John, Morico, and Philip—about whom virtually nothing can be known with certainty. Masseo may have been a knight from Perugia. Later speculation places the entrance of better-known early brothers like Juniper, Rufino, and Leo at this time, but the best early sources are silent on them. Francis himself decided whom to admit, and he accepted just about anyone who asked. Nearly all were laymen rather than clerics, and as far as we can tell, they came from the same class as Francis, mercantile and generally well-to-do. They were men who gave up their possessions, not men born poor.

Thus by the time the community moved to the Porziuncula, Francis's spiritual world had become very different than it was five years earlier, when he had prayed alone before the cross in San Damiano. His conversion had been a private experience, a reorientation of his sensibilities. His response had been to serve the lepers he had previously detested. Then Bernard and Peter arrived, moved by similar religious conversions. Francis's response to this unexpected development was to seek help from God through a popular divination, the random opening of the missal at San Nicolò. The result was a radical call to leave everything beyond. Unsure whether this was a delusion or a vocation, and with Bishop Guido out of town, the three men went to Rome. There, instead of receiving a simple approval, they were told to preach penance and were made clerics.

Then followed a period of debate and some confusion over the role of preaching in the new movement. Francis felt the weight of the new responsibilities thrust upon him. The decision to occupy a church of their own and establish something like a traditional religious life seems to have been made by their leader alone. Rather than being guided by some theory or a vision, Francis made concrete decisions and choices in response to particular events. In doing so, he used the models available to any thirteenth-century Italian: the practices of a brother of penance, the forms of traditional monastic observance, the itinerancy and preaching linked to the movements of the "Apostolic Life" in the previous century, and the liturgical functions typical of all clerics. The one thing this seemingly random spiritual bricolage had in common was Francis himself. Unlike earlier founders—Benedict, Augustine, Bernard—Francis presented his followers not with a coherent rule, but with himself. At the Porziuncula, the members of the new community would have to discover for themselves what this meant for them. And Francis would have to discover what it meant for himself as well.

[3]

THE PRIMITIVE FRATERNITY

1209–1215

Biographers speculate much on how Francis understood his mission in the early days of his movement, what his debts were to earlier spiritual masters, and how he conceived of the group of followers he collected. Fortunately, at least for his self-understanding, Francis left us a spiritual testament for this period. It is the "Earlier Exhortation to the Brothers and Sisters of Penance," popularly called "The First Letter to All the Faithful." Usually dated between 1209 and 1215, it was probably written somewhat after 1210, because it implies that Francis had already gained some reputation as a spiritual guide. Written for lay penitents generally, it was also directed to his followers, who at this time still described themselves as the "Penitents from Assisi."

Francis as a Spiritual Leader

Francis always saw a sharp break between the way he lived when he "was in his sins" and the life he lived after he "left the world." The same contrast is evident in the Exhortation. Its language is deeply scriptural, almost a pastiche of biblical quotations, but Francis's personal passion shines through the conventional language. He divided this little treatise into two parts, one addressed to "those who do penance" and the second to "those who do not do penance." In the first part, Francis lists four characteristics of the repentant: "[They are those Christians who] love the Lord with their whole heart, with their whole soul and mind, with their whole strength and love their neighbor as themselves; who hate their bodies, with their vices and sins; who receive the Body and Blood of our Lord Jesus Christ; and who produce fruits worthy of repentance. O how happy and blessed are these men and women!" In short, the repentant follows the two great commandments, practices bodily asceticism, receives communion regularly, and does good works. Francis, however, transforms this conventional medieval piety into a mystical vision. A sinner who takes up the penitent life receives God as his Father and Jesus as his spouse. Impregnated by the Holy Spirit, the penitent gives birth to Christ in the world. Envisioning this transformation transported Francis into ecstasy: "O how glorious it is to have a holy and great Father in heaven! O how holy, consoling, to have such a beautiful and wonderful spouse! O how holy and how loving, gratifying, humbling, peace-giving, sweet, worthy of love, and above all things desirable: to have such a Brother, such a Son, our Lord Jesus Christ!"

In contrast, the unconverted deceive themselves and work their own eternal destruction: "They are held captive by the Devil, whose children they are, and whose works they do." Unless they repent, they will be damned: "See, you blind ones, deceived by your enemies—the World, the Flesh, and the Devil—because it is sweet for the body to sin and it is bitter to serve God, for every vice and sin proceed from the heart, as the Lord says in the Gospel. You will have nothing in this world or in that to come!" The deep chasm between Francis in sin and Francis repentant has become a paradigm for all humanity. Indeed, if Francis had a message for his little group of brothers and those who observed them, it was to choose life over death and to present that choice to others by "works of repentance." The vision is almost Manichaean in the black-and-white contrast between the elect and the damned. Yet this fearful dualism is saved by God's superabundant forgiveness to Francis. Moreover, what he has chosen all can choose.

In spite of the fearful, indeed terrifying, challenge of his Exhortation, many observers found Francis engagingly attractive. Perhaps it was because of his intensity. The increasing number of followers certainly suggests Francis's great personal magnetism. On the other hand, Francis seemed to have none of the qualities usually found in a leader, religious or otherwise. He seemed positively averse to the responsibilities that his movement's success forced upon him. When he eventually undertook new projects, like establishing a stable community at Santa Maria degli Angeli or sending out followers on preaching tours, he did so more out of a sense of obedience to the pope than out of personal conviction that it was the right thing to do. Francis founded his movement in spite of himself.

Whether the brotherhood should grow or not seems never to have crossed his mind, at least as he reveals it in his extant writings. His concerns were always directed toward the individuals who joined him. When one of them was sick, he was present; when another was discouraged, he consoled him; when someone was hungry or cold, he was there to minister, but more as an example to others than as someone in charge. When, near the end of his life, Francis reflected on the early days of the movement, he focused on only three aspects of it: the members gave up everything they had, literate brothers recited the Office "like other clerics," and all did manual labor to support themselves. None of this seems very idealized or romantic, although Francis seemed a bit nostalgic when he recorded it.

Francis made a further remark about the primitive life, one that seems almost trivial at first glance: God had revealed to him a greeting: "May the Lord give you peace." We even have a physical example of Francis using it. He put it on parchment for Brother Leo in a short autograph letter of blessing written during his final illness. He used it when he greeted the birds of Bevagna before his famous "sermon to the birds." This phrase was not a command or a didactic instruction; it was a prayer. Its use placed Francis within a medieval "peace movement" going back to the period of the Gregorian Reforms in the eleventh century, but its use as a greeting was revolutionary in its novelty. The only parallel any contemporary could recall for such a greeting was a religious vagabond who had passed through the city of Assisi sometime before Francis's conversion, shouting "Peace and Good!" as he went.

Francis claimed that he had learned the greeting from God alone, which may mean, as it does for his "form of life," that he found it in the scriptures and that it was approved by the Church. A form of it is indeed found in Numbers 6:24–26, but the more likely source is Christ's own instruction in Luke 10:5–6 that the disciples invoke peace on every house they visit. The latter form had become the liturgical formula used by priests in the visitation of the sick: *Pax huic domo.* Unlike that formula, however, Francis's greeting did not use the imperative as a priest's blessing would have; rather, setting aside any priestly authority, he prayed that God grant the hearer peace. Something about this greeting was so disturbing and novel that when Francis was traveling with one of his early brothers, perhaps Bernard or Giles, people reacted with confusion or anger at it. The reaction was such that the brother with him asked him not to use it anymore.

Nevertheless, the negative response that the blessing seems to have received suggests that when the brothers used it, they seemed to be inappropriately taking to themselves a priestly prerogative, or perhaps their hearers heard an implicit rebuke of themselves as peace breakers. Medieval preachers linked peacemaking with repentance, as they usually saw personal moral failure or heresy as the root of civic unrest. This was such a commonplace that Francis may have understood Pope Innocent's commission to preach penance as an approbation of the peace greeting that God had revealed to him. One thing that distinguishes Francis from earlier and later medieval peacemakers was his absolute lack of any program of legal or social reforms. He did not diagnose the moral roots of social disease or civil unrest. Rather, he prayed to God to remove them. Once it became clear that Francis claimed no authority over others, that he had no particular religious program to impose, and that he passed no judgments on hearers' behavior, the greeting worked an unexpected effect. Combined with Francis's presence, it effected an inner peace in many who heard it. That his words and presence gave a profound internal peace underlies Francis's magnetism for the men and women of Assisi and communal Italy.

On the Road around Assisi

Francis and his first followers found ways to put Christ's words into practice in their plain, literal sense. Bernard, who had ample resources, sold them and distributed the money to the poor; Peter, who had less, gave what he had. After the move to the Porziuncula, the brothers continued to visit and assist at local leper hospitals. The brothers took menial jobs in return for an offering of food or other supplies, although they seem to have generally avoided taking these alms in cash. Near the end of his life, Francis emphasized the importance of manual labor as a means of support and as a way to keep busy and avoid temptations. That he favored manual labor over getting support by seeking alms suggests that begging was not the brothers' primary source of support in the early period. Among his own manual works, Francis rebuilt or repaired any number of abandoned chapels in the Assisi *contado*. Such buildings provided places to sleep and pray in seclusion and at a distance from the bustle of the city.

Soon the brothers began to travel beyond Assisi and its immediate environs. Sometime after the 1209 trip to Rome, intending to go on pilgrimage to Santiago in Spain, Bernard and another brother, perhaps Peter, wandered north to Florence, a four- or five-day walk. Once they reached the city, they went door to door, asking for shelter. One woman refused them access to her house but finally let them sleep in the bakehouse under her portico. Her husband reacted badly, thinking the two were a security risk. His wife replied that, at least in the bakehouse, there was not much to steal besides the firewood. Following a practice known to be typical among contemporary brothers of penance, the two rose early, around three or four o'clock, and went for Matins in the neighborhood chapel. That morning, when the woman showed up for Mass, she found the two men already in the church, doubtless reciting their Pater Nosters before the crucifix on the choir screen.

After Mass a local man of some resources named Guido, who often distributed alms to the paupers present, approached the two Umbrians to give them a coin. They refused it, much to the woman's surprise. When Guido asked why they didn't take alms like all the other beggars, Bernard replied that they had willingly chosen to become poor for the love of Christ. They had not been born that way and were not looking for money. They would, they said, work for food or shelter. This was a totally unexpected answer, since even monks, the "poor" of the Church, accepted alms. Guido and the woman were so impressed by the answer that both offered them lodging during their stay in Florence. Perhaps remembering the woman's husband's negative feelings, they stayed with Guido.

At the time of the brothers' visit to Florence, Francis walked overland to the Marche of Ancona. We know virtually nothing about this journey. But we do know something about another trip he took about this time with Brother Pacifico, a recruit from that region who had been a troubadour in the world before his conversion. The two men stopped to work at a leprosarium near the abandoned town of Trevi. This journey would have happened before 1215, when the town was rebuilt. One evening, after ministering to the lepers, Francis and Pacifico went to Bovara, another abandoned village, and entered the church of San Pietro. The two sang Compline in the abandoned building, after which Francis asked Pacifico to return to the leprosarium so that he could spend the night alone in vigil. The next day, Pacifico returned to find Francis still awake, inside the church's chancel screen, praying before the altar. Pacifico, as a lay brother, stayed outside to pray before the rood cross until Francis came out of the sanctuary.

This story confirms other reports we have about the friars' travels in this period. They wandered from town to town, working with their hands and serving lepers; they sought solitary refuges for prayer; and they passed nights in local churches, where the clerics among them said the Office. To those who witnessed them the brothers must have seemed like pious tramps. Occasionally the brothers spoke about their love of God and their decision to do penance, but this was to individuals, not groups or assembled congregations. Francis sang songs in praise of God in his bad French. Some observers may have been edified, but the more common reaction was that of every age when confronted with vagabonds: avoidance and annoyance. There was nothing to distinguish these unkempt and scruffy brothers from petty thieves or mentally unstable paupers. Women avoided them. The life was hard, but at least Francis, being away from Assisi, had become an unknown, no longer subject to abuse from his family and neighbors.

Much as Francis may have wished to obey the pope's command to preach penance, and even if biographers describe the little band as preachers from the beginning, most of what went on as the friars wandered about was sporadic personal contact with people like Guido and the unnamed woman in Florence. None of the original band, except the priest Silvester, had ever spoken in public or addressed a crowd. It is not surprising that Francis relied on his innate ability to make dramatic gestures and to win hearers by his enthusiasm and sincerity. We hear of Francis or his followers stripping themselves in public or preaching "naked," which probably means in their undergarments. Eyewitnesses describe Francis dancing with excitement as he sermonized, or making animal noises when he spoke, as he did later in his famous Christmas talk on the Babe of Bethlehem at Greccio.

Early biographers, writing after the order had become international, suggest that vast numbers of men came to join Francis in the first few years, but, in fact, there is no real evidence for this. For at least three years after 1209, the Franciscan movement remained little more than an odd band of penitents somehow linked to Santa Maria degli Angeli in the *contado* of Assisi. As late as 1216, when the visiting prelate Jacques de Vitry observed the Franciscans with approval, they were still found exclusively in central Italy. When the brothers wandered off to other cities, people received them with suspicion, sometimes even driving them away with curses and blows. When asked who they were, or if they belonged to some new religious order like the Humiliati or Poor Catholics, they could reply only that they "were penitents and born in Assisi." The people made the same mistake that Pope Innocent probably did. They assumed that they were, like those two new orders, groups of lay preachers, perhaps converted from heresy.

Lay penitents were not institutionally organized at this time, and thus the brothers' answer revealed merely their generic status as penitents, and their city of origin. The movement was in no way an "order," nor, it seems, even a confraternity. After their travels, the brothers did come together at the Porziuncula. But this was just one of any number of abandoned churches they repaired and stayed at. It is easy to forget how different the brotherhood was, in spite of papal approbation, from a traditional religious order. Even after acquiring the Porziuncula, the brothers wandered about without fixed residences. They had no superiors to hold them to account, save for Francis, who was himself often away on the road or in seclusion in the woods. In short, the group was on the periphery of medieval penance and pilgrimage culture, inhabiting the world of pious wanderers. Its reputation was mixed at best.

Even some of those attracted to Francis found it hard to understand his way of life. On one occasion in the Marche, a man came to Francis and asked to join the group. Francis told him, as he had Bernard of Quintavalle, to give all he had to the poor. The man went and gave his possessions to some of his less well-off relatives. On his return, Francis rejected him, calling him, as he had the slothful brother at Rivo Torto, "Brother Fly." Family had no privileged claim in Francis's view and certainly not in almsgiving. Few communal Italians ever understood this attitude, for it was attachment to family, not a taste for high living, that Francis struggled with in his followers during these years.

Compassion for those in need was always primary to Francis, and this led him at times into self-contradictory behavior. On a visit to a small town in the Assisi *contado*, Francis was sweeping dirt out of churches with a broom. A man named John, who was a rather simple plowman, asked for a broom so that he could sweep too. When he then asked to join the band, Francis told him to dispose of his goods. However, when John set out to give the family ox to some paupers in town, Francis intervened to prevent the family of poor *contadini* from losing their livelihood. What might have seemed infuriating inconsistency to "Brother Fly" made perfect sense to Francis, for whom true poverty, not relative poverty, always had a claim on compassion. For his own part, this John became known for his simpleminded imitation of Francis's behavior, even in things like spitting, coughing, and other gestures. In response, Francis took to calling him "Saint John." Only the most peculiar, or gifted, of brothers could merit that kind of praise from the founder.

Francis assumed that his followers would learn by imitation. Giving them rules or structures to follow was not merely difficult for him; it placed him in a position of superiority that he found painful. He never could formulate his program into rules or present his followers with clear guidelines for behavior. This was especially true in this early period, when many of the attitudes he would later adopt had not yet been clarified and solidified. New followers were to give up their worldly goods, work with their hands, and not receive cash in payment. Nevertheless, even Francis himself seems to have received alms in coin, especially for the repair of churches and for the needs of the sick. Years later, when he was sick at Cortona, Francis gave away his cloak to a beggar, and when the brothers wanted the beggar to return it for Francis's use, the founder insisted that they pay him for it. Apparently they were still handling coins, even at that late date.

Francis was never a rulemonger, even in matters as dear to him as poverty. His disciples had to watch him closely and do their best to get the drift. Their leader's own call to leave the world was so intense, so personal, that he never could explain it fully, much less sketch out a program to make it practical or concrete. The determination to abandon his autonomy and become totally dependent on God for what might happen meant that, even had he been able to concretize his vision into specific directives, he would have been horrified to give orders or instructions to others. To do so would have made him greater than others, and thus no longer a "lesser brother."

Although the brothers were not quick to act on Innocent's commission to preach after returning from Rome, it is clear that they had begun doing so by the beginning of 1212 in the cities of Umbria. This was the movement's first real exposure to the public, and had the brothers not had some success as preachers, Francis's movement might have remained a small movement of hermit penitents around Assisi. Francis and his brothers "preached penance," that is to say, they urged people to reform their moral lives and go to confession. Untrained, and in some cases hardly literate, they had little to say about doctrine (other than to promote a Catholic devotion to the sacraments), and they largely avoided exegesis of scripture. Francis was fiercely orthodox himself, but there is no trustworthy report of him preaching against heresy. On one occasion, when a Dominican pointed out to Francis a biblical text that was useful for refuting heresy, he simply replied that if the simple Francis himself could become a model of holiness, people tempted to error could be confirmed in their faith by that alone. We are told that the Dominican went away "edified."

Just as Francis never proposed a social reform program, so he never presented a religious one. His authority came from his submission to God, and his greatest sermon was always his own life. Eventually, he and his followers picked up some homiletic techniques and were able to produce sermons organized by theme and divisions on the conventional model, but such sophistication was impossible in this early period. Francis always preached more by example than by words. The men he attracted in these early days must have found him a very difficult act to imitate. Sent off with no preparation, and with very little in the way of travel plans, they did what they could. One senses that Francis cared little about success or failure, at least as those around him would have assessed either.

The brothers' preaching transcended personal morality. Like all "penance preachers" of the period, they urged peace and reconciliation. With time, their words took on a political and social flavor, but such flavor was absent in these early years. Somewhat later, perhaps in 1221, well after Francis had become famous, a well-recorded sermon against civil faction in Perugia shows Francis the peacemaker in action. While he was preaching in the city piazza to a decent-sized crowd, a group of young knights came racing through the square, scattering the crowd and jeering at Francis. They yelled that he was from Assisi, and so allied with an exiled faction. Francis pointed out, doubtless to the delight of the crowd, that these young troublemakers were the cause of bloodshed and mayhem in the city and that God would not leave their wrongdoing unpunished. The crowd must have been even more delighted when Francis told the men to reform their lives and make restitution for the damages they had caused before they could be reconciled to God. If they did not, Francis declared, God would punish them with civil war, and their violence would redound on their own heads. Inspired by Francis's words, the citizens of Perugia rose up a few days later and drove the unruly knights from the city. The result was a violent conflict in which both factions destroyed each other's property. Given his prediction of war, the peace preacher became known as a prophet as well. Francis's reputation spread.

Francis was always more a man of actions and gestures than of carefully crafted words. Indeed, it was his delivery and his persona that most affected his hearers, rather than the words he spoke. One man who heard Francis preaching in the Piazza Maggiore of Bologna in 1222 remembered the sermon for its enthusiasm and incitements to action rather than for its theological or biblical message. The topic of the sermon was angels and demons, but Francis used the occasion to implore his listeners to change their minds and do penance with their bodies—something they as human beings could do that angels and demons could not.

Francis was also known for the enthusiasm with which he addressed crowds, occasionally dancing and even breaking into song. Indeed, singing (always in French) was one of Francis's gifts, and it came more naturally to him than sermonizing. Sometimes he would take up a stick to use as a make-believe violin and bow it with his right hand as he sang. Music, however, was never a mere recreation or entertainment for Francis; invariably, his mind would turn to spiritual matters, and he might even end up in tears over the ultimate gift of God, his Son's death on the Cross. It is telling that even after years of public speaking, Francis chose to mime his last sermon to the nuns of San Damiano, not using any words. Asked to preach one last time to the sisters, Francis recited the penitential psalm, the Miserere, sat on the ground, and sprinkled ashes on his head. Doing penance made a better sermon than talking about it.

Preaching brought with it greater exposure, and for a man with Francis's magnetism and attractive personality, especially as stories of prophecy began to circulate, his reputation for holiness and access to God spread. Francis did not encourage the growth of any cult, but once an audience had been created, he lost control of his public persona. Sometime after his return from Egypt, he preached to the people of Terni in the piazza outside the bishop's palace. Bishop Ranieri, appointed by Pope Honorius in 1218, came to see the celebrity. At the end of the sermon, the bishop himself stood up to address his people. He called to mind the debt that the town owed to God for allowing them to hear the words of this "little poor man, lowly and unlettered," but still sent by God. Afterward, Francis went with him into the church and typically fell to the floor to kiss the bishop's feet. He thanked him for not calling him a "saint." Like any number of medieval holy men, Francis had already in his lifetime become viewed as a saint, with the power to work miracles and intercede before God for others.

This name of "saint" put Francis in a position of spiritual superiority to others, something that pained him deeply. We are told:

> Often when blessed Francis was honored and people said, "This man is a saint," he would respond to such expressions by saying: "I'm still not sure that I won't have sons and daughters." And he would say: "If at any moment the Lord wanted to take back the treasure he has loaned to me, what would I have left except a body and a soul, which even non-believers have? I must believe, rather, that if the Lord had granted a thief and even a non-believer as many gifts as he has given me, he would be more faithful to the Lord than I."

Francis's reputation for holiness began at home among the brothers, not in the piazza. First and foremost, however, Francis was a compassionate brother, especially for those who were tempted, spiritually troubled, or depressed. It was an age that ascribed depression to diabolical powers, and Francis had a special gift for consoling those who suffered from it. One brother, a longtime companion of Francis, resorted to fasting, scourging, and repeated confessions, seeking to escape the torment of his lack of devotion and piety. Francis perceptively noticed that the man's cure was not helping; if anything, it was making his matters worse. He therefore forbade the friar to go to confession and told him to content himself with saying seven Pater Nosters a day.

Doing what he was told, the man found that the dark cloud lifted from his soul. One can only imagine the relief he felt at being told that he was not to blame and that he did not have to torment himself any longer. The brother considered it a miracle, and so it was. Stories of Francis's gift for what would later be called "spiritual direction" spread outside the community. The abbot of Santa Giustina near Perugia sought Francis out while traveling near Assisi and begged him for prayers. After he departed, Francis began to pray. While the abbot traveled home, he experienced a wonderful joy and warmth and was moved to praise God. Again, a gentle encounter was counted a miracle. And as such the abbot recounted it in sermons to his monks.

It did not take long for Francis's skill to become known outside the world of professional religious. A young noblewoman from Limisiano with an abusive husband trailed after the brothers as they passed by the town. Word of this reached Francis, and he waited for her. She begged his blessing, saying she wanted to become a nun. Whatever she wanted, Francis could not tell her to abandon her husband. He did the best he could, holding up Christ's Passion as a consolation for her trials and promising to pray for her. He told her to go home and seek God with her husband. As she approached her house her husband came out and demanded to know where she had been. She explained that she had been to see Brother Francis, and that he had told her to go home so that she and her husband might strive to save their souls together. Undoubtedly surprised by what he heard, his temper suddenly changed, and he confessed that he would try to follow the saint's direction. In the end, he and his wife took vows of celibacy and devoted themselves to the life of lay penitents. Years later, they died on the same day, considered saints by their neighbors.

Once a reputation for holiness was established, the popular demand for miracles followed. There is no evidence that Francis ever cultivated this reputation, but his acts and gestures would be viewed as causing the miracles typical of a saint. The most primitive miracle collection shows this happening to Francis, almost in spite of himself. On one occasion, when a brother was suffering from seizures, Francis took pity on him and prayed over him, a simple act of piety. The illness departed, never to return. Word spread. At Gubbio, a crippled woman begged him to come and visit her. Ever tenderhearted, Francis came; the woman then touched him and was cured. Another woman, at San Gemini, was afflicted with epilepsy. Her husband came to Francis and the brothers to ask for help. After the brothers had prayed with the man and he was still not satisfied, Francis went himself to visit the stricken woman. Fulfilling his office of deacon, Francis recited an ad hoc prayer of exorcism, since epilepsy in the Middle Ages was generally considered to be caused by demons. Immediately, the demon departed, and the woman returned to health. On another occasion, a child at Toscanella was wasting away. The parents begged Francis to lay hands on him. Francis, who was passing through, came and blessed the boy. He later recovered, and all ascribed the cure to Francis's saintly power.

Francis realized that if he became known for healing, he would become a center of attention and a celebrity. Neither was easy to combine with his goal of being the "least of the brothers." At Arezzo, a woman hovered between life and death in labor. When Francis, perhaps intentionally, did not take the road past the woman's house, her brother went and got the bridle of the horse Francis had been riding. It did the trick: when applied to the woman, she recovered. Hearers and observers found ways to procure miracles on the sly. They would bring Francis food to bless—a seemingly harmless gesture—but then they would put the food in circulation for curing the sick. At Gualfreduccio near Città di Pieve, a man got some threads from Francis's habit and dipped them in water to pass out for the sick to drink: cures followed. In spite of himself, Francis was pressed into performing cures. At Narni, a man named Peter was struck with paralysis for five months. Knowing Francis's dislike of performing cures, he had a message sent to the bishop so that he would order Francis to visit and bless the man. Francis did, and the man recovered.

Stories and reports from the first few years at the Porziuncula are very hard to interpret, but one theme stands out: Francis was having difficulty adapting to his new role as a leader of a religious movement and a public person. For over two years, Francis struggled with what later biographers opaquely called "a serious temptation of spirit." He often left the community to seek refuge in the woods nearby, spending time alone in prayer. On one occasion, he was seen wandering through the woods near the Porziuncula sobbing. When asked what was wrong, all Francis could say was he wanted to wander through the whole world like this, "crying and bewailing the Passion of the Lord." To one observer, his eyes seemed so red from sobbing that they were filled with blood. The Lord's Passion was Francis's passion. Francis's response to spiritual dryness was a typically medieval one: he began to fast, inflict physical penances on himself, and spend longer periods in prayer, mostly at night when most of the brothers had gone to bed.

Francis spoke of these temptations as his "flies," the same label he used for troublesome brothers. The link does not seem accidental. If one thing is clear from these stories, it was Francis's desire, at least on occasion, to get away from the brothers. His seclusion and desire to wander away, at the very time when his little band was growing and developing into something resembling a traditional religious order, arose not merely from an internal conflict, but also from his inability to deal with the new challenges of leadership. He was sorely tempted to abandon the brotherhood and flee. Francis seemed to have regressed to the spiritual state that typified his life just after his conversion, when he could find solace only before the cross at San Damiano. Only when praying before the altar and accepting the cross of temptations did he find relief and peace. Those around him noticed the change.

Finally, Francis decided that he had to embrace his cross in a new way. He resolved to leave Assisi and travel to the Holy Land, perhaps there to find martyrdom for preaching the name of Christ. In the summer of 1211, accompanied by an unnamed friar, he went overland to the Adriatic coast, where he found a ship leaving for the Orient. Having convinced the ship's captain to take them on board, they set sail, but within days of leaving port, a major storm blew up and forced the ship into port on the other side of the Adriatic in Dalmatia, perhaps at Dubrovnik or Split. Since the two men could not find a ship leaving for the Holy Land that late in the summer, they begged sailors departing for Ancona to take them along. Unsurprisingly, the captain refused to take on board two scruffy vagabonds with no money to pay their way. In a typically impulsive decision, they stole on board the vessel and stowed away. Yet another storm broke, and the vessel remained at sea for several days, failing to make the brief crossing. Francis came out of hiding and shared the food he had brought along, which did something to reconcile the sailors to their unwanted cargo. Finally the ship made land on the west coast of Italy. Francis was back in his homeland, his plan to escape thwarted.

The Conversion of Clare

Within six months or so of his return to Assisi, Francis found two men who became his lifelong confidants and his support in difficult times. One was the priest Leo; the other was Brother Rufino. The first became Francis's chaplain and confessor; the second was first cousin of an aristocratic woman of Assisi, the niece of Monaldo, lord of Coriano. She was Clare di Favarone di Offrediccio, a woman from the very class of landed aristocrats that the young Francis had imitated and longed to join socially. There is no evidence that Rufino had anything but a close and peaceful relationship with his family. Perhaps he was the source of Clare's knowledge of Francis and his movement. In any case, one day Rufino came to Francis to explain that his kinswoman wanted to meet him. Francis had never contemplated a women's branch of his movement: he had hardly anticipated a movement of men. We may guess that he expected the young woman to take up the life of a sister of penance, not to join him and his small group at the Porziuncula.

Clare was, we understand, some eleven years younger than Francis, aged about eighteen in 1212, when the approach was made. Hers was an age when thirteenth-century Italian women were carefully guarded by their parents, especially by aristocratic parents, in preparation for marriage or entrance into a convent. Francis agreed to meet Clare and talk about her plans. A meeting was arranged unbeknownst to Clare's parents; she would come escorted by a chaperon, Bona di Guelfuccio, while Francis would come with his current *socius,* Brother Philip Longo of Arti. Lady Bona eventually accompanied Clare to a good number of clandestine meetings, during which Francis urged the young woman to take up a life of penance. Beyond that, we have no idea what went on during their conversations, all other reports being late and legendary. The eventual result, however, was a plan for Clare to "leave the world," just as Francis had nearly seven years earlier.

On Palm Sunday morning, 1212, Clare attended Mass at San Rufino with the women of her family and received her palm branch from the hand of Bishop Guido. He gave it to her personally, because, it seems, in a fit of distraction she had failed to join the women's line for the distribution of the palms. Perhaps Guido knew what was going on, and this was a signal that he approved. That night, accompanied by her sister Pacifica (Bona had departed on pilgrimage to Rome), Clare left the family's house though a security door. This required moving away the bricks and beams blocking it. The choice of this exit, rather than the usual street door, suggests that Clare left home against the wishes of her parents or at least without their knowledge.

Clare and her sister arrived at the Porziuncula during the night. They found Francis and the community waiting for her in prayer before the candlelit altar. Francis cut the young woman's hair and gave her a habit like that of the brothers, but with a veil. Before the ceremony, as Clare later recounted herself, she made profession of religious obedience for life directly to Francis. Francis, like other religious leaders of the time, considered it normal that those entering monastic life make a vowed life commitment before they entered. There was nothing unusual about Clare's profession, except that there was absolutely no provision for a woman to live at the Porziuncula. Francis now faced a new problem: what to do with his first female disciple. As on several other occasions of need, he turned to the Benedictines. He placed Clare among the nuns of San Paolo of Bastia, which was about two and a half miles outside of Assisi on the road to Perugia. Their party arrived at the nunnery late at night, because Clare could not stay till morning at Santa Maria degli Angeli. This arrangement must have been planned well ahead of time, but it was, at best, a temporary expedient. Clare's family soon found her at San Paolo and challenged her decision. She warned off her father and uncles by showing them her shaven head. They seem to have acquiesced in the decision without further protest.

Within a couple of days, Francis moved Clare again, this time to the Benedictine nuns of Sant'Angelo of Panzo, a mile-and-a-half trip out on the opposite side of Assisi. This monastery was under the jurisdiction of the abbot of Subasio, to whom the Porziuncula belonged. Francis seems to have made the new arrangements through his own landlord. At Sant'Angelo of Panzo, Clare was joined by her sister Agnes, again without parental consent. This time the family arrived with soldiers to take both women home by force. Again, Clare succeeded in sweet-talking her father. He went home without his daughters. Francis then arrived publicly to perform Agnes's vestition and take her profession of vows. Francis's next move strongly suggests that Bishop Guido had been in on the plan from the beginning. Within a couple of months, Francis settled the two women on their own at the cathedral chapter's church of San Damiano. It became the first convent of the female Franciscan movement. With episcopal protection, the women could live in peace. Use of the church may have been the pious bishop's last gesture of support for Francis and his movement, for by September of that year he seems to have died, and another bishop, also named Guido, was serving in his place. At Clare's request, Francis prepared for the sisters a "form of life" that sounds very much like his own *praepositum* of 1209. By it they were charged to "follow the perfection of the holy Gospel."

Strangely, from this point until his last illness, Clare completely disappears from Francis's life. We understand that they exchanged letters, and that, in his last illness, Francis returned to San Damiano to see the sisters, but there is no evidence of any other visits. Francis had bowed to her request to do penance, professed her as a nun, and given her a rule of life. Then he left, romantic elaborations in modern biographies notwithstanding. Supervising the growth of the Poor Ladies of San Damiano and defending their call to live a life of absolute poverty would become Clare's responsibility alone.

Only once, in a letter to Agnes of Prague of 1238, does Clare tell us anything of her correspondence with Francis. She wrote that he had directed the sisters to observe the Lenten fast year-round, except on Sundays, Christmas, and feasts of the Virgin and the Apostles, and to mitigate it for the sick. The advice seems almost generic in its traditionalism, though very typical of Francis's liturgical piety. That something so unexceptional would be the one communication from Francis that Clare chose to quote suggests that in her case, like that of the brothers, it was Francis's actions and personality, not his words or instructions, that spoke most directly to her.

It took Francis about a year to arrange for Clare's final settlement and the regularization of the Poor Ladies' life at San Damiano. Freed of that responsibility, probably in the fall of 1212 or winter of 1213, Francis again decided to leave Assisi. This time, Francis decided not to risk sea travel; he would reach Muslim lands and possible martyrdom by the land route through Spain. He set out for Andalusia, intending then to go on to Morocco. There he planned to preach to the court of the Miramamolin, as the Almohad caliph Muhammad al-Nasir was known in western Europe. This Muslim leader had been defeated in July of 1212 by the combined Christian forces of Iberia under the leadership of Alfonso VIII of Castile at the battle of Las Navas del Tolosa. The victory suggested that Christian missionaries might now have access to Muslim lands in the West.

Francis's new escape plan was no more successful than his earlier one to Syria. Before reaching Spain, perhaps before leaving Italy, Francis fell gravely ill and had to return home. Muhammad al-Nasir himself had already died at

Marrakesh in early 1213. This was news that Francis had probably not heard. Perhaps he learned of it when he reached the Iberian border. It provided another reason, besides illness, to go home.

Francis Faces New Growth

On 8 May 1213, Francis received a gift, perhaps motivated by his need for spiritual refreshment when responsibilities of administration became burdensome. Count Orlando of Chiusi, a member of the powerful Caetani family, granted, by an oral gift to Francis and his friars, the possession of an isolated mountain in the Tuscan Apennines, just above the valley of Casentino. Its name was La Verna, or, in Latin, Alverna. The count, we understand, gave the mountain "solely out of devotion," so that "Francis and his brothers might live there." Orlando often gave Francis hospitality when he traveled in the region, and he treasured the items that the founder used during those visits. That Francis received such a generous donation from a member of the Italian aristocracy confirms that his movement was now attracting the attention of men from the highest classes.

The period from 1213 to 1216 is the most obscure period in Francis's life. This is unfortunate, as it is the period in which Francis first had to deal practically with the growth of his movement and provide for a brotherhood that extended beyond Assisi. It is telling that during this period Francis's fellowship finally received a set name. The earlier, purely descriptive phrase "Penitents from Assisi" seems to have been replaced by the title "Lesser Poor," in contrast to the "Catholic Poor" of Bernard Prim and the heretical "Poor of Lyons." Perhaps Francis did not like the comparison implied with these other groups, because by 1216, he had begun to call his followers the *Fratres Minores,* which is best expressed in English as the "Lesser Brothers."

This standardization of their name happened in the wake of the Fourth Lateran Council, which met under Pope Innocent from 11 to 30 November 1215. That council required that all religious orders hold "chapters," meetings so called from the practice of reading a chapter of the Bible at their opening. These were to follow the format and purpose of the chapters held by the Cistercian monks, who would themselves serve as advisers for groups new to the practice. It is not impossible that Francis attended the council in person, although the first evidence for this is an unsupported assertion to that effect by the Spiritual Franciscan Angelo Clareno in the fourteenth century. Some modern historians have also suggested that Francis drew up a new version of his Rule in the wake of the council, but again there is no contemporary evidence for such a project. In any case, already after the return from Rome in

1209, Francis and his followers had gathered at the Porziuncula periodically during their journeys. It would be hard to call these early gatherings "chapters," as the word was used in Church legislation like the statutes of the Lateran Council. Canonically formal meetings on a regular basis would come for the Franciscans only after the council.

During the summer of 1215, even before the Lateran Council had met, another milestone was reached: Cardinal John of San Paolo Colonna died at Rome. He had advised Francis even after the return to Assisi in 1209. Through him, Francis and his group had become known in Rome and welcome at the houses of some of the cardinals. Within a year, on 16 July 1216, Pope Innocent died while with his curia at Perugia. The bishop who had supported him, the pope whom he considered his spiritual father, and the cardinal who, more than any other, had become the protector of his movement were gone. Francis was alone, even if surrounded by a growing crowd of friars, imitators, and perhaps even sisters.

Soon after, the newly elected bishop of Acre in Syria, Jacques de Vitry, arrived in Perugia, expecting to be consecrated by the pope. Instead, he found that the pontiff's body had been left lying in state in the cathedral, and, during the night, thieves had stripped the corpse and left it naked and decaying. The sight gave him pause and set him to thinking about the transitory nature of human glory. Jacques would be consecrated bishop by Innocent's successor, Honorius III, on the Sunday after his installation as pope. Jacques was impressed by Honorius's piety and generosity, but the papal curia seemed to him a den of power-hungry lawyers, consumed totally with lawsuits and politics.

The one happy impression that Umbria made on Jacques was the presence of a new religious movement, as yet unknown in France, that was attracting men and women from all classes. These practitioners of a new form of religious life were known, Jacques was told, as the "Lesser Brothers and Sisters." He probably did not completely understand the revolutionary development. His letter on the movement, written a couple of months later from Genoa to his friends back in Liège, is the first eyewitness description of the Franciscan movement. He reported that the members of this new movement spent their nights in prayer and vigil and that during the day they went from village to village and town to town seeking souls for Christ. Wherever a group of the brothers arrived, others wanted to join them. All the clergy, he said, including the pope and cardinals, held them in high esteem. According to Jacques, Francis's followers could be found in Tuscany, Umbria, and the kingdom of Naples. He asserts that they met yearly to eat together, exchange mutual support, and draw up statutes for themselves, which were then sent on for papal approval.

Among those attracted to the movement was a Cistercian monk of Casa-mari, Dom Nicholas, a penitentiary of the pope, who joined them, only to be recalled to curial administration because the needs of the Curia took precedence over his pious desires. Jacques seemed to think those Roman priorities mis-guided. Oddly, the new bishop of Acre never mentioned the founder himself; at this point he had probably never met him. For Jacques, it was the followers that merited attention. Things had changed for the movement since before the Lateran Council. Before Jacques' letter, there is no evidence that the Franciscan movement had any effect outside of the valley of Spoleto. From the day that Innocent sent the first three friars home to see if God would prosper their in-tentions until Jacques' observations, there is no direct evidence that the Roman Curia and the pope ever paid them any attention. Now they were active in central and southern Italy and known in Rome.

Although Jacques describes a regularization of the brothers' life—for example, the convocation of "chapters"—he still describes a very fluid world. He knows of no established settlements of the men and mentions women followers who live in hospices near the cities, supporting themselves by manual labor. The movement sounds very free-form, perhaps consisting mostly of men and women who loosely associated with Francis and his brothers but lived lives of penance on their own. Only the meeting of chapters hints at the Porziuncula as a center of activity, and it is nowhere mentioned by name in the letter. Even the name "Lesser Brothers and Sisters" sounds unofficial, being merely "what they call themselves." Some historians suggest that the "Lesser Sisters" sound rather suspiciously like the Beguines Jacques knew back in the Low Countries, for whom he was now seeking papal approval. Most likely, however, given the loose organization of the brotherhood at this stage, there were penitents of both sexes who imitated Francis and sought his advice. These are the kind of pious lay folk to whom Francis addressed his "Earlier Exhortation to the Brothers and Sisters of Penance." In the midst of the flurry of activity Jacques describes, Francis himself is oddly invisible.

When Jacques sat down some five years later to describe the same events in his *Historia Occidentalis,* he would get Francis's name wrong, calling him Francino, not Francesco—this even after the bishop had met him personally in Egypt. Nevertheless, this period of early Italian growth was the work of Francis himself, and not, like the exponential expansion of the movement throughout Europe in the next few years, the work of his followers. Beginning as a voluntary outsider on the margins of Assisi, Francis had already become a religious figure of note in central Italy. It was not, for him, a happy situa-tion: even Jacques noticed that the "Lesser Brothers," no doubt imitating their leader, were "grieved, indeed troubled, to be honored by the clergy and laity more than they wished."

Growth was aided by Francis's difficulty in turning down those who came to him asking to join. He had no training as a preacher or administrator, much less as a novice master. Jacques de Vitry's successor as cardinal bishop of Tusculum, Eudes of Chateauroux, would later marvel: "If anyone considers what Francis did after his conversion, he will only discover folly. Isn't it pure folly for a man who knew nothing about it and had no experience of it to found an order? Isn't it folly and madness to preach to the Saracens and—what am I saying!—to the Christians themselves?" Yet Francis eventually set out to preach and from the beginning accepted new recruits. Jacques himself tersely commented that "he admitted everyone indiscriminately." When Francis was challenged about his lax admissions policy and the absence of any spiritual training for his recruits, he replied, as was his usual habit, with a slightly off-color parable. There was, he said, a country woman who had become the lover of a great king, and by him she had a son. Eventually, as the son grew up, she went to the king, who admitted the paternity and arranged for the boy's support. Francis went on to say that since God had impregnated him by his Word and given him many spiritual sons, God himself too would have to provide for them.

The self-deprecating tone of the anecdote sounds very much like Francis. The willingness to act and let God provide describes him perfectly. Francis's own impatience with religious strategy and planning is reflected in another incident set in the period "when Francis first began to have brothers." He found that the brother cook, perhaps at the Porziuncula, was putting beans in water to soak the night before they were to be prepared, the usual culinary practice. Francis, noticing that this was "taking concern for the morrow," instructed him to wait until after Matins had been sung on the morning of the day they were to be used. Given that beans need a good six hours of soaking to be usable, this was cutting it short, but the cook obeyed Francis. We hear that Francis's followers continued to follow this directive "for a long time, especially when they lived in cities."

Francis struggled with his need to follow Christ's less practical directives, yet not think well of himself for doing so. Once while walking through Assisi, a beggar woman asked Francis for his cloak, and he immediately gave her the one he was wearing. Afterward, he went before the brothers and confessed to his vainglory over the incident. Francis lived on the edge of spiritual comfort, not merely on the edge of physical destitution. Much as the later recounting of this story made it an exemplum for less perfect Franciscans and other clerics, the tension here was not, for Francis, in discomfort with others' failure to live up to his lofty vision of the Gospel. It was his recognition of his own inadequacy. But Francis's own purity, in comparison to the worldly and often litigious clergy of his day, appealed to the wave of reforming zeal that had swept Latin Christendom since the eleventh century. The perfection of its evangelical life lay behind the movement's swelling number of recruits. But, in central Italy, the original draw had been Francis's unique and attractive personality alone.

[4]

EXPANSION AND CONSOLIDATION

1216–1220

B Y 1216, FRANCIS had become a religious celebrity, at least in central Italy. A small sign of this celebrity is visible today in the Church of Santa Maria Maggiore in Assisi where an inscription from that year dates repairs in the sanctuary "to the time of Bishop Guido and Brother Francis." As his movement grew, Brother Francis found himself increasingly removed from the hermit life in the woods that he lived at the time of his conversion. After this date Francis's own writings and the stories told about him show the world of solitude and nature to which he was always drawn slowly slipping away.

Francis and Nature

Francis felt a deep union with living creatures, who, like the lilies of the field and the birds of the air, lived the Gospel precept of complete reliance on God spontaneously and naturally. Whether he considered them a model for religious or not, they followed the Gospel of complete reliance on God better than some of Francis's followers. Here was a "religious community" that needed no leader and no correction. No wonder Francis felt a union with them that eluded him with his human brothers. Francis's appreciation of nature was not, however, guided by metaphors, however biblical. He experienced creation directly and intensely, a reality sometimes hidden by the symbolic use of animals in his writings. He loved living things; they moved him to prayer and, most typically, to compassion, especially toward animals themselves. His first response to nature was to praise its Creator and to love the creature. Animals were for him a gift, not an opportunity for homilizing or appropriation. When speaking of Francis's relationship to nature, those who knew him personally said nothing about his preaching to the birds. Rather, what impressed them was his deep affinity for creatures, his habit of speaking to them with affection, and their attraction to him. He was like them in his great simplicity.

When Francis used images from nature in his own writings, he did so in two ways. First, he used phrases and similes drawn from scripture: "sheep among wolves," "the birds of the air," and, later, "the ox and the ass" in the tableaux of the manger at Greccio. Second, he was fond of giving animal names to friars as a means of criticism: "Brother Fly" for a lazy and worthless brother; "Brother Ass" for his own body when it was proving recalcitrant or troublesome. This language, while often critical, had a playful element that brings us close to Francis's affinity with nature. Both of these uses of nature images come together in one of Francis's most famous dreams, one he used to criticize his own failures. He dreamt of himself as a little black hen, who was comically unable to shelter her numberless scattering chicks under her wings. For Francis, the dream symbolized his own inability to provide and care for all the friars of this rapidly growing movement. He identified himself as the weak little creature, an identification both self-critical and playful. He took his inspiration from scripture, for Christ used a very similar image when speaking of Jerusalem: "Jerusalem, Jerusalem, you who kill the prophets and stone those sent to you, how often I have longed to gather your children together, as a hen gathers her chicks under her wings, but you were not willing" (Luke 13:34). But Francis blames only himself, not his wayward friars. That Francis experienced such a complex and beautiful image in a dream shows that identification with creatures came naturally to him. As a "servant of all," including natural creatures, Francis avoided using nature or natural imagery for teaching others, other than in labels like "Brother Fly." When he used nature homiletically, in preaching or teaching, the images were biblical, rather than experiential.

In his love of God's creation, Francis encountered nature as a unified whole. Near his death, when he composed the "Canticle of Brother Sun," he referred to the celestial bodies and the four classical elements (earth, air, fire, and water); he made no mention of any living creatures but no doubt saw them as part of the whole of creation. In his other writings, Francis mentioned creation and animals only rarely. He only twice gave rules as to the use of animals by his followers: they were not to ride horses, and they were not to keep pets. These rules are only partly about poverty; they encouraged friars not to treat animals as objects or possessions. And, in the case of horseback riding, his rule distanced the friars from the proud world of chivalry. Even when sickness compelled him to ride, Francis always preferred a donkey. Near the end of his life, in a very revealing gesture, he urged the brothers to put out special food for the birds and beasts at Christmas so that in their own way they might rejoice at the birth of the Savior.

In his writing, Francis adopted nature imagery from scripture, not from nature directly. In the five passages outside of the Rule where he mentions animals, only once does he go beyond imagery from scripture, and it is to hold up animals as an example of obedience to God. There is not a hint of pantheism in Francis's approach to nature. Animals praise God by their being and are a model of obedience to God; they are not, like the Eucharist, identified with God himself. They remain creatures. There was another limit to Francis's identification with nature, again with scriptural rules. In accord with the Gospel precept to "eat what is put before you," Francis, alone among medieval religious founders and reformers, permitted the eating of meat—a rule he followed himself. He was emphatically not a vegetarian.

Francis took spontaneous joy in his encounters with animals, especially when they responded to him. Once at the Porziuncula, while staying in the cell that would, after his death, be occupied by the gardener, Brother Ranieri, he found a cricket on a branch of the fig tree outside his door. He coaxed it onto his finger and said: "Sing, my sister Cricket!" The little creature sang. For an hour he held the cricket with pure delight. For a whole week, each morning when he came out, he found what seemed to him the same cricket, and it would sing for him. This brought him great consolation. Eventually, he allowed the creature its freedom. He "gave her permission" to go wherever she wanted. She took off and flew away.

Francis's respect for animals' freedom and dignity shows him at his most sensitive and attractive. He could not bear the thought of a living creature caught in a trap or destined to be killed, even for food—despite his rejection of religious abstinence from meat. As Francis and the brothers walked the highways of Umbria after a rain, he would stop to pick up and move worms that had crawled on the road to escape the water. He could not bear the thought of people stepping on them. He expressed the same compassion to animals brought to him or the brothers for food. Once, at Greccio, a brother brought in a hare caught in a trap, doubtless proud of having provided a meal for the community. Francis took the hare, held it, stroked it for some time, and then went out and released it. The small creature must have found a sense of security beside Francis, for it would not leave his side; even when chased off, it found its way back to his feet. Eventually, he had one of the brothers take it to the deep woods. Offerings from outsiders he also set free. While crossing the lake of Rieti, a fisherman offered him a tench (*tinca*). Francis accepted "Brother Tench," but then dropped him back in the lake. A familiarity with animals, reminiscent of Adam in the garden of Eden, was part of the conventional medieval model of sanctity, but Francis exhibited something more, a personal affection and love of them. In a world where nature was typically exploited as a source of resources or feared as dangerous, those who knew him commented on Francis's affection for animals and delight in creation.

On occasion, Francis pointed to animals as an opportunity to reflect on the Gospels and their message. Once while walking with Brother Paul to Osimo, where the brother was minister, they passed a peasant with a flock of goats, in the midst of which was a single lamb. Francis recalled Christ's allegorical use of sheep and goats, and since this lamb reminded him of the Lamb of God, alone among the Pharisees and high priests before his Passion, he began to weep. Brother Paul bought the lamb with alms they had been given, and the two brothers presented it, safe, to the bishop of Osimo. For Francis, lambs were always images of Christ, but above all their innocence and weakness aroused his affection and compassion. Once in the Marche, he came upon a peasant bringing two lambs to market. Horrified to hear that they were to be sold and killed for food, and moved by their pitiful cries, he traded his cloak for the lambs. Even Thomas of Celano avoided allegorizing this touching story in his retelling.

Above all, Francis loved birds, larks in particular. We have a saying attributed to Francis in which he gives reasons for this particular affection:

> Our Sister Lark has a hood like a religious and is a humble bird, who gladly goes along the road looking for some grain. Even if she finds it in the animal dung, she pecks it out and eats it. While flying, she praises the Lord, like good religious who look down on earthly things, and whose life is always in heaven. Moreover, her clothes, that is her feathers, resemble earth, giving an example to religious not to wear clothes that are colorful and refined, but dull, like earth.

This kind of moralizing seems unusual in Francis's attitude toward animals and is less an attempt to teach a lesson than to explain the reason for his spontaneous delight and affection.

Once while traveling near Bevagna in the Spoleto valley, Francis spied a large flock of birds in a field by the side of the road. Delighted by them, he approached and addressed them with his familiar greeting, "The Lord give you peace." He was even more delighted that they did not fly away, even as he walked into their midst. He voiced great praise to God for this and urged his sister birds to do so too. This was something they did, singing, spreading their wings, and taking flight as he blessed them with the sign of the cross. This incident, later elaborated into the famous "Sermon to the Birds," exemplifies Francis's relationship to nature: delight at its presence and greater delight when animals did not fear him, both leading to praise of the Creator who made them.

Integration into the Life of the Church

As long as Francis and his followers remained a local movement in the Spoleto valley, they were principally answerable to the bishop of the diocese in which they had their base, Assisi. By 1212 this was Bishop Guido III, the successor of the Guido who presided over Francis's conversion, who is conventionally referred to as Guido II. The later Guido had a very different personality from his predecessor. He was of a more irascible temperament, and his reign was filled with lawsuits exerting his rights, especially in respect to religious orders and hospitals. He was, however, supportive of Francis and his movement and visited the Porziuncula often, sometimes arriving unannounced at Francis's own cell.

By 14 May 1217, the day of the brothers' annual chapter, when, we are told, Francis still did not have very many brothers, the movement had grown large enough that it could now fulfill Christ's command to preach the Gospel to all nations. Francis selected leaders, to be called "ministers," to lead groups of brothers outside of central Italy to other places where the Catholic faith was practiced. Groups went to the areas of Italy where the movement was not yet known, that is, to Lombardy and Venetia in the north. Francis dispatched other groups to France, Germany, Hungary, Spain, and other regions beyond the Alps. This major missionary effort was not the first dispatch of brothers abroad. At the previous chapter of 1216, Francis had appointed the lay brother Elias of Assisi (usually referred to incorrectly as Elias of Cortona) to lead a small missionary group of friars to the Crusader lands of the Middle East. They accomplished the very journey that Francis had attempted, without success, a couple of years before.

The missions dispatched by both chapters were very much ad hoc affairs; there was no administrative division of the brotherhood into geographic provinces at this date nor any clear chain of command, and Francis himself remained the sole brother responsible for admitting new members to the movement. These journeys were very much personal projects of the brothers involved, not a corporate project. In this they resembled the travels that Francis and his followers had been taking since their first settlement at Santa Maria degli Angeli. The mission to Germany had about sixty friars in it. Six other expeditions, including that bound for Syria, are reported in the sources, so we might guess how many followers Francis had in 1217. If each mission was on the scale of that to Germany, then three hundred to four hundred brothers were involved. Reports suggest that less than half of Francis's followers stayed in central and southern Italy. So Francis's whole brotherhood probably still numbered fewer than eight hundred in the spring of 1217.

After the departures of the brothers for foreign missions and other parts of Italy, only a handful remained at the Porziuncula in Umbria; well under a hundred, perhaps fifty or fewer. Now, released from the burden of directing and guiding a large group of brothers at Santa Maria degli Angeli, Francis felt free to travel abroad himself. With little if any consultation, Francis left Umbria and set out for France. His destination had personal and spiritual motives. Francis already had some facility with the French language and had loved its poetry and songs since his youth. He told the brothers another reason for his choice of destination: the Catholics in France had a greater devotion to the Blessed Sacrament than those of any other land. Devotion to the Host, which had been a growing part of Francis's spirituality since his conversion, seems the determining factor in his decision. It was natural that Francis chose, among others to go with him, Brother Silvester, the first priest to join the brotherhood. Francis would never be without the Eucharist on his journey.

Traveling north on the Via Francigena, the group arrived at Arezzo, where factional divisions had broken out in street fighting. Unable to enter the city, and sensing demonic influence in the civil strife, Francis asked Silvester to pray a prayer of exorcism over the city. Later they would find that the unrest had receded soon after, convincing Francis that the factionalism was indeed demonic; but not yet knowing that peace had been restored, the group continued on to Florence. On reaching that city, Francis heard that Cardinal Hugolino of Ostia was there, exercising the office of papal legate for Tuscany, Lombardy, and the Marche of Treviso. The cardinal had just seen his attempted reconciliation of Genoa and Pisa collapse. As was his habit with ecclesiastics, Francis went to pay his respects to the cardinal, who was very busy with internal factional problems in Florence and, perhaps, with repression of heresy.

The two men had never met before. Hugolino, through his work in the Roman Curia, was not unaware of the growing brotherhood of penitents in Assisi. He may have gotten reports through sympathetic cardinals like John of Santo Paolo Colonna or from the new bishop of Assisi, Guido III, with whom he had been involved in a canonical matter during May of 1217. His most likely informant at the papal court was the appreciative observer of the Franciscans, Jacques de Vitry, the French theologian recently elected bishop of the Crusader stronghold of Acre in Syria. That the cardinal made time for Francis shows that he was sympathetic to a new and radical religious movement, but that does not mean that Francis got much of his time. Their interchange seems, to put it kindly, rushed and curt. Hugolino was shocked to hear that Francis had sent his brothers abroad and now intended to abandon the small group left in Assisi. Francis remained adamant; he tried to explain his purpose and protested that his failure to go would shame him before his missionary brothers.

The cardinal would have none of it. He ordered Francis to return home and fulfill his major responsibility: leadership of his growing movement. Francis's personal leadership was imperative, the cardinal said, because, at the Curia and among the hierarchy, there were men less disposed to the new movement than he. Francis, with his habitual deference to ecclesiastics, agreed to obey. Hugolino sensed Francis's disappointment, which was hardly hidden, and offered as recompense his services as canonical adviser and as advocate at the Curia. Francis accepted the offer and invited the cardinal to attend the next Pentecost chapter at the Porziuncula. Francis seems to have thought that if he could not go to France, then the man who prevented that journey could now help him with his burden at home. Hugolino accepted the invitation. His responsibilities as legate would leave him free to attend only the chapters of 1218 and 1219. Francis sent Brother Pacifico and several others on to France, and he returned to Assisi.

The cardinal's meeting with Francis seems accidental, but his reaction to Francis's decision to abandon Assisi shows that he understood the founder's central role in his movement. Francis's "form of life," which had been "conceded, but not confirmed," was still probationary. The movement's growth in numbers had reached a point where "some" ecclesiastics were concerned about the brothers' orthodoxy, submission, and discipline. Francis himself found it ever harder to oversee his now far-flung disciples. Hugolino's command to return, much as it frustrated Francis, was an ad hoc reaction to these circumstances. But the cardinal's attendance at one or two Porziuncula chapters signaled a major change in the status of Francis, his movement, and its relations to the hierarchy. The cardinal's was to be a new, solemn, and authoritative presence.

Francis Dispatches Letters and Missions

Within a year of his return to Assisi, Francis composed his first extant letter. Something had triggered his decision to go to France, where the Eucharist was venerated properly, and now he was unable to go. Instead, he dispatched this letter, the first of his two "Letters to the Clergy." Its language is heated, pained, and almost frantic in tone. In it he includes himself among the clergy, a good indication that he had already been ordained to the deaconate. What motivates him is the same passion that sent him on the road to France: his love of the Eucharist. He is outraged at the "great sin and ignorance some have toward the most holy Body and Blood of our Lord Jesus Christ and his most holy names and words that consecrate his Body." How that sin expressed itself, and its remedy, he made clear: "Let all those who administer such most holy mysteries, especially those who administer them illicitly, consider how very dirty are the chalices, corporals, and altar linens, on which his Body and Blood are sacrificed. It is placed in many dirty places, carried about unbecomingly, and ministered to others without care. Even his written names and words are at times left to be trampled under foot." Francis directs that the Host be kept in a "precious place" and locked up, and that scraps of parchment with the words of scripture or the name of God be collected and put in suitable places. Those receiving his letter are to clean their altar linen and polish their chalices without delay. This theme reappeared regularly in Francis's writing, but seldom with such passion and anger.

Francis returned to the theme of reverence for the Eucharist in other writings about this time. His "First Admonition," even if influenced by the mystical understanding of the Mass found in Cistercian writers as some suggest, is authentically Francis's own. For him, the change of the elements from bread and wine to Christ's Body and Blood was like the Incarnation. Christ gives himself to those viewing the Host or receiving communion as literally as he allowed himself to be seen and touched by the apostles. By this giving, he is with believers until the end of the age. The locus of Francis's "mysticism," his belief that he could have direct contact with God, was in the Mass, not in nature or even in service to the poor. Thus his harsh words for those who ignored the Eucharistic presence are unique: he never used such language about peace breakers or those who oppressed the downtrodden, deeply as those sins pained him. Francis always preferred to speak by actions and gestures rather than words: he expressed his reverence for churches by sweeping and cleaning them. In response to clerical failure to keep the Host in honorable containers, Francis once tried to have his friars bring precious pyxes to all the regions where they were active. He asked that these be used to reserve the Host when other decent containers were lacking. One can imagine the effect of Francis's poor followers, with their miserable habits, presenting silver pyxes to parish clergy for the reservation of the Sacrament. It would have been a striking gesture, if the brothers, in fact, obeyed Francis's wishes.

If the context of the letter was his ordination to the deaconate, which gave him an access to the altar that he had lacked even as a tonsured cleric, his sensibilities may have been scandalized to see firsthand that the Host, which he had adored from afar, was treated with such disrespect and indifference by the priests at whose Masses he now served. On the altar in front of him were the cheap and tarnished chalices and filthy linen that these priests considered good enough for use in worship. Francis's sense of decency and beauty, which he had mortified by choosing to live amid poverty and outcasts, had not been deadened. Its object was no longer fine garments and meals for himself, but items dedicated to the Lord who had died for him.

In his "Letter to the Clergy," Francis spoke warmly of reverence for priests as well as for the Blessed Sacrament. He demonstrated his devotion by kissing the hands of any priest he met: consecrated with sacred chrism, they handled the Host. For the Host itself Francis practiced acts of reverence that, although not uncommon in France, were just becoming popular in Italy. He begged the brothers who met a priest on horseback, especially one carrying the Blessed Sacrament, to kiss the horse's hooves rather than wait for the priest to dismount. Francis wanted that "subjection to all," which was so much a part of his conversion, to be a lived reality among the brothers.

Francis's anger at slipshod priestly service was only unusual in its early date, for by midcentury similar blasts of outrage would issue from other Italian penitents and pious laypeople. The clergy struggled to keep up with such increased spiritual fervor among their people. Finally, on 22 November 1219, Pope Honorius III, in his decrees *Sani cum Olim* and *Expectavimus Hactenus,* required just what Francis was calling for: clean and proper instruments for Mass, reservation of the Host in a precious locked container, and the wearing of proper vestments when administering it. Pope Honorius was still a bit behind the times in his command that people bow before the reserved Sacrament and during the Elevation at Mass. Months earlier, Francis, expressing the lay piety of the time, directed them to kneel. We do not know if Honorius knew about Francis's letter, but Francis heard about the papal decree. He rewrote the original letter to reflect this new legislation after he returned from the East in 1220. Two years later, his agitation for proper reverence of the Host had not diminished.

Beyond its rubrical concerns, Francis's first letter gives a window into his developing spirituality. His earlier piety had focused on praying before the Crucifix, repairing or cleaning churches, and reverence for priests. All involved symbolic or mystical manifestations of the Crucified Lord: churches as the place where God chose to dwell, and priests because they have the power to draw Christ down from heaven during Mass. Francis's piety has now focused on God's most tangible manifestation in the world: the Host itself. Francis was developing an ever greater sense that God is present to Christians in the Sacrament, and that it was to be reverenced above all other presences. In both the Host and Christ's words, the work of Calvary is delivered to the believer. The Host is Christ's real Body, the same one that suffered and died for us. The sacred words that especially concerned Francis are those used in the canon of the Mass and found in the Last Supper narratives of the New Testament. These record his action of offering himself to his disciples "on the night before he suffered."

Modern observers find Francis's growing concern about the writing on scraps of parchment somewhat embarrassing or perplexing. Even pious Christians today have lost this sense of the concrete divine presence. In the thirteenth century, however, this attitude was not some oddity that Francis had picked up from Jewish or Muslim practice. For Christians of his age, the words of scripture were not merely didactic reminders of past events or moral norms. As divine words, they were a locus of power. Merely pronouncing them, as when the bishop read the beginning of the four Gospels toward the city gates facing the four points of the compass during springtime Rogation processions, put demonic powers to flight. When used by Brother Silvester over the city of Arezzo, the divine words could, by their very power, end civil strife. Now, when Francis began to chant from the book of Gospels as a deacon, he himself proclaimed and enacted the words of power. A perplexed brother once asked Francis about his practice of collecting such scraps of parchment, and he replied: "Son, I do this because they have the letters that compose the glorious name of the Lord God, and the good that is found there does not belong to the pagans nor to any human being, but to God alone, to whom every good thing belongs." This identification between names and the realities they signify was not only a commonplace in medieval sensibility; it spoke to Francis's profound sense of God's presence in the concrete here and now, and in the most commonplace of things and events. For a layman like Francis, only marginally able to write, letters themselves were mysterious and somehow sacred: friars knew well that when Francis made a mistake in writing, he let it stand, rather than "killing the letter" by crossing it out.

Before, as a simple cleric singing the Office, he had chanted the psalms of David; now, as a deacon, he read the very words of Christ. At Solemn Mass, he did so facing north—the direction of darkness and, for medieval minds, paganism, and thus putting both to flight. That certain clerics treated these powerful and holy texts with disrespect outraged Francis's acute spiritual sense. To leave sacred books on the floor or in dishonorable places was, in its own way, as sacrilegious as the desecration of the Host. Ever more intensely, Francis associated his own experience before the Cross, his transforming encounter with the lepers, and the divine commission to live the Gospel perfectly with the immediate, unmediated presence of Christ given to each Christian in Word and Sacrament.

Jacques de Vitry described Francis and the brothers as meeting once a year for mutual encouragement and missionary planning. At these meetings, Francis gave a sermon or spiritual instruction, usually without much preparation, but rather as the Spirit moved him. Some fragments in the collection known as Francis's *Admonitions* probably reflect concerns he voiced during these gatherings. If he ever became stern, it was when he reminded the brothers that they were to look down on no one, cleric or lay, who lived a more comfortable life than they did: they were to be lesser brothers, not merely in their actions, but also in their view of themselves. By refusing to pass judgments on others, an act that placed one above another, friars could find the inner peace necessary to use Francis's peace greeting with sincerity. While deference to the Host and priests came easily to Francis, refraining from judgment did not. In fact, in his unwilling role as leader, he was now obliged to correct others' faults. His followers did not accept criticism easily.

On one occasion, at a chapter, Francis declared that he would only be a true lesser brother if, after giving a sermon at a chapter, the brothers rejected it out of hand and then threw him out of the meeting, and, most importantly, he then recognized that this was what he truly deserved. The fervor with which he repeated this teaching suggests that the brothers had rejected his instruction often enough, even if they had not gone so far as to expel him from a chapter. Rather than cease passing judgment, the brothers found it easier to conform to conventional religious practices and adopt savage penances, fasts, and disciplines. It is telling that the only fault for which Francis was known to rebuke his followers directly was their overuse of physical penance when it harmed bodily health or, worse, replaced the lesser brother's obligation to view himself as subject to all others, as never their equal, much less their superior.

There were pressing matters of administration and governance to be addressed, but, by talent and temperament, Francis found himself unsuited to the task. He began to rely on friars with organizational skills, as well as on the experts in theology and canon law whom he invited to the chapters, following the recommendation of the Lateran Council. Those invited included, very likely, Cistercian monks and, at the chapter of 1218, perhaps Cardinal Hugolino.

Within a year after the 1217 dispatch of the brothers, discouraging reports were received about the missions, with the exception of that closest to home in northern Italy. One problem was the brothers' complete lack of linguistic preparation. The sixty brothers who went to Germany with the minister Brother John of Penna discovered that, when asked if they were hungry, saying "ja" was an excellent response. But when asked if they were Cathar heretics from Lombardy, they also answered "ja," and the result was imprisonment, beating, and worse. In Hungary, where the language barrier was even greater, the brothers were attacked by robbers, who took their cloaks and then beat them because they had no money. They gave up their tunics, but they were beaten even worse. Finally, they sacrificed their undertrousers, but to no good effect. After begging clothing to cover their nakedness, this group also went back to Italy. Other missionaries returned to Italy, equally frustrated and battered.

In areas where Romance languages were spoken, the brothers fared a bit better. The men who reached Paris were also suspected of heresy, but they were able to explain themselves well enough to the bishop and his university consulters that they were left in peace. Even then, they had to procure a confirmation of their orthodoxy from Pope Honorius. The group that went to Spain, where the language was closest to Italian, avoided the problems encountered elsewhere. Within two years, however, brothers of this group reached Muslim lands in North Africa, only to be martyred.

The missions, however unsuccessful, did have a telling result. Francis and his movement became both known outside of Italy and a subject of talk. By 1219 one English preacher, Odo of Cheriton, could already speak of Francis as though all his hearers knew who he was and what he was like. Odo used him as an example of someone who guilelessly spoke his mind to everyone, including popes. He also knew that Francis was fond of using parables and stories for instruction. Although he lived in far-off England, Odo's perception of Francis was correct.

The traveling brothers found that they were treated no better by the clergy than by the laity. For ecclesiastical authorities, the problem was that the brothers could show no rule formally approved by the pope. The 1209 concession of the original form of life was provisional and probably available in no written text. As the disheartened friars returned home, bitter and frustrated, Francis found that they did not consider passive acceptance of rejection as a virtue. Some came to him, probably at one of the Pentecost chapters, to ask that he request a papal privilege granting them access to areas where they had encountered resistance, and even the right to preach without episcopal permission. Francis reacted sternly and rebuked them for not accepting their rejection without complaint. Prelates were to be won over by the brothers' obedience and humility, not by papal orders.

When Cardinal Hugolino attended the chapter, probably in 1218, the friars came forth in procession to meet him. He dismounted from his horse and came in state to the Porziuncula church. He celebrated pontifical Mass, which the friars sang, and for which Francis served as deacon and sang the Gospel. Francis was probably ordained between his first encounter with the cardinal during the summer of 1217 at Florence and this 1218 Pentecost chapter. The ordination fits with Cardinal Hugolino's other actions at this time to improve the brotherhood's standing with the hierarchy.

Francis's stern rejection of appeals to the Roman Curia does not seem to have stopped the brothers from going behind his back and asking Hugolino for help. The cardinal got an earful from the brothers about the behavior of Church authorities. Cardinal Hugolino's response to friars' complaints, even if he fell short of getting a papal command that prelates were to receive the brothers, angered Francis greatly. Hugolino procured a papal letter of recommendation certifying the brothers' orthodoxy. Nevertheless, this regularization of the movement in the Church accomplished by Hugolino gave Francis a freedom he previously lacked. Following the Pentecost chapter of 3 June 1219, Francis finally fulfilled his longtime hope to go abroad, preach Christ to unbelievers, and perhaps even to achieve martyrdom. In late June, the founder appointed two vicars, men who would lead the brotherhood in Francis's name while he was away, Gregory of Naples and Matthew of Narni, and set out for the Middle East.

Francis Abroad

The recapture of Jerusalem, lost to the Muslims during the Third Crusade in 1187, had been a project of Pope Innocent III and was now that of Honorius III. Finally, after years of frustrated planning, Crusader forces were in position to move against the Ayyubid sultan of Egypt, Malik al-Adil (1145–1218), known to the Franks as "Saphadin" from his honorary title "Saif al-Din." Al-Adil had risen to power during the unrest and civil war that followed the death of his brother Saladin. He united Egypt and Palestine by his victory at the battle of Bilbeis and was declared sultan. He cultivated good relations with the Crusader states and fostered trade. Nonetheless, he held Jerusalem, the object of the Crusades, and, by 1217, Christian leaders from Europe and Syria had forged an alliance with Keykavus I, the Seljuk sultan of Rum in central Anatolia, who sought to expand his control south into Syria. He would place pressure on the sultan in Palestine, while the Crusaders attacked the Egyptian delta directly. This invasion of Egypt would become known as the Fifth Crusade. In June of 1218, the Crusader forces reached the Nile Delta and besieged the port of Damietta. The city was to serve as a base for an assault on the Egyptian capital at Cairo.

After organizing Egyptian and Palestinian troops in the north, al-Adil took the field against the invaders, only to die on campaign in September. In spite of his advanced age, al-Adil had been a very capable general and effective commander. His son, Malik al-Kamil (1180–1238), was far less effective and energetic. Rather, he was known for clemency and humanity. In 1219, Cardinal Pelagius Galvani of Albano arrived to take leadership of the Crusader forces, which had become divided by rivalry and faction. Al-Kamil offered to negotiate, suggesting an exchange of Jerusalem for the lifting of the Crusaders' siege and their departure from Egypt. Secular leaders of the Crusade, in particular John of Brienne, titular king of Jerusalem, were inclined to accept the offer. The cardinal believed that lasting security was impossible without removing the Egyptian threat and that the sultan's deal offered nothing to help Christians living under the Muslim yoke. He vetoed the offer.

During this stalemate, Francis arrived in Egypt, accompanied by a companion, Peter of Cataneo (so called from his birthplace, Gualdo Cataneo near Bevagna), a jurist who had recently entered the order. Francis's trip to Egypt, although unique because it involved the movement's leader, was part of the missionary projects of the chapter of 1219. If the route of his journey east was typical, he left from Bari or Brindisi in southern Italy. His ship then followed the coast of Greece, passed along the north shore of Crete, and probably put in for supplies at the Crusader stronghold of Rhodes or Acre. From one or the other, it then made the passage south to the Nile Delta. Some Franciscans had already arrived with the Crusaders, and others now followed with Francis. Late sources name Brother Illuminato and Brother Leonard as among them. Unlike the situation during his ill-conceived trip to France, Francis's appointment of the vicars had ensured that his absence would not cause administrative problems for his brotherhood.

When Francis arrived, the Crusader army was besieging Damietta. Contact with the military life of the camp profoundly disturbed him. It brought on premonitions of disaster and evoked memories of his own traumatic military experiences. He voiced his anxieties to one of his companions, probably Peter of Cataneo, asking what he should do. The friar told Francis to follow his instincts, so the somewhat out-of-place little monk set off, wandering about the camp and loudly voicing his anxieties to the soldiers, with, it seems, no little animation. To the rough Crusader troops, he became something of a joke; to their leaders, he seemed a feckless threat to morale. Francis's fears proved well founded: the Crusader army suffered a major defeat before the city walls on 29 October. Later retelling turned this incident into a fearless announcement of visionary prophesy, while modern writers often reconfigure it as pacifistic, antiwar preaching. Francis's real motivations seem very personal, not visionary or ideological.

Whatever the case, Francis was no coward. He soon asked permission to cross enemy lines, enter the Muslim camp, and preach Christ to the sultan al-Kamil. The cardinal flatly refused the request. Death was the usual punishment for those who attempted to convince Muslims to abandon their religion, as it was for any Muslim who apostatized. Francis was undaunted; he and his companion—late sources identify him as Illuminato—continued to harass the cardinal, arguing that since they would go only with his permission, not by his command, he could not be blamed for anything that happened to them. The cardinal, a high ecclesiastical diplomat and administrator, knew little or nothing about Francis or his movement. He had no way of knowing what their intentions were or what result their infiltration of the Egyptian camp might have. He again rejected their request, saying that he had no way of knowing if their project was of God or the devil. Eventually, tired by their persistence, Pelagius said he would not stop them from going, but that they were under no circumstances to tell anyone that he had any connection to their mission.

The cardinal was ostensibly washing his hands of the matter, saying in effect: If you are harmed, imprisoned, or killed, do not expect any help from me. But his primary concern was to prevent al-Kamil from thinking that the friars' visit implied some change in his hard-line position of no negotiations. The secular leaders of the Crusade may well have hoped that Francis's journey would reopen the possibility of a negotiated settlement. Francis was probably oblivious to the political implications of his endeavor. In any case, the unarmed Francis and his companion left the Crusader camp, crossed the Nile, and approached the Muslim fortifications. Egyptian guards, assuming that the men were deserters who wanted to renounce their faith and accept Islam, took them in charge. When it became obvious that the two men had no intention of accepting Islam, the guards began to maltreat them. Francis, who knew no Arabic whatsoever, began to shout the one word he did know—"Soldan"—over and over. Finally, the bemused soldiers took him to al-Kamil.

Every report says that the sultan received the friars well, no doubt hoping that they were, in fact, a new embassy charged with reopening negotiations. He would have recognized them as Christian clergy by their tonsure and religious garb. The sultan, undoubtedly communicating with the brothers through a translator, asked if they were an embassy from the Crusaders, or if they intended to accept Islam, or perhaps both. Francis skipped over the question about messages from the leaders of the Crusade and got immediately to the point. He was the ambassador of the Lord Jesus Christ and had come for the salvation of the sultan's soul. Francis expressed his willingness to explain and defend Christianity. This was not at all what the sultan wanted. He replied that he had no time for theological discussions and that he had plenty of religious experts who could show the two men the truth of Islam.

Francis was delighted to find a larger audience for his message and agreed to discussions, saying that if the sultan and his advisers were not convinced by his presentation, they could cut off his head. Some of the sultan's religious advisers were summoned to present the faith of Muhammad to Francis. He replied by stating his own faith. The reaction was swift: Francis was tempting them all with apostasy and was therefore dangerous. The Muslim experts unanimously advised the sultan to execute both of the Franciscans for preaching against Muhammad and Islam. They warned him not to listen to them, as even that was dangerous. The religious leaders then withdrew. Francis did make some impression, either positive or negative, on one of the Muslim religious leaders present. The jurist Fâkhr ad-Din al-Fârisi had his involvement with al-Kamil in the "affair of the monk" recorded on his tombstone.

Al-Kamil, however, did not execute or dismiss the two friars. Rather, left alone with the two friars and, probably, an interpreter, the sultan seems to have been impressed by Francis's sincerity and willingness to die for his beliefs. He also probably hoped that once they finished ventilating the religious matter, there might be an opening for political negotiation. Thus there began a long conversation between Francis and the Muslim leader. Francis continued to express his Christian faith in the Crucified Lord and his promise of salvation. Al-Kamil continued listening politely, doubtless occasionally probing to see if the little Italian's homilies masked a political feeler. In spite of his advisers' hard line, the sultan had little reason to take offense at Francis's expression of faith, for, as Jacques de Vitry himself remarked, Muslims had no objection to praising Jesus, who was a prophet for them too, as long as the speaker avoided any suggestion that Muhammad's message was false or deluded. Francis himself never spoke ill of Muhammad, just as he never spoke ill of anyone. Later, when other Franciscans crossed over the battle lines and preached against Muhammad, they were fortunate to escape with merely a flogging.

After several conversations over a number of days, and finding that this discussion was making no political headway, the sultan decided to end it. He made a final offer: if the brothers would stay and accept Islam, he would see that they were well provided for. Francis and his companion flatly refused, saying again that they had not come to convert but to preach Christ. So, in a typical act of Middle Eastern hospitality, al-Kamil had a table set out with precious cloth and gold and silver ornaments and offered the two men their pick of them as gifts. Much to the sultan's surprise, Francis explained that their religion forbade them to accept any precious gifts, money, or property. On the other hand, he would be happy to accept food for the day. Whether or not he asked Francis to pray for him, as some Christian sources claim, al-Kamil was pleased to provide them with a sumptuous meal, after which he ordered them deported to the Crusader lines.

Francis may not have converted the sultan, but he and his companions did make a deep impression on the Christian clergy present in Damietta, including Jacques de Vitry, bishop of Acre. Much to the bishop's displeasure,

Don Ranieri, rector of the Crusader church of St. Michael at Acre, abandoned his master to join the Franciscans. Two other clerics attached to his party, Colin the Englishman and Michael of the Church of the Holy Cross, also joined Francis. In a letter dated later in February or March 1220 to friends at home, de Vitry ascribed the rapid growth of Francis's movement to their failure to screen and test applicants and to the friars' willingness to send enthusiastic, if unprepared, men to all parts of the world. In the bishop's opinion, too many of those attracted to the movement were unstable, enthusiastic youths, unready for the risks of itinerancy and uncloistered religious life. When Francis merely attracted lay brothers in rural Umbria back in 1216, the bishop of Acre had good words for the movement. Now, in light of Francis's imprudent zeal in crossing enemy lines, and his willingness to take runaway clergy into his ranks, de Vitry's views were more mixed. He wrote to his friends that it was all he could do to keep his chanter John of Cambrai, his cleric Henry, and several others from joining Francis. These defections are part of the exponential increase in numbers that the brotherhood experienced following the missions out of Italy in 1217.

Francis's impact on the bishop of Acre's clerics was short-lived, however, because he soon departed from Egypt. Some time after the Crusaders' conquest of Damietta on 5 November 1219, Francis chose to leave. The horror of the sack that followed the breach of the walls probably brought on painful flashbacks from his own experiences as a soldier at Collestrada. As Francis had arrived near the end of August, his stay in Egypt thus lasted at most two or three months. A number of Francis's followers remained with the Crusaders and were even given charge of a church in the city of Damietta. He himself went on to Syria, where Franciscan missionaries had arrived two years before.

Once he had arrived in Syria, Francis received disturbing news from home. In his absence, his vicars, Gregory and Matthew, had instituted what today seem trivial changes in penitential discipline. Following the general Church discipline then in force, the brothers abstained from meat on Friday, the Catholic fast day. To this Francis himself had added abstinence on Saturday, also a traditional day of penance in the Latin Church. On other days, they could eat meat. The vicars decided that on the nonfast days the community should eat only meat that was spontaneously given them in alms, and not procure any on their own, and that they were to eat no meat, even from alms, on Mondays. In addition, on Wednesdays and Fridays, they were now to abstain from dairy products as well as meat, unless these were spontaneously given to them. A certain lay brother, outraged that the vicars were adding proscriptions to the form of life, stole a copy of the legislation and, without any permission, fled Italy.

He arrived in the Orient only to find Francis sitting down to lunch with Peter of Cataneo and several others, most likely in the Crusader stronghold of Acre. The meal included meat, as, prior to this new legislation, the day had not been one of abstinence. The brother confessed his sin of taking the legislation and leaving Italy without "an obedience." Overlooking the brother's shocking conduct, Francis read the new legislation and turned to Peter, who was a canonist by training. He asked him, giving him the honorary title for a legist, as he often did in jest: "Lord Peter, what should we do?" Peter replied, no doubt with a smile: "Well, Lord Francis, do whatever pleases you; you have the power here." Francis replied: "Then let's eat what is put before us, as the Gospel says." The group, including the lay brother, then sat down to lunch. This new legislation, which went beyond biblical and public ecclesiastical norms, went against Francis's firm conviction that the brothers should live by the Gospel alone.

Francis, it seems, never visited Jerusalem during his trip to the Levant, for there is no record that he ever incurred the statutory excommunication imposed by Honorius III on Christians who visited the Muslim-controlled city. If he visited any other sites in the Holy Land, the best reports are silent on it. Within a short time, possibly in early March or early April, Francis departed for Italy, along with Peter of Cataneo, Elias of Assisi, and a new friar admitted by Elias, Cesarius of Speyer, probably from Acre.

[5]

FRANCIS RETURNS HOME

1220–1221

F RANCIS RETURNED HOME from the Middle East, probably in late spring of 1220, to face demons, both internal and external. He arrived sick, most likely with malaria and a variety of infections, illnesses that would become progressively worse till his death. Physical illness was not his gravest burden. Changes made to his rule of life while he was away proved that, without his presence, practices that clashed with his vision could be introduced almost unnoticed by his followers. Without that disobedient lay brother, he might not have discovered the deviations introduced by his vicars, Gregory of Narni and Matthew of Naples, until much later. Now, on return, Francis faced a situation even more devastating for him personally. He could not escape his role as leader and teacher of the movement, and this meant passing judgment on errors and making corrections, something totally contrary to his nature and to his spirituality. Headship in his rapidly growing movement seemed contrary to the Gospel, which required him to be "less" than all others, subject to them in all things. Leadership made others subject to him. Spiritually, this was an intolerable burden, one he wished to be rid of as quickly as possible.

Francis and the Cardinal

The twelve months from spring 1220 to spring 1221 were Francis's *annus horribilis,* the most painful year of his life. Under the leadership of Gregory and Matthew, and what seems like a council of more senior friars, the movement was changing in ways that gave Francis pause. The leaders had instituted some new ascetical practices; the most important of these, because symbolic and regular, were the new dietary regulations, which had triggered Francis's early return from the Middle East. Although they did not impose the vegetarianism normative in all other religious orders, the new rules limited eating of meat and dairy products on days when Church law did not forbid it. There was absolutely nothing particularly "monastic" in these new regulations. Observance of abstinence on days other than Friday was a common lay practice and a very ancient one at that. The brothers had probably come in for some criticism from the devout laity when it was found that they ate meat. The new dietary regulations were modest steps toward conforming to pious expectations.

Piety did not bother Francis. What offended him was the imposition of regulations not found in scripture; in particular, the abridgment of Christ's command to "eat what is put before you." More problematically, this dietary change allowed the friars to avoid criticism and invidious comparisons with other religious who did abstain. For Francis, following the Gospel involved opening one's self to just this kind of criticism. The problem was not that the brothers were becoming monks, much less that they were fasting and abstaining; it was that they were unwilling to endure the humiliation of pious misunderstanding.

And the dietary changes were not the matter that most upset Francis. On his return to Italy, he made two other troubling discoveries. One of his early followers, Brother John of Cappella, had gone off on his own and formed a community to serve lepers. It consisted of a mixed group of paupers, lepers, pious men, and even women. This loose organization and its involvement with the poor often appear to modern observers to be a repeat of the founder's activities soon after his conversion. What could be wrong with such a development? But the issue of proper care for the lepers continued to eat at Francis, even after John's group had been abolished, as we will later see. We will probably never know what lay behind Francis's harsh reaction to John's project with the lepers. Perhaps he feared negative public opinion, because the friar was breaking the "quarantine" imposed on these outcasts. But this seems rather unlikely for the leader of the "lesser brothers." Or, more likely, John's leper project threatened to professionalize such service, thereby allowing most friars to avoid it. Or, perhaps, important as his experience of the lepers had been, and as much as he wanted friars to serve them, the last thing Francis wanted was for his order to become a group of social workers or hospital attendants. The lesser brothers were called to live according to the Gospel, not to perform a particular kind of charity.

Meanwhile, another early follower, Brother Philip Longo, who was responsible for Clare and the Poor Ladies, had petitioned the Holy See to grant letters of protection for the nuns, giving him authority to excommunicate anyone who disturbed them. Why this bothered Francis is easier for us to understand. Such a strategy was exactly the kind of dependence on authority to resist evil that Francis wholly rejected. A lesser brother, following Christ's command to turn the other cheek, was not to resist evil under any circumstance or in any way.

This medley of developments—dietary asceticism, social work, and papal protection—caused dissension, which in turn divided the brotherhood. The controversies so upset Francis that he found himself unable to confront his vicars or the wayward brothers directly. Instead, he ran for help. As so often in his life, Francis explained his predicament by the metaphorical elaboration of a dream. He recounted that he had dreamt he was a small black hen, and under him so many chicks were hatching that he could no longer keep them all under his wings. As that hen desperately tried to cover and protect her brood, her young kept popping out from under her and running away. The meaning was all too clear: Francis could not perform the task of mother hen that God had given him. He had failed.

As he did after the Bible divination at San Nicolò, Francis went directly to the pope. He sought out Pope Honorius and his curia at one of the papal cities, probably Viterbo or Orvieto. That Francis could gain immediate access and address the pontiff directly shows how far we are from the first visit of 1209. Rather than knock at the door of the papal chambers, he waited outside until the pope came out on his own. Francis greeted Honorius with the words "Father Pope, may God give you peace!" The pope replied: "May God bless you, my son." Francis explained that he understood how busy Honorius was, and knew that it was impossible to consult him on every detail of life in his movement. He had only one request: "You have given me many popes!"—by which Francis meant his imperious brothers—"Give me one now in your place to whom I can talk when I need to, who can discuss my affairs and those of the Order." The pope asked whom he had in mind, and Francis immediately replied: "The Lord of Ostia"—Cardinal Hugolino.

Honorius honored Francis's request. Hugolino had already been advising Francis and the brothers and had attended at least one Pentecost chapter; with this request his role would change dramatically. The cardinal would exercise direct authority over the movement in place of the pope. In practice, this meant advising the founder and implicitly backing up his decisions with papal authority. Francis wasted no time in unburdening himself of his problems to Hugolino, his new "pope." As Francis went home to Assisi, the papal problem-solver acted with dispatch in Rome. He revoked the letters Philip Longo had procured imposing canonical sanctions on those who disturbed the Poor Ladies. He got the papal curia to reject Brother John of Cappella's project to form an order for lepers and those who served them. The rejection of the project was not gentle, which shows how seriously Francis took this infraction. John, we understand, left the Curia humiliated for his presumption, never to return to the brotherhood.

Francis did not like to make his authority felt; Hugolino had no problem doing it for him. But there was never any question where the real authority and power lay. About this time, Jacques de Vitry wrote of Francis and his movement in a report we have already mentioned. He now understood Francis to be the head of an international organization. De Vitry had, years earlier in his letters, spoken of the Franciscans as a loosely organized movement with little in the way of structure other than an annual chapter. Now, in the *Historia Occidentalis,* he described Francis's leadership as monarchical. The titles he used for Francis were fluid—*summus prior, magister, superior, fundator*—but this reflects his difficulty fitting Francis into conventional models of religious authority. De Vitry was well acquainted with the new religious movements of the time, but he had never encountered a group whose identity was so tied up with the personality of its founder.

And this founder was himself uncomfortable with his position of leadership. Francis's unwillingness to lead was in great part the cause of the chaos into which his movement had drifted while he was in Egypt. The brotherhood sensed itself without a leader, helpless and abandoned. Rumors of Francis's death were put to rest by his return. His inability to lead was remedied by Hugolino, an ecclesiastical authority who shouldered the burden of responsibility. As Francis settled into his new role, he turned for support to the friars who had accompanied him back from the Middle East: Peter of Cataneo, Cesarius of Speyer, and Elias of Assisi, all men with legal and administrative skills. All three played central roles during the coming year. With the cardinal, they served as part of Francis's private council, a kitchen cabinet, advising him and executing his decisions. This inner body was made up of men with the same kind of practical learning found in Peter, Cesarius, and Elias. Francis chose no advisers from the simple pious priests like Brother Leo or the unlettered lay brothers like Brother Giles. The circle of Leo and Giles—and their modern admirers—never accepted or understood Francis's choice. But the choice was Francis's own and his alone. Knowing his own limits, he chose wisely.

Before his departure for Egypt, the brothers had complained to Francis that prelates did not always receive them well and that a papal privilege might help. Francis rejected the idea then, and, on his return, he had Brother Philip's bulls for the nuns squelched without hesitation. But he did leave unchanged an accommodation to practicalities begun before his departure. A sympathetic ear at Rome, probably Cardinal Hugolino, had raised the status of the movement with the pope, and the first extant papal letter concerning the Franciscans had been the result. It was a simple letter of introduction, not a privilege or a protection. *Cum Dilecti Filii,* issued by Pope Honorius on 11 June 1219, came just after the Pentecost chapter of that year, perhaps even before Francis had himself left for Egypt. As it is addressed to Francis by name, it is likely that the request was made with his knowledge, even if without much enthusiasm on his part. The letter does nothing more than remind bishops that they are to receive Francis's followers as "faithful Catholics." It says nothing about letting the brothers preach or about letting them establish residences, but papal patronage has a power by itself. The appointment of Hugolino was another sign of that patronage.

Jordan of Giano, a friar who wrote a precious eyewitness chronicle for this period, reports that as soon as Hugolino had been appointed and the trouble-makers corrected, Francis immediately announced that a chapter would be held at the Porziuncula the following spring; it would be the largest and most important meeting of the brotherhood to date. Hugolino took a direct role in the brothers' affairs and, it seems, the preparation for this chapter. After the cardinal's appointment by the pope as responsible for the movement, Hugolino sent letters vouching for the Franciscans to the bishops, and he seems to have urged other cardinals to do so as well. The second papal letter for the Franciscans, *Pro Dilectis Filiis,* issued by Honorius on 29 May 1220, came in the midst of this letter-writing campaign and was probably part of it. The pope was direct. For the first time, he called Francis's movement an *ordo,* a canonical religious order, and he instructed the bishops to admit the brothers and allow them to take up residence. This was a weapon that the friars could use against those who resisted them.

It is telling that Francis never had these first two letters repealed. Near the end of his life, in his Testament, Francis rejected with anger any future requests for papal letters of protection, but there is no evidence that he ever rejected or criticized these first papal briefs. They were somehow different from the protection and power of excommunication sought by Brother Philip; they lacked the coercive language and appearance of power so unbecoming to a lesser brother. As the year progressed, Rome's involvement in the new order increased. On 22 November 1220, Pope Honorius directed a new letter, *Cum Secundum,* to the friars and in it forbade "priors and custodians" of the Franciscan Order from admitting new members without completion of a yearlong novitiate, the canonical probationary period of training and testing for new members. Honorius imposed a similar regime on the Dominicans at the same time. His lack of direct familiarity with the Franciscans is shown by his use of the Dominican term "prior" in the letter. The Preachers, like Francis, had been professing applicants immediately, before even clothing them with the habit. Francis encountered problems with unwisely admitted friars, especially after his return from Egypt, and he may well have desired greater screening of applicants himself.

Cum Secundum did not address Francis by name, so he was spared a papal rebuke, but his well-known practice of "admitting anyone" who wanted to join his movement lies behind the letter. Jacques de Vitry had already criticized the abuse in 1216. The papal letter took from Francis his position as the sole determiner of who could join the movement, a prerogative that he had already shared with his vicars before he left for Egypt. Francis came back all too aware of the results of his carefree policy; there is no evidence that he resisted this change either. The same letter permitted Franciscan superiors to inflict canonical censure (excommunication or interdict) on brothers who wandered off without an "obedience." This letter was directly related to the internal life of the order and the discipline of a religious rule.

The letter, with its direct reversal of Francis's admissions policy, may well lie behind Francis's trip to Rome and visit to Cardinal Hugolino in the late fall of 1220. Later legends embroider this visit with stories of Francis begging food instead of eating at the cardinal's lavish table. This dinner became the context for another invention, Francis's encounter with the founder of the Dominicans, Dominic Guzman, who supposedly offered to merge their movements and met with Francis's rebuff. These stories, for which there is little solid evidence, belong very much to the world of legend. What really did happen during the visit was more important and of more lasting significance.

Recognizing that the Curia had little direct knowledge or contact with the Franciscan movement and its practices, Cardinal Hugolino decided to introduce Francis personally to the cardinals and ecclesiastics of the Curia. Francis's movement was large and growing. He was now internationally known by name, and an appearance in Rome would put a face on the brotherhood. Francis's "order" was still functioning as a confraternity with provisional papal approbation. It was still loosely organized, governed by a "rule" that had only verbal approval from the now long-dead Innocent III. The brotherhood needed to become an established religious order of the Catholic Church, in status equal to the Benedictines, the Cistercians, and the newly founded Dominicans.

Cardinal Hugolino decided that the best way to introduce Francis was to have him preach before a papal consistory. The very idea terrified

Francis, who had, during his first visit in 1209, addressed the Curia only through his proctor, Cardinal Colonna. Francis argued that he was incapable, "unlettered and ignorant." This was something of an overstatement. Francis was by this time a deacon and sang the Divine Office daily in Latin. Hugolino insisted, and he suggested that Francis could memorize a written text and deliver it from memory, if he preferred. Francis hesitantly agreed. But when Hugolino presented him to the Curia, Francis's memory failed him. He spoke from the heart, extemporaneously and movingly, so excited by the vision he was expounding that he seemed to be dancing with enthusiasm. The cardinal was very likely chagrined: he would look foolish for wasting the Curia's time with such a rustic. But Francis had been right all along—reading from a written text was not his style. Contrary to the cardinal's anxiety, the pope and cardinals were captivated and edified. Francis's preaching of Christ and repentance moved the clerical bureaucrats to tears.

No source describes the business transacted during this visit to Rome, but most likely Francis, with his canonist, Peter of Cataneo, and his secretary-editor, Cesarius of Speyer, consulted with Hugolino and other experts about the "form of life" that he now undertook to write. The "rule" under which the brothers had lived since 1209 had grown in a haphazard way from the short Bible passages permitted to Francis by Innocent. Earlier chapters had added some material; other provisions Francis added himself, always in response to concrete situations and problems. The proposed rule to be presented for official papal approbation would have to be carefully edited and reworked and made more general and systematic. Such abstraction and logical reorganization, by its nature, risked losing the direct and concrete quality of the founder's own experiences, choices, and perceptions. The strain such revision imposed on Francis was great. He considered himself inadequate to the task of planning and governance—the black hen with too many chicks. Francis was, without knowing it, groping for a charter that would allow the order to exist without his presence.

The strain came to a head during Francis's stay with Leo Brancaleone, a cardinal who was a close collaborator of Hugolino. The source for this visit gives no year, but the events fit well with Francis's visit to Hugolino in late winter 1220. Brancaleone, the cardinal priest of Santa Croce, had served with Hugolino as papal delegate in northern Italy and, like him, was impressed by Francis and his movement. While staying with Hugolino, Francis accepted an invitation to spend a few days at Brancaleone's residence, perhaps as a Lenten retreat. The cardinal of Santa Croce had a tower in the city walls where Francis could pass time in prayer. The rain and cold of the Roman winter made it unwise for Francis to travel, given his unstable health since his return from

Egypt. Brother Angelo Tancredi, an early follower who was Francis's current companion, urged him to accept the offer. The cardinal's tower would be like a hermitage in the city. Using the language of the "Rule for Hermitages," which Francis was also composing at this time, Angelo would be the "mother," tending to the founder's material needs, and bringing him food, while Francis, the "son," would spend his time in prayer and seclusion. It seemed a workable arrangement.

On the very first night in the tower, Francis began shouting to Angelo for help. He found Francis bathed in sweat, probably running a high fever, and nearly delirious. This may well have been a bout of the malaria that he had contracted in Egypt, but for Francis the torment was above all spiritual. He recounted for Angelo a series of violent satanic attacks that seemed like physical beatings. He begged Angelo to stay with him, because he was afraid to be alone. The two men stayed up the entire night. Francis poured out his heart to Angelo, asking why, though he could think of no serious sins, God had allowed his "police" (*gastaldi*), the demons, to torment him. Francis speculated that as God sometimes used his police to torture those who had sinned unknowingly to force them to examine their consciences with greater rigor, he must be guilty of some forgotten sin. This popular demonology was very much typical of Francis. We have no direct testimony about what was eating at Francis's conscience, but his actions the next day give us some idea. Very early the next morning, Francis went to Cardinal Brancaleone and told him that he could no longer stay in Rome: he had to return to the brothers. The little black hen had committed, or was about to commit, the sin of abandoning his flock. The cardinal respected his visitor's decision and let him leave.

Francis and Angelo set off on the road to the brothers' *locus* at Fonte Colombo near Rieti. There he would work on the revision of the Rule. As Francis was weak, he rode a horse, while Angelo walked along beside him. Other than for eating and sleeping, Francis got off the horse only to recite his Breviary with Angelo, often standing soaking wet in the late winter rain. As they traveled, Francis pondered the devilish attack in Cardinal Leo's tower. The "Assisi Compilation" of stories puts these words in Francis's mouth:

The devil is delighted when he can extinguish or prevent the devotion and joy in the heart of a servant of God that spring from pure prayer and other good works. For if the devil can have something of his own in a servant of God, he will in a short time make a single hair into a beam, always making it bigger, unless the servant of God is wise, removing and destroying it as quickly as possible by means of contrition and confession and works of satisfaction.

If these words really indicate Francis's spiritual perceptions, we can see him shaking off his nagging scruples about how his plans would affect the brothers. He was preparing himself for the hard choices and painful labor that lay before him.

Francis Resigns

After six months or so of work on his Rule, during a routine community chapter at the Porziuncula in the fall of 1220, Francis dropped a bombshell on the brothers. The founder announced his intention to relinquish leadership of the order and appoint Brother Peter of Cataneo as his replacement. A supposed eyewitness later described the event: "'From now on,' [Francis] said, 'I am dead to you. But here is Brother Peter of Cataneo: let us all, you and I, obey him.' Then all the brothers began to cry loudly and weep profusely, but blessed Francis bowed down before Brother Peter and promised him obedience and reverence." So Peter of Cataneo became Francis's vicar, a title previously used by Gregory of Naples and Matthew of Narni. But unlike that earlier arrangement, the founder remained very present and visible. Francis now claimed to place himself under Peter's obedience, and he began to speak of himself as having a new role. Rather than a leader who would give directions, he would be an exemplary brother, one who would give the brothers a model of humility and obedience. Repeatedly, he would assert that he wanted a "guardian," even a novice, assigned to him whom he could obey in all things. The leader and founder would now be below even the lowest of novices. These novices were, since *Cum Secundum,* not even professed and could be dismissed at will from the order.

In theory, it was a striking role reversal. Francis, the little black hen, had handed over responsibility for the brothers to others and was now free to return to the life he preferred, that of a simple lesser brother, subject to all and superior to none. No one was deceived, much less the pope and the Franciscan leadership. Francis remained the de facto leader. During his lifetime, Francis intervened in the movement's governance, legislated for it, and corrected the order's leaders. He now did so with good conscience because he was no longer "officially" in charge and so not "above" the others. Francis's vicars in fact recognized their subordinate role and never used the later title "minister general" during his lifetime. They remained "vicars" of the founder, not leaders in their own right. Everyone knew the truth, as Peter did when he said to Francis in Syria: "You have the power."

Resigning and providing replacement leaders did not resolve the crisis that had developed during Francis's absence in Egypt. The founder's behavior as a "subject," if anything, made the crisis worse. Peter of Cataneo was not strong willed, and, in any case, it was difficult to stand up to Francis when he had made up his mind to do something. According to one report, Francis once found himself in the position of having to tell his "superior" how to order him around. Francis had returned to the Porziuncula to find that Brother James the Simple, a not very bright brother of whom he was particularly fond, had brought home a leper to dine with the community. James was living at the leprosarium, and Francis had assigned this particular leper to his care because his illness was very progressed, and James had no qualms about touching his sores and cleaning them. On the other hand, Francis was realistic enough to see that if people knew that there were lepers around the church, they would avoid coming there. In addition, James's habit of wandering around in public with lepers had become a topic of popular derision.

Francis, probably still working through the crisis of John of Cappella's delinquency, directly rebuked the simple brother, saying: "You should not take our Christian brothers"—Francis's name for lepers—"about in this way since it is not right for you or for them." Mild as this correction was, that he made it at all was totally contrary to Francis's desire to be "subject to all," and it embarrassed both James and the leper. Struck with remorse, Francis immediately went to Peter of Cataneo, confessed his fault, and demanded that Peter impose on him a penance he himself had chosen, eating out of the same dish as the leper. "Brother Peter so venerated and feared, and was so obedient to blessed Francis, that he would not presume to change his obedience, although then, and many other times, it hurt him inside and out." The situation was truly bizarre. Francis, subject to all, was telling superiors what to command him to do. "Brother Peter and the other brothers saw this, grew very sad, but did not dare say anything out of fear of the holy father." Francis's behavior, rather than providing an example of docility, was, by public admission, something that inspired fear in his "superiors."

More and more, Francis struggled with the burden of "exemplarity" that he had taken on. During that winter of 1220, he suffered repeatedly from "fevers," probably the malaria that he had contracted in the East. During these sicknesses, he was allowed food with meat and soup made with meat broth. Even though Francis's model of life did not involve abstinence, and, even in vegetarian religious orders, meat was allowed to the sick, Francis became convinced that he was giving a bad example. After a sermon in the main piazza of Assisi, he told the audience not to leave. He took Peter of Cataneo and another brother into the duomo of San Rufino and produced a bowl of ashes and a rope. He told the brother to lead him back to the piazza by the rope and then sprinkle the ashes on his head while Francis confessed his "fault" to the crowd.

The unnamed brother flatly refused. "Brother Peter said to him: 'Brother, in what concerns you and me, I cannot, and should not want anything else except what pleases you.'" Francis's ever-cooperative vicar, weeping, took the rope and bowl and did the job.

Much as Francis would have preferred it, his example could not serve as a model of life for the other brothers. The order was now large and international; many brothers would never meet the founder personally. In addition, the leadership needed something more abstract and practical as a guide to discipline and behavior. The decision to remove himself from leadership created new tensions and spiritual dilemmas for Francis. It signaled the beginning of the recurring bouts of temptation and spiritual suffering that characterized his last years. Francis ascribed this horrible period to diabolical attacks, even obsession. Sometimes the attacks were physical, leaving Francis exhausted. At other times they were internal and approached a crisis of faith. It is probably not wrong to trace them, at least in part, to a troubled conscience. Much as Francis recognized his inadequacy as the administrative head of a huge international order, he could not let go of the need to be an example of life for the brothers "God had given him." Only in solitude and prayer did he find any relief, a refuge that, by isolating him from the brothers and depriving them of his example, probably further fed his doubts and temptations. God had given him a burden that he could not carry, and he could find no escape from it, even in retirement.

More Letters and a Spiritual Testament

One way that Francis addressed the confusion among the brothers that he found when he returned to Italy in the spring of 1220 was to write letters to groups for which he had a special concern. Although often described as a "layman" and so from a predominantly "oral" culture, which to some extent he was, Francis was also an Italian, and the ability to read and write had come earlier to the peninsula than to northern Europe. In Francis's time, most Italian city men could read, if not write. His medieval biographers describe him writing letters, and we possess two of his autographs, both somewhat after this period. Most of his letters, like these two autographs, were short and personal. Those letters that Francis wrote on his return to Italy are precious testimony to his spiritual state at the time. They illustrate his major concerns after the crises created by Philip Longo, John of Cappella, and his vicars. Two of them are revisions of his earliest extant writings. The revisions show how Francis's ideas had evolved over the past four or so years.

Although Francis wrote in Latin, and all his letters show the polish of the scribes and editors on whom he relied, the ideas and content are his. Indeed, the more polished the Latin, the more important he seems to have considered the communication. The more formal the letter, the more we can trust the content to be under his intentional control and not accidental jotting. Francis himself developed, with help, a personal Latin style often characterized as the *stilus Ysidorianus,* a kind of rough-and-ready rhetoric that depended on repetition, parallel clauses, and occasional rhymed prose. Francis's Latin thus has striking parallels to his vernacular compositions, such as the "Canticle of Brother Sun," which uses precisely the same rhetoric. This style is also that of the Latin Psalter, which Francis sang or recited every day for several hours during the Divine Office. Francis modeled his style on the Sacred Text, another example of his desire to follow not his own will, but God's. His Latin is that of the biblical language, not that of theologians or canonists, or even modeled on the language of vernacular poets. The Latin Bible formed Francis as a writer.

Francis wrote letters to priests, Franciscan ministers, and the podestas of Italian cities, all probably during the year 1220. All of his addressees were in positions of leadership and able to form public opinion, within and without the order. In one letter, a revision of his earlier letter to the clergy, originally penned before his departure for Egypt, Francis emphasized again respect for the Blessed Sacrament and the quality and cleanliness of the vessels and linens used at Mass. This time he was able to include a direct reference to the decree of Pope Honorius III, *Expectavimus Hactenus* (22 November 1219), in which the pope commanded that the Sacrament be reserved in a fitting and secure place and that those passing before it bow in reverence, especially at the Elevation. When a priest carried it to the sick, attendants were to go before him with a torch or candle to call people's attention to the Eucharistic presence. It must have gratified Francis to see that his own horror at the scandalous indifference of priests toward the reserved Sacrament and their sloppiness in celebration of Mass had found a powerful ally in Rome. He was probably somewhat disappointed to find that the pope imposed only a bow (the clerical gesture), rather than a genuflection (the lay style preferred by Francis) at the Elevation. Francis added his own stern warning that priests who failed in these duties would "be found to render account to the Lord Jesus Christ."

Not satisfied with writing to priests, Francis also wrote a circular letter to the local superiors in his order, the custodians. In it he made them directly responsible for ensuring that Franciscan communities properly reverenced the Eucharist and had worthy vessels and appointments for Mass. Typical of his unwillingness to place himself (or his brothers) in a position superior to priests, he instructed the custodians, who would often be lay brothers, to "humbly beg the clergy to revere above all else the most Holy Body and Blood of our Lord Jesus Christ." In addition, he returned to a theme first mentioned in the letter to priests from before his departure for the East. He begged recipients to pick up and keep in a place of reverence any piece of parchment on which was written one of the holy names of God (Lord, Jesus, Holy Spirit, etc.) or the words of institution ("This is my Body"; "This is the chalice of my Blood") used in the consecration at Mass. Here cooperation of the clergy was not needed; any friar could show reverence to the holy words. Writing as much to nonordained brothers as to priests, Francis expressed in this letter his own spiritual preferences, without concern for clerical tradition. Instead of Pope Honorius III's bow, Francis insisted: "In every sermon you give, remind people about penance and that no one can be saved unless he receives the most holy Body and Blood of the Lord. When it is sacrificed on the altar by a priest and carried anywhere, let all peoples praise, glorify and honor on bended knee the Lord God, living and true." This instruction on sermons, whether by ordained or unordained brothers, shows his determination to encourage the more dramatic and humbling act of kneeling before the Sacrament in place of the older bow. Francis was himself a leader in this new lay style of prayer and reverence. He considered this message so important that within the year he wrote again to the custodians, reminding them of the instructions in his first letter and again reminding them to preach reverence for the Sacrament, whether this was in the piazza before people or in sermons before "podestas, consuls, or other rulers." That he wrote twice on this topic to those in the best position to make his will known is a window into the founder's frame of mind at this time.

We have from Francis one other message written in 1220, an appeal to the very rulers to whom his friars were to preach repentance and devotion to the Eucharist. Addressed "to the podestas, consuls, and other rulers" of cities, the letter is short and stern, a reminder of death and judgment:

> Reflect and see that the day of death is approaching. With all possible respect, therefore, I beg you not to forget the Lord because of the world's cares and preoccupations and not to turn away from his commandments, for those who leave him in oblivion and turn away from his commandments are cursed and will be left in oblivion by him. When the day of death does come, everything they have will be taken from them. The wiser and more powerful they were in the world, the greater will be the punishment they will endure in Hell.

He then turned to his favorite topic in this period, the Eucharist, writing that "therefore" they should receive communion with fervor and foster honor to the Lord among those they rule. "If you do not do this, know that, on the day of judgment, you must render an account before the Lord your God, Jesus Christ." Some have suggested that the strong emphasis on impending death in this letter is the result of his experience of battle during the Crusade. But Francis already had a firsthand experience of military slaughter at the battle of Collestrada in his youth, and death in squalor and pain was something he encountered daily in his ministry to lepers. Physical death, however brutal, was for Francis merely the pale image of the eternal death of hell. The preaching of penance, now one of the works of his movement, was about the latter, not the former.

These letters tell us much about Francis's concerns at this time, but his true "spiritual testament" for this period is the short treatise known as the "Later Admonition and Exhortation to the Brothers of Penance." This tract, probably written soon after Francis's return in the spring of 1220, reworks the "Earlier Exhortation to the Brothers and Sisters of Penance" of 1210 and, in the care and eloquence of its Latin, shows that Francis intended this as a lasting statement of his views on penance and the spiritual life. It was addressed, not to all laypeople, but to a special group, the Brothers and Sisters of Penance, to which he had belonged from the time of his conversion. Like his letter to priests, this document needs to be read along with its earlier version to detect the changes in Francis's ideas over the past five years.

Like the "Earlier Exhortation," this tract is in two parts: the first, to those Christians practicing the virtues and the sacramental life; the second, to those who neglect them. In the new version, both sections show careful theological and biblical elaborations, although the elaborations are much more extensive in the first section. Additions to the second section are mostly short, with the exception of a new meditation on death and the importance of proper deathbed confession and satisfaction for wrongs. These changes in the second section amount to a rather conventional exhortation to sinners to make a "good death."

Most important in the Later Exhortation are the extensive elaborations of the first part, that addressed to the already pious and penitent. The Earlier Exhortation opened by describing its intended audience as those who "do penance, love God and neighbor, receive the Eucharist and hold their bodies in contempt"; the Later Admonition elaborates extensively on each of these themes. Francis opens with a long section absent from the Earlier Exhortation, a meditation on the Incarnation and its links to the Eucharist. Here Francis gives theological expression to concerns that, in his shorter letters, might seem a fussy fixation with rubrics and liturgical norms. Now Francis meditates on how the Word of the Father, exalted above all creation, humbled himself to take flesh from the Virgin, an act which was "to choose poverty." This is the only mention of "poverty" in Francis's letters of 1220–21, and this "poverty" is not linked to giving up property, simplicity of life, or living only for the day. Francis identifies this poverty with the very physicality of the human condition taken on by the Word.

Nor does Francis dwell on that "poverty" in itself. Rather, he passes to how the Word made flesh gave himself to his followers on the night before his Passion, when he took bread and wine, and, by the words "This is my Body" and "This is the Blood of the New Testament," gave himself over to his disciples as food. Jesus's act of self-giving is, again without elaboration, linked to his sacrifice and death on the Cross for sinners. The Chalice of his Blood given to the disciples is the same one that Jesus spoke of in his prayer to the Father: "Father, let this chalice pass from me," as his "sweat became as drops of blood flowing down upon the earth." At that Last Supper, then, Jesus instituted the Eucharist so that, as victim on the altar of the Cross, he could "give us an example, so that we might follow in his footsteps."

The Later Exhortation highlights a theme that is consistently present in Francis's postconversion life: the imitation of Christ's act of self-offering, which becomes real and tangible "in all the churches of the world," above all in the Eucharistic sacrifice. Christ at the Last Supper commanded his disciples to do as he did, to speak his words over the bread, and so, in eating it, receive his True Body. To take into one's self the Living and Crucified Body during communion, to venerate it at the Elevation during the Mass, and to do so worthily, was to experience the true poverty that was embraced by the Word: human flesh, torn and suffering, bleeding and dying, for others.

It horrified Francis that some were indifferent or even hostile to Christ's command: "Those who do not want to taste how sweet the Lord is and who love the shadows more than the Light, not wanting to fulfill the mandates of God, have been cursed. It is they of whom the prophet wrote: 'Cursed are they who turn away from your mandates.'" I know of no other place where Francis describes others as "cursed." After pointing the way to self-emptying that is the Sacrament, Francis reintroduces, virtually verbatim from his earlier letter, the great commandment of Christ to love God above all things and one's neighbor as oneself, explaining that love of God is identical with that poured out in prayers of adoration before God "day and night," by which believers become adorers of him "in spirit and in truth."

Francis's second major revision of the Earlier Exhortation comes after this meditation on Christ's work and the Sacrament. Francis had previously linked "penance" almost entirely to fasting and corporal mortification of the body, making it almost an end in itself. Now, in the more developed teaching of the Later Exhortation, he links "penance"—now explicitly understood within the context of sacramental confession to a priest—directly to preparation for reception of communion. Beyond sacramental confession, Francis focuses on three specific acts of penance. Those who are in positions of power, who can impose their will on others, are to withhold their authority and exercise mercy rather than judgment. Those with possessions are to give them up by almsgiving. And, finally, all believers, even those without power and property, can abstain from their "vices and sins" and practice fasting and prayer. He writes: "We must be Catholics. We ought to visit churches frequently and venerate clerics, and revere them, not so much for their own sake, for they may be sinners, but on account of their office and administration of the Most Holy Body and Blood of Christ, which they sacrifice on the altar and receive and minister to others." The logic, or better poetic associations, in Francis's thought have taken us full circle. The subordination of the Christian to the Church makes sense only because Christ has chosen to use its clergy, sinners as they are, to make his own self-emptying present to the world through the Mass. To participate worthily in this is, for Francis, what it means "to love God above all things."

Another lengthy section of the Later Exhortation is devoted to the love of neighbor. Francis explains that love of neighbor, indeed love of enemies, means that we "deny our very selves and place our bodies under the yoke of servitude and holy obedience." One is only truly "lesser" than those one is obliged to obey. Love of others means to do their will, not one's own. This subordination of will alone makes one a "lesser brother." Among the brothers, those who exercise authority subordinate their wills to those they rule, by "showing them mercy, as they would want done to themselves." Only after explaining obedience as the ultimate mortification does Francis bring up corporal penance and contempt for the body. Meditation on the body, which in his greatest act of humility, God himself assumed, will make us recognize that we are all "wretched and putrid, fetid and worms." Bodily penance is only real when it teaches us that "we ought to be slaves and subject to every other human creature for God's sake." Physical mortification is never an end in itself.

Francis left the closing section of the first part of the Earlier Exhortation unchanged in the Later. This is the only place where he saw no reason to develop his thought. It consists entirely of a concatenation of quotations from what biblical scholars call the "Priestly Prayer" of Jesus in John 17:1–26. In that prayer at the conclusion of the Last Supper, Jesus offered himself, and his disciples by association, to God the Father as a sacrificial offering to reconcile the world. Francis made this biblical prayer his own, asking God that he and his followers be made perfectly one in the Father so that, while in the world but not of it, all would see not them, but the one who sent them, and come to be where they already were, with him in the splendor of God the

Father. That splendor still remained in the Word, even after the Son humbled himself to take on human flesh and all its limitations and sufferings. In sharing those limitations and sufferings, the faithful follower of Jesus shares his splendor.

Brother Elias and the 1221 Chapter

Brother Peter of Cataneo died on 10 March 1221, after serving as Francis's "superior" for less than six months. As his new superior, Francis chose another of the friars who had returned from the East with him, Brother Elias of Assisi. Of all Francis's decisions, later observers have found this choice the most difficult to understand. Elias had none of Francis's virtues and a good number of vices besides. He was imperious and uncharismatic. To the later Spiritual Franciscans, he was lax and self-indulgent. To later Franciscan clerical leaders, he was an uncouth lay brother. In fact, Francis's choice made perfect sense and showed his astute self-awareness. While Francis lacked any ability at organization and administration, Elias was a born administrator. While Francis suffered horrible spiritual crises every time he was called upon to give orders, Elias took great delight in command. Francis found in Elias the exact skills and temperament that he himself lacked.

Like the choice of Hugolino as his "pope," in whom Francis found the man with the legal skills he himself lacked, the choice of Elias compensated for Francis's own perceived weakness in administration and command. In addition, Elias was, like Francis, by rearing and outlook a layman. They shared the same horizon, the culture of communal Italy, not that of the monastery or the classroom. If Francis ever made a wise decision in his life, it was his choice of Elias as his vicar. If he ever made a poor one, it was the failure to anticipate what would happen after his death when Elias became, on his own, leader of the order. But long-term planning was never Francis's strength. For now at least, the partnership worked well.

Elias assumed the role of vicar soon after Peter's death in March, and he presided at the Pentecost chapter at the end of May 1221. This was the largest assembly of brothers up to this date. Jordan of Giano, who was present and gives the best report, places the number present at three thousand, which is high, but not impossible. Even novices attended the chapter, a sign of the uncloistered and yet unformed nature of the Franciscan novitiate. Brothers ate in shifts at twenty-three tables and lived in the open in makeshift quarters. The people of Assisi responded with great enthusiasm and generosity to Francis and his followers, and by the end of the weeklong event the friars had to turn away food and other offerings.

Cardinal Hugolino was in Lombardy at this time, but Cardinal Ranieri Capocci, a former Cistercian monk, now cardinal deacon of Santa Maria in Cosmedin, was the ranking ecclesiastic present. There were other bishops present as well, and probably representatives of other religious orders. At the cardinal's direction, one of the other bishops present celebrated Mass, at which Francis sang the Gospel in his function as deacon. Francis preached to the assembled brothers on a text from Psalm 143: "Blessed be the Lord my God, who trains my hands for war." Francis applied this text to moral struggles, but, so soon after his return from the Crusade, he probably drew on his experiences there for examples or comparisons.

Throughout the chapter, Francis, who in his own mind had relinquished his position of leadership, sat at the feet of Brother Elias, who was seated in a chair, symbolizing his presidency over the assembly. Whenever "the Brother," as it was customary to call Francis, wanted to say something, he would tug on Elias's tunic. Elias would bend down to let Francis whisper what he wanted communicated in his ear, and Elias then communicated it to the assembly. Brothers later ascribed this routine to Francis's bad health and weakness. But that weakness had not prevented him from serving as deacon and preaching, so it seems likely that this odd arrangement allowed Francis to exemplify humility by abandoning the chair, and to avoid giving directives by having Elias do it. Elias, who enjoyed giving orders, played his part well. Nothing at the chapter happened without Francis's approval, for he was "the Brother," beyond any mere superior, prior, minister, or vicar. There would be many ministers and vicars, but there would always be only one "Brother."

A friar at the chapter, we are told, had been praying over and over for God's deliverance of his Church from the heresies of the Lombards and the murderous pagan "furor" of the Teutons. This very prayer shows that the mostly Italian friars knew very little about Germany, since, except in the Baltic and far eastern areas, the Germans had been Christian from the eighth century or earlier. Nevertheless, this simple prayer reminded Francis of some unfinished business. As the chapter drew to a close, the Brother tugged on Elias's tunic. The long, difficult journeys of the German pilgrims traveling to Rome had shown Francis that they too deserved the presence of the friars, just like the Catholics of Spain, France, Italy, and Oltremare. But the difficulties encountered by earlier missions to Germany implied that those sent might be treated badly. He instructed Elias to emphasize that only those who were willing to take on an obedience greater than that of going to Oltremare should offer themselves for this mission. The appeal was successful; some ninety volunteers offered to go.

The assembling of the German mission in early June 1221 was marked by a festive atmosphere. The friar who had prayed against the Teutonic "furor" was sad that the names of the friars killed by the Muslims in Spain had never been recorded, so he ran about asking all those joining the new mission for their names and where they were from, thinking that it would a great thing to recount how he had known the "German Martyrs" before their departure. One of the missionaries he approached was Brother Palmario of Monte Gargano, who replied with his name and then said: "And you are going with us!" Brother Cesarius of Speyer, who had been chosen to lead the mission, agreed with the choice. So, in spite of his protests, Brother Elias gave the brother an obedience to go to Germany, whether he wanted to or not. And so he went. And we lost one of our best witnesses of Francis's life. That friar was Brother Jordan of Giano, the chronicler and one of Francis's editors. From this date on, although his chronicle is important for the friars' history in Germany, it contains no more eyewitness material on Francis.

[6]

RULES AND RETIREMENT

1221–1223

FROM HIS RESIGNATION in the fall of 1220 until the Pentecost chapter in the spring of the following year, Francis spent much of his time revising, with the help of Cesarius of Speyer, the document that we know as the "Earlier Rule," the "Rule of 1221," or the *Regula non Bullata*. That Cesarius could leave for Germany after the chapter suggests that this project was completed by that time. Although scholars speculate much about this rule, we really know little about the legislation that lay behind it. How the legislation in it was enacted, how it was redacted, and who besides Francis and Cesarius contributed to the final product remain very unclear. We cannot even be sure it was discussed at the 1221 Pentecost chapter. No evidence exists to confirm or deny its presentation there. Nevertheless, the Earlier Rule is important as evidence for Francis's concerns in 1221 and 1222 and for background to the "Later Rule" or *Regula Bullata,* which would be approved by the pope in 1223 and became the official Rule of the Franciscan Order.

It is uncontested that eleven years after Francis's initial approach to Pope Innocent III in 1209, his movement had no confirmed "rule," but rather a "form of life" merely "conceded" provisionally by the pontiff. That the movement might eventually receive a formal canonical rule or statutes was probably implicit in Innocent's promise that he would "do more" for the brothers after it was seen whether or not God would prosper their work. Strictly speaking, the true founding of the Franciscan Order happened only with the formal approval of the Rule. Till then, the movement was loosely organized, heavily dependent on the founder, and more a confraternity than a traditional religious order.

Francis's Working Paper

The movement's existence and development depended very much on Francis himself, even after his "resignation." Lacking a formalized rule and without a functioning system of governance, the movement could not exist on its own. Francis suffered spiritually and emotionally from the demands this put on him, and his decision to cast the Rule into a final form was undoubtedly motivated, at least in part, by his desire to step down from a position of authority. At least initially, composition of the Rule was not something that Roman authorities or the more senior brothers imposed on him. Like his resignation of leadership, writing the Rule was Francis's own decision. He undertook it because only an approved rule could free him of personal leadership responsibilities so that he could become, as he wished, the "least of the brothers."

Composing a rule was a task for which Francis could hardly have been less suited. Francis was many things, but he was not a legislator. And his task was great. Growth had exposed his movement to just criticisms: lack of conventual life and proper formation, friars abandoning religious life or wandering about without permission, and even heresy. All these criticisms, save the last, were well founded. There is no good evidence in contemporary sources for heretical brothers, just as there is none for violations of poverty, save when nonfriars were at fault in building lavish houses for the brothers. The papal requirement of a novitiate, consisting of a year of training for new friars before they made vows, had come on 22 September 1220, when Honorius III issued *Cum Secundum Consilium*. The first clear evidence for appointment of local, if not regional, superiors soon followed. Francis's work on the Earlier Rule belongs in the context of these reforms. The decision to discipline and regularize his formless mass of followers, which would result in making them more autonomous and less dependent on him, would be Francis's own.

Redaction of the Earlier Rule took place principally during the winter and spring of 1221, roughly the same time as the composition of the "Later Admonition and Exhortation to the Brothers of Penance," which I described in chapter 5. (Indeed the language and phrasing of both documents are remarkably similar.) Also, at about the same time, the Brothers of Penance, until this time a loosely organized group of lay penitents, had their own *memoriale* or "rule" drawn up and presented to the pope for approval. Later legend would turn this independent lay movement into the body of pious laity that would later become known as the Franciscan Third Order, but Francis had no direct hand in that document. Francis probably did serve as an inspiration for the group, as he had originally been a member of it.

In reality, the Earlier Rule was not a canonical rule at all. It is best understood as Francis's "working paper" in the project of establishing a form of life that could be lived by the brothers independent of him. There is no evidence that any Franciscan chapter ever discussed or voted on the document, and Francis seems never to have submitted it to the pope for approval. Moreover, the term "lesser brothers," which appears only once, does not yet even seem the name of the organization. The Earlier Rule is a composite document, made up of disparate material composed at different times in response to very particular issues facing the brotherhood. Francis was no doubt the primary author as to the content, but the early followers who attended the chapters at the Porziuncula also contributed to it though their comments, discussions, and actions. Some sections, such as the one on manual labor, seem outdated in light of actual conditions in the early 1220s; rather, they seem to be relics of a period when the movement consisted of lay penitents living on their own. Important as manual labor was to Francis—and he would praise it in his Testament—by 1220 the Franciscan movement had become very diverse. It included priests, missionaries, and preachers, some well educated. Manual labor would remain part of the Franciscan way of life, but by this date it could no longer be one of its defining characteristics. Sometime after 1223, in his letter to Anthony of Padua, Francis himself would begrudgingly allow study and theological teaching to replace manual labor, at least for an educated friar.

The Earlier Rule is not an abstract statement of the founder's vision. Francis, a man intensely affected by his personal experiences and environment, would have been hard pressed to produce an abstract exposition of his "way of life." The document is divided into twenty-four chapters and composed in grammatically correct Latin, which means that it underwent revision by Cesarius of Speyer and other literate friars. It features numerous biblical quotations to illustrate and express the author's vision, something that makes perfect sense, since Francis understood God to have revealed to him his way of life, at least in part, through the *sortes biblicae* at San Nicolò church. Although Francis probably depended on the theologically literate Cesarius for the quotations, they express Francis's vision very directly; they are hardly embellishments. In spite of the many hands involved in its composition, the Earlier Rule was Francis's project and reflects, above all, his concerns, needs, and worries of the early 1220s. Its complexity reflects his struggle to put into written form the kind of life he had been living and the way he wanted his followers to live after he had retired from leadership.

The first note that Francis strikes in the Earlier Rule is obedience. In 1209 he had personally promised obedience to Pope Innocent and his successors, after which all the brothers professed obedience to Francis and his successors.

Accordingly, the first chapter sums up the brothers' life as follows: "The rule and life of the brothers is this, namely: 'to live in obedience, in chastity, and without anything of their own' and to follow the teaching of Christ." The phrase "to live in obedience, in chastity, and without anything of their own" is identical to that used by Innocent III when he approved the rule of another new order, the Trinitarians, in 1198. In content it is no more than the traditional monastic vows. Francis then summarizes the "teaching of Christ" by quoting a series of biblical texts that encapsulate his initial conversion experience. The injunction to "leave all things" and "take up the Cross" and follow Christ (cf. Matt. 19:21; Luke 18:22) overlaps and parallels the texts revealed in the *sortes biblicae.*

To these texts, Francis adds Gospel passages that declare those unworthy of Christ who do not hate mother, father, and family (Matt. 16:24), and those who do not leave all things for him (Luke 14:26). If any texts summarized Francis's experience of leaving his family and entering the life of penance, they were these. In essence, Francis's decision to become a lay penitent remained the foundation of his movement, and he had no problem linking that to the traditional monastic vows of poverty, chastity, and obedience, using a verbal formula that had already received papal approval on at least one occasion. As he would say in his Testament, God had revealed his life to him, and the pope had approved it for him. The result is wholly conventional and monastic, on the one hand, and, on the other, a commitment to follow literally the hardest of Christ's hard sayings.

The remainder of the Rule addresses diverse concerns, some of which Francis also addressed in the "Later Admonition and Exhortation to the Brothers of Penance" and in the letters he wrote at about the same time. Chapters 20–23 ring changes on very familiar themes of Francis. In chapter 20 he dwells on the importance of auricular confession to priests, or to laymen when priests are unavailable, a common medieval devotional practice that did not imply that this removed the need to repeat the confession to a priest when one could be found. Chapters 21–22 amount, oddly enough in a rule, to a model sermon on repentance. They are heavy with biblical quotations urging hearers to turn from sin, forgive their enemies, and embrace a life of self-denial. Francis follows this with a homiletic exegesis of the parable of the sower and an extended quotation from Christ's "Priestly Prayer," a favorite biblical passage of Francis, as seen in his earlier writings. Chapter 23 is an extended prayer of praise for God, very personal in tone, which in its litanic form bears a strong resemblance to prayers just becoming common in Italian manuscripts of personal devotion. Francis delights in listing the hosts of heaven; the orders of the Church hierarchy, clerical and lay; the attributes of Christ; and the ways he would praise God. Chapter 24 concludes the document.

When we compare chapters 20–24 with Francis's earlier writings, we find that some of his favorite spiritual themes have now been integrated into a seamless whole with a flowing rhetorical structure and unity. The spirituality begins with penance, personal and sacramental, moves to the ecclesiastical context of the life of penance, and then looks ahead to the glory of the saints in heaven. Some scholars have suggested that Francis prepared this section of the Earlier Rule as a "testament" for his followers just before he went to Egypt. Although not impossible, it seems more likely that Francis produced these chapters after his return from Egypt, when he was trying to create a written version of his "form of life."

By contrast, the materials in chapters 2–19 seem practical and concrete, directed at very specific issues facing the brothers at various different times. For example, chapter 3 deals with the recitation of the Office and fasting, regulations essential because of Cardinal Colonna's tonsuring of Francis and his two followers. Chapter 2 concerns the novitiate, a discipline that Pope Honorius directed the fraternity to adopt in November of 1220. Chapters 4 and 5 deal with the office of minister and correction of the brothers. This office was a response, about the time of the trip to Egypt, to the growing size of the movement, which prevented Francis from having direct contact with all the brothers. This problem was already acute by 1216, when Hugolino told Francis not to go to France but to return to Assisi.

Particular symbolic concerns—for example, that the friars not ride horses (chapter 15) or that superiors not be called "prior" (chapter 6)—sit uncomfortably next to longer sections on manual labor (chapter 7) and the preservation of chastity (chapters 12–13). Chapter 11, on avoiding the sin of detraction, resembles the outline of a spiritual conference, one that Francis might well have given as an exhortation during a chapter at the Porziuncula. Two chapters of this practical section treat missions to the Saracens (chapter 16) and preaching (chapter 17) and again address those topics from the point of view of their spiritual foundation and temptations. They represent Francis's reflections on the preaching mission he had received from Innocent in 1209 and on his own experiences with the Crusade. In short, it is probably not far from wrong to see these central chapters as particular pieces of legislation, assembled by Francis as the norms of a "rule," and bookended by chapter 1 and chapters 20–23, in which Francis summarizes his deeper personal and spiritual concerns.

In its homiletic tone, its concrete particularities, and its chaotic order, the Earlier Rule seems exactly the kind of personal document that Francis would have produced, left to his own devices. Reading it carefully can dispel certain misconceptions about his focus in this period. For instance, the legislation on books and the Office casts his life at this period and that of the brotherhood in a very different light from the reminiscences of his companions thirty years or more after his death, when the issue of books had become part of the controversies over poverty. Francis's concern in 1221 was that books represented an aspiration to clerical status and ordination, not some violation of poverty. So chapter 3, placed immediately after the clothing of novices, requires the friars, both clerical and lay, to recite the Office. It specifically provides that those who can read, even if laymen, may have Psalters. On the other hand, those who cannot read should not have any books at all. They are to recite sets of Pater Nosters in place of each of the liturgical hours. The implicit message is clear: lay brothers should not strive for "higher" position by learning to read and becoming clerics. They should stay as they are; but clerics who join the fraternity are to continue in that state. This passage reflects the following reminiscence of Francis in his Testament: "We clerical brothers said the Office as other clerics did; the lay brothers said the Our Father."

The Earlier Rule also addresses the most pressing issue facing Francis's movement at the time: the role of superiors and the nature of obedience. Francis's own spiritual development was characterized by a burning desire to subject his own will to God, the Church, and all others—to become truly a "lesser brother, subject to all." He recognized that authority over others could be corrupting and that those exercising it might not merely err, but even command what was objectively sinful. The obedience of the subject in the monastic tradition was never absolute, and the early constitutions of the Dominicans, redacted before Francis compiled the Earlier Rule, provided that sinful commands were void, and subjects had an obligation to correct superiors. In contrast, for Francis, obedience to God and the Church, by which he meant the hierarchy, was absolute. If a bishop or priest treated the brothers wrongly, they were to accept it as chastisement; if he commanded something sinful, they were not to resist, but to shake the dust from their feet and depart. They were not to resist a sinful command but to flee it.

The Earlier Rule is not, by any means, the only place where Francis discussed obedience. In a saying of Francis, which seems to predate the Earlier Rule and is preserved as the third item in the collection called his *Admonitions,* he elaborated on one of his foundational biblical texts, Luke 14:35, the command to renounce all things to follow Christ. He read this renunciation as principally about destroying self-will through obedience, not as about abandoning property. Drawing on traditional monastic sources, he balanced the total surrender of will by the religious to his superior with the proviso that sinful commands need not be obeyed. Nevertheless, he worried about religious who construe their superiors' hard commands as sins and so "return to the vomit of their own will."

Francis's teachings in his *Admonitions* reflect his views on obedience while they were still in flux. By 1221, the experience of leadership had tempered those views. The personal spiritual issue of obedience to superiors had to be supplemented by mechanisms for settling controversies over obedience within the brotherhood. In the Earlier Rule, after charging ministers to act as servants rather than superiors, and insisting that the brothers not obey obviously sinful commands, Francis provided that when a superior acted according to the flesh, not the spirit, the subjects should admonish him three times, and if that failed, bring the grievance to the attention of the annual Pentecost chapter. Although he does not quote it, Francis had found in Romans 8:4 a biblical method of correction for dealing not just with erring friars, but also with erring superiors. Medieval canon law knew this procedure as the "Evangelical Denunciation." One first confronted the erring privately, then with another witness, and finally in the public forum. Above all, the ministers themselves were to scrutinize their own behavior constantly and remember the Lord's words that those who would be first should put themselves last. That true spiritual authority came from putting one's self below others lies at the heart of Francis's insistence, first seen in this document, that those in charge not be called "prior," which meant one "above" or "ahead," but rather all were to be "lesser brothers."

Chapter 18 of the Earlier Rule provided for annual assemblies or "chapters" of the brothers. In so doing, it marks a milestone in the development of governing structures, as it offers the first formal discussion of a chapter in Francis's writing. Jacques de Vitry, in his letter of 1216, spoke of the brothers gathering for a "chapter" once a year. By the time he redacted his *Historia Occidentalis* sometime after 1221, he spoke of the friars as having one or two "general chapters" a year. In the earliest days of the movement, such meetings were fluid and ad hoc. Before the Earlier Rule, we find no direct evidence for any particular meetings other than the one annual Pentecost chapter. The Earlier Rule formalized norms for local regions: friars were to gather with their local minister on the feast of St. Michael the Archangel in September. We know that one of these local chapters was convened on 29 September 1221 at Trent by Cesarius of Speyer, the minister of the German mission.

The long-traditional chapter on Pentecost at the Porziuncula now took on a special role. It was no longer merely a local assembly of the brothers, as it seems earlier to have been; the Rule now required all ministers from the other parts of Italy to attend it every year, and those abroad at least every three years. This is among the most practical and canonically sophisticated sections of the Earlier Rule, and it is likely that Cesarius of Speyer, or even Cardinal Hugolino, had a hand in its formulation. But Francis himself recognized that this kind of institutionalization was necessary if he were ever to relinquish his role of general superior and become one of the "least of the brothers." Whoever wrote it, Francis approved it.

The Earlier Rule is also the first datable writing of Francis in which he speaks about poverty directly, and it shows that his ideas were still developing and rather flexible. In chapter 8, he makes explicit what his behavior had already taught: the friars are not to work for money or to receive it in alms. They are to treat coins as no better than the mire under their feet. Specifically, Francis orders his followers to avoid soliciting funds for any purpose, even for the needs of the lepers who were so dear to his heart. But Francis immediately modifies this hard rule and allows the collection of alms for lepers when there is dire necessity. "But let them beware of money," he cautions. The conflicted state of this passage reflects Francis's interior struggle. He despised money and coins, but even his gut revulsion could not stop him from making an exception for the lepers, perhaps the most excluded and marginalized group in his society.

Francis next discusses begging as a way of supplying material needs, when the manual labor that he assumes to be the normal means of support fails. Friars were to beg because it placed them in the position of the despised and powerless—it was a kind of mortification, a way to become a "lesser brother." The sense that charity toward those in need can trump the rule against accepting coin offerings is again confirmed by Francis's permission to work for pay and even to accept cash when there is an "evident need of the sick brothers." It must have pained Francis to make these exceptions, but charity for those in special need—lepers or the sick—was a greater rule.

As with obedience and poverty, Francis's treatment of preaching and missions shows him grappling with changes in his movement since the first followers joined him. When he speaks of the brothers "going through the world" in chapter 14, he connects this with the biblical injunctions to take nothing, to accept as food whatever is put before you, and not to resist evil. These passages were not only connected to the *sortes biblicae* at San Nicolò; they underlie the earliest descriptions of Francis's postconversion activities. Doubtless he preferred to present the biblical quotations alone as his "mission statement," but his unexpected commission to preach granted by Pope Innocent required more. The pope's charge presented a problem for Francis; preaching, after all, implies that the speaker knows something that the hearers do not. Even more, the effective preacher wins acclaim from his hearers whether he wishes it or not, and such acclaim can lead to a reputation, as it did for Francis, as a healer or miracle worker.

Francis's reflections on preaching in chapter 17 reveal his fears about these temptations. Friars are to preach only with permission from their minister; they are to stop when it is withdrawn. They are not to rejoice in any positive results, but to humble themselves. It is better to preach by actions than words; even then, positive results should be ascribed to God alone. The unrelentingly admonitory quality of this chapter is striking. It parallels Francis's wish that those who go among the Saracens (chap. 16) should live quietly among them and spread Christianity by example, especially during persecution, rather than by preaching. Francis in 1221 was still struggling to reconcile Innocent's commission to preach with the form of life revealed to him at his conversion.

It was around this time, or perhaps a little later, that Francis produced a small rule governing the life of friars in hermitages. Hermitages were not places of total isolation; rather, they were remote residences where two or three friars could withdraw and focus exclusively on prayer. This practice was a throwback to the kind of life he, Bernard, and Peter were practicing when they journeyed to Rome in 1209. Stories about Francis after his return from the East often place him in a hermitage or on the way to one. At such times, Francis could escape the demands of administration and, for short periods at least, return to something of the early days after his conversion. In this document, Francis sketches his ideal of the eremitic life, one not totally solitary, but quasi-communal in form. In the longest section, he outlines the structuring of the day by the liturgical offices, which are to be done together, not in private. However much solitary prayer appealed to Francis, even in the "desert" he favored above all the vocal prayer of the Church.

In the "Rule for Hermitages," Francis used a traditional active–contemplative division of labor. One friar was to stay home and pray, while the other was to take care of material needs. But Francis gave this division of roles a novel twist. First, the two brothers were to exchange roles periodically, and more important, the one in charge, the active friar, was to be considered the "mother"—not the "father"—and the other, the contemplative, was to be the "son." Francis was a man of his time in his stereotyped view of mothers as nurturers and fathers as disciplinarians, but he was also capable of startling reversals of traditional roles. In the hermitage, the "superior" was to be feminine, a nurturer, not an authority, much less an authoritarian like Pietro di Bernardone. Oddly, too, given the medieval hierarchical order in which contemplation was higher than action, the "mother" was to be the active friar, not the contemplative. If correction was to happen, it came from the superior displaying good behavior, not by issuing corrections. No role of leadership was to be permanent. Temporary exemplarity was the one form of leadership that Francis could accept with a wholly clear conscience.

Using the traditional image of Mary and Martha as a model for the division of activity and contemplation, he divided the roles as "mother" (Martha) and "son" (Mary), thereby making the active role superior to the contemplative: Mary subordinate to Martha. The "mother" was responsible for dealing with the outside world and protecting the "son" from being disturbed. The use of maternal imagery here reflects Francis's own image of himself as the mother hen trying to protect the brood of chicks that are his friars. It also echoes the parable he told, in reference to his lax admissions policies, in which he compared himself to a poor woman whose sons are the products of her union with the great king. Even in the hermitage, the "sons" are to practice the self-abasement of begging. Francis directs that they may break silence and speak to their "mothers" so that "they can beg alms from them as poor little ones for the love of the Lord God." Neither role is permanent: "mothers" and "sons" should take turns and exchange roles "as they have mutually decided."

Revision and Approval of the Rule

As Francis revised the Rule, he continued to function as head of his move-ment, even though Peter of Cataneo was formally recognized as his vicar. Peter, meanwhile, found it hard to order Francis about; he made mistakes in doing so, at least from Francis's point of view. In the early 1220s, the friars gen-erally did not have Breviaries, but they did have Psalters and Gospels for use in the Office. On one occasion in late 1220 or early 1221, an at-best semiliterate novice who wanted to learn to read approached Peter and asked to have use of a Psalter, but the novice also wanted Francis's approval. Francis's reaction was immediate and negative. In the received version of the story, Francis had a horrible crisis of conscience because he failed to prevent a "violation of the Rule." He ran after the novice, threw himself down on the ground, and ac-cused himself of sin for not preventing the novice from having the book.

Peter, who was educated and probably a trained canonist, had no problem with friars studying. The novice's request reflected a desire for the kind of self-improvement that would eventually become normal and expected. Francis had nothing against clerics—he was a cleric himself—but friars in the lay state should remain there. From very early on, there were priests in the movement; this bothered Francis not at all. But the unordained were not to strive for or-ders either. When brothers began to aspire to clerical status or ordination, their striving showed they were no longer true "lesser brothers." Such striving lies behind Francis's outburst in chapter 3 of the Earlier Rule, where he ordered lay brothers not to have Psalters but to content themselves with reciting Pater Nosters, like other illiterate laymen.

Francis not only concerned himself with policy on issues like books and status: he also had to deal with particular problems referred to him by local ministers and superiors. This too forced him to rethink his Rule. Sometime before Pentecost 1221, Francis wrote his "Letter to a Minister." Some local minister had written to Francis, or it had been reported to Francis, that the minister was so frustrated with those under his charge that he wanted to resign and go live in a hermitage. This was a temptation Francis understood well. He reflected on the superior's responsibility to correct erring subjects and the problems presented by their disobedience. The standard he set was high. The superior is to consider it a grace when his subjects disobey him or treat him badly. Accepting this burden as sent from God will be "more than a hermitage for you." In addition, Francis directed the minister to forgive any friar, no matter how much he has sinned, and, should the friar not ask forgiveness, offer forgiveness anyway. He was to encourage other ministers to act the same way.

The counsel is noble in sentiment and reflects Francis's wish that a minister should be the least of the brothers and "subject to all." Nevertheless, rejoicing in subordinates' disobedience as a gift sent from God and forgiving those who might have no intention of reforming may have been a fine spiritual discipline for the minister, but it was a formula for spiritual and community disaster in a large religious organization. Most manuscripts of this letter resolve the tension by adding a section in which "Francis" suggests a piece of legislation for the next Pentecost chapter that gives practical means of disciplining delinquents. That this form of the letter tells the minister to preserve the suggestion and propose it suggests that the recipient, at least of the expanded letter, was indeed Elias, the vicar as the chapter of 1221 approached. One suspects that this practical proposal may have come from the vicar himself, rather than from Francis.

Francis, in the longer version, binds under obedience any friar "who has sinned" to go and confess it to his superior. If he does not do this on his own, his brother friars are not to discuss or publicize the issue but are under obedience to take him to the superior. The superior is to treat him with mercy and impose no penance other than the injunction to "go and sin no more." In addition, friars are all obligated to confess to a priest (or to another brother until a priest is available), even if they fall into merely venial sin. Cleverly, Francis has now relieved the superior (and himself) of the task of correcting subordinates. The task of discipline has devolved to the brothers. The role of the superior is so hedged about with qualifications that it is hard to see how he could, on his own, deal with the recalcitrant. Nevertheless, we are on the way to the practical solutions of the Earlier Rule. Specifically, chapter 5, with its more systematic procedure for delinquents and its enhanced punitive powers for superiors, reflects Francis's further progress in confronting the complexity of discipline in a mass movement.

I have discussed the incidents of the novice's Psalter and the frustrated minister because they are the best examples of Francis dealing with practical problems following his return from Egypt, and both produced extant legislation. Francis finally confronted the problem of leaders making wrong decisions and brothers exhibiting bad attitudes. In both cases, Francis accomplished what he was least skilled at: drafting legislation. Francis needed help in this process, and his companions of this period were not all helpful. Peter of Cataneo, for all his legal training, seems to have been hopeless at governance. Cesarius of Speyer was no canonist. As a result, the Earlier Rule, while very much a personal expression of Francis's character, remained too homiletic, too disorganized, and ultimately too sketchy to serve as a "constitution."

For Francis, God had spoken through the biblical texts revealed to him in 1209. Francis had trouble enough systematizing this revelation himself. Nevertheless, it seems that he continued to try to perfect the document, even presenting it for discussion at the chapter of 1222. During that assembly, some of the friars seem to have suggested that Francis use one of the older approved rules as a model. He reacted with some heat and told his advisers that he did not want to use any model, not that of Augustine, Bernard, or Benedict, but to do it his own way. God had, he said, wanted him to be a "new fool in the world." Those who wanted anything more, he declared, would be punished by God's "police," the demons. Francis then took two friars, Brother Leo, his confessor and confidant, and Brother Bonizzo of Bologna, to the hermitage at Fonte Colombo near Rieti for the final revisions. Bonizzo is an obscure figure; Leo, at least, was educated enough to be a priest. One wonders how much help these companions were. We do not know if others went along, but Elias and other friars likely visited Francis as he worked.

While in reclusion at Fonte Colombo Francis struggled to revise the 1221 document into one that could serve as a constitution for his order. The result of this revision, what is known as the "Later Rule," was finally approved by Pope Honorius on 8 November 1223 and betrays the hand of a ghostwriter with training in canon law. Ad hoc pieces of legislation, like that proposed in the "Letter to a Minister" or those found jumbled in the Earlier Rule, have undergone a careful revision. Over the fifteen months between the chapter of 1221 and the approbation of 1223, Francis received help from men with training in Church law and administration. The experience of his revision was frustrating for Francis. He needed help, but the experts were experts, because they knew canon law and the practice of older religious orders.

In the end, Francis depended more and more on a non-Franciscan, his friend Cardinal Hugolino. The cardinal was a man whom Francis trusted. In addition, Hugolino had never been a member of an older order, so he came to the work of revision with an open mind, unformed by previous styles of monastic life. It is a sign of Hugolino's increasingly close work with Francis that on 29 March 1222, Pope Honorius issued *Devotionis Vestrae Precibus,* the first privilege to the movement. It was one to which Francis had no objection. The privilege granted the friars the right to say the Divine Office even in places where public religious services were forbidden because of an interdict. This was exactly the sort of "privilege," the right to pray, that Francis could accept.

By the spring of 1223, Francis had produced the document that he always considered "his Rule," and to which he always directed his followers as the expression of his ideal. This is somewhat surprising, since, in external form at least, the new Rule is quite different from the working paper that was the Earlier Rule. It is much shorter, just over a quarter the length of the earlier document. Gone were nearly all the sections in which Francis spoke in his own voice: the homiletic and spiritual exhortations, the confusing and contradictory attempts to balance practicality with the demands of poverty, and the personal expressions of piety and prayer. Sections like that on admissions to the novitiate (chapter 2) show the hand of a trained canonist and lift norms directly from canon law. The provision on modifying clothing according to the climate of the place where the friars live (chapter 4) borrows from the Rule of Benedict, while that on contact with nuns (chapter 11) betrays the influence of Cistercian regulations. Although not modeling the new Rule on earlier rules, Francis was willing to borrow from them when they were helpful. Hugolino helped Francis find voices in the monastic tradition that could still authentically become his own.

The Later Rule reveals how much the brotherhood had changed from the early days at Rivo Torto, and not merely by increase in numbers. Above all, it serves to rationalize the internal governance of the brotherhood. The role of superiors and chapters (chapter 8), disciplinary procedures (chapters 7 and 10), and choir obligations (chapter 3) are spelled out and clarified. These sections show most clearly the influence of someone like Hugolino. Although the Later Rule leaves the office of preaching open to all friars, certain provisions work against preaching by the lay brothers. In the Earlier Rule, for instance, superiors merely monitored preaching for orthodoxy and risk of scandal, but in the Later Rule they grant a formal "ministry of preaching" to worthy friars. This gave superiors a practical veto power over preaching by lay brothers. Chapter 11 (where the phrase "I strictly command" rather than the usual "Let the brothers" reveals Francis's own hand) forbids the brothers to enter houses of nuns without permission of the Apostolic See. The threat of scandal was undoubtedly behind Francis's strong language here, but the effect is to regularize the previously free-form (and so potentially problematic) relations between the friars and nuns. Growth in numbers demanded these developments. Many modern observers decry these changes, but only a hopeless romantic could think that the now huge international brotherhood could have remained un-changed from what it was in 1209, like some fly in amber. Francis was no romantic, and the Later Rule reflects that fact.

Francis's own language reveals these changes, but also an underlying conti-nuity. In 1209, of course, Francis and his two followers were a free-form group of lay penitents with no real formal status. During their visit to Rome, the three men were unexpectedly tonsured and given permission to preach, thus becoming clerics. Soon others joined them, but their way of life underwent no particular change except that the clerics among them began to recite the Of-fice. The movement was not an "order" in the traditional sense: they were not monks like the Cistercians or canons regular like the early Dominicans. Fran-cis originally referred to his group as a *fraternitas,* which was one of the names given to groups of lay penitents. Although outside observers soon spoke of the movement as a *religio* or "religious movement," Francis himself continued to use the word *fraternitas* and even employed it in the Later Rule, which employs the word *ordo* (order) only once and in that case only loosely.

Francis and Hugolino did not think they were creating a rule for an "order" in the traditional sense. Francis was certain that his group was some-thing wholly different. Nevertheless, with the approval of the Rule, the papal curia began to think of the Franciscan movement as an "order" and treated it accordingly. The brothers thought of themselves more and more as an "order," like the Cistercian monks or the Norbertine canons. Even Francis began to use the word occasionally, and he never objected to it. This linguistic shift reveals the progressive institutionalization of Francis's personal aspiration to follow Christ perfectly. It is hard to see how else he could have passed his vision on to a body of several thousand men.

With the canonical status of an approved order, the Franciscans began to act less like a confraternity. The decision, enshrined in chapter 3 of the Later Rule, that they would celebrate the "Divine Office according to the rite of the Roman Church," was a change of great consequence. Before 1223 the broth-ers had conformed their prayers to local liturgical practice, just as groups of lay penitents did. In Assisi, the brothers had followed the liturgical uses of Bishop Guido and his chapter. And they still did, since Guido, like the friars, adopted the Roman liturgy in about 1223. Francis still thought of himself as following his bishop's lead. But now friars beyond Assisi were distinguished liturgically from the priests and clerics who surrounded them, just as the Cistercians, the Carthusians, and (eventually) the Dominicans would be by their corporate liturgical homogeneity.

The Franciscans were the first order to use the Office of the Roman Church outside of Rome and its environs. This liturgical branding, so to speak, gave the order an international identity based on clerical liturgical practice. Francis seems to have accepted this development without any difficulty. Perhaps he even favored it. In any case, by the end of the year, he received his own personal copy of the Roman Breviary as a gift from an anonymous official of the Roman Curia who had used it from 1216 to 1223. Francis had the Mass Gospels of the year bound into the back of this volume for his devotional reading each Sunday. He used this Breviary until his death, when it passed to the friars, who used it until Francis's companion Brother Leo finally gave it to the sisters of San Damiano. It can still be seen in a reliquary in Assisi today.

In spite of this perhaps inevitable institutionalization, the Later Rule did not remove many revolutionary elements of Francis's way of life. Some of these, Francis himself further radicalized by his own actions. While working on the Rule, he also traveled, visiting the friars and preaching. On one occasion he traveled to Verona, and on his return to Umbria he intended to pass through Bologna, but when he heard that there was a new "house of the brothers" there, he sent a message commanding them to abandon the house. In obedience, even the sick were "thrown out" into the street, and Francis showed his displeasure by avoiding the city. He only later relented and gave permission for them to move back into the house when Hugolino announced in a sermon that he, not the brothers, was the legal owner of the building.

A repeat of this reaction to new residences occurred at Assisi in 1222, probably during preparations for the Pentecost chapter. The people of Assisi, knowing that many friars would come for the assembly and have no place to live, constructed a large dwelling for them. Francis, returning to find the construction almost finished, protested against it by going up on the roof, tearing off the roofing tiles, and throwing them down. He ordered the other friars to come up and help him destroy the building. Only when knights from the commune shouted up that the house was the property of the city and that Francis was destroying public property, did Francis stop and come down from the roof. These two incidents are the only occasions for which there is certain evidence that Francis was reacting to the brotherhood's slow deviation from its original simplicity of life, in short, the first violations of poverty. Near his death Francis would again cry out in his Testament against friars' accepting overly lavish residences.

Francis's anxiety about dwelling places that could compromise the friars' poverty plagued him until his death. The incidents involving the Bologna and Assisi houses were the first skirmishes in what would become the controversy over poverty that would rack the order some forty years after Francis's death. During his life, however, there is no good evidence that the later abuses of handling of money through agents, storing and consumption of sumptuous food, or use of fine clothes had yet appeared, but the acquisition of imposing residences, at least in Bologna and Assisi, was a sign of problems to come.

These painful events left clear traces in the Later Rule. The section on residences in the Earlier Rule seems casual: "Wherever the brothers may be, either in hermitages or other places, let them be careful not to make any place their own or contend with anyone for it." The parallel of the Later Rule is sharper. In chapter 6, that on houses and almsgiving, Francis wrote: "Let the brothers not make anything their own, neither house, nor place, not anything at all." The phrasing is not casual: Francis is speaking with vigor and determination. The growing number of friars required larger places to live in, but the friars are absolutely forbidden to "make it their own"; it will remain the property of others, as was the case in Bologna and Assisi. But Francis allowed such vicariously owned property only with the sorest of misgivings. The Later Rule expresses as forcefully as Francis ever did his burning zeal to have them live in the world as pilgrims and strangers. If the exponential growth of the order forced Francis to allow friars to take shelter in large buildings belonging to others, it is hard to see how he could have forbidden it.

Contrary to the common misconception, the Later Rule is stricter on poverty than the 1221 draft. In chapter 4, that on money, Francis closed the loopholes we noted in the Earlier Rule that allowed the brothers to accept cash alms for aid of lepers and the sick. Now they are not to do so directly or through intermediaries. Rather, the ministers are to rely on "spiritual friends" when they need to care for the sick. "Spiritual friends" would later become an institutionalized means of controlling large resources, but in 1223 the "friend" was not a kind of legal agent for the brothers. Rather, he was an acquaintance on whom they could rely for help. Francis was no longer willing to allow charity to trump his desire that the friars never handle money. The brothers would no longer stockpile coins; they were now to be dependent on others, exactly what Francis wanted. Chapter 4, in a similar way, makes the parallel legislation of the Earlier Rule more rigorous.

While maintaining the requirement that those brothers who can work with their hands do so, the Later Rule drops the concession that they might have personal tools of their trade. In contrast to manual labor, begging is now very much emphasized, and it is assumed that all friars will practice it primarily as a self-abasement and spiritual discipline, not merely as a supplement to manual labor. In part, this probably reflects the growing number of clerics and intellectuals entering the order, men who would probably never be able (or willing?) to support themselves by manual labor. This is a major shift in focus and marks the beginning of the process by which begging would eventually become, in place of physical work, the primary marker of poverty for the movement, something still not the case in 1223.

With the growth of the order came new friars from diverse backgrounds, some of whom were poor enough that even Francis and the friars seemed better off than their families. While Peter of Cataneo was vicar, the mother of two friars, probably her only sons, turned to Francis for help. He went to Peter and asked him to find something to help "our mother"—the term Francis used for the mother of any of the friars. Peter replied that the only thing at the Porziuncula that could be sold for alms was the New Testament they used for the lessons at Matins. Francis instructed Peter to give it to her to sell. Considering Francis's overriding concern for having suitable service at the altar and his dedication to the Office, it must have been a difficult decision. As brothers joined him, Francis now felt an obligation to their families, something unimaginable in the days of San Damiano and Rivo Torto, when he had rejected the idea that friars would give their possessions to blood relatives. Again, circumstances, here vocations from destitute families, caused the founder to rethink his original approach.

The friars certainly discussed the final draft of the Rule at the Pentecost chapter of 1222. We do not know if it was discussed again at the chapter in June 1223. Nevertheless, by the end of the summer, the document had been sent to Rome. As the curial official most directly involved with the Franciscans, Cardinal Hugolino probably served as Francis's proctor in petitioning Pope Honorius to approve the final draft of the Rule. The pope did so in the bull *Solet Annuere* on 29 November 1223. This bull of approbation is why the Later Rule is often called the *Regula Bullata* in contrast to the unapproved Earlier Rule of 1221.

Francis himself was not in Rome when Pope Honorius approved the Rule. He was probably at Rieti or a nearby hermitage. The bull itself is a curial form letter into which the Rule has been inserted, a format that shows the routine nature of the event. This was a common bureaucratic procedure for approving requests from religious orders, when legislation was submitted to Rome for approval. Unlike Innocent III's approval in 1209, which was tentative and above all concerned Francis's personal and spiritual scruples, *Solet Annuere* signaled that the movement was now an established religious order of the Catholic Church. In a legal sense, the bull ended the probationary period granted by Innocent. Francis always spoke of this papally approved text as his Rule. For him it was the definitive form of life he wished to pass on to the brothers.

With the active and self-possessed Elias as his vicar, and a papally approved Rule, Francis now devoted himself more and more to his new self-appointed task: acting as a model for the brothers. Until nearly two years later, when he would retire to La Verna, the order was in the odd position of having two superiors: Elias, who was responsible for making sure the friars lived according to the letter of the Rule, and Francis, whose life and behavior presented a second, unwritten rule. Sometimes these two "rules of life" were in conflict; sometimes they supported each other.

Francis Prepares to Retire

Francis remained involved in the life of the friars and nuns, even in what seem insignificant institutional matters, after the approbation of the Rule. For example, on 16 June 1223, five months before the approval, he participated in the legal business of drawing up a deed for a convent of the Poor Ladies. In addition, while Elias and the ministers were in charge of day-to-day governance, more serious matters were regularly passed by Francis for his advice. This bureaucratic shuffle meant that application of discipline was sluggish. On 18 December 1223, Pope Honorius III wrote, asking about lax enforcement of excommunications applied to delinquent brothers. Slowly, however, either by design or by circumstances, Francis's direct involvement in the order diminished.

The brothers themselves had conflicted attitudes toward the founder. They revered Francis and wanted to think of him as their leader. But as he became sicker and insisted on being subject in obedience to the "handlers" who cared for him, these friars not only controlled his life, but more and more they claimed to speak for him on matters of the Order. Francis remained in control, more or less, of his own day-to-day existence. By mid-December 1223, he decided to leave the hermitage near Rieti, where he had been living, to travel to Greccio for Christmas. If the story of a fisherman giving him a water bird while rowing across the lake describes this trip, he traveled by boat.

Greccio during that Christmas season witnessed one of the most touching and revealing incidents in Francis's life. Two weeks or so before the feast, Francis called on a certain John of Greccio, with whom he was familiar, and had him erect a grotto modeled on Bethlehem, with straw-filled manager, ox and ass, and an image of the Child Jesus. He placed it within the church's choir screen, near the altar. On Christmas night the townspeople gathered by torchlight to contemplate the scene. The friars sang the Vigils of the Nativity, which at that time immediately preceded the Midnight Mass. Francis served as deacon for the Mass, and, after singing the Gospel, he entered the pulpit and preached on the Nativity of the Savior.

Overcome with emotion, Francis pronounced the words "Babe of Bethlehem" in such a way that those hearing thought they could hear the bleating of the sheep around the manager scene. He picked up the figure of the Child, held it in his arms, and presented it for the devotion of those present. John of Greccio thought he saw the previously lifeless image vivified and remade as the living Christ Child. At the end of the service, those present entered the sanctuary and took pieces of straw to keep as relics. Reports circulated that sick domestic animals that ate the straw recovered their health, and that women in labor touched with it had easy deliveries. The Little Poor Man of Assisi was already on the way to becoming a miracle-working saint two years before his death. After his canonization, an altar in his honor would be built over the site of the Greccio manger.

The humiliation of the Son of God, who became a child in the stable amid squalor and domestic animals, was for Francis a model of spiritual perfection. The one who had died for sin on the Cross chose to be born a weak child, subject to all. Francis wanted animals, and even inanimate creation, to share in the joyful celebration of Christmas. On one occasion, not long after, he declared that were he ever to meet the emperor, he would ask him to enact a law obliging people to put out seed for the birds at Christmas and give their domestic animals an extra ration of feed. In 1226, when Christmas Day fell on Friday, a traditional fast day, Brother Morico spoke of the day as a penitential one, forgetting it was the festival of Christmas. Francis challenged him and ordered him never to call the twenty-fifth of December "Friday" but always "Christmas." "I would want the walls to eat meat on that day, so, at least on the outside, they can be rubbed with grease!" Francis stayed at Greccio until the spring, when the weather and his health had improved enough to allow him to do a final preaching circuit in the Marche. It would be his last pastoral journey.

[7]

THE WAY OF THE CROSS

1223–1225

A FTER POPE HONORIUS approved the Rule in November 1223, Francis gradually withdrew from the community of his brothers. Those who describe him in the ensuing years paint a picture of a deeply conflicted man. The charismatic, joyful spirituality of his youth did not wholly disappear, nor did his intense identification with the Cross. But he became more distant and withdrawn, even, as he became sicker, refraining from exercises of conventional piety. He was becoming ever more intractable and more easily frustrated, occasionally even lashing out at those around him. Later hagiographers, in particular those of the Spiritualist tradition, attribute his moments of bad temper to laxity among his followers and betrayals of his ideal of poverty. But there is no good evidence for such corruption among the brothers.

Francis's struggles seem more personal and internal. His erratic behavior was rooted in the painful realization of his own faults and shortcomings. He, the least of the "lesser brothers," struggled constantly to be a good model for the friars, becoming thus spiritually superior to them, that is, no longer the "lesser brother." The task to which he had set himself was internally inconsistent, and so impossible. Then there was his frustration with his caregivers, and their impatience with him. The result must have been an invisible but real spiritual crucifixion.

Francis Withdraws from Leadership

From late 1223 to spring 1224, Francis stayed at a hermitage in the little town of Greccio. This place was one of his favorite retreats, especially because of the humility of the friars' dwellings there. There was one cell in the hermitage smaller and poorer than the rest, the "lesser cell," and it was Francis's favorite. He probably spent Lent there in 1224. He remained in the cell continuously, probably out of his need for solitude and his declining health. He even recited the Divine Office there in private, leaving the cell only for meals. In the one known exception to this, he left the cell to bless a brother from Rieti who had come to see him and stood outside crying because he could not enter. During the winter months, Francis not only declined physically but suffered from insomnia and extreme spiritual and mental distress.

In an effort to help Francis, his lay friend John of Greccio, who had earlier helped him construct the first crèche, gave him a feather pillow so that he might sleep with greater comfort. The gift backfired. One night Francis called out to his companion, who was sleeping in the next cell, and complained bitterly that he could not sleep. He blamed this on a devil in the pillow, and in a fit of anger he threw the offending object at his companion. The friar picked it up and went out into the garden. There he was overcome by an uncanny feeling that rendered him immobile for some time. He finally threw the pillow away and returned to tell Francis. Francis was now sure that the devil had destroyed his prayerful recollection after recitation of Compline. The pillow demon also stopped him from sleeping.

The best report of the event with the pillow records Francis's words: "The devil is very cunning and subtle. Because, by the mercy and grace of God, he cannot harm me in my soul, he wanted to disturb the needs of the body by preventing me from sleeping or standing up to pray, in order to stifle the devotion and joy of my heart so that I will complain about my sickness." Those who retold the story were convinced that Francis was troubled by the luxury of the pillow, viewing it as a poverty violation, but this is an interpretative gloss and unfounded. Taking Francis at his own words, he saw his growing insomnia, spiritual dryness, and lack of patience as the work of the devil, not the result of self-indulgence. Gentle-spirited as he was, he was horrified that he had treated his companion with rudeness. Whatever was driving this interior torment, his only recourse could be to divine mercy.

On 18 March 1224, less than three months after the approval of the Rule, a group of friars became priests, making them the first friars to be ordained. The group included the chronicler Jordan of Giano, who tells us of the event. A second event, one that would facilitate admission of more candidates with clerical aspirations, happened at the Pentecost chapter of June 1224, at which Francis himself seems to have been present. Where previously only Francis or his vicar could admit novices, this authority now devolved onto the provincial superiors. Unlike Francis, who was a deacon, and his vicar Elias, who was a lay brother, more and more of these superiors would be priests. They had few qualms about admitting young men who aspired to that higher state. Considering Francis's attitude toward illiterate lay brothers who merely wanted to learn to read the Psalter, one might wonder what he thought about unordained novices now aspiring to become priests.

The first steps toward the clericalization of the Franciscan Order had begun. More than any supposed deviation from Francis's views on poverty, this development would transform the order into something Francis never imagined. That Franciscans were now to be ordained meant that they had to be trained. Even before the approbation of the Rule, friars were agitating for lectures in theology from those who had such training. Studies implied a change in the style of life inherited from Francis, who, although literate and ordained a deacon, was never a man of books, other than the Bible and those of the liturgy. And those books were, for him, objects of devotion rather than scholarly study. This transformation later Conventuals and Spirituals both accepted with little or no difficulty.

Francis showed respect, even exaggerated respect, to theologians, as he did to bishops and clergy generally. Nevertheless, he always considered manual labor more suitable to a friar than mental labor. Study seemed to him much harder to combine with prayer than physical work. Eventually, Francis himself complied with the brothers' demands, and not long after the approval of the Rule, he addressed a short letter to a learned ex-Augustinian, Anthony of Lisbon. This friar had entered the order inspired by the martyrdom of the first Franciscan missionaries to the Spanish peninsula. The world today knows him as Saint Anthony of Padua. Francis wrote:

> Brother Francis sends greetings to Brother Anthony, my bishop.
>
> I am pleased that you teach sacred theology to the brothers provided that, as is contained in the Rule, you "do not extinguish the spirit of prayer and devotion" during study of this kind.

Francis used the term "bishop" for professors of theology, and the Latin phrase Francis used in his letter, *legere theologiam* (translated here as "teach theology"), literally means "to give academic lectures in theology." The quotation is from Later Rule 5, where it actually applies to manual labor. While Francis's motives were most likely to provide instruction for ordained friars who needed to preach and hear confessions, this assimilation of intellectual to physical labor was a revolution.

The implications of this move were even greater than the practice of ordaining friars to the priesthood. Francis had chastised an illiterate novice for wanting to read. He had written into the Earlier Rule that only those friars already literate could have books, and those books were to be liturgical ones. By this short note he put his seal on a revolution within his order: he allowed academic study. And he expressed himself as "pleased" to do so. One might wonder if he realized the implications of his act. Later friars came to see the results of this decision, and not all of them were pleased.

By summer of 1224, Francis's health was in rapid physical decline. He was not an easy patient. He chafed at the singularity of the accommodations his caregivers made for his disabilities and tried to turn them into public acts of humiliation. When he had to accept food cooked in lard during St. Martin's Lent in the fall, because oil caused him digestive problems, he insisted on broadcasting this "luxury" to all and sundry who visited the hermitage. He did the same when those caring for him prepared any special food required by his illness. During one of his last winters, his caregivers lined Francis's tunic with fox fur to give his stomach some protection against the cold. He chastised them and insisted that another layer be sewed on the outside of his tunic so that all would know about it. He discarded this tunic as soon as weather permitted. When the brothers tending him tried to apply ointments or other palliatives, he resisted and complained that his conscience was bothered by attention to his bodily needs. Only when one of the friar nurses reminded him that he could not serve God without his body did he relent.

As a superior, Francis had found it difficult to formulate clear directives because he was loath to command. Now as a subject, when others were placed in authority over him, he found it difficult to follow their directions. Illness intensified Francis's interior struggle to combine total submission to others with his status as the moral exemplar for the brothers. His urge to correct the defects in those around him intensified, and although he worked hard to control it, he struggled with the temptation to use his power harshly. To one of the brothers he acknowledged the temptation and admitted, almost wistfully, that grace alone kept him from lashing out: "There is no prelate in the whole world who would be as feared by his subjects and brothers as the Lord would make me feared by my brothers, if I so wished. But the Most High gave me this grace: that I want to be content with all, as one who is lesser in the religious life." It was a weakness that he could not always control. When his tenders were careless, or he found fault with their words to him, he withdrew into isolation and prayed for help. Francis insisted that other friars, even novices, be placed over him to command his obedience, yet they had to struggle to figure out what commands they had to issue to avoid frustrating him. In the end, he asked the vicar to remove all his assigned tenders on the grounds that their care made him "singular." Rather, he insisted, it was better to be ordered about by anyone who happened to show up, or by whoever happened to be traveling with him from place to place. Such inconsistent attention also meant that if one tender gave him instructions that he disliked, the next might well change them.

By summer 1224, Francis was still able to travel, but he was beginning to realize that he would not recover and that his death, if not imminent, was not far-off. He was staying at Foligno with Brother Elias, and, in the middle of the night, the vicar awoke from a troubled dream to find Francis very sick. Thomas of Celano reports that Elias's dream was of a venerable priest in white who instructed him to tell Francis that he had only two years to live. The prophecy would prove to be correct.

On Mount La Verna

Throughout his life Francis retreated to remote places and hermitages to refresh his soul by prayer, mortification, and solitude. In his final illness, he was harassed by visitors, often more curious than pious, wanting to see him or benefit from his prayers. To escape this burden, he determined to go into seclusion. He announced that he wanted to do a "Lent" in honor of God, the Blessed Virgin, and Saint Michael the Archangel, whose coming feast would fall on 29 September. As Francis's health was so bad that he could not travel on foot, he left the hermitage, perhaps that at Foligno, where he was staying with Elias, and rode a borrowed horse to La Verna, the mountain hermitage he had received as a gift years before. After he reached the mountain, he had his companion, a certain Brother Peter, take the horse back to its owner. As Peter was going through the *contado* of Arezzo, he passed near the house of a woman suffering in hard labor. Her husband, who wanted Francis to pray over his wife, had to be satisfied with borrowing his horse's bridle from Peter. He placed the reins around his wife's stomach, and she delivered with ease. Francis, not yet dead, was already viewed as a saint with miraculous powers.

The first night on the mountain, ever anxious about whether his choices and actions were in accord with God's will, Francis begged for a sign. It came the next morning. On leaving his cell he was greeted by birds, not in a large flock, but one after the other, each singing, as if for him alone, a lovely song of welcome. It was the sign that he had hoped for. Nevertheless, the sign did not fully soothe his troubled soul. He complained to his companions that he was attacked each night by demons and suffered horrible temptations. To one he said: "If the brothers knew how many trials the demons cause me, there would not be one of them who would not have great pity and compassion for me."

It is not clear that those with Francis understood his anguish and desolation. The small group of closest companions, which included Brother Leo, his confessor, and perhaps also Brother Illuminato and Brother Rufino, seemed caught up in their own worries about the state of the order. But witness to their state of mind comes only thirty years or more after Francis's death. In those later memories, the stay on La Verna was romanticized and reimagined as a return to the simple life at Rivo Torto in the early days of the Franciscan movement. The reality was more complex. Sometime soon after arrival on La Verna, Francis, not satisfied with the sign of the birds, sought God's will through the *sortes biblicae,* the Bible divination to which he had turned at the beginning of his conversion. He placed a copy of the Gospels, perhaps that bound into his Breviary, on the altar of the hermitage and prayed for divine guidance. Francis made the sign of the cross and took up the book. Three times he opened it, each time finding a passage treating the Passion of Christ. Francis would spend his time in seclusion meditating deeply on the Passion of the Lord, whose Cross he had chosen to accept and take up as a model of life. Francis passed about a month on La Verna, entering ever more deeply into the mystery of the Lord's Passion and death.

As Mass was not said daily on La Verna, Francis asked, according to his usual custom when he could not attend Mass, that a brother read him the day's Gospel before he took his principal meal of the day. This reading was his daily spiritual nourishment, the subject of his solitary meditations. Perhaps out of weakness, Francis became more and more passive as his "retreat" progressed. Unwilling or unable to react to what was happening around him, he turned ever more in on himself. One day, after reading the Gospel for Francis, the two brothers returned to the kitchen cell to find that the cooking fire had spread to the roof. The cook called for help to extinguish the blaze, but Francis simply grabbed a piece of hide he used as a cover while he slept and fled to the safety of the nearby forest. Fortunately, other brothers saw the smoke from a distance and came running to put out the fire. Francis's attachment to his comforter left him deeply disturbed. After he had eaten, he declared to the brothers: "From now on, I don't want this hide over me since, because of my avarice, I did not want Brother Fire to consume it." This act of "avarice" continued to nag at Francis throughout his illness, even as light and fire became harder and harder for his eyes to bear.

Francis's prayer, always focused so intently on the sufferings of Christ, became ever more so. Christ's Passion gave him strength in his own illness and consoled him in his temptations. An example of this can be seen in Francis's little devotional work known as the "Office of the Passion." Although he probably composed this work over a long period of time, it gives us some idea of his prayer on La Verna. To create it, Francis compiled verses from the Psalms that figuratively described Christ's life from Holy Thursday to Easter Sunday or presented responses to events in that narrative. Virtually nothing is from Francis himself; rather, he allows scripture to guide his meditation. Nevertheless, the work is creative and original. For example, Francis is the first to call the Blessed Virgin the Spouse of the Holy Spirit, a remarkable and original title.

The Office of the Passion is divided into two parts: a Passion Cycle, focused on the liturgical office of Good Friday; and a Resurrection Cycle, focused on that of Easter. Francis intended that the user recite a section after each hour of the Divine Office, and the two parts were to be used during different seasons of the year. That of the Resurrection was for use from Easter to Pentecost, during Advent and Christmas, and on solemn feasts. The rest of the year, which included the time he spent on La Verna, the Passion Cycle was to be used.

Each hour's meditation begins with a Marian antiphon, invoking her aid and that of Saint Michael, the two saints to whom he had dedicated his La Verna retreat. The verses for the night prayer of Compline focused on the desolation of Christ, who was abandoned by his followers in the Garden of Gethsemane. The verses for Matins are less coherent, but they highlight themes of self-emptying tempered by confidence in God. At Prime, he focused on verses that invoked God's justice and mercy in the face of Pilate's condemnation of Jesus. Terce consists of Psalm selections related to the scourging and crowning with thorns, while Sext focuses on Christ's abandonment and desolation in the face of his betrayal and condemnation. Fittingly, None, the hour recited at midafternoon when Christ died on the Cross, describes the division of his garments, his cry for drink, and his death. In this hour, the images are graphic, horrible, and tragic, but for Vespers Francis chose instead Psalm passages of rejoicing and vindication—in the Cross, which, as John's Gospel teaches, is Christ's exaltation and his victory over sin and death. We can imagine Francis living through the events of salvation each day on La Verna, whether he did so using these verses or through the freedom of his personal prayer alone. Each day on the mountain Francis identified himself more and more with the mysteries he was contemplating.

One morning, after leaving his cell, Francis told his companions that he had received a strange but consoling vision. He had seen a "man" who had six wings like a seraph, just as these angelic beings are described in scripture. Francis identified it as indeed a seraph. As he gazed on the apparition, Francis wondered what it meant. Even more than the sign of the birds, the gracious look the seraph gave him brought him peace and consolation. At the same time, this otherworldly being seemed fixed to the Cross, a sight that terrified him. The contradictory character of the vision, consoling yet frightening, confused Francis and left him anxious. It was probably this conflicted state that led him to break his general practice of never revealing to others what God showed him in prayer. Francis was deeply moved by the vision. He asked Brother Rufino to wash the stone above which the seraph appeared, and anoint it with oil. This kind of special veneration for the concrete places where God's presence was manifest is very much typical of Francis's piety.

After this vision, Francis began to manifest strange marks on his body. On the palms of his hands and on the top of his feet, there appeared protruding bits of flesh that resembled nothing so much as nail heads. On the base of his feet and the backs of his hands, other outgrowths appeared resembling nail points. In his side, there appeared a wound that dripped blood. The phenomena on Francis's hands and feet did not issue any blood. Instead they seemed darkened protrusions of flesh. Francis concealed the marks, but later, probably after he had left La Verna, some of his companions discovered them. On one occasion, Brother Rufino was washing him and chanced to touch the wound in the side. Francis recoiled in pain, pushed the hand away, and cried out to God for help. He commanded Rufino never to reveal the wound to anyone. Francis's vicar Elias probably saw the side wound on at least one occasion, but he also never mentioned it to others while Francis lived.

These physical marks reproduced the very wounds of Christ, the same wounds on which Francis meditated daily. They were as painful physically as his inner trials were spiritually. Like those trials, he revealed them only to his closest companions, and then only under a seal of silence. Soon after Francis's death and the revelation of these physical marks, they became known as the "Stigmata of St. Francis" and were an important fixture of devotion to him as a saint. Given the reports by his companions and the testimonial document signed by a score of Assisi citizens who viewed the wounds after Francis's death, virtually all modern historians conclude that they were real. Nevertheless, almost immediately after the announcement of the marks to the world, critics, especially outside the Franciscan Order, raised doubts about them. They seemed to some an almost blasphemous assimilation of Francis to Christ. Even when they admitted the existence of the marks, some considered them self-inflicted or the result of some other kind of fraud. Most famously, the humanist Petrarch, in a letter of 9 November 1366 to Thomas of Garbo, suggested that the stigmata were not impressed by the seraph but caused by intense meditation on the Passion, an idea common among modern historians who prefer psychological explanations to spiritual ones.

Miraculous or not, the form of the marks is difficult to square with some natural cause: unlike the later paintings of them, they were not holes in

Francis's hands and feet. It is difficult to imagine a fraud or psychologically in-
duced condition that would take such an unusual shape as fleshy nail heads. In
any case, the stigmata were the culmination of Francis's life since his conversion: a search for total conformity to Christ. He spoke little or not at all about
his private experiences in prayer, and he warned his followers not to do so.

Although Francis said little or nothing about his encounter with the seraph,
Brother Leo tells us that soon after the event he composed a series of "Praises
of God," giving him thanks for the event. These praises have come down to us
in Francis's own hand. Leo himself had been hoping for something of this type
from Francis that would serve as a kind of relic or talisman for him when he experienced his own temptations. Francis's composition was spontaneous and not
requested by Leo. One day Francis asked Leo for parchment and ink to write
down some verses that he had been meditating on in his heart. He wrote them
on the tiny scrap of vellum (about 4 x 5.5 inches, or 10 x 14 centimeters) in
his unlettered mercantile calligraphy. He used a crude wide-nibbed pen, hard
strokes, and wide spacing. Nevertheless, the form of his letters was regular.

Francis folded the scrap and handed it to Leo, telling him to keep it until
his death. It exists today in a reliquary at Assisi in the basilica of San Francesco.
Later, on the back of the parchment, Francis added a short blessing for Leo
consisting of Numbers 6:24–26, seemingly influenced by a liturgical prayer for
penitents. Francis added to the quotation, according to Leo, a Tau cross over
a sketch of a skull—certainly meant to evoke the Cross on Calvary. Contrary
to Francis's instruction, Leo did not keep the parchment with him his entire
life; rather, he passed it on, along with Francis's Breviary, to the sisters of San
Damiano about the year 1256.

True to his reticence about personal experiences, Francis never directly alluded to the seraph vision in his own writings. Historians, however, have suggested that the praises of the Leo parchment record Francis's own response to
the stigmata. The praises are a series of acclamations, loosely parallel in structure, typified more by pleonasm than by any other rhetorical device. They
resemble other Italian lay devotional compositions of the mid-thirteenth century. The text is in Latin rather than Italian and employs scriptural language,
both qualities typical of contemporary lay compositions. But the praises have
some very distinctive characteristics, seemingly unique to Francis alone. This
autograph is the closest we will ever come to a prayer that was uttered by the
saint's lips.

Francis focuses all his attention on the Father, who is the Triune God,
King of Heaven and Earth. While the object of his praises is the exalted God
of Gods and the Highest Good, the attributes chosen are those that reflect
not the divine majesty, but the effects of God's presence on the individual

Christian: patience, humility, security, rest, gladness, joy, hope, and temperance. God is all the riches needed for human sufficiency. The way of the Cross leads to consolation and refreshment. This is not the way a modern person would think of the painful imposition of the stigmata on Francis's sick and weakened body. For Francis his sufferings are not physical disabilities, but ultimately an experience of God on the Cross. The suffering is a positive experience of divine presence, and its fruit is good: "You are our Hope; you are our Faith; you are our Charity. You are all our sweetness." This was what the Cross had become for Francis two years before his own death.

Francis Descends the Mountain

Sometime near the end of September 1224 Francis ended his retreat and came down from the hermitage on La Verna. His health had declined greatly, and he now needed what amounted to nursing care, so he went to Assisi to be cared for in his illness by the sisters of San Damiano. The Franciscan world to which he returned was in rapid flux. Pope Honorius had issued *Quia Populares Tumultus* on 3 September 1224, granting friars the use of portable altars in their residences, thereby facilitating the celebration of Mass. This was followed on 18 September by a letter to the bishop of Paris, chastising him for hindering the friars from using their portable altars. We do not know how much Francis knew of these developments, but, as far as we know, he had never objected to this privilege. Indeed, his chaplain Brother Leo made use of it in various hermitages so that he could celebrate Mass for Francis. Nevertheless, the rebuke of the bishop of Paris was exactly the kind of papal protection Francis consistently rejected.

His retreat and return are the background to the "Letter to the Entire Order," which was, in a way, Francis's public farewell address. The Latin is carefully crafted, although colloquial enough to suggest it is Francis's own work, not much revised by his secretaries. After a formal greeting in which he kisses the feet of the brothers, Francis arrives at his issues and concerns. The first concern would be familiar to anyone who has read his other letters. All possible reverence is to be had for the Body and Blood of the Lord, and priests who celebrate Mass are to do so with the utmost care. In treating the celebration of Mass, Francis's tone is urgent, indeed harsh and peremptory. Like the priests of the Old Law who violated the laws of temple sacrifice, priests of the New Covenant who celebrate unworthily are damned and cursed. He elaborates on the priestly office in a long section, extolling its dignity and the exalted nature of the priestly calling. Although not a major theme in early letters, Francis's well-known reverence for the clergy is reflected in his words.

In his final words to his followers, the issue he found most pressing was not poverty, not obedience, but proper reverence for the Eucharist.

Francis is responding to events that were out of his control: the provision of portable altars, the first Franciscan ordinations, and papal commands that bishops allow ordained Franciscans to celebrate Mass. Speaking to "my priest brothers," he reminds them that they stand in the place of the priests of the Old Law and are like the Blessed Virgin. She, sinless, carried Christ in her womb. They too must be without sin when they touch him with their hands. He wrote: "As the Lord God has honored you above all others because of this ministry, for your part, love, revere, and honor him above all others." The whole cosmos should tremble with fear before the work of the priest.

Then, almost from nowhere, comes a command that must, like other special commands of Francis, be related to some particular contemporary event: "I admonish and exhort you in the Lord, therefore, to celebrate only one Mass a day according to the rite of the Holy Church in those places where the brothers dwell. But if there is more than one priest there, let these others be content, for the love of charity, at hearing the celebration of another priest, because our Lord Jesus Christ fills those present and absent who are worthy of him." After Francis's exaltation of the Mass and the priestly ministry, this seems a strange injunction, limiting the number of celebrations of Mass. It is possible that Francis was concerned that daily celebration of Mass by every priest in a community would create a "clerical class" raised up above the others in the order. That is how many modern interpreters read the command. After Francis's death, the ordained friars would remove the lay brother Elias from office and essentially "clericalize" the order. But there is nothing in the letter to confirm such an interpretation.

The command comes after Francis's exaltation of the priesthood above every human office, and, more important, it is immediately followed by urgent instructions to use only the cleanest linens and properly prepared vessels in worship. As in previous letters, he raises his often-repeated concern that parchment with biblical phrases and the name of God also be honored and protected. Francis's limitation of the number of Masses in a friary to one a day thus comes in the middle of the long treatment of reverence for the Mass, not one concerned with distinctions among the friars. Most likely, with the growing number of clerics and the facilitation of daily Masses by the privilege of portable altars, Franciscan celebration of the liturgy was becoming routine and sloppy, the very sin that Francis had so abominated in the clergy. It was, in fact, the only one he ever chastised them for. And now carelessness in celebrating Mass had appeared among his own friars. Rather than waiting in line to rush through their own private Mass in assembly-line fashion, or even to mumble Mass at a side altar while the other brothers are chanting the Office (a not-uncommon solution to the multiplying of Masses), friar priests were to take turns celebrating the solemn sung community liturgy with deacon, subdeacon, and all the proper ministers and rites. And they were to do so with the greatest of care. Otherwise, they risked damnation.

The remainder of the letter shows that Francis intended it as his farewell to the friars. He acknowledged his own sinfulness, confessing his sins to God, the Virgin, Elias the minister of the Order, and "to the priests of our Order and my other blessed brothers." He accused himself of violating the Rule in particular, not by violations of poverty, but by his failure to say the Divine Office correctly, "out of negligence, or because of weakness, or because I am ignorant and stupid." His own confession is of a piece with the sins he detected in the priest brothers: failure to discharge properly the liturgical duties of their exalted religious calling. He commanded Elias to make sure the Rule was obeyed, that clerics said the Office properly, and that all brothers lived in peace, just as he would. As he had promised to do all these things, he expected no less of the other brothers. If any refused to do so, then he would consider them neither his brothers nor Catholics. He refused even to speak with such brothers until they repented and did penance.

After commanding Elias and the ministers to keep this letter and have it regularly read to the brothers, he closes with a prayer. The words have uncanny echoes of those in his earliest recorded prayer, when he was kneeling before the San Damiano cross at the time of his conversion. It was his final blessing as head of the order:

> Almighty, eternal, just, and merciful God, give us miserable ones the grace to do for you alone what we know you want us to do and always to desire what pleases you. Inwardly cleansed, interiorly enlightened, and inflamed by the Holy Spirit, may we be able to follow in the footprints of your Son, Our Lord Jesus Christ, and, by your grace alone, may we make our way to you, O Most High, who lives and reigns in perfect Trinity and simple unity, and is glorified as God Almighty, forever and ever. Amen.

At the same time that Francis was composing this testamentary letter, he found time to write a short personal note to Leo. Preserved today in the duomo of Spoleto, the note is in Francis's own hand, making it, along with the "Praises of God," the only relics we have of the saint's pen. His writing has become tortured and irregular. Some suggest that the pain of the stigmata had begun to take its toll on his ability to write. The occasion for the note grew out of some earlier conversation between the two men, perhaps as they were coming down from La Verna. Francis encourages Leo to trust in God's guidance when trying to find the proper way to live obedience and poverty. Ever hesitant and dependent on the founder, Leo had found it hard to accept this advice in the past. Taking on the role of "mother" to "son" outlined in his Rule for Hermitages, Francis writes: "I am speaking, my son, in this way—as a mother would—because I am putting everything we said on the road in this brief message and advice. If, afterwards, you need to come to me for counsel, I advise you thus: In whatever way it seems better to you to please the Lord God and to follow his footprint and poverty, do it with the blessing of God and my obedience." In essence, Francis was telling Leo not to feel obliged to come to him with his every hesitation and question. The "son" needed to develop spiritual maturity. It was a hard message, and Francis seems to have decided that the command to stop coming to him for advice was too harsh. Before dispatching the letter, he added a couple more lines. They are in different ink and in an even more pained and crabbed hand: "And if it is necessary for you, for your soul, for some consolation to you, and you want to come back to me, come." He signed the note with his special seal, the Tau-shaped Cross. Even now, as his health rapidly declined, Francis could not turn away a troubled soul. Leo kept the letter on his heart for the rest of his life—it is today badly worn and soiled—as a protection and talisman. It was a decision that Francis, with his almost superstitious reverence for the written name of God, would have approved.

The "Canticle of Brother Sun"

As winter drew on, Francis stayed in a little hut of reed mats attached to the church of San Damiano. The cold hastened his decline in health. Brother Elias pressed him to get medical treatment and move to a place where his convalescence could be better managed. Francis's eyes were now severely affected by light, even at night, but it was "not the season" for eye surgery, which would have to wait until warmer weather in the spring. So for fifty days, probably until late March of 1225, Francis stayed in his drafty hut day and night. It appears that he was suffering from trachoma or perhaps conjunctivitis, in addition to the malaria he had contracted in Egypt and malnutrition from his fast on Mount La Verna. The squalor attracted vermin and mice, which attacked him as he tried to sleep at night. By day they infested and defiled his food. Francis became convinced that they were no ordinary vermin, but a trial sent by the devil himself.

Francis identified his temptations with the trials of Christ and told the brothers that he wanted to compose new "praises of God" expressing his will to rejoice in the tribulations. It would be a poetic completion of the *lauda* he had composed on La Verna and, like that composition, a reaffirmation of his embrace of Christ's Passion. The work he composed, the "Canticle of Brother Sun," is the first great poem of the Italian vernacular. It is among the first of the vernacular *laude* that characterize the lay devotion of later medieval Italy. Francis, in this great composition, paid homage to the Sun, to Light, and to Fire, the very forces that caused him the greatest physical pain. In it he addressed God the Father as subject of all praise. Christ and his Cross recede into the background but are taken for granted.

Most High, all-powerful, good Lord,
Yours be the praises, the glory, and the honor, and all blessing.
To you alone, Most High, do they belong
And no one is worthy to mention your Name.
Praised be you, my Lord, with all your creatures, especially Sir
Brother Sun,
Who is the day, and through whom you give us light.
And he is beautiful and radiant with great splendor,
and bears a likeness of you, Most High One.
Praised be you, my Lord, through Sister Moon and the stars,
in heaven you formed them clear, and precious and wonderful.
Praised be you, my Lord, through Brother Wind,
and through the air, cloudy and serene, and every kind of weather,
through whom you give sustenance to all your creatures.
Praised be you, my Lord, through Sister Water,
who is very useful, and humble, and precious, and chaste.
Praised be you, my Lord, through Brother Fire,
through whom you light the night.
And he is beautiful, and playful, and robust and strong.
Praised be you, my Lord, through our Sister, Mother Earth,
who sustains and governs us,
and produces fruit with colored flowers and herbs.
Praise and bless my Lord and give him thanks
and serve him with great humility.

Oddly, this composition, which enumerates and gives God praise through the celestial bodies (Sun, Moon, and Stars) and through the four Aristotelian terrestrial elements (Air, Water, Earth, and Fire) makes no mention of any living creature, unless one counts the mention of Fire as an oblique reference to the fiery seraph on La Verna. Francis could not shake off the sense that animal creation, so dear to him, had, like the mice and vermin of his cell, somehow become infested by demons who attacked and tempted him. For a lover of animals and nature, this was a torment. Francis also composed a melody for the Canticle, and the earliest manuscript we have of the poem has musical staves above the words. Sadly, the music was never copied in and has been lost. The Canticle was Francis's musical, as well as spiritual, testament to the world.

Whatever light the Canticle throws on Francis's physical sufferings, it is above all a prayer, a prayer of thanksgiving. Although the translation above renders the Italian preposition *per* as "through," and so Francis, in a kind of mystical way, praises God "through Brother Sun" and the other elements, it might also, if not more correctly, be rendered as praising God "for" the elements. Francis needed to praise God "for Brother Sun" and "for Brother Fire" because these were the very cause of suffering in his eyes. To praise them was to praise the Cross of Christ and to give voice to the sensibilities that lay behind liturgical compositions like the Office of the Passion. Francis never composed any prayer or poem without the language of the liturgy and Bible in the back of his mind. There are the strong resonances between the "Canticle of Brother Sun" and the "Canticle of the Three Young Men" (Dan. 3:57–88 in the Vulgate), which he sang every Sunday morning in the Divine Office at Lauds, and Psalm 148, the *Laudate Dominum,* which he sang every day in the same liturgical hour. Both songs charge creation and all living creatures to praise their Lord. In the "Canticle of Brother Sun," Francis joined his voice with all creation and praised God with and through it as well.

Francis's musical testament was for him a living text, and on two occasions he added to it. The first addition came soon after its composition. Even in his reed hut, Francis could not escape the chaotic world around him. He heard that the podesta of Assisi, Don Oportulo, and Bishop Guido had fallen out, probably over court jurisdiction. The bishop had excommunicated the podesta, and the podesta had made it a crime to have legal dealings with the bishop. Now, civil strife was added to Francis's trials—his physical pain, the pestilential vermin, and the bitter winter cold. He responded using the one faculty he could still make use of, his voice. He added a stanza to his Canticle, praising those, who like Christ on the Cross, forgive their enemies and dwell in peace. In humility, he accounted himself with the evildoers that fomented civil war. All needed divine help to endure evil and find peace:

> Blessed be you, my Lord, through those who give pardon for
>   your Love,
>   and who bear infirmity and tribulation.
> Blessed are those who endure in peace
>   for by you, Most High, shall they be crowned.

He sent word that the podesta and his curia were to assemble outside the bishop's palace. Don Oportulo complied. He probably expected Francis, already a saint in popular eyes, to issue an arbitration on the affair, perhaps even one in his favor. Such mediation in civil affairs by holy men was not unknown in the mid-1200s. Francis instead sent two brothers to sing the Canticle in the presence of both parties. The podesta was so affected by the gesture that he rose, announced that he was withdrawing his grievances, and fell prostrate at the bishop's feet, asking forgiveness. The prelate had no choice but to ask forgiveness in turn. They embraced and exchanged the kiss of peace that, to the common mind and also at law, signified the end of a feud. We have this story from eyewitnesses; the friars who recounted the story signed it "we who were with him." Francis changed the poem once more, just before his death, but for now it ended with a prayer of reconciliation and peace.

As spring came on, pressure mounted on Francis to leave San Damiano for medical treatment. He was troubled by his inability to visit the sisters and encourage them, and he had to leave them. So again, as he had for the bishop and podesta, he turned to poetry. The result, the "Canticle of Exhortation," is his testament for Clare and her sisters, the women he had converted to the life of penance. Recalling that they had been called from all parts of the world, he asked them to "live in truth" and in holy obedience, to cultivate the Spirit within, and to ignore the world without. He charged them to use discernment in disposing of alms they received, the only mention, albeit oblique, of poverty in his poems. As to those who are sick and those who care for them, he implored them, as he did the authorities of Assisi, to "bear it in peace." These are words he probably meant as much for himself and the brothers as for the sisters. Finally, he prayed that all would be crowned in heaven, along with the Virgin Mary, who was the model for all nuns.

It was his good-bye message for Clare. In June of 1225, Francis capitulated to the demands of his vicar Elias and Cardinal Hugolino. He would leave Assisi and go to Rieti for medical treatment.

[8]

FROM PENITENT TO SAINT

1225–1226

Failed Medical Treatments

F RANCIS LEFT THE monastery at San Damiano in June 1225 and took up residence at the hermitage of Sant'Eleuterio, near the village of Condigliano, just outside of Rieti. Among his various ailments, he was now nearly blind, hardly able to eat, and suffering probably from ophthalmia, a severe inflammation of the eye and the mucous membranes that line the inner part of the eyelids. The pain and sensitivity to light caused by this inflammation were excruciating. Struggling with his disabilities, he found it hard to reconcile himself to his loss of energy and independence. From his sickbed, he repeatedly urged those around him: "Let us begin, brothers, to serve the Lord God, for up until now we have done little or nothing." Mostly, he spoke nostalgically about returning to service of the lepers, the work during which he had discovered his vocation. A group of friars, chosen from those closest to Francis, were assigned to care for him. He was not a cooperative patient. They urged Francis to consult with physicians, the very reason he had been moved, but now he flatly refused.

On one occasion, the brother assigned to Francis suggested that one of the companions might read to him from the scriptures. "In that way," he said, "your spirit will rejoice in the Lord and receive great consolation." Francis's desire to hear the Gospel of the daily Mass was well known, but in this case, seemingly fed up with the pious mothering, he snapped back at the brother: "I have already taken in so much Scripture that I have more than enough to meditate and reflect on. I don't need any more, my son: I know Christ poor and crucified." He then quoted, as he did often during his illness, the psalm of David: "My soul refuses to be consoled." Francis's behavior in illness seemed almost willfully contrary. As he became worse, he refused not only medicine, but food as well. He admitted that he could eat only specially prepared food, but when the brothers went to the trouble of preparing it, he refused to eat it. He rebuked his caregivers, saying that he had to be a model for others and avoid the particularity of the special foods that alone he claimed to be able to eat. Although it was now getting on into summer, Francis suffered from the cold. For added warmth, he had his single tunic lined with patches, but even this small indulgence weighed on his conscience.

Sometime after late June 1225, Brother Elias, exercising his authority as vicar, ordered Francis back into the city of Rieti to get medical attention from physicians who specialized in eye problems. Francis, now unable to walk, traveled on horseback. When the party arrived at the city, they found the Roman Curia in residence. So, in order to give Francis greater privacy, Elias decided that the medical intervention on Francis's eyes would be performed at the hermitage of Fonte Colombo. On one evening, after an extended medical consultation, Francis asked the brothers to give dinner to the doctor. They were embarrassed by the meager fare, but as they sat down to dinner, a woman arrived "with a large basket filled with beautiful bread, fish, crab-cakes, honey, and freshly-picked grapes, which had been sent to Brother Francis." The brothers recorded the arrival as a miracle. Although Francis found it difficult to enjoy even the simplest of pleasures, he rallied himself, trying to be a better patient. He admitted that, in spite of his stomach problems, he might eat some shark (*squalo*), a dry bland fish, should it somehow become available. Caregivers tried to accommodate him. They had Brother Gerardo, the minister in Rieti, send a delivery man to Francis with a basket of shark and crab cakes that had become available in town. Francis was able to eat at least some of it.

For all his troubles, Francis did not lose his love of music. One day, after being moved into Rieti to the house of Theobaldo Saraceno, he was sitting with a brother who had played the lute before entering the order. Francis confessed that although he knew that secular lute music was a worldly vanity, and he feared giving a bad example to the brothers, he wanted the brother secretly to get a lute and play a song to which words praising God might be put. The brother demurred, saying that if word got out that he was playing the lute again, people would think he had reverted to his worldly life as a troubadour. That night Francis got his wish: someone in the street below his window began to play the lute in the most beautiful fashion, and did so for over an hour, even though it was past curfew. Francis in his innocence thought it a miracle, and so it was reported. Perhaps the troubadour brother had undergone a change of heart and decided that Francis's needs had overridden his own scruples. Events like this soften the picture we have of Francis's sometimes impatient and uncomprehending demeanor as reported by those who nursed him.

The ophthalmia eventually reached the point that Francis had to wear a piece of cloth sewn across the front of his hood to keep his eyes in total darkness. Even firelight caused him severe pain. But this pain, which he saw as an opportunity to share in Christ's sufferings, produced behavior that appeared strange and conflicted to outsiders. On one occasion at Fonte Colombo, Francis sat near the fire to warm himself from the cold. His companion noticed that the underdrawers that Francis wore under his habit had caught fire as he warmed himself. When he tried to put it out, Francis resisted. The caregiver had to shout for the guardian to command Francis to let him extinguish it. Francis knew that the attention required because of his insomnia and his disabled condition weighed on the brothers who served him. Sometimes the burden on them became obvious, and they grumbled: "We cannot pray, and we cannot put up with all this work." If we are to believe the later report, on one occasion at Fonte Colombo, Francis even consoled his caregivers with the thought that they were, by their generosity, making God their debtor. Francis himself would make sure that the Lord properly repaid them in heaven!

The consulting doctor told Francis that he needed to cauterize the flesh of his face from the jaw to the eyebrow of his weaker eye. Francis begged that the treatment be put off until Brother Elias had arrived. This gave some delay to the frightful surgery. Finally, sometime before Cardinal Hugolino left Rieti with the Roman Curia on 31 January 1226, he added his voice to that of the brothers urging the operation. Francis at last consented. When the doctor had heated the iron to red hot, Francis is said to have addressed the fire: "My Brother Fire, noble and useful among all the creatures the Most High created, be courtly to me in this hour. For a long time I have loved you and I still love you for the love of that Lord who created you. I pray our Creator who made you, to temper your heat now, so that I may bear it." Having made the sign of the cross over the iron, Francis indicated that the doctor could proceed, and the brothers fled the room. The cauterization was intended to stop the drainage from his eyes, but it had no effect at all. Another doctor recommended that the patient's ears be pierced, which was done, also to no effect. Nor was Francis left alone in his misery. People from the nearby village of Sant'Elia came asking for the water used to wash his eyes so that they could sprinkle it on oxen afflicted with "falling sickness" (basabove). They were refused, but one enterprising peasant sneaked in the next morning and stole the water used to wash Francis's hands. The oxen, it is reported, were healed.

After these fruitless medical procedures, Francis was moved to the palace of the bishop of Rieti. This move was intended to isolate the patient and allow closer and more careful control of his behavior. If anything, it made Francis more accessible to those with needs and requests. Giving away his clothing was the one act of charity Francis still had the power to perform, much to the chagrin of his handlers. Once a poor woman from Machilone, who also suffered from eye problems, came to Rieti to see the doctor but did not have the money to pay the fees. The doctor himself told Francis about her. Francis ordered one of the brothers to take his mantle and give it to the woman, along with the community's supply of bread. While generous and exemplary, this behavior, given Francis's weakened condition, had a self-destructive side. Only a direct order from the guardian prevented him from giving her his patched tunic as well. It was not the only time that Francis's handlers had to replace some piece of clothing that the now-shivering Francis had given away.

Sick as Francis was, people with health problems were brought to him for prayer and healing. Among them was Gedeone, a cleric of the Rieti curia. Known for his worldly life, Gedeone promised to amend his life in return for a cure. Francis's prayers and blessing were reported to have cured his debilitating back pain, but his evil living remained unchanged. By early fall, most likely to give Francis some seclusion and rest, the friars moved him to the little town of San Fabiano, where they placed him in the house of the poor parish priest, well known to the brothers. This move did nothing to stop the exhausting parade of well-wishers and visitors to Francis's sickroom. Members of the Roman Curia, including a number of cardinals, marched through his room on a daily basis. The poor priest had a vineyard next to his house, and when the curialists passed through it—it was almost time for the harvest—they plucked grapes to eat. What they did not eat, they trampled underfoot. The friars who were with Francis reported later that he had calmed the distraught priest, promising him that his harvest would be even greater than usual, in spite of the predations. And so it came to pass.

Francis spent the entire winter of 1225–26, most likely in Rieti, recovering from his surgery. Around the beginning of April, the ministers decided that Francis should go to Siena, a larger city, to seek further medical attention. Francis made the trip, accompanied by one of the doctors who had been attending him. Along the way, while passing through the plain of Rocca Campiglia, three poor women asked them for alms, which the doctor provided. Francis, who always sought the divine even in the humblest of places, identified the three as a manifestation of the Trinity, sent to support him in his trials. When the party reached Siena, they stayed at the friars' residence, which was newly constructed on land donated by a certain Lord Bonaventura. Francis stayed in one of the cells there, the conditions of which were probably no better than the squalid poverty of his cell at Rieti.

Whatever medical attention he received at Siena seems, like that at Rieti, to have been of little or no benefit. One evening in his cell, Francis began to vomit blood. The vomiting continued through the entire night. Diagnosis at such a distance of time is hard, but he had perhaps developed a gastric ulcer aggravated by malnutrition and stress, or cancer of the stomach. Most likely, it was the result of malarial cachexia, a general wasting and decline in body mass. Any of these afflictions, in Francis's weakened condition, would have been fatal. Francis himself sensed the severity of his condition and that he needed to prepare the brothers, not only for his death, but for life afterward.

Word that the Francis was in critical condition eventually reached Brother Elias, who dropped his business and rushed to the founder's side. The ever-practical Elias suggested to Francis that he compose a final message for the brothers. Francis, who was never good at long-term planning or programmatic instruction, must have understood the gravity of the situation, for he made a first attempt at composing a "testament." He called for Brother Benedict of Piratro, who was a priest, and so able to read and write, and asked him to "write that I bless all my brothers, those who are and who will be in the religious order until the end of the world." Whatever else Brother Benedict wrote has been lost, but reporters summarized Francis's instruction to the brothers this way: "May they always love each other; may they always love and observe our Lady Holy Poverty; and may they always remain faithful and subject to the prelates and all the clerics of Holy Mother Church." The use of the term "Lady Poverty" is here suspect, as it appears in no writing from Francis's own pen, but the spirit of the summary is probably accurate. Francis also charged the brothers to avoid giving scandal to anyone. These same themes would reappear, some with greater urgency, some with less, in Francis's conversation and dictation over the next six months.

In midsummer, as quickly as it had worsened, Francis's sickness abated. He was able to travel with Brother Elias to the hermitage he had founded at Celle in 1211 near Cortona. But within a very short time, his abdomen began to swell, a sign of dropsy, and he could no longer stomach food. He still made the gestures of charity so integral to his nature. While at Celle, he gave away his cloak to a poor man. His caregivers must have been relieved that it was summer and they did not need to find a replacement. Finally, he begged Elias to take him home, back to Assisi.

The Return to Assisi

By late July or early August, after returning to his hometown, Francis stayed first at the Porziuncula. But after only a very short stay, the friars took him to their newly constructed house at Begnara near Novara. The summer heat in Assisi probably prompted the move. Francis stayed there for "many days," perhaps as long as a month. His dropsy became worse, especially in his legs and feet. News of his decline reached Assisi, and the citizens themselves intervened, sending a group of knights to bring Francis home, lest he die abroad, and they lose control of his relics. On the way home, stopping for the night in a village of the Assisi *contado*, the knights could not find any stores open to buy food. They did, however, receive abundant food when they went, at Francis's urging, door to door begging for it. The locals were doubtless delighted to help a man they already considered their local saint. The knights took Francis to the Assisi bishop's palace. The bishop was away, but the accommodations there were more suitable for a sick man and ensured that he was close to medical care. At night they put armed guards around the palace so that should Francis die, they could prevent even the brothers from carrying off the body. The Little Poor Man had become civic property.

Francis, still sensitive to music, repeatedly asked the brothers to sing the "Praises of the Lord" for him. At night, the guards could hear it being sung. Brother Elias, who was attending Francis, once remarked that while their joyful tone might well express Francis's own lack of fear about death, the singing of the "Praises" gave those hearing it a false idea of how sinners should approach their own mortality. Elias speculated on what people thought: "How can he show such joy when he is so near death? He should be thinking about death." Francis replied that since Elias's prophetic dream at Foligno two years earlier, he had constantly meditated on death, but that now, while he could, he wanted to praise God: "Let me rejoice in the Lord, Brother, and sing his praises in my infirmities, because, by the grace of the Holy Spirit, I am so closely united and joined with my Lord, that, through His mercy, I can well rejoice in the Most High himself."

The friars were caught up in the townspeople's expectation that Assisi would soon have a local saint in heaven as intercessor and miracle worker. One day, the brother caring for Francis commented on his fur-lined sackcloth cap and his extra sackcloth tunic: "You will sell all your sackcloth to the Lord for a good price! Many canopies and silk coverings will hang over this body of yours, now clothed in sackcloth." Francis, a man of his age, was no fool and could see what was going on around him. He replied, probably with resignation more than expectation: "You're right, because that's how it will be."

Although it seemed hopeless, doctors continued to call on the palace for consultation on Francis's case, usually finding they could do or say little to help. Among the doctors was one Don Bongiovanni of Arezzo, whom Francis had met before. They even had a little private joke going, because Francis, respecting Jesus's statement that "no one is good save God alone," always addressed the doctor as Giovanni rather than Bongiovanni—that is, "John" rather than "Good John." After hearing the usual medical circumlocutions about his condition, Francis finally demanded that the doctor tell him the truth. He was no coward and could face it. The doctor admitted the reality and made what turned out to be a lucky guess at how long Francis had to live: "According to our assessment, your illness is incurable and you will die between the end of September and the fourth day before the Nones of October," that is, 4 October. To which Francis stretched out his hands and uttered words he was soon to add to the Canticle of the Sun: "Welcome, my Sister Death!"

According to the custom of the age, those attending a dying man, especially members of the family, had the responsibility to insure that the dying performed the acts of penance and devotion that characterized a "good death." The sick person needed to face the reality of death directly and make amends for his sins, thus edifying onlookers and providing a model for others. One brother serving Francis, with remarkable bluntness, reminded him that he was dying and that the brothers visiting him expected to see an edifying death worthy of remembrance. Francis, in spite of his own misery, was determined to unite his own joy in God with Sister Death, whom he was now awaiting. So he told the friar: "If I am soon to die, call Brother Angelo and Brother Leo so that they sing to me about Sister Death." The result was the final strophe of the Canticle of Brother Sun:

> Praised be you, my Lord, for our Sister Bodily Death,
>   whom no one living can escape.
> Woe to those who die in mortal sin!
>   Blessed are those whom Death finds in your most holy will,
>   for the Second Death shall do them no harm.

In his last recorded poetic utterance, Francis is unchanged in the central conviction of his conversion. Leaving the world to do penance was not just a personal choice. It was, at least in his case, essential to his eternal salvation. Had he died, as he put it, "in his sins," he would have been damned. So too those around him. The stanza recalled what he had earlier written in a homiletic, but also very poetic and impassioned, section of the Earlier Rule:

> Blessed are those who die in penance,
>   for they shall be in the Kingdom of Heaven.

Woe to those who do not die in penance,
  for they shall be children of the Devil,
  whose works they do.
And they shall go into everlasting fire.

Now, as he himself lay dying, he reaffirmed the decision made so many years ago, to "do penance" and so "leave the world." He had become a model, but also a warning, for his brothers. They now waited expectantly for the relics his body was soon to become.

Francis's Testament

A last preparation for death remained, the composition of a will or a testament. Doing so was part of the rituals of making a "good death," since in a last testament the Christian could atone for any wrongs he had done in life. Francis had probably given directives to the brothers on previous occasions to follow after his death, but they would now take his words down in writing as definitive. Dying men were to make provision for the dispersal of their goods. Francis had only one possession of significance, his Breviary. This he had already given to Brothers Leo and Angelo so that they could read it to him, since he was nearly blind. Brother Leo would keep it after his death.

Francis had more important spiritual goods to bestow on his brothers. He tried to describe his experiences from his conversion to the present day, and to reflect on the issues the friars now faced. Francis, following the usual deathbed convention of calling learned assistance, asked an unnamed literate friar to take down his thoughts. The friar did so, translating them into Latin as a notary would have done for any dying Christian. Francis offered neither a series of bequests nor a systematic vision for the future of the order, but something more precious, the gift of his own life. Francis spoke of the first days of his conversion, recounting how "when he was in his sins," to see lepers was bitter to him. And how God brought him among them and changed his whole perception. The bitter sight of lepers had become sweet.

Francis then focused on the spiritual gifts that God gave him when he "left the world." First, his "faith in churches," which inspired him to elaborate a prayer in their honor, drawing on the Liturgy of Holy Week: "We adore you, Lord Jesus Christ, and for all your churches, which are in the whole world. We also bless you, because by your Holy Cross you have redeemed the world." Francis lived in no abstract universe. God was found in physical places, churches, just as he had died in a particular place, Calvary, and in a particular way, on the Cross. Next, God gave him such faith in the priests that ministered in those churches, so long as they "lived according to the form of the Catholic Church," that he wanted to have them as his lords. This he linked not to any particular holiness of their lives, but to the reality of the Eucharist, which they celebrated. Of utmost importance, he said, the Host should be honored above all things and kept in a fitting place. So too any scrap of parchment with the name of God or a biblical text on it was to be preserved and honored. Finally, he recorded his faith in theologians. Respect for churches, priests, the Eucharist, and Catholic theology: these were the things that Francis wanted his followers to remember as the fruits of his encounter with the lepers and his choice of penance.

Francis then recounted, with seeming surprise, that God had sent him followers and showed him a new path to take: "And after the Lord gave me some brothers. No one showed me what I should do, but the Most High himself revealed it to me, that I ought to live according to the form of the Holy Gospel. And I had it written in a few simple words, and the Lord Pope confirmed it for me." Francis then described the simplicity of life in the early days. The friars had given all they had to the poor; they were satisfied with a simple habit with one tunic and a cord; clerics said the Divine Office, and the lay brothers recited Pater Nosters. All worked with their hands, as much to avoid idleness as to get their daily bread. Finally, he wrote: "The Lord revealed to me a greeting, that we are to say: 'The Lord grant you peace!'"

Recounting his early days, Francis spoke without any sense of pressing urgency or concern but as he went on revealed his passion, even anger, at the thought of deviations from the humility and simplicity that he had chosen to embrace. The series of almost peremptory orders that follow in the Testament provide an insight into the changes and developments that were tormenting Francis along with his illnesses. He imposed two commands on the brothers:

> Let all the friars beware of themselves, so that they receive almost none of the churches, the poor tiny dwellings and all the buildings, which are constructed on their behalf, unless they would be such as befits holy poverty.
>
> I firmly command all the friars by obedience, that wherever they are, they do not dare to seek any letter in the Roman Curia, by means of themselves or by an interposed person.

Francis's tone here suggests that his words were provoked by actual events, not abstract speculation. Other evidence confirms this. Since about 1221, witnesses reported Francis's anger at the brothers' apparent appropriation of buildings in Bologna and Assisi. It was by a sleight of hand that Cardinal Hugolino and the commune of Assisi had circumvented Francis's reaction by claiming to retain ownership for themselves and merely let the brothers use the buildings. Francis recognized that the friars would be offered other houses to live in, and he does not condemn that. There is no evidence that the places of the brothers in Assisi or Bologna were extravagant or "violations of poverty." Francis did not suggest otherwise. Rather, he focused on how admiring donors could subvert simplicity by their generosity, and the brothers could collude in the sham. And he needed to "warn" the friars about this.

But more pressing and dangerous to Francis's mind—as his use of the phrase "I command under obedience" reveals—was the brothers' habit of invoking papal protection and ecclesiastical privileges. This abuse was real, and the past year had seen the papacy responding to requests for help, either from Franciscans or their friends. On 4 October 1225, Pope Honorius III extended the legal privilege of clerical immunity to Franciscan clerics and instructed the archbishop of Milan to have a friar released from jail. On 7 October 1225, the pope had directed the archbishop of Toledo and territorial princes to support and defend Franciscans active in that archbishop's diocese. On 2 January 1226, the pope had directed secular authorities to protect Franciscan missionaries. Finally, on 17 March 1226, he also allowed fines for usury to be applied to support the Franciscan missions.

More than a hypothetical violation of poverty, these privileges placed the Lesser Brothers in positions of power over others. No longer would they be "subject to all." Paradoxically, this situation forced Francis to place himself in the very position he most disliked, that of a superior giving instruction and orders to others. Here was the same status climbing and self-promotion that Francis had condemned in the lay brother who wanted to learn to read, and which had provoked his outburst about this in the Earlier Rule. Francis's tone implied that this was already a lost cause. His pain is palpable.

It was natural for Francis to turn to his own condition. He reminded the brothers that he wanted to live in obedience to his vicar and to the local superiors. But he did ask for one thing: that a cleric be with him to read the Office to him. This clerical obligation was followed by a second outburst, one that modern writers call the "Penal Section" of the Testament. The ailing founder's hard words may have been triggered by the heretical preaching of a certain renegade Franciscan, Brother Paul, at Colle Val d'Elsa in 1224, but improper recitation of the Divine Office was the first item on Francis's mind:

And those, who might be found that do not perform the Office according to the Rule and want to vary it in another manner, or who are not Catholics: let all the friars, wherever they are, be bound by obedience, that wherever they have found any of these, they are to present them before the nearest custodian of that place, where they have found him. And let the custodian be firmly bound by obedience to guard that one strongly, just like a man in chains, day and night, so that he cannot be snatched from their hands, until he, in person, presents him into the hands of his minister. And let the minister be firmly bound by obedience to send him by means of such friars, that day and night guard him as a man in chains, until they present him before the lord of Ostia, who is the lord, protector and corrector of the whole brotherhood.

For modern readers this passage is among the most startling in all Francis's writings. No other issue, certainly not the quality of domiciles, provoked such an invocation of authority and preemptory command. Not only is it harsh, but Francis preempts the authority of the local bishop in enforcing orthodoxy and remands delinquents—those who committed liturgical abuses or transgressed dogmatic orthodoxy—directly to the Roman Curia in the person of Cardinal Hugolino. Francis was fearful about the orthodoxy of his brothers, but he expressed this fear in a typically lay manner. It was not theological options that came to his mind, but rather whether the friars properly celebrated the Divine Office. This concern resembles Francis's anxiety that friars show proper respect for priests and, above all, for the Corpus Domini, the Sacred Host. Every aspect of the public worship of the Church was sacred and had to be kept inviolate. For Francis, Catholicity was about things and actions, not just about ideas. His greatest fear, as he lay on his sickbed, was that those who came after him would replace this homely piety with the pride of intellectualized abstractions and assumption of religious status.

This was not a misplaced fear. Francis closed his Testament with a long— and often quoted—passage, explaining that it was not a "new rule," but an admonition to observe the Rule in "a more Catholic way." Above all, friars were not to add anything to the Rule, or to gloss it. They were to observe it simply, without trying to divine unwritten intentions or meanings from the words. If they could accomplish this, then they would be truly blessed.

Last Days with the Brothers

Around mid-September of 1226, Francis asked to be taken to the Church of St. Mary of the Little Portion, the Porziuncula, to die. This small church, so closely connected with Francis's first days after his return from Rome in 1209, was especially dear to him and represented the joyful days with his first followers after his conversion. It was there that the life of the order had begun, and where God had first multiplied its members. It was natural that Francis would want to die there, with his brothers, rather than in the bishop's palace, with physicians and outsiders. The brothers carried Francis on a litter, since he could not walk or ride. As they left the city and passed by the hospital, he asked that they place the litter on the ground and face it toward the city. He could see his hometown only with difficulty, so impaired was his eyesight. Although Francis had chosen to leave his family and the city of his birth, which he had served in war, he always remained a man of his commune. He would always be Francis, one of "the penitents from Assisi," as he had been described to Pope Innocent. Francis prayed for his city and those who lived in it, giving them a parting blessing. At San Damiano, Francis's first woman follower, Clare, had fallen seriously ill. Word of this came to Francis, and he sent her a message of consolation and blessing. At the Porziuncula, the friars placed Francis in one of the cells. The death watch began.

The week before his death, Francis put his last affairs in order. He was now alone with his brothers, in particular with an unnamed brother who had been a physician in his earlier life. He was so exhausted that he instructed this brother to make the decisions about what he was to eat and drink. More urgently, he asked that a priest brother be with him at all times, not only to read his Divine Office for him, but so that he could go to confession if any forgotten sin should come to mind. The friars tried to make Francis as comfortable as possible, even rushing out to pick parsley for him when he thought that eating some would help his digestion. It seems to have helped a bit, although Francis did scold the cook for not going out immediately to find it in the dark. To the end, Francis remained a difficult patient.

No outside visitors were permitted to see Francis, with one exception, a woman whose importance to him is known only from the stories told about the days immediately before his death. She was Jacoba de' Settesoli, a matron of means from a prominent Roman family. Perhaps this woman belonged to the circle of pious Roman women that included the recluse Sister Pressede, of whom Francis was also very fond. Jacoba had provided Francis with lodging during his visits to Rome, and he remembered her with great fondness. She was probably the only woman with whom Francis ever developed a close friendship, one so close that he even called her a "brother" and excepted her from the rules excluding women from the cloister. He asked the brothers to send her a message, informing her of his impending death. He asked that she prepare him a gray shroud for burial, modeled on the burial robe used for monks of the Cistercian Order. In a moment of nostalgia, Francis also asked her to send him some of the confection of almonds and honey that the Romans called *mostacciolo* that she used to make for him during his visits.

In fact, word of Francis's decline had already reached Jacoba. Before his message could even be sent, she arrived at the friary. Asked what to do about the arrival of a woman, Francis, as in the past, told them that the rule of cloister did not apply to her, especially since she had traveled so far to see him. As it turned out, she had already bought gray cloth for the shroud, incense and wax for the funeral rites, and all the ingredients needed to make the *mostacciolo*. The brothers took her offerings to make the shroud and funeral candles. She prepared the confection, but Francis was now so sick that he could hardly eat any of it.

Soon after, perhaps that very night, Francis experienced such pain that he could not sleep. The following day was not a Thursday, but Francis thought it was. Thursday had been the day of Christ's institution of the Eucharist at the Last Supper, and Francis decided this was a suitable day to take formal leave of his brothers. He called them all around him, and, "beginning with one brother," which was probably his vicar Elias, he blessed them all. He asked for a loaf of bread, which he blessed. He was so sick that he could not break it himself, so he asked the brothers to do so for him and to give a piece to each brother. They were to eat it together, calling to mind both the absent brothers and those who would join the Order in the future. Francis then blessed them all. It was Francis's Last Supper. "One of the brothers kept a piece of that bread, and after the death of blessed Francis," we are told, "some people who tasted it were immediately freed from their illnesses."

Then, or very soon after, following the common practice for the dying, Francis asked to be clothed in sackcloth, placed on the floor, and sprinkled with ashes. He then asked that a brother read over him the Passion of Christ from John's Gospel, which, following the medieval death customs, one brother was already prepared to do. On Saturday evening, just before nightfall, a great flock of larks circled the cell where Francis lay, filling the air with their songs. The lark was Francis's favorite bird, because, as he often said, they had a brown "habit" and a "hood," just like a friar, and because they constantly sang the praises of God, just as good religious do in the choir office. That night Francis died. It was the third of October, 1226.

From Death to the Altar

That night the friars kept the traditional vigil over the founder's body, reciting the Psalter and other prayers for the dead. The next morning, when they laid Francis out for those arriving from the city to view, they noticed that his limbs were still soft and supple, as if he were still alive. This was the first marvel recorded after his death. Years later, many other marvels were added to Francis's death narrative. Among them were visions of him ascending to heaven, seen not only by the brothers but also by the bishop of Assisi himself. For the first time, the brothers in general discovered the stigmata, and they showed the marks to those present, which may have included officials of the commune. Brother Elias would soon announce the wounds in a circular letter to the friars. The few earlier examples of such wounds were known to be fraudulent or self-inflicted, and even among the brothers there was a certain incredulity about such an extraordinary event. Cardinal Hugolino himself remained doubtful, something that even Saint Bonaventure admitted some forty years later. Nonetheless, the witness of the fortunate laypeople who saw them, and the oddness of the nail heads, which would not be expected in self-inflicted wounds, eventually triumphed over skepticism.

Within twenty-four hours, the townspeople and clergy formed a funeral procession, which brought Francis's body into town. They carried olive branches and sang hymns. They went first to the church of San Damiano. There they removed the iron communion grille so that they could hold up the body for Clare and the sisters to touch and kiss. The nuns' veneration lasted about an hour. From San Damiano, the cortege entered the city and went to the church of San Giorgio, where a Requiem Mass was sung, and the body placed in a stone coffin that Brother Elias had purchased and set up well ahead of time. Although Francis would probably have preferred a rude wooden box, like that used to bury the founder of the Dominicans, Saint Dominic Guzman, under the feet of his friars in Bologna, Elias's choice was not unsuitable. It was a rather rough ancient stone sarcophagus that had been used as a drinking trough for domestic animals.

The body was placed inside with a stone pillow for Francis's head. Then, iron gratings in the form of a cage were fastened around the coffin to close it. As the original cover of the sarcophagus had long been lost, the grating replaced it. Those visiting the shrine in San Giorgio could peer through the small holes in the grate and see the holy body within. Although they could not touch it, they could insert cloths to touch the relics. Some dropped in small votive objects. When the coffin was opened in the nineteenth century, several small coins, beads, and a ring were found at the saint's feet. It would be romantic, if unlikely, to suppose that the ring belonged to Jacoba. At least, as a love gift, it is somewhat less incongruous than the coins. Francis's body remained at San Giorgio for four years, entombed in the church's crypt. During that period the stone coffin was placed within a larger wooden box, the *arca*, that could be opened on special occasions or for the devotion of the faithful. This must have been a very sturdy and permanent structure, as the stone coffin weighs about 490 pounds.

The *arca* was raised off the floor to about chest level on four legs and thus allowed the faithful to crawl under it—a very common practice at thirteenth-century saints' shrines. This arrangement with the tomb raised off the floor occasioned Francis's first posthumous miracle, on the very day of his entombment at San Giorgio. A young girl who had suffered for over a year with a deformed neck was brought in and placed underneath the *arca*. Her neck suddenly returned to normal, and, in shock and surprise, she ran off crying. A permanent depression remained in her shoulder, to show where her head had been while twisted out of position by her deformity. Oddly, the friars made no petition for his canonization. Rather, the first movement came from Francis's old friend, the cardinal protector, but not until two years after his death. Perhaps Hugolino was too busy fortifying the order with privileges and protective bulls, a good number of which date to the first two years after Francis's death. He had many other distractions.

On 19 March 1227, Cardinal Hugolino was elected Pope Gregory IX, as the brothers believed Francis had predicted. Within six months, the new pope himself was in exile from Rome, fleeing the army of the emperor Frederick II, who had invaded Italy. The pope went first to Rieti, then to Spoleto, and then to Assisi. Finally, from 13 June to 13 July, he was able to find safety and peace in Perugia. In a consistory of cardinals held there on 16 July 1228, Gregory declared the Little Poor Man a saint of the Catholic Church. He wrote: "The life of this saint does not require the evidence of miracles, for we have seen it with our own eyes and touched it with our hands." Three days later, he announced his decision to the world by the canonization bull *Mira circa Nos*.

Brother Elias, who had resigned as the minister of the order for this purpose, began construction of the great basilica of San Francesco at Assisi. He worked quickly, and, by the spring of 1230, the grand new church was ready to receive the saint's body. That year, Pope Gregory was finally able to return to Rome. In May he traveled to Assisi to preside at the translation of Francis's body to its final resting place. The pope went first to the church of San Giorgio to venerate Francis's relics in their original shrine. It was intended that the body be translated to the new basilica in the presence of the pope and many dignitaries, both ecclesiastical and civil, but Elias seems to have caught wind of a Perugian plan to steal the body during the translation. At least that was the story that circulated. No special precautions had been taken to protect the relics while they lay at San Giorgio.

In any case, Elias must have been planning the security of the new depository for the relics well ahead of time. Three days before the planned translation, on 25 May 1230, in the dead of night it appears, the friars moved the body to the basilica and entombed it there. They did so without informing the pope, his attendant cardinals, the commune, or any of those who had traveled from distant lands for the occasion. A pitlike chamber had been carved into the rock below the floor of the basilica's transept crossing, on the spot over which the current high altar stands. The stone coffin, encased in its gratings, was lowered into this space. Workmen placed a great travertine slab on top of the coffin and secured it in place with three iron bars that were inserted and cemented into the stone side walls of the pit. A second, tightly fitting stone was then cemented in place on top, completely sealing off access to what lay below. On top of that, yet a third monolith was sealed in place with concrete. This stone seems to have been at floor level, in a small "confessio" or access chamber. One entered it most likely down a short flight of stairs in front of the medieval high altar, much as one does at the tomb of St. Peter at the Vatican. Whatever the original arrangement, this third stone, when finally uncovered in 1828, was found to have its upper surface well worn by the feet and knees of countless pilgrims. Thanks to Elias's careful planning, the relics of the Little Poor Man would be protected from profane eyes and Perugian thieves for the next six hundred years.

Although, even in the Middle Ages, not all found the cult of Francis to their taste—peasants in far-off Spain initially rejected him as a "merchant" saint—his Franciscan brothers spread devotion to Francis wherever they went, and he soon eclipsed all the other saints of his age in popularity. And the Little Poor Man's splendid shrine became a popular destination for pilgrims, and for tourists. So it remains, perhaps ever more so, to this day.

[FOR FURTHER READING]

This is not a bibliography on Francis; rather, it is a series of suggestions for English-speaking readers who have found this life interesting and want to read more. I categorize these books under four headings.

Original Sources

Those who would like to sample the medieval sources for Francis should start with the following, which are listed in chronological order of composition. All of these texts may be found in the excellent translation collection *Francis of Assisi: Early Documents* [FA:ED] (New City, 1999–2002).

The Writings of St. Francis
The First Life by Thomas of Celano
The Anonymous of Perugia
The Legend of the Three Companions
The Second Life by Thomas of Celano
The Major Legend by Bonaventure
The Little Flowers

There are many other texts in FA:ED, and they are all worthy of consideration. Those interested in the writings of Saint Clare of Assisi and the sources for her life may find them in *Clare of Assisi: Early Documents: The Lady,* ed. Regis Armstrong (New City, 2006).

Recent Works by Major Francis Scholars

Some of these are biographies, but most are studies on the interpretation of sources and issues in scholarship. Manselli still represents the only sustained attempt to discover the Historical Francis, the project of this book.

Rosalind B. Brooke, *The Image of Saint Francis: Responses to Sainthood in the Thirteenth Century* (Cambridge University Press, 2006). A fine set of studies on the images of Francis in literature, hagiography, and art.

Lawrence S. Cunningham, *Francis of Assisi: Performing the Gospel Life* (Eerdmans, 2004). By a theologian, an unsentimental presentation of Francis as an inspiration for contemporary Roman Catholics.

Jacques Dalarun, *Francis of Assisi and Power* (Franciscan Institute, 2007). Not a biography, but a thoughtful study by a major Francis scholar.

Jacques Dalarun, *The Misadventure of Francis of Assisi: Toward a Historical Use of the Franciscan Legends* (Franciscan Institute, 2002). How medieval sources reinterpret and misinterpret the saint, and the implications for Historical Francis projects, but not a new biography.

Francis of Assisi: History, Hagiography, and Hermeneutics in the Early Documents, ed. Jay Hammond and Joseph Chinnici (New City, 2004). Essays on interpreting the early sources.

Chiara Frugoni, *Francis of Assisi* (Continuum, 1998). A short, rather generalized life, with special emphasis on medieval artistic interpretations of the saint.

Jacques Le Goff, *Saint Francis of Assisi* (Routledge, 2004). Not a biography, but four previously published essays on Francis and his times.

Raoul Manselli, *Saint Francis of Assisi* (Franciscan Herald, 1988). Probably the best critical life of the saint, but difficult reading for beginners and often surprisingly uncritical of some sources.

Thaddée Matura, *Francis of Assisi: Writer and Spiritual Master* (St. Anthony Messenger, 2005). Not a biography, but a careful study of Francis as a spiritual writer.

Michael Robson, *Saint Francis of Assisi: The Legend and the Life* (Chapman, 1999). A thoughtful if conventional biography, seemingly untouched by the accomplishments of Manselli.

Roberto Rusconi, *Francis of Assisi in the Sources and Writings* (Franciscan Institute, 2008). Francis as he is presented in the sources, rather than the Historical Francis.

Richard C. Trexler, *Naked before the Father: The Renunciation of Francis of Assisi* (Lang, 1989). A major, if narrowly focused, work on Francis and his family, with Freudian considerations.

Classic Biographies and Literary Contributions

None of the versions of Francis presented in these biographies would now be considered "scientific," either because of new knowledge of the sources or because the authors take an uncritical approach to them. But these works do give an idea of how interpretation has developed over the past hundred years. They are arranged chronologically to reflect that development.

Paul Sabatier, *Life of Saint Francis of Assisi* (1894; latest repr. Fili-Quarian Classics, 2010). The work that began the modern search for Francis. A Romantic image, uncritical by modern standards.

Johannes Jørgensen, *Saint Francis of Assisi: A Biography* (1907; latest repr. Husain Press, 2009). Long the most popular Catholic reply to Sabatier. Francis as a faithful churchman, with little criticism of the sources.

Father Cuthbert of Brighton [Cuthbert Hess], *Life of Saint Francis of Assisi* (1912; latest repr. Kessinger Publ., 2008). Similar to Jørgensen as a popular Catholic biography of the early 1900s, apologetic in tone.

G. K. Chesterton, *Saint Francis of Assisi* (1923; latest repr. Ignatius Press, 2002). A literary classic, perhaps more Chesterton than Francis.

John R. H. Moorman, *Saint Francis of Assisi* (SCM, 1950). A readable retelling of the conventional narrative by an Anglican historian.

Arnaldo Fortini, *Francis of Assisi* (1959; repr. Seabury, 1981). Although wholly dated as a biography, this abridgement of the massive work in Italian by a mayor of Assisi draws on important archival material.

Michael de la Bedoyere, *Francis of Assisi: The Man Who Found Perfect Joy* (1962; repr. Sophia Institute, 1999). A Catholic devotional classic, not historical in purpose.

Omer Englebert, *Saint Francis of Assisi: A Biography* (Franciscan Herald, 1965). The best synthesis in the tradition of Jørgensen and Cuthbert. Raphael Brown's appendices are still invaluable.

Julien Green, *God's Fool: The Life of Francis of Assisi* (Harper & Row, 1987). A popular biography by a well-known novelist, not original scholarship.

Louis De Wohl, *The Joyful Beggar: Saint Francis of Assisi* (1958; repr. Ignatius Press, 2001). A popular devotional novel.

Nikos Kazantzakis, *Saint Francis* (1962: repr. Loyola Press, 2005). Another novel, but perhaps one of the most commonly read books about Francis.

Some Modern Interpretations

These authors have little interest in reconstructing the Historical Francis; rather, they approach the saint from a perspective that is explicitly theological, spiritual, political, economic, or otherwise interpretative. So long as it is understood that they are more informative about modern concerns than about the thirteenth-century Francis, they can make interesting reading.

Leonardo Boff, *Francis of Assisi: A Model for Human Liberation* (Crossroad, 1982). How Francis's choice of voluntary poverty subverts capitalist hierarchies, by a liberation theologian. An interesting contrast to the work of Wolf below.

Jacques Dalarun, *Francis of Assisi and the Feminine* (Franciscan Institute, 2006). Francis from a feminist perspective, by a leading Francis scholar.

Adrian House, *Francis of Assisi: A Revolutionary Life* (Paulist Press, 2003). Francis as a spiritual radical, beyond institutions, by a journalist.

Richard Rohr, *Hope against Darkness: The Transforming Vision of Saint Francis of Assisi in an Age of Anxiety* (St. Anthony Messenger, 2001). Francis's possible significance for modern psychological dilemmas, by a popular spiritual writer.

Roger D. Sorrell, *Saint Francis of Assisi and Nature: Tradition and Innovation in Western Christian Attitudes toward the Environment* (Oxford University Press, 1988). What Francis might contribute to ecological spirituality.

Donald Spoto, *Reluctant Saint: The Life of Francis of Assisi* (Viking Compass, 2003). A popular study by a biographer of Hollywood celebrities, often insightful as to Francis's psychology.

Kenneth Baxter Wolf, *The Poverty of Riches: Saint Francis of Assisi Reconsidered* (Oxford University Press, 2005). How Francis's choice of voluntary poverty reinforced capitalist hierarchy, by a medieval historian. An interesting contrast to the work of Boff above.

[PART II]

Sources and Debates

[PRELIMINARY NOTE]

FOR EACH CHAPTER, I provide, in summary form, a discussion of the medieval sources and scholarly controversies that lie behind the narrative of the biography. I have not included this material in the text of the biography, lest the narrative become fatally burdened by digressions and controversial academic issues. In the essay entitled "On the 'Franciscan Question,'" I discuss the history of modern scholarship on Francis and position this project within it. Then, for each chapter, I present the sources and academic debates that lie behind my reconstructions. These excurses should be considered something like long footnotes, commenting on the narrative. Their topics are linked to the corresponding chapter by page numbers. These notes are by no means exhaustive, but I think that I have flagged most of the issues that would interest scholars and informed readers trying to understand the Little Poor Man of Assisi.

I have adopted an abbreviation system for the sources and scholarly literature that will, I hope, save space and make it easy for the reader to identify the works cited. For medieval sources, I use the abbreviations from *Francis of Assisi: Early Documents* [FA:ED] (New York: New City Press, 1999–2001), the best available set of English translations. These abbreviations are listed immediately after this preliminary note. I normally cite by section and paragraph numbers rather than page numbers, so that readers can find the passages in any edition or translation they wish. If I had quoted or summarized the hundreds of source texts I cite in this study, it would have grown to an absurd length. I suggest that these commentaries be read with editions of the sources to hand, or, for those without Latin or Italian, the fine translations in FA:ED. For modern scholarship, I give the author's name (or book title for collections) and original publication date in parentheses. The bibliography is alphabetized using these short citations. English translations are used wherever possible.

Finally, some words of thanks. First, I would like to thank Cornell University Press and, in particular, its editor-in-chief, Mr. Peter J. Potter, who read and commented on every chapter of this book, for constant support and advice. I also thank the University of Virginia, where, as Professor of Religious Studies and History, I was granted research leave during the academic year 2007–8. This made possible most of the research for this book. During that sabbatical, I was hosted for three months at the Franciscan Institute of St. Bonaventure University by its director, Fr. Michael F. Cusato, O.F.M. He is in no way to blame for anything I have written about his Holy Father Francis, unless it is true and holy. My Dominican brothers at the Università Pontificia di San Tommaso d'Aquino (Angelicum) in Rome were generous hosts for much of that year. Finally, the members of my community at St. Albert the Great Priory, Oakland, California, have unflaggingly supported this project and have been the best of brothers while I completed my writing and revisions.

[ABBREVIATIONS]

1C	Thomas of Celano, *Life of St. Francis*
1LtCl	Francis of Assisi, "First Letter to the Clergy"
1LtCus	Francis of Assisi, "First Letter to the Custodians"
1LtF	Francis of Assisi, "First Letter to the Faithful"
1MP	*The Mirror of Perfection, Shorter Version*
2C	Thomas of Celano, *Remembrance of the Desire of a Soul*
2LtCl	Francis of Assisi, "Second Letter to the Clergy"
2LtCus	Francis of Assisi, "Second Letter to the Custodians"
2LtF	Francis of Assisi, "Second Letter to the Faithful"
2MP	*The Mirror of Perfection, Longer Version*
3C	Thomas of Celano, *Treatise on the Miracles*
AC	"Assisi Compilation"
Adm	Francis of Assisi, *Admonitions*
AF	*Analecta Franciscana*
AFH	*Archivum Franciscanum Historicum*
AP	"Anonymous of Perugia"
AS	*Acta Sanctorum*
BF	*Bullarium Franciscanum*
BlL	Francis of Assisi, "Blessing for Brother Leo"
CA:ED	*Clare of Assisi: Early Documents*
ChJG	Jordan of Giano, *Chronicle*
ChTE	Thomas of Eccleston, *Chronicle*
CtC	Francis of Assisi, "Canticle of the Creatures"

CtExh	Francis of Assisi, "Canticle of Exhortation"
ER	Francis of Assisi, Earlier Rule (*Regula non Bullata*)
ExhP	Francis of Assisi, "Exhortation to the Praise of God"
FA:ED	*Francis of Assisi: Early Documents*
FLCl	"Form of Life" of Clare
L3C	*Legend of the Three Companions*
LCh	Thomas of Celano, "Legend for Use in the Choir"
LCl	*Legend of Saint Clare*
LJS	Julian of Speyer, *Life of St. Francis*
LMj	Bonaventure, *The Major Legend*
LP	"Legend of Perugia"
LR	Francis of Assisi, Later Rule (*Regula Bullata*)
LtAnt	Francis of Assisi, "Letter to Anthony of Padua"
LtL	Francis of Assisi, "Letter to Brother Leo"
LtMin	Francis of Assisi, "Letter to a Minister"
LtOrd	Francis of Assisi, "Letter to the Entire Order"
LtR	Francis of Assisi, "Letter to the Rulers of Peoples"
OfP	Francis of Assisi, *Office of the Passion*
PC	*Process of Canonization of Saint Clare*
PrCr	Francis of Assisi, "Prayer before the Crucifix"
PrOF	Francis of Assisi, "Prayer Inspired by the Our Father"
PrPov	"The Privilege of Poverty"
PrsG	Francis of Assisi, "The Praises of God"
RH	Francis of Assisi, "Rule for Hermitages"
SalBVM	Francis of Assisi, "Salutation of the Blessed Virgin"
TestCl	Testament of Clare
Test	Francis of Assisi, Testament
TPJ	"True and Perfect Joy"

On the
"Franciscan Question"

I N WRITING A biography of Francis of Assisi, the author must come to terms with problems posed by the medieval sources—what has traditionally been called the "Franciscan Question." Before that, however, the biographer must confront an even more basic problem. Francis was, and is, a canonized Catholic saint. He remains a model for Christians generally and for Franciscans in particular. As De Beer (1963), 242, and Vauchez (1968), 84, long ago noted, the oldest witnesses to Francis, in particular 1C, tended to make him so uniquely holy and blessed by God that he became inimitable. As Miccoli (1991), 242, has noticed since then, miracle and prophecy stories became ever more important for later biographers, because they proved the saint's exceptional holiness. This extraordinary and miraculous Francis remains very much alive among modern devotional writers. Modern non–Catholics, like Sabatier (1894) or, more recently, Merlo (1992), 545, have, for very different reasons, emphasized the uniqueness and inimitability of Francis. So he stands alone, somehow disconnected from his place and time, transcending historical categories.

The inimitable Francis was, nevertheless, a model for the medieval Franciscans who compiled his legends. Modern secular writers assume that Francis has something to teach their readers, or that he presents a model worthy of imitation. There remains also a temptation to turn Francis into the mouthpiece for ideas or ideologies he never espoused. This practice started early and still thrives. Merlo (1993b) has catalogued a rogues' gallery of exploiters of Francis for modern religious views or political agendas. Merlo (1993a) comments trenchantly on the then current state of affairs in Italian Franciscan studies.

Those who read English need only glance at the December 1981 issue of *Sojourners* to see a similar situation in American appropriation of the saint. There, pop-culture "fans" of Francis, like John Michael Talbot, Robert Coles, Colman McCarthy, and Sr. Joan Chittister, enlist the Little Poor Man for their various ideological projects. Among them, Richard Rohr (1981) alone questions the parade of stereotypes, only to propose a pacifist-feminist Francis with no apparent sacramental life: in short, a late twentieth-century secular liberal. Even when a thoughtful appropriator, such as Newman (1985), attempts to separate legend from fact, he can still find the distorting fictions of director Franco Zefferelli's *Brother Sun, Sister Moon* (1972) a "beautiful" presentation of Francis. I will not belabor the obvious problem here.

More sophisticated is the reworking of Francis by modern Franciscans for the internal purposes of their order, a project that began before the saint's death. Manselli (1980), 151, rightly observes that medieval Franciscans were less interested in facts about Francis than in presenting a saint useful to their religious life, or at least to that of some particular faction within the order. This kind of twisting was insidious because Francis was, indeed, a Franciscan. These medieval propaganda products usually have some verisimilitude. A sophisticated modern version of such a project may be seen in Lambertini-Tabarroni (1989), and in other writers who want to bring the Francis of history into "conversation" with modern theological or spiritual concerns. Of course, merely being a Franciscan in no way excludes a scholar from doing serious, detached historical analysis. Indeed, modern academic work on Francis rests on a foundation built, almost exclusively, by Franciscan historians. They were among the first to seek the "Historical Francis."

Attempts to detect the Historical Francis over the past hundred years have uncanny similarities to attempts to reconstruct the "Historical Jesus." Dolcini (1994), 15, briefly notes the parallels; Manselli (1980), 8–11, has focused on them at length. Some, like Clasen (1967), have come to the conclusion, a common one among "Historical Jesus" scholars in the 1960s and 1970s, that Francis sources are so "theological" that no historical reconstruction is possible. Pellegrini (1977), 303, would have the product of "Francesco storico" scholarship be the history of the ways people perceived the saint after his death, not any factual details of his, perhaps unretrievable, life. This would turn a biography of Francis into the history of his medieval hagiographers (and modern biographers).

I think we can do more than that. Merlo (1992), 549, notes that, as for Jesus in the first century, the sources for Francis in the twelfth to thirteenth centuries are much better than those for any other spiritual leader of his age (e.g., Dominic or Valdes). And, unlike Jesus, we have actual writings by Francis—in fact, a large corpus of them. But even his own writings do not give us an unvarnished Francis. They represent the founder's concerns at specific times and places and represent his reactions to concrete events. Had he written an autobiography, it too would have adapted remembered events and facts to his own subjective purposes. We are fortunate that much of what he wrote was not intended as self-portrayal.

It is possible to construct a Historical Francis, but the limits and difficulty of such a reconstruction must be faced directly. Manselli (1995), 25, rightly rejected the contention of Bihl that 1C presented the "real Francis," while other sources introduce some particular slant or interpretation. Even the saint's first biographer had an agenda. In an article published already in 1969, Manselli gives a good orientation for issues involved in retrieving Francis from the legends. All medieval reports about Francis were written for a purpose and for an audience; every reporter had a particular perspective. Some biases are more obvious and wrongheaded than others, but there is no uninterpreted Francis. That includes the Francis of this book.

A Francis reconstructed by critical historical method is not the "real Francis"; this Francis is also an interpretation, albeit of a particular kind. A Historical Francis is one whose construction is governed by the modern historical method. What the historian can do is strip away, or at least discount in part, hagiographic stereotypes, political concerns of reporters, and simple factual errors in the sources. Dalarun (1996), 258, claims that the resulting Historical Francis will be "rougher, livelier, sharper," and "more appealing." In part, this sounds to me like academic romanticism, but there is much truth here. Honesty must admit that, as a medieval Italian Catholic, the Francis produced by the historical critic could just as likely be a rather unappealing man. It would not be odd if modern sensibilities found some aspects of such an alien person uncomfortable.

Modern Scholarship on Francis

The Search for the Historical Francis is not new, and it is worthwhile to review it briefly. A very good introduction to the history of how Francis has been understood, reunderstood, and misunderstood from his death to the year 2000 is found in the "General Introduction" of FA:ED 1:11–31. I urge readers to consult it. Manselli (1995), 21–35, is a good companion to the FA:ED introduction. More detailed, but not necessarily better, is Stanislao da Compagnola (1973), esp. 223–513, which covers the modern period to that date. *Studi francescani* (1993) is a good collection of essays on the state of the question at that date. I do not intend in this essay to repeat that overview. Those who would like a concise bibliography for the period after 1995 may find it conveniently in Vauchez (2009).

Dalarun (1996), 24–29, is useful for the origins of the Franciscan Question—that is, the project of source criticism starting in the late 1800s. A quick sketch of the major names and approaches is in Merlo (1992), 549. Pellegrini (1988), esp. 324–26, is very useful on the two major approaches to the Franciscan Question. One group, represented by Moorman (1976), Clasen (1966), and Cavallin (1954), tried to determine which medieval sources were earliest (and so most "authentic"). One might call this the philological approach; it is currently out of favor. The other approach, represented by Campbell (1967), Desbonnets (1983), Brooke (1970), Manselli (1980), and Pásztor (1973), tried, more modestly, to reconstruct the original forms of the testimonies.

By the 1980s, these two projects had run their course, their results as good as we are going to get. A mere early date is not a guarantee of "authenticity." Detecting or reconstructing lost "eyewitness" testimony has also come to look less and less possible. I am skeptical about reconstructing or identifying eyewitness testimony if that means it is more "objective." Each pericope in the collections, no matter how close to "first person," needs to be evaluated individually for its ideological purpose, its intended audience, and the way it reformulates earlier material.

As most academic readers have encountered scholarship on Francis, they should be aware of the methods and presuppositions of each period and "school" in the Search for the Historical Francis. The prescientific writing on Francis, which began with 1C in 1228 and extended to the late 1800s, may be called "hagiographic." It was written to glorify Francis as a Catholic saint. Nonetheless, already by the time of Bonaventure, it was obvious that Francis's own writings and the early lives, while not presenting wholly contradictory narratives, presented contrasting images, as well as chronological and factual conflicts. Hagiographers sought to harmonize the disparate material into a more or less coherent story. They found it hard to reject any anecdote, however ill founded or far-fetched, and they usually treated different versions of the same story as reporting distinct incidents. The Francis received by the nineteenth century was that of Bonaventure's *Legenda Major*, a nearly wholly derivative text; that of Bartholomew of Pisa's *Liber de Conformitate,* which remodeled Francis's life on that of Jesus, often retailing wholly invented parallels; and that of the collection of stories known as the *Fioretti,* which Dalarun (1996), 71, has rightly called the "combat manual" of fourteenth-century schismatic (and often heretical) Franciscans.

By the late 1800s, some critical work and much collecting of sources had been done, especially by Franciscans, but no attempt had been made to synthesize the material until the French liberal Paul Sabatier produced his *Vie de St. François d'Assise* (1894). Sabatier's Francis, founded principally on witnesses from the Spiritualist Franciscan tradition, was a religious genius, misunderstood and exploited by the "institutional Church." This Francis was a remarkably modern individualist, a romantic seeker, anachronistic to medieval Italy. Nevertheless, Sabatier was the first to evaluate and interpret the sources critically. He created the modern study of Saint Francis. He also generated violent reactions among Catholic scholars, in particular among the Franciscans.

Reaction to Sabatier dominated all serious writing on Francis from the 1890s to the Second World War. Stanislao da Compagnola (1973), 305–6, insightfully divided the followers of Sabatier into the *medievalizzanti,* who emphasized Francis as a medieval personage, more or less alien to modern sensibilities and perhaps even "heretical," and the *modernizzanti,* who wanted him to be a source of modern (i.e., postmedieval Christian) sensibilities. All followers of Sabatier agreed in placing Francis in conflict with the medieval Catholic Church, or at least in discontinuity with it. Opposed to these were the Catholics—Johannes Jørgensen (1907) is probably the best—who wanted to save Francis as a Catholic saint, orthodox and spiritually edifying to those of post-Tridentine spirituality. As Dalarun (1996), 32, observed, no scholar today can accept the anachronistic dichotomy between the romantic Francis of the Sabatier school and the saint's medieval Italian Catholic culture. But Francis was also a particular and unique spiritual personality; he cannot be routinely assimilated to some model, even medieval, of Catholic piety. As Manselli (1995), 23, wisely wrote, "We have not to reply to or refute Sabatier, but to free ourselves from him."

By the 1920s, the Franciscan Question in its technical and philological sense had come to dominate research on Francis. It was clear that the issues raised by Sabatier, his admirers, and his critics could not be resolved until all extant sources for Francis were identified, critically edited, and studied carefully. Kajetan Esser, Sophronius Clasen, Théophile Desbonnets, David Flood, and Stanislao da Compagnola were the great contributors to this project, through their editing of texts and their philological criticism of them. In the conference proceedings published in *Povertà* (1969), Raoul Manselli and Pietro Zerbi summarized the achieved consensus. All previous biographies, even Sabatier's, were "hagiographic" rather than historical. We may add that even biographies produced well past the millennium, as the editors observe in FA:ED 1:35, were usually written ignoring Francis's own writings, with the exception of the Rules and the Testament. The favored hagiographic sources for popular lives were both late and strongly theologically driven, the *Little Flowers* and Bonaventure. The earliest life of Francis, by Thomas of Celano (1C), was a distant third as a source.

Raoul Manselli (1965) reviewed the study of Francis from 1945 to 1965 and thoughtfully appraised postwar scholarship. He concluded that only two projects of general significance were produced in the period: the collection of essays *Unvergleichliche Heilige* (1958), edited by J. Lortz, and the multivolume biography by Arnoldo Fortini (1959). Neither was satisfactory. The Lortz volume still presented an anachronistic, unmedieval Francis; Fortini's scholarship was still "nei limiti di quella scritta nell'ormai lontano 1929." More significant for later scholarship would be the edition of Jacques de Vitry and Esser's work on the Testament. For the early Franciscans, however, Rosalind Brooke (1959) finally broke away from interpretations based on Spiritual propaganda of the early 1300s.

No modern biography could be written until the Franciscan Question was resolved to general satisfaction. Pietro Zerbi (1971) and the papers by Manselli, Grau, Baldelli, Esser, Delaruelle, Selge, and Serban published in *San Francesco* (1971) all reflected a consensus that more philological study was necessary before any attempt at a chronology of the sources, much less a biography, could be undertaken. Desbonnets (1967), 273–316, had earlier made a similar claim. In the conference papers published as *Questione francescana* (1974), Manselli and Grau agreed that all attempts at biography to date had done little but harmonize *legendae*. The consensus was that a study of the Historical Francis, given the debates on the sources, was still impossible.

Nevertheless, two years after the 1971 conference, in his volume of the Einaudi history of medieval Italy, Giovanni Miccoli (1974), 734–93, made the first systematic attempt to disentangle the "Francis of History" from the "Francis of Church Tradition." This project was developed and expanded in his 1983 article "La proposità cristiana di Francesco d'Assisi"—reprinted in Miccoli (1991). In Dalarun's opinion, Miccoli's short biography is probably still, with Manselli (1982) and Frugoni (1998), among the most useful today, to which I would add Vauchez (2009), which I will discuss presently. The methodological revolution of Miccoli's project was to privilege Francis's own writings over the legends. In the same year, a similar project to retrieve Francis's own vision appeared in Desbonnets (1983). Neither project, however, was a full-fledged biography. Both were studies of Francis's mind-set and vision, not his life. Somewhat earlier, De Beer (1977) had actually attempted to write a biography of Francis, using only his own writings and nonhagiographic contemporary reports. The result was very short, mostly a summary of Jacques de Vitry. More was needed.

To write a life required reconsideration of the legends, their composition, and the influences on them. Four scholars dominated that project: Raoul Manselli on the Assisi Compilation texts, Ovidio Capitani on the social environment of Franciscanism, Chiara Frugoni on iconography, and Jacques Le Goff on Franciscans and cities, although he focused principally on France. A contemporary overview of the state of the question in the 1970s is Langeli (1977), who is especially appreciative of Miccoli. Merlo (1993b) is probably the best overview of this period in retrospect. Pellegrini (1988), esp. 329–46, summarized trends in the 1980s: discussion of the *Sitz im Leben* of the sources, form criticism of pericopes, and redaction criticism of reports. In the later scholarly roundtable "Francesco storico" (1993), major Italian Francis scholars discussed Raoul Manselli (1980) and his contribution to work on the *Nos qui cum eo fuimus* sources, that is, the collection of stories found in AC that are signed "We who were with him." Discussion focused on the extent to which Manselli believed these texts could yield a "Francesco storico." Although Edith Pásztor ("Francesco storico" [1993], 365) argued that this was not Manselli's goal, Merlo and Capitani asserted that something like that was intended.

Indeed, soon after his publication on the *Nos* texts, Manselli (1982) did publish his interpretation of the Historical Francis, the first new synthesis since Sabatier. It opened a new period in Franciscan studies, which has continued to this day. Unfortunately, due to the author's struggle with cancer, the biography was rushed out in a rather imperfect form and without notes. It privileged the *Nos* texts as the witnesses closest to the Historical Francis, second only to Francis's own writings. Manselli's Francis, like Sabatier's, is still in conflict, now no longer with the Church, but with the reality that surrounded him. In spite of its strengths, the book is confusing, hard to read, and too uncritical of the theological agenda of the *Nos* reports. And Manselli still tended to read back later realities into Francis's earlier life. An appreciation of Manselli's accomplishment comes from comparison with contemporary biographies by the two great leaders of Francis studies in the 1960s and 1970s. Flood (1983) read Francis through the lens of liberation theology, and Desbonnets (1983) drew far-fetched comparisons of Francis with Teilhard de Chardin and popular writing on physics. Manselli stands alone.

Dolcini, in *Frate Francesco* (1994), 29 n. 61, has noted that models of Francis in conflict with "uncomprehending" institutions still dominate writing on the saint. For Grado Merlo, Francis is still in conflict with the "institutional Church." For Raoul Manselli, the conflict was with the Proto-Conventuals of his own order. I am inclined to see all this as anachronistic retrojection of later conflicts into the later years of a man who was himself highly conflicted. If there was an external conflict in his later years, it was over the growing clericalization of the order, not over routinization per se nor about abstract visions of poverty. In this I agree with Cracco (1982), who long ago warned against accepting the older conflict models uncritically.

Merlo (1991a), Capitani (1991), 449, and Paciocco (1986), 138–40, all see Miccoli as the first step beyond the philological trap of the Franciscan Question. But what followed him (Manselli excepted) was a subjective world of experiences and reminiscences. Merlo concludes that the "Francesco storico" has vanished in the procession of voices. As Dalarun (1996), 37–38, has observed, Manselli remains the only truly critical biography. In contrast, again to Manselli, is the well-reviewed Robson (1999), which, while interesting and readable, does not present a new portrait, and it is far less critical of the sources than Manselli, whose accomplishments Robson seems not to know. Had Manselli lived ten years longer and had the time to refine and perfect his project, my biography would probably not have been written.

In part, the reason for this gap in the scholarship is that scholars after Manselli mostly shied away from reconstructing the Historical Francis. Miccoli (1991), a collection of eight previously published essays, initiated the trend among Italian scholars that dominates today. The "memories of Francis" in the writings of his hagiographers are contrasted with the saint's experience as recorded in his own writing, principally represented by the Testament. Frugoni (1998), similarly, focuses on the way Francis was envisioned in artistic monuments. For Dalarun (1996), 42–43, these two scholars, along with Manselli, represented the current state of the question of the Historical Francis in the 1990s. The similarity to Historical Jesus studies is obvious. Francis studies are often reduced to literary analysis, bypassing Francis the man as hopelessly lost to us. Dalarun (1997), 11, summarized the state of Francis studies as it still stands at the time of my writing: "Today historians no longer seek to reconstruct a universal, coherent, single image of the one true Francis, following the rules of critical methodology. He has become more inaccessible. Narrowly defined or thematic studies have taken the place of biographies."

The one exception to Dalarun's summary is now Vauchez (2009), whose biographical section, pp. 25–222, presents what might be called the first scholarly narrative life since Manselli. He is extremely good on presenting comparisons and cultural contexts, but his life remains typically cautious about going behind the texts of the sources to the man who lies behind them. Instead, Vauchez presents hagiographic reworkings of events, flags elements clearly legendary, and weaves the saint's life together in a broad-brush way. The result is masterful, and, for those who read French, this is now the biography of choice. Still, from my perspective, the work represents a retreat from Manselli's attempt to retrieve the Historical Francis. I understand that an

English translation by the Franciscan Institute of St. Bonaventure University is under way.

Otherwise, biographies of Francis have become the realm of nonhistorians. I will not even begin to catalogue the interpretations foisted on Francis by various theologians, ecologists, journalists, and other popular writers since 2000. Their Historical Francis is most often that of the Sabatier school, spun for various contemporary purposes. Those who want a sample of the better attempts should consult "For Further Reading," which follows chapter 8 in this book.

Sources for a Life of Francis

We now need to examine the kinds of medieval sources available for the Historical Francis. For an extended overview, see Beguin (1979), 107–244, or, in English, the introductory essays found in FA:ED, volumes 1–2. Scholars like Manselli (1980), 12–30, conventionally divide the major sources into four groups: (1) Francis's own writings, (2) unsystematic collections ("Legend of Perugia," the Lemmens "Mirror," and the Little "Mirror"), (3) systematic collections (*Three Companions,* "Anonymous of Perugia," Mirror of Perfection), and (4) official compositions (Celano 1, Celano 2, Bonaventure). This division has merit, and I will follow it.

Following Manselli (1982) and Marini (1989), any attempt to retrieve the Historical Francis must privilege his own writings over what others wrote about him. For an introduction to the textual issues involved in editing Francis's writings, see Esser-Oliger (1974). Next, one should privilege anything with a claim to have been first written down before 1260 over what is later. That date excludes, for almost all purposes, Bonaventure. On Bonaventure's theological and pastoral project, which was to produce a Francis who was above all a mystic, and so inimitable for friars living very different lives in teaching and church administration, see Dalarun (1996), 254, who draws much from Gilson (1940), 81–82. We will consider as pre-1260 the stories in AC, even though the one manuscript of that compilation is dated to 1310, since much of its contents does seem to have been originally composed in the 1250s or earlier.

Nevertheless, reports composed in the mid-1240s and later—L3P, AC, 2C—must, as I will explain later, be used with great care. This does not mean that earlier material like 1C or AP does not require careful reading, but the problems with those texts are less grave, since some controversies that color later compositions have not yet arisen. For completeness, I will here mention four other very early sources: Julian of Speyer's *Life of St. Francis* (1232–35),

Henri d'Avranches's *Versified Life* (1232–39), and Thomas of Celano's "Legend for Use in the Choir" and the *Divine Office for St. Francis* by Julian of Speyer (both early 1230s). These are early but contain virtually nothing not already found in 1C.

Citing a remark of Attilio Bartoli Langeli in 1974, Dolcini (1994), 6, emphasized that Francis's own writings must have first place, something obvious, but in practice ignored for everything but the Rules and the Testament. Francis's writings have been exhaustively studied, but, with the exception of Manselli (1982), to this date no construction of the Historical Francis has made a systematic attempt to privilege them. Even they must be examined with care. Some documents, like ER, are filled with material from other pens, here Cesarius of Speyer. Most of Francis's writings were at least edited by others to improve the Latinity. But as Scivoletto (1977), 120, points out, the presence of a learned Latin *cursus* does not exclude the possibility that the contents of a document comes from Francis himself.

Francis's presentation of himself in a composition like the Testament is just as much an interpretation of the man as the Francis of the hagiographers, but at least the concerns revealed are those of Francis himself. Merlo (1992), 547, rightly notes that those who observed Francis sometimes noticed things about him that he did not notice himself. This is simple human nature and should not surprise us.

In a special place, although sometimes overlooked, are the "minor" sources for Francis that appear in non-Franciscan chronicles and offhand remarks. These are described in Di Fonzo (1982), 7. The writings of Jacques de Vitry are the most important of the minor sources, followed by the chronicles of Jordan of Giano, Thomas Eccleston, and the writers on the Fifth Crusade. These are all precious because they are relatively uninfluenced by the "mythology" of Francis the Saint and by internal Franciscan political concerns. They do bring in other concerns, but these are usually easier to detect. I am less sure than Miccoli (1991), 194, that we should reject Esser's dictum that non-Franciscan reports are more trustworthy than Franciscan ones. However, they are at least mostly free of internal Franciscan politics. Minor only in its length is Jordan of Giano's *Chronicle,* which is not only by an eyewitness with little seeming stake in later Franciscan politics, but also the best chronological resource for the central part of Francis's life.

The unsystematic or private collections present their own set of interpretative problems. In terms of the scholarship, these documents have become very much identified with the project of reconstructing the dossier of stories supposedly transmitted to the minister-general Crescentius of Iesi and the supposed writings of Brother Leo preserved on *cedulae* mentioned by later Spiritualist writers like Peter John Olivi and Ubertino da Casale. Pásztor (1973) surveys views on the hypothetical "Scritti Leonini," which some believe can be reconstructed from materials in AC and later related compilations.

I am skeptical about the value of reconstructing such hypothetical documents. Menestò (1993), 251–52, emphasizes that the "oral" nature of the unofficial collections made for great plasticity in retelling: the political agenda of the last reteller of a story may be far from the original realities. Pásztor (1973), 204–11, rightly observes that what is missing from the studies of Delorme, Clasen, Moorman, Brooke, and Desbonnets is a sense that there has been a deformation of Francis's words by oral transmission. The change of *Sitz im Leben* between 1244 (Crescentius) and 1266 (Bonaventure) was profound, and little of the material in the unsystematic collections predates Bonaventure, at least in the form in which we have it.

The Franciscan Question, which focused intensely on the unsystematic collections and their relation to the writings of Brother Leo, is fundamentally closed. Dalarun (1997), 187, is right that to call AP, AC, and L3C "Leonine" is absurd, since they are not a single corpus and represent diverse ideologies. As Pellegrini (1982b), 242, wrote, all scholars now basically agree on the following: (1) all sources are composite; (2) there was an oral transmission and collection of stories in response to Crescentius's letter; (3) any original dossiers that resulted from these collections have vanished; (4) every collection we have is posterior to 2C, even if it contains older material; (5) the "Letter of the Three Companions" that prefaces L3C is an important witness to a collection, but its link to L3C is dubious. In short, mere presence in a particular collection does not make a report "authentic"; every report must be evaluated individually. This is true, even if (*pace* Manselli) the report is "signed" by supposed eyewitnesses.

It is worth mentioning in passing that the earlier consensus on dating and relationships between the extant documents has now been confirmed by Desbonnets (1999), a massive computerized quantitative study of linguistic patterns. The results are the following: 1C and Celano's "Legend for Use in the Choir" are close; 2C stands linguistically between AP and 1C; the texts identified as LP and the *Speculum* form a group; and L3C and AP are close. The only surprise is that LCl resembles nothing in the texts ascribed to Celano; he is probably not the author. I now turn to the major sources individually.

1C: Thomas of Celano, Vita Prima,
commonly called Celano 1 (1228–1229)
This is the first, as well as the first "official," biography of Francis and was written shortly after the saint's death. Dalarun (1996), 101, has noted how unusual

this document is as the first vita commissioned by a pope—in a period when papal canonization itself was rare. That papal commission still makes it suspect to some. Starting with its condemnation by Sabatier, 1C has been subject to continuous criticism. Dalarun (1996), 111–27, sees the first part of 1C as a literary rewrite of the autobiographical remarks of the Testament. He identifies the probably apocryphal but debated Letter of Elias as Celano's source for the saint's last sickness, and the canonization inquest as the source of the miracles. Rightly, he complains that the work is overtly conformed to hagiographic stereotypes.

Nevertheless, as Di Fonzo (1982), 6, notes, 1C is, for a hagiographic product, rich in interpretable dates. The source is precious for this chronological information, although, as Pellegrini (1977), 300–301, notes, Celano's dating cannot always be taken at face value. Clasen (1966) has shown how to disembed precious information from the stereotyping. When the text reports incidents without reworking them according to hagiographic stereotype, the reporting is blessedly clean of ideological and political spin. This allows us to use the text as a control on ideological reworkings of the same incidents in later writers.

AP: John of Perugia, The Beginning or Founding of the Order and the Deeds of Those Lesser Brothers Who Were the First Companions of Blessed Francis in Religion, commonly called "Anonymous of Perugia" (1240–1241)
On this work, see Di Fonzo (1972) and Beguin (1979), who critically edited the document. Following Beguin, the document is to be dated between 4 Mar. 1240 and 22 Aug. 1241. The attempt to place AP after 1287 by Cavallin (1954), 255, is not convincing. Di Fonzo (1972), 180–201, considers AP to be 1C plus a "florilegium" of anecdotes (since lost). Dalarun (1996), 179, calculates its contents as 40 percent from 1C and 60 percent new material. Thanks to Di Fonzo (1972), 373–75, 396–409, we now know the work's author: Brother John of Perugia, companion and confessor of Brother Giles. This explains the extremely good material it contains on Francis's conversion, his first followers, and the early days of the brotherhood. AP is an extraordinarily important source for the early period and shows little sanitizing or reworking according to hagiographic stereotype. It is much to be preferred to 1C (or any source other than Francis's own writing) for the period 1210–1221. On the relation of AP and 1C, see Beguin (1979), 109–36. It is perhaps the oddest lacuna in Manselli (1982) that he does not use AP.

AC: The "Assisi Compilation" (1244–1260)
Although the manuscript containing this collection is late, 1310, what it contains is much older. Thus I treat it next. The codex has been edited in

diplomatic form by Bigaroni (1992), whose first edition was severely criticized by Gattucci (1979) and by Pellegrini (1982b), 238–39. Gattucci should be consulted even when using the 1992 edition, which corrected many typographical errors and textual problems flagged by critics.

Unfortunately, most interest in AC until the 1980s was as a quarry for collecting pericopes to include in hypothetical reconstructions of the supposed "Legend of Perugia" that was (or was not) compiled from a dossier of reports sent to Crescentius of Iesi. A classic example of this kind of dossier reconstruction remains Campbell (1967). On reconstructing LP, from Delorme to Brooke, see Gattucci (1979), 791–811. Gattucci (1979), 867–70, also presents a synoptic table of LP editions and Bigaroni's text. Dalarun (1996), 204–6, speaking honestly, says that the "Legend of Perugia" is "an artificial construct" and a "working hypothesis," but "a plausible one." LP is the "Q Document" of Francis studies, much discussed, but never actually seen.

Much of this reconstruction was driven by the conviction that if a report was in LP, then it must have a very good claim to be "authentic." Brooke (2006), 104–9, who edited a version of LP, reevaluates the "authenticity" of the supposed dossier that LP represents. She still supports it, albeit with greater reservations. I reject that conclusion. The stories and logia of Francis usually identified as in LP are disparate. Each item, no matter what its provenance, needs to be examined on its own merits. This represents the consensus of modern scholars, even those who continue to speak of the "Legend of Perugia" as a source. I will not use the hypothetical text as such. The document we have is the Assisi Compilation, and so I will call it.

In fact, a large part of AC is lifted wholesale from 2C and provides no independent witness. Dalarun (1996), 206, catalogues the origin of material usually identified as in the 117 chapters of LP; with the exception of 6 from 1C, 1 from AP, and 4 from L3C, the rest are unique to AC (although different versions of some of these also appear in 2C). The supposed LP texts might include reports by those who knew Francis directly. Manselli (1980) is the most convincing attempt to detect parts of AC that can claim to be eyewitness reports. Among the AC material, he focused on the reports signed *Nos qui cum eo fuimus*. None of these reports are in 1C; 2C contains some, but only as borrowed from whatever source the compiler of AC was using. Nearly all these reports concern the period of Francis's final illness and death, although a couple might be dated to the early 1220s. For that late period they are precious, especially since they provide witness to a period lacking in AP and very schematic in 1C.

Nevertheless, these AC texts have a powerful ideological flavor. In their preserved form, they are the products of the Proto-Spiritualist party and place that party's political agenda into Francis's mouth, going so far as to create long speeches on poverty for him. They mock or vilify what has been called a "Spiritualist rogues' gallery" of traitors and corruptors. There is nothing like this abuse in Francis's own writings. Each *Nos* text must be read with great care to filter out this later agenda. Miccoli (1991), 237–38, points out a number of ways these elderly eyewitnesses had lost touch with the early days they romanticize. They have trouble understanding the role of manual labor in the early period. They idealize the Porziuncula into a model of exemplary monastic observance. They are frustrated that Francis was silent on issues they consider crucial to the life of the order, above all, the kind of food eaten by friars. Perhaps most tellingly, they replace Francis's model of living with the poor with having compassion for the poor. And they present early Franciscan life as in overt or implicit contrast with a corrupt institutional Church and compromised Franciscan Order. Dalarun (1996), 217, remarks on the anachronism of this: there is no sign of conflict between Francis or his followers and the "institutional Church" during the saint's lifetime (and beyond). On the origin of this anachronistic view of the early order among the Proto-Spiritualists, see Burr (2003).

L3C: The Legend of the Three Companions (1241–1247 or later)

There are twenty-two manuscripts in two traditions of this document, described and edited by Desbonnets (1974). Both recensions probably depend on a lost original. If 1C has been the unloved orphan of Francis studies, this document was long the favored child. Perhaps a bit harsh, but reflecting the current consensus, is Brown (1965), 356, who calls L3C a "literary forgery." The famous "Greccio Letter" from the "three companions" themselves, dated 11 August 1246, with which L3C opens, is probably authentic, but what follows the letter cannot be the collection of stories supposedly sent by Leo, Angelo, and Rufino. They describe the collection as not in any particular order—in short, not a biography. Since what follows is a carefully constructed narrative, not an unstructured collection, and one that depends on 1C, AP, and Julian of Speyer for over 60 percent of its material, it cannot be the original. Di Fonzo (1972) and Beguin (1979) show that the use of AP is extensive. In the current form, the author of the extant document may have even used Bonaventure, or at least that is Desbonnets' conjecture. For material shared with 1C and AP, these are to be preferred, as L3C harmonizes and conflates those sources, as Beguin (1979), 164, has shown.

What does not come from 1C and AP often parallels 2C. Beguin, Di Fonzo, and Miccoli all agree that, when parallel, 2C is a later version of the source (now lost) used by L3C, but that the final redaction of L3C is itself almost certainly later than 2C. Desbonnets (1974), in his edition of L3C, who is followed by Trexler (1989), 34, believed that 2C used L3C, and so dated it

to before 1247. After extensive study, Cavallin (1954) concludes that Di Fonzo
and Beguin are probably right, and that both 2C and L3C used an earlier
source. This means that L3C received its final form after 1247. I tend to agree,
but the issue is unimportant. Whatever its date, L3C contains the shared material in a rawer form than 2C. So for the parallel passages, it is usually a better
place to start.

As Dalarun (1996), 196–97, has noted, L3C is especially well informed
about the town of Assisi and the earliest period up to 1210. So, although the
conflations with 1C and AP must be controlled, L3C is probably the best
source for Francis's early life.

2C: Thomas of Celano, Remembrance of the Desire
of a Soul, commonly called Celano 2 (1245–1247)
This second life by Thomas of Celano was compiled between 11 August 1245
and its adoption as the official life of the saint on 13 July 1247 at the Lyon
general chapter. It contains 131 sections not found in 1C, AP, L3C, or AC.
These earlier sources contain more primitive versions of the shared material,
although each pericope must be evaluated individually. The unique material
generally highlights controversies within the order or concern the stigmata.
Dalarun (1996), 132, rightly notes that the controversy material reflects conditions in the 1240s, not during the life of Francis. Its function in the life is to
foster unity and order among the divided friars at the time of its composition.
Such passages must be treated with skepticism as anachronism, much like the
poverty rhetoric in AC. Dalarun notes that the Francis of 2C is a more stereotyped "monastic" miracle-working saint than the Francis of 1C. Landini
(1968), 100, has noted that issues of clericalization (pretty much absent in earlier sources) take on a larger role in this document, again mirroring the 1240s.
Attached to 2C is Thomas of Celano's *Treatise on Miracles,* often called Celano 3.
It contains five stories (all posthumous) not found in earlier documents.

De Beer (1963), 273–74, notes that some of the developments and concerns
about decline detected in 2C were already present by 1230 in Celano's "Legend for Use in the Choir," but that the big change in 2C is the presence of
long "speeches" by Francis, a trait shared by AC. It is safe to conclude that the
speeches are in both works literary devices, not historical reports. In addition,
2C avoids stories in his sources that might be viewed as suspect by Church
authorities or by academic theology. The Francis of 2C is a much more conventional saint. Tellingly, Miccoli (1991), 227–28, points out the concern for
decadence in the order found in 2C. Some slight concern existed in 1C, but by
the 1240s, a concern about decadence affects all reports: AP, AC, L3C, and 2C.
We should be cautious about naively reading this concern back into Francis

himself. He had concerns, but they were not likely to be identical to those of his followers fifteen years after his death.

Dalarun (1996), 219, observes that Celano was never able to synthesize the confusing and contradictory material at his disposal; it is no surprise that 2C was a failure. Nonetheless, it can sometimes add details and context to stories found elsewhere in more schematic form.

Handling the Sources

Before I sketch the principles employed to deal with this confusing mass of material, it is useful to raise the question of partisanship and bias in the sources. As Manselli (1980), 34, noted, commenting on the first round of Historical Francis debates, there is nothing more "authentic" in the "Spiritualist" reporting favored by Sabatier (1894) than in the "Conventual" reporting favored by Tamassia (1909). All compilers had a vision and a purpose. There is no "unbiased" source, including Francis's own writings. This does not mean the reports are worthless or fiction (although some are), but it does mean that every source must be read with its purpose, author, and audience in mind. To some extent, this means that the age of the Franciscan Question, when the dream was to find the most "primitive," "unbiased," "true" source, has passed. As Menestò (1993), 266, observed, if by the Franciscan Question we mean reconstruction of a pure, original, unbiased text that lies behind the extant documents, it is impossible. We must, however, order and relate the sources. Happily, this has pretty much been accomplished. Over one hundred years of debate have not been in vain.

Pellegrini (1988) is an extended essay on the hermeneutics of reading Francis sources. He covers the development of a more sophisticated reading during the twentieth century and gives a good general overview of criteria for evaluating medieval reports. As I mentioned earlier, the attempts to reconstruct the Historical Francis bear striking similarities to the Quest for the Historical Jesus. The shifts in Francis studies usually parallel developments in Jesus studies within ten to fifteen years, as Dalarun (1996), 111, has observed. Historical Jesus studies today are roughly divided into two camps: one that emphasizes "discontinuity" and "embarrassment" as a guarantee of historical authenticity (an approach popularly identified with the "Jesus Seminar"), and another (dominant in mainline scholarly work) that gives a place to multiple independent attestation and conformity to the cultural realities of the first century.

So too, in Francis studies, some biographers privilege stories that present Francis as acting oddly or espousing extreme, even heretical, opinions and practices (this tendency goes back to Sabatier), while another school (identified with Sabatier's opponents) focuses on the *Sitz im Leben* of the report and reminds us that Francis was, first of all, a medieval Catholic. According to Pellegrini (1982b), 247, the movement toward placing Francis and reports on him in their cultural context has been dominant since the 1980s. I favor that trend.

Individual reports presenting a strange or inconsistent Francis, or one who seems extreme, do, however, merit credence. It is unlikely that his pious followers made them up. Nevertheless, we should immediately discount any report where the "extreme" Francis is mouthing or enacting the agenda of some later Franciscan party. Such reports usually arose within a Proto-Spiritualist or Spiritualist milieu and are a form of propaganda. Conversely, Sabatier was right in discounting reports that turned Francis into a traditional monk or a conventional "churchman." These reports reflect later political realities just as much as the radical Francis of the Proto-Spiritualists does. Miccoli (1991), 233, reminds us that the first question to ask about a text is why it was written or saved.

No report gives us mere raw facts. Miccoli (1991), 298–300, lists a set of influences on the way an author constructs a report on Francis or why a collector prefers one. I cannot do better. These are (1) internal politics of the Franciscan Order, (2) growing institutionalization, (3) older hagiographic models, (4) theological considerations, (5) persistence of elements from earlier sources, and (6) personal spiritual or religious preferences of the author or collector. Merlo (1992), 546, adds that we must be careful to control the "official" biographies (1C and 2C) for the influence of the image of Francis in the canonization bull *Mira circa Nos,* which certainly had a strong influence on those collections. I would caution, following De Beer (1963), 282–85, that rejection of any event merely because it reflects earlier hagiographic models is wrong. Francis knew the hagiography of his time; he also knew the scriptures. If he seems to be acting like Jesus, this may be more than just the hagiographer's intrusion of convention. Francis may have thought it proper to imitate his Savior. Many medieval Christians did.

Finally, as a general principle, I want to emphasize my agreement with Pellegrini (1977), 304–7, who argues for favoring the earlier sources over the later. This may seem obvious, but the dismissive treatment of 1C in Francis scholarship goes against this principle. It was harder to fool people about Francis's desires in 1228 than it was in 1250. Nearly all the reports are hagiographic, and what is true for the compiler of a saint's life may not be so for a critical historian. There is no source that is privileged per se. But when Francis is acting in ways that are contrary to the hagiographic conventions, or when he is shown engaged in unbecoming behavior after his conversion (e.g., berating a brother who is ministering to him when sick), we should pay careful attention.

Conversely, when Francis acts according to conventions of medieval religion that seem alien to moderns (e.g., believing in diabolical obsession), there too we need to pay attention. In the first case, this is because it is unlikely to be made up; in the second case, because modern prejudices might lead us to dismiss the report.

A good number of events in Francis's life are preserved in more than one report. These doublets are sometimes very different. The principles I follow in choosing the version to follow are the normal ones of historical criticism. When one report is the source of the other, the original is usually to be preferred. When one version is allegorized, and the other is not, the bare text is preferred. When a story lacking in the miraculous is reworked into a miracle, the down-to-earth version is more trustworthy. I have no doubt that Francis did things that even today might be considered marvels, but hagiographers will give even the most jejune event a miraculous spin, because saints work miracles as part of their job description. I am especially skeptical of stories that have Francis playing the prophet about betrayals of his vision or conflicts in the order long after his death. These prophecies seem obviously *ex eventu,* especially when they serve to confirm the Franciscan politics of those recounting them.

I would like, in conclusion, to summarize the times when my strong inclination is to reject a report, at least in its payoff or implications. First, when the report seems to score points in later Franciscan controversies; second, when the story seems to be crafted to communicate some particular theological position; and third, when the author tells us directly what the story means—such interpretations are self-evidently the author's. Finally, and most important, I am highly skeptical of all reports that suggest no real development in Francis's ideas after his conversion. Even modern biographers as critical and solid as Manselli have been willing to read Francis's later ideas back into the period right after his conversion. The result is a Francis who stands outside of the events around him, and who tries to impose on his followers a vision perfectly formed at his conversion. This is a hagiographic topos: the sinner perfected by grace. There is very much to suggest that Francis spent much of his time groping for solutions to situations that he did not expect to encounter. Careful reading suggests that much of the time Francis had to react to new, concrete situations; he did not carry out some abstract vision or plan.

ON CHAPTER ONE

M ANSELLI (1982), 28–61, covers the period of this chapter, but he reads the evidence differently in many ways. As his work is closest to mine as a critical biography, at the beginning of each chapter, I will flag where we cover the same material. I will also flag for each chapter André Vauchez (2009), the best current scholarly biography of Francis. The material of this chapter is covered by Vauchez (2009), 25–62. For both works, I will comment directly, however, only on the major disagreements concerning facts, chronology, and interpretation of sources.

Francis's City, Home, and Family

Medieval Assisi (pp. 3–5)
The foundational study of Francis's family is Bracaloni (1932). Manselli (1982), 20–27, sketches conditions in Assisi at the time of Francis but errs on the identity of Conrad of Urslingen. More complete on the physical environment of medieval Assisi, but in Italian, is Bracaloni (1914). For a short review of the politics of this period, see Brown (1965), 420–21, who follows and corrects Fortini (1959), 1:1:134–64. Flood (1983), 11–13, also has an overview of this period. In French, Vauchez (2009), 25–40, is very complete on Assisi and its social and political life. These last four authors, however, overemphasize the "feudal" versus "mercantile" aspects of civic conflict. On Assisi in the time of Francis, see also Bracaloni (1914) and Langeli (1978). The most accessible short overview of the city in English is

probably Brown (1981). On medieval Italian cities generally, Hyde (1973) remains the best short study.

Francis's family home (p. 5)

Brown (1965), 385, identifies the controversy over the house of Saint Francis as one of the most bitter and unedifying of the last century. Archaeological discoveries, reported in Muscat (2005), § 12.4–12, have finally, we hope, put this controversy to rest. Excavations under the Convento di San Antonio on Via San Paolo uncovered the remains of the walls of the old Platea Nova, which is now covered by the Torre and Palazzo of the Capitano del Popolo, the Costanzi house, and the Sacro Convento itself. These walls are now open to public view. Central to the debate was the expansion of the Piazza del Mercato to form the Piazza Nuova in 1228–29. Householders affected by the construction included the sons of Francis's brother, Angelo di Pica, a merchant like his father, Pietro.

The San Nicolò house had first been identified as Francis's birthplace by Fortini (1959), 1:1:112, using documents of assessment and land conveyance in the Assisi archives. For a summary of the debate about Francis's birthplace before the archaeological discoveries during the late 1990s (which answered his call for an "impartial" investigation), see Muscat (2005), and Brown (1965), 407–19, esp. 418–19. Bracaloni (1943), 247–53, who wrongly argued for the authenticity of the Chiesa Nova house, edits the document trail. For a transcript of the 1229 tax assessment for the family house (6£ 10s luchese—the highest tax on a house in Assisi was 11£), see Bracaloni (1943), 247–48. This document is Assisi: Archivio Comunale, segnata M.1, fol. 4 (now in the Biblioteca Comunale). Older scholars had attempted to link these documents to houses on the sites of what are today the two sanctuaries of St. Francis, the Chiesa Nova (with its supposed cell where Francis's father imprisoned him) and the oratory of San Francesco Piccolino (location of the stable that was supposedly the saint's birthplace). These sites are found to the east and south of the Piazza del Comune.

Francis's family (p. 5)

Francis and his early biographer Thomas of Celano (1C 4; 2C 31) were very conscious of his commoner origin. On attempts to provide Francis with noble lineage (for both sides of his family), see Bracaloni (1932), who rightly rejected these. Fortini (1959), 2:197, and Trexler (1989), 11–12, reject noble ancestry for both sides of the family. Brown (1965), 400–401, dispatches the old attempts to identify Francis's mother with a noble family from Picardy in France. De Beer (1963), 73, summarizes the evidence that Francis's father was not noble: 1C 13

(Francis is *impar* to a knight); 2C 31 (he was not noble like Bro. Leonard); 2C 34 (the family did not socialize with older noble families). De Beer considers vainglory, the desire to be a "noble," Francis's principal youthful fault.

Francis's father, Pietro di Bernardone (p. 6)

Brown (1965), 397–99, outlines what is known about Pietro di Bernardone. Fortini (1959), 2:102–12, describes his land investments. Mockler (1980) tries to problematize the conventional image of Pietro. The best dating for his death is before 1215, when his son Angelo appears without patronymic as "Angelo di Pica." Trexler (1989), 10, suggests Pietro's rural origins based on 1C 53.

Francis's mother, Pica (pp. 6–7)

See Trexler (1989), 9–17, on Pica's family. When a member of an Italian family died, it was common to "remake" the deceased by naming the next child born after that person. So Angelo's remaking of Pica in his son Piccardo allows us to date her death between 1204 and 1211. Fortini (1959), 2:95, suggests that there were several children in the family because of the reference to "other children" in L3C 9.

The argument that Pietro traded on Pica's dowry is the principal thesis of Trexler (1989). Barbero (1990) argued that Trexler's identification of the "Angelo documents" with Francis's family was merely conjectural and (ibid., 843–46) that "pater" is the antecedent of the "eius" modifying what Francis is to renounce in 1C. No one doubts that all the sources have fashioned the renunciation story as a conflict between father and son. Were this merely a legal case about Francis's claim on the inheritance from his father, however, Pietro could simply could have disinherited him, allowing more or all of the wealth to go to Angelo. The archival evidence has now confirmed the extent of Pica's family's wealth in contrast to Pietro's own. Barbero is thus unconvincing. I know of no other attempt to discredit Trexler's conclusions. See Bracaloni (1943), 248–49, on the 1253 division of Angelo's property between Piccardo and Giovannetto di fu Angelo di Pica. Piccardo di Angelo later became a syndic for the basilica of San Francesco: Fortini (1959), 2:96.

Birth and Youth

Francis's birth and baptism (p. 7)

Scholarly consensus on Francis's birth date is that nothing more specific than 1181/2 is possible. Brown (1965), 373, who prefers 1181, summarizes the arguments both ways. Di Fonzo (1982), 46, makes a valiant effort to establish a more specific date (between December 1181 and February 1182); others try to tie the day to the saint's "name day" on the feast of the Nativity of John the Baptist (24 June). Di Fonzo (1982), 40–42, is good for the technicalities of the dating arguments. Abate (1949) traces the development of the rich complex of late medieval legends that came to cluster around Francis's birth, itself supposedly in a stable and foretold by a beggar pilgrim's prophecies, the historicity of which he does not question. Modern critics have relegated these legends to the world of pious myth. I agree.

If Francis was baptized in 1181, the date of that event would be 5 April; if the event was in 1182, it would be 17 April. The acrimonious debate between Abate (1949) and Fortini (1959) about Francis's baptism is outlined in Brown (1965), 405–6. In any case, Francis could not have been baptized at his parish church, San Nicolò, much less at San Giorgio, which was a hospital chapel, because they were not baptismal churches. Bracaloni (1943), 8, correctly identifies the cathedral as Assisi's only baptismal church in the 1180s. For Easter baptismal practices in high medieval Italy, see Thompson (2005), 320–35.

Francis's name (pp. 7–8)
Sources like L3C 2 and its parallel, 2C 3, report that Francis was baptized John and renamed by his father; they also record that his mother prophesied his later holiness. Bihl (1919) long ago demonstrated that the name Francesco was not at all as rare as 2C 3 suggests, but was common as a proper name and a place-name. But he does not reject the idea that Giovanni (John) was the saint's baptismal name. De Beer (1963), 179, notes the biblical typology of the name John in L3C, where it first appears, although he does not rule it out as Francis's original name. The biblical typology that controls the saint's name change makes me very suspicious of its historicity.

Francis's education (p. 8)
Dalarun (1997), 191, accepts the report in L3C 9 that Francis was his mother's favorite; if we are to believe the story of his spiteful treatment by his brother Angelo in L3C 23, there may have been some sibling rivalry. That Francis was educated at San Giorgio is based on its use as his burial place (1C 127), rather than on any direct evidence. For sensible comments on what we can really know of Francis's education, see Scivoletto (1977), 108 n. 8. As De Beer (1977), 33, notes, sources often play up Francis "illiteracy" to make him fit the model of the "illiterate fishermen" who were the apostles of Christ. On Francis's ability to write in Italian and Latin and his calligraphic style, see Langeli (1994).

Francis's character (pp. 7–9)
AP 3 and L3C 2 report Francis's entrance into the merchant trade and place it before the battle of Collestrada (summer 1202). See 1C 2, AP 3, and L3C 3 for

contrasting descriptions of Francis's youthful character. My hermeneutic here, and throughout this book, is that proposed by De Beer (1963), 294, 299–300; hagiographers clean up contradictory actions and odd behavior by making them symbolic of spiritual realities. On De Beer's method, see also Miccoli (1964), who refines some of De Beer's comparisons by rejecting the theological glossing of events. The historian should trust the facts reported, especially when odd, but ignore the theology that explains them away.

On the diverse views of the youthful Francis in the sources, see Cracco (1982), 107–11. 1C 1–3 is based more on hagiographic models than direct reports. In it, Francis's youth is bad in all respects; his conversion is the result of illness and a spiritual struggle. I agree with Dalarun (1996), 197–207, that L3C seems to report firsthand, or close to firsthand, information on Assisi and Francis's family and works it into the chronology of 1C. L3C shows a more mixed family background, but Francis still struggles to find his mission. Nevertheless, L3C adds prophetic elements and presents a picture of a man destined to become a saint. These are theological glosses. 2C rewrites L3C's narrative even further: the family remains mixed, but Francis is good from the beginning, gets his mission as a result of a direct call from God, and responds immediately.

My characterization of the preimprisonment Francis generally follows L3C, as the least theologically rewritten. I discount prophecies by Francis's mother and Francis's predestination to sainthood as theological commentary.

Francis's "sins" (p. 9)
There has been a long-running debate on how "debauched" the young Francis was. 1C 1–2, with its generalized "evil youth" patterned on Augustine's *Confessions,* is the only source for a debauched Francis, although it is perhaps confirmed by 1C 3's reference to his *lubrica aetas.* 1C woodenly patterns its report on Test 1–6, as Dalarun (1996), 104–7, observes. 1C uses Augustine's *Confessions* to expand on the Testament's phrase "when I was in my sins." The pattern is clear: 1C borrows the description of the habit from the Testament; the kissing of the San Damiano priest's hands in 1C parallels the Testament's praise for Roman priests; rebuilding churches parallels Francis's respect for them in the Testament, etc. It is just this fidelity to the Testament that, for me, gives 1C whatever credibility it has for this period. 1C conforms any informants' stories to Francis's own narrative.

De Beer (1963), 69–74, summarizes the debate on Francis's "sins." Some older writers discount the implied sensuality of 1C (Bihl), some elaborate on it (Jørgenson, Englebert), and others are undecided (Sabatier, Gratien). Manselli rejected the sensual Francis, but Dalarun (1996), 122–23, was willing to entertain it, only finally to reject it, at least in a sexual form. I would consider a "debauched Francis" at best unproved. Of his sex life, we know absolutely nothing. But there are nonhagiographic confirmations for the descriptions of Francis and his friends reveling. Fortini (1959), 1:1:116, confirmed the existence of youthful eating and drinking fraternities in Assisi like those alluded to in L3C 8 and 2C 7. Desbonnets (1983), 67, notes that the documents mentioning the "society of the wand" date only to 1382 and 1416, but this does not mean we should exclude the witness of L3C to them for the early 1200s; as a source it is quite good on Assisi civic culture.

The poor beggar (p. 9)

The incident of rudeness to the beggar in the family shop is found in AP 4 and L3C 3; cf. 1C 17. De Beer (1963), 50, correctly reads the parallel of the poor beggar incident in 1C 17 and L3C 3. C2 5 is a doublet, where an ordinary beggar is replaced by a poor knight. For 2C this functions literarily as a lead-in to Francis's military dreams. I thus accept only the ordinary beggar story.

Military Adventures

Francis and chivalry (pp. 9–10)

Francis served in the army; did he have "chivalric" aspirations? Cardini (1976), 151–58, 168–70, notes that AC never uses military allegory but does have Francis quoting the Arthurian legends. In contrast, L3C is filled with such rhetoric. Pásztor (1985), 54, is skeptical of the chivalric images and aspirations ascribed to Francis by 1C and L3C; Dalarun (1997), 205–10, notes that L3C and AC are the sources for courtly language in the later tradition and that Francis's own writings lack it. I agree that this characterization of Francis seems too much like the thirteenth-century stereotyped merchant longing for noble status to be very trustworthy. But such aspirations are not impossible. Francis was indeed a thirteenth-century merchant.

The function of chivalric images in sources for Francis, with some attempt to detect the historical reality, is the subject of Cardini (1976), esp. 175–80, where he is less skeptical than Dalarun or Pásztor. Cardini leaves unsettled the question of how much is hagiographic embroidery, but he emphasizes the military quality of male life in the communes. Manselli (1980), 63, for his part, rejects the Miles Christi image of Francis, at least as found in 2C, but he says nothing on Francis's preconversion aspirations. Francis did, after all, serve at least once as a soldier.

The battle of Collestrada (p. 10)

For Umbrian politics before and after Collestrada, see Brown (1965) and Flood (1983), 11–12. On Francis's participation in Collestrada, imprisonment, and

subsequent illness, see L3C 4; cf. 1C 3. Fortini (1959), 2:178, rejects the assertion of L3C 3 that Francis was prisoner for only a year, because the truce was
not signed until August 1205. Actually the war did not end until 1210. We do
not have enough information to reject the L3S report.

The "Dream of Arms" (p. 10)

This dream is reported in 1C 5, AP 5, and L3C 5. 1C and AP are oldest; L3C
is derivative; for more on the relationship of the texts, see Desbonnets (1972),
91. The simplest version is that of 1C, which Brooke (2006), 139, considers
probably closest to the original events. The sources (especially L3C) make
this dream symbolic of Francis's later status as a Miles Christi, thus giving the
founding of the Franciscan movement a chivalric character. On the dream,
see Cardini (1980), esp. 15–28, on the prophetic elements hagiographers tend
to read back into Francis's dreams and their attempt to turn this dream into a
"conversion experience." Cardini (1980), 22, sees the chivalric dream as symbolically antibourgeois. It is interesting that the later writers—AP, L3C, and
2C—omit or diminish 1C's description of Francis's illness, while they embel-
lish the dream, turning the house into a palace and loading it with theological
significance. The less allegorical version of the dream is most likely the most
primitive.

The Apulia excursion (pp. 10–11)

As the early hagiographers describe it, the "Dream of Arms" helped restore
Francis's joyful outlook. Rather, I suspect, it triggered a spurt of activity that
presented itself as a restoration of his previous demeanor but was actually a
form of the "avoidance" noted in what we now call post-traumatic stress disorder. See National Center for PTSD (2010), where the symptoms described
are remarkably like those assigned to Francis by 1C 3–4: feeling numb, including loss of affection for friends and delight in things previously enjoyable;
increased emotional arousal, including sleep problems; lack of concentration;
avoidance, keeping away from people; and reliving the experience, including dreams. I would understand the Dream of Arms as part of something like
PTSD, which would make that dream not only wholly believable, but very
disturbing to Francis.

   Following AP 5, Beguin (1979), 111, sees the Apulia excursion as a carefully thought-out "change of career," resulting from Francis's meditation on
the Dream of Arms. Francis's erratic behavior before and during the expedition seems to rule out such a careful calculation. But I agree with Beguin's
decision to follow AP 5 in putting the dream at the beginning of the preparations, not in the middle, as 1C does. Compared to 1C, AP is generally well

informed on this period, and the disturbed Francis would have been grasping at straws. 1C 5 explicitly states that he had to "force himself" to go on with preparations. The PTSD parallels are again striking. There is debate over the exact date of the Apulia excursion, on which see Di Fonzo (1982), 61–64.

On Francis's gift of his horse and arms to the poor knight (L3C 6; 2C 5) and its modeling on the life of Saint Martin of Tours, see Fortini (1959), 1:1:228–31. This erratic behavior fits so well with Francis's state of mind that I accept it, in spite of the use of a hagiographic model. I do very much, however, doubt the theological gloss that this was another example of Francis's generous spirit. It was simply the kind of erratic behavior the veteran was exhibiting at this time.

There is much speculation about the commander whom Francis planned to join. No count appears in 1C or 2C. AP speaks of a "comitem gentilem," with no proper name. L3C turns "gentilem" into a proper name. LMj 1.3 backtracks to "quemdam liberalem comitem." Brown (1965), 425–26, Manselli (1982), 48–50, and now Vauchez (2009), 46, all identify the count as Walter of Brienne, brother of John of Brienne, king of Jerusalem, who was later much devoted to Francis and became a Franciscan tertiary. Di Fonzo (1982), 60, accepted "Gentile" as a proper name, and so identified him as Gentile of Pagliara, Count of Manoppello. He rejected the identification as Walter of Brienne, who was killed 14 June 1205 while fighting in Apulia after his conquest of the region in 1201. I too reject this identification. Aside from the question of who was fighting in Apulia in the spring of 1205, I have my doubts about whether this "count" ever existed, at least as a player in the planning by the anonymous Assisi nobleman and Francis.

The "Dream of the Master or Servant" (p. 11)
This dream, lacking in 1C, is recounted in AP 6, L3C 6, and 2C 6 and becomes, in the later two sources, a prophetic dream about service of God. In AP it is not explicitly a dream, but more a bedtime conversation with an unidentified someone. Francis's squire would be a logical interlocutor. Nor does AP suggest that the "lord" and the "servant" here are anything but human figures. This form, the most primitive and nontheological, seems most convincing to me.

The sale at Foligno (p. 11)
On the return from Spoleto, see 1C 6–8; AP 6–7; L3C 7–16; 2C 6–11. The chronology of Francis's stop at Foligno to sell his military supplies is perhaps one of the most controversial choices I will make in this biography, and I know that I am dissenting from virtually all modern biographies of Francis, including Manselli (1982), 49–57, whom I very much respect.

Beguin (1979), 114–16, virtually alone, argued for trusting AP, against Di Fonzo, who tried to finesse the text's Latin to harmonize with the other sources (see FA:ED 2:36 n. c). I believe not only that the received Latin version of AP is the original, but that AP is also correct on the chronology. AP 7 places the sale of property at Foligno on the way back from Spoleto, with no return to Assisi first. 1C has a return to Assisi, but the report is very brief and consists mainly of Francis trying to decide what to do and praying in caves with an anonymous friend. L3C 6–15 and 2C 6–10 interject a large mass of material at this point. 2C omits the entire Foligno sale story. My conclusion, admittedly tentative, is that Francis sold his horse and finery on the way home. The incident was not that important in Francis's spiritual development; it was yet another of his vacillations. Francis's sale at Foligno, the first big town on the way north, was simply a logical way to disburden himself of unneeded gear.

Sketchy as it is, 1C still deserves consideration as the earliest version. It has Francis return to Assisi, then go to Foligno, then return to Assisi. This presents problems on several levels. 1C knows virtually nothing about the return and sale but, wanting to emphasize poverty (the sale of goods and giving away of money), it literarily provides the Foligno sale with a spiritual buildup by placing it after the story of Francis praying in caves for inspiration. The theological concerns, and the literary structure that highlights them, are obvious. AP has no theological agenda of this type. De Beer (1963), 285–86, has also listed the inconsistencies and contradictions in 1C 7 and concluded that this version of Francis's return to Assisi is simply unbelievable as written. Celano could not have known about Francis's prayers in caves where no one else was present. In 1C, Francis converts and then reconstructs San Damiano for no apparent reason; then, when talking to the San Damiano priest, Francis refers to the Franciscan Order before it has been founded. Celano was obviously struggling to make sense of an incoherent story.

If one wants to accept the traditional chronology founded on 1C, then, as Bertoli (1993), 167, suggests, the L3C version is more coherent than 1C, because the to-ing and fro-ing can be explained by the speaking cross at San Damiano. This is exactly why I completely distrust L3C on this; that source inserts a miracle to resolve the incoherence in 1C. L3C also interpolates a number of preconversion stories into 1C's gaps. I will discuss these stories in the next section, "The great L3C intrusion." By introducing the miracle of the speaking cross at San Damiano as the sale's trigger, L3C 13 makes the sale a response to Francis's divine and precocious conversion to poverty. Yet at this point in all the narratives Francis has not even renounced his inheritance! The early appearance of the poverty theme in 1C, L3C, and 2C is proleptic.

Readers who want a consideration of what the incident might mean, if it really happened the way 1C describes it, may consult Manselli (1982), 54–57, who also accepts the speaking cross as a historical event. I agree with Beguin (1979), 115–16, in his reading of AP, that Francis merely wanted the priest to hold the money for safekeeping, and then, when he met resistance, just went off, abandoning the money.

The "great L3C intrusion" (p. 11)

Given the theological motives that the four sources have for structuring their narratives as they do, and my decision to accept the AP version of the Foligno sale, the major question is how to treat the "great L3C intrusion" (sections 7–15) between Spoleto and the Foligno sale. This intrusion greatly expands on 1C 7's short mention of Francis praying in caves. It is historically hard to believe that a mere sale of merchandise (or even a horse and arms) would have triggered the violent reaction by Francis's father that all the sources report. In contrast, when L3C 7–15 places Francis's erratic and downright bizarre behavior after the Foligno sale, Pietro di Bernardone's growing exasperation with his son makes excellent sense. Two parts, however, of the "great L3C intrusion," L3C 11 (parallel with 2C 9) on the lepers, and the obvious retrojection of later spiritual habits in L3C 14–15, are out of chronological order and reflect the postrenunciation Francis. I will discuss the leper incident later. I think that L3C's other erratic behavior makes perfect sense as the trigger for Pietro's wrath. It is very significant that when Celano reworked the earlier material in 2C, he omitted the entire Foligno sale. He understood that it was not the central event he had originally made it.

AP 7, 1C 9, L3C 13, and 2C 11 recount the story of Francis abandoning the Foligno sale money at San Damiano. 1C says that the money was to be "given to the poor." L3C 13 and 2C 10 omit that reason and say that it was to be used to restore San Damiano in response to Francis's misunderstanding of the speaking cross's request to "rebuild my church." I consider the speaking cross to be a theological elaboration on PrCr, crafted to make sense of the sudden trip back to Foligno that these narratives require. Bertoli (1993), 169–70, considered the 1C story of the abandoned money an elaboration on TestCl 10–14, because of the prophetic mention of the nuns at this point in this source.

AP is more modest. It merely says that the money was left at San Damiano for safekeeping; no secret motive is revealed. De Beer (1963), 54, correctly observes that in the two earliest versions (1C 9 and AP 7), the gesture is spontaneous and even capricious. This is the least theologized version of the event. So this embarrassing fact seems likely to be historical. Of the two versions, I follow AP as more likely to be from a witness with personal knowledge.

Francis in Crisis

Sources

The four earliest sources for the period after Francis's return from Apulia in 1205 until the arrival of his first disciples in 1208 (1C, AP, L3C, and 2C) present the events in conflicting chronological order and theologize them in diverse ways. The most extended essay on the narratives of Francis's "conversion" is De Beer (1963), which Miccoli (1964) finds superficial and lacking. Those interested in the contrasting chronologies and theologies of the sources can find them quickly summarized in Frugoni (1984), which also includes analysis of LMj and the frescoes ascribed to Giotto in the Assisi basilica. I agree with Manselli (1995), 29, when he urges that we focus on Francis's interior state, rather than external acts, during this period of his life.

1C has a rapid movement from "sin" to "conversion," which is God's work more than Francis's. But, having relatively little material to work with, 1C employs hagiographic stereotypes. The result is a conversion from generic sin to generic grace. L3C fits a series of dislocated incidents into 1C's chronology between Francis's return from Apulia and the renunciation of his inheritance, tracing Francis's long struggle to find a way to serve Christ. For L3C, the conversion becomes Francis's victory over his mercantile lust for money. For example, the speaking cross at San Damiano triggers the Foligno sale (Francis has to disburden himself of possessions); in contrast, the 1C sale was the result of a finished conversion from "sin." Frugoni (1984) does not deal with AP, which constructs Francis's "conversion" as one from chivalric vanity to personal humility. In AP, the Foligno sale is the beginning of Francis's conversion, not its conclusion. The divergences among the major narrative sources indicate that the confused events during Francis's return from Apulia did not explain themselves.

Francis in turmoil (pp. 12–13)

Francis's erratic behavior and our sources for it are the following: distractions while partying, L3C 8; 2C 26; giving away food from the family table, L3C 9; 2C 27; the Rome pilgrimage, L3C 10; 2C 28; hiding in caves to pray, 1C 7; L3C 12; 2C 11; taking refuge at San Damiano, 1C 9; L3C 13, 16; 2C 11.

All these sources have strong poverty themes. I doubt Francis had any clear plans for the future at this point. Trexler (1989), 44–45, correctly notes that even if Francis intended to give the sale money away, he still failed to do what he would later require of Bernard: sell everything and give it to the poor. There is no good evidence that Francis had a conversion to poverty at this point in his life. Whom did this money belong to, Francis or his father?

This question becomes important only if we take the San Damiano cash as the motive for Pietro's wrath. I doubt that either Francis or Pietro would have been legalistic about ownership at this point. Francis was still a member of the family, and when he had previously given away military trappings, that does not seem to have caused much of a rift with Pietro. I suspect that Pietro's anger with Francis was not about the Foligno sale or the money from it. I will consider the real issue later. Dalarun (1996), 199, rejects the Rome pilgrimage story in L3C as an anticipatory account legitimizing Francis's later trips there. I do not see it as anticipatory, but I am uncomfortable with the precocious emphasis on poverty in the reports.

Francis's spiritual moves (p. 11)

Francis's internal tribulations on returning to Assisi are graphically described (and carefully theologized) in L3C and, more concisely, in 2C. 1C 7 has a short parallel passage that adds nothing to those two passages. Stripped of the theological interpretations, which make Francis's every step a God-guided, even predestined, journey from holiness to holiness, the events themselves paint a vivid picture of a thirteenth-century Italian layman drawing on traditional piety and practice to confront a bitter spiritual desert. The same PTSD-like symptoms that marked Francis on his return from Perugia continue and are, in some ways, intensified. As this continuity has verisimilitude, I follow L3C (and its parallels).

The "prayer before the crucifix" at San Damiano (p. 11)

My recounting of Francis's time at San Damiano includes the text of PrCr (FA:ED 1:40) as it is found, in Latin, in two L3C manuscripts: Barcelona, Biblioteca Central, MS 655 (ca. 1405) and Fribourg, Bibliothèque des Cordeliers, MS 23J60 (ca. 1406). There are many Italian versions of this prayer, all apparently translations from the Latin. Both L3C 14 and AC 78 portray Francis as convulsed with compassion for the crucified Christ, and sobbing as he prayed before the San Damiano cross. Whether the San Damiano cross spoke to him in words or not, prayer before it reordered the young man's emotions and aspirations. On AC 78 (and its derivative parallel in the "common" recension of L3C 14), see Manselli (1980), 159–62, who places it early in Francis's life, not late or after the stigmata. I agree.

At San Damiano: "Rebuild my church" (pp. 11–12)

During Francis's prayer at San Damiano, both L3C 12 and 2C 10 include the famous speaking crucifix that gave Francis a mission to "rebuild my church." I consider this event theological elaboration, and not historical, for several reasons: (1) It is absent in the two earliest and most sober lives, 1C and AP. (2) It is meant to explain theologically what appears to be random behavior (church repair). (3) Most importantly, it is crafted as a prophecy of Francis's future role in "saving the Church." L3C proleptically ties the event to that document's emphasis on Francis's almsgiving as a precursor of Franciscan absolute poverty. So, in that text, it functions as the divine commission that Francis's greedy father cannot understand. I will not commit myself to claiming that Francis did not have some mystical experience of some sort during prayer (perhaps he did), but the incident's clear literary function in L3C counts against it as historical.

That since his return Francis had been soliciting advice from Bishop Guido is admitted (with reluctance, because God is really guiding the saint) in L3C 10. That Francis has become, or will soon become, a penitent, subject to the ecclesiastical forum at law, seems obvious in L3C 19, in which the city remands his father's case to the ecclesiastical court. It is possible that he was a brother of penance by this time, but the Fratres et Sorores de Penitentia were, in 1206, still a very young and unformed movement. However, independent penitents attached to churches were already common: see Thompson (2005), 77–82. It is just as likely that Francis was simply a *conversus,* a private penitent attached to a local church, here probably San Damiano. But there was little difference between a *conversus* and a brother of penance at this date.

Francis "Leaves the World"

On the date 1205 (p. 14)
My use of 1205 here depends on the date of Francis's "conversion," on which much ink has been spilled. Whatever actually happened in Francis's early life, the "conversion" is essential to the calculation of dates in 1C, and it seems clear that 1C intended the "conversion" to be Francis's hearing of the Gospel at San Damiano. Depending on how one calculates from Francis's death in early October 1225, using 1C 109's formula "conversionis suae tempus iam erat viginti annorum spatio," the year of the conversion could be either 1205 or 1206. Di Fonzo (1982), 20–39, reviewed the debates and found that, among previous authors, Franciscan scholars favored 1205 by 6 to 2, while non-Franciscans favored 1206 by 5 to 4.

Although this debate is hardly over, I find Brown (1965), 369–73, the most convincing. He puts the 1C conversion in 1206, and I calculate dates accordingly. This date makes sense of the largest number of 1C's relative dates when these can be correlated with known absolute dates. Using Brown's hypothesis, only two of 1C's dates do not work; one is the use of the calendar year for a date given after Francis's death (perhaps related to use of the canonization bull?), and the other is the traditional dating of the "Mass of the Apostles," which I consider a red herring, as I will explain later.

Now, Celano considered the "conversion" to have been in summer, but we know that Francis's decision to "exire de saeculo" (Test 3) happened "soon" after his encounter with the lepers, which is recounted in 1C 17. And, as we know from 1C that Francis's renunciation was followed by snowy weather, the renunciation would better be placed in winter 1206 (snow during the fall in Assisi seems less likely). Readers who want more details may consult Brown.

Francis hides from Pietro di Bernardone (pp. 14–15)
1C says that Francis hid in a pit "in the house" (which would seem to be the San Damiano priest's house); L3C says he hid in a cave. This cave story seems something of a doublet with the cave of 1C 7 and L3C 12. 2C 9 (the parallel of these two passages) speaks only of seclusion, not of caves, and it omits the entire hiding incident. There is nothing like this in AP. I am uncomfortable with the whole story, especially the cave/pit part of it. Perhaps the origin of the story is that it took Pietro a month to track down his son's whereabouts, and so Francis must have been hiding someplace. Francis's capture, "house arrest," and escape are recounted in 1C 11–13 and L3C 16–18, but omitted in 2C.

The reader will notice that I have a rather sympathetic view of Pietro di Bernardone in his problems with his son. All sources agree that both his parents loved Francis, but they did so "carnally." That is to say, they did not immediately recognize what the hagiographers, especially 1C, take as a given: that God was guiding Francis, who was already on the way to becoming a great saint. I do not fault the parents for that, nor do the modern historians summarized by Pásztor (1985), 52–54. Dalarun (1997), 191, notes that later sources (L3C; 2C) make Pietro worse and Pica better. As Trexler (1989), 13, observes, this conforms to the hagiographic stereotype of the "good mother, bad father." As Manselli (1980), 14, concluded, later sources also reflect the order's desire for better relations with the family of Pica's son Angelo after Francis's death. I agree with Dalarun (1996), 113, that the Pietro of the sources is a more complex figure than he is usually presented as being.

What did Francis renounce? (pp. 15–16)
Most people's images of the renunciation before the bishop have been formed by paintings or (worse) movies and television. 1C 15, AP 8, L3C 19, and 2C 12 elaborate on the legal process of Francis's renunciation. 1C makes a point of the fact that Francis is twenty-five and therefore of age. Trexler (1989), 34–37, emphasizing Francis's majority, has him renouncing a claim to the Foligno sale cash because it was his father's money, and Francis did not want contact with

funds contaminated by Pietro's usury. Such contamination would be doubly bad for one in the religious state. This is a possible reading of the bishop's advice to Francis in L3C and 2C. But I do not think much can be made of this, since in both L3C and 2C the money at stake is the purse from Foligno—not the inheritance, as in 1C—and one might just as well consider it "tainted" because it came from the sale of the horse and arms.

In our oldest source—1C 15—it is Francis's "inheritance" (whether from mother or father is not said) that is at stake in court, and not the Foligno sale money. L3C and 2C make the story turn on the sale money so as to highlight Pietro's greed for a purse of cash with little value. In contrast, 1C tells us Francis happily returned the purse, but that this did nothing to change Pietro's attitude. The two court actions by Pietro (before city and bishop) were not over proceeds of the sale, as L3C 19 suggests.

Rather, I find the further contention of Trexler (1989), 27–34, 59–65, that the money at stake was Pica's dowry completely believable, in spite of the criticisms of Barbero (1990). Barbero's contention that the Foligno money belonged to Francis may be correct, but no historian now considers that sum part of the legal action before city or bishop. No source before LMj 2.4 describes Francis as renouncing his "paternal" inheritance. Trexler (1989), 71–102, shows that Pica and family members appear in the earliest paintings of the renunciation, those at Assisi, implying they are involved. Only in later art does the encounter get reduced to Francis versus Pietro alone. The famous fresco of the event in the Assisi basilica is nicely analyzed by Brooke (2006), 377–78.

That Pietro could have lost much of his business assets to the unstable Francis if Pica died goes a long way to explain why he took his son to court (twice). Cardini (1976), 191, compares Bishop Guido's action of covering Francis with the rituals of joining a chivalric society; it is more reasonable to see it as based on a rite of religious procession among the *conversi*.

Francis and the robbers (p. 16)
De Beer (1963), 107–10, notes Francis's sense of freedom in 1C after the renunciation. Francis's wanderings after the renunciation are reported only in 1C 16, where they directly precede his encounter with the lepers in 1C 17. The parallel encounters with lepers are L3C 11 and 2C 9. Dalarun (1997), 203— quoting Cardini (1976), 196, and with Cardini (1983a), 57–58—thinks that the "chivalric" language used by Francis in the encounter with the robbers is "a genuine cultural impulse." Although I am skeptical that this language is really Francis's, the phrase "Herald of the Great King" seems about as authentically Franciscan as one can get.

Francis and the lepers (pp. 16–17)
That 1C 17 has the right chronology, as well as the least reworked version of the leper incident, seems obvious. L3C and 2C reverse the order of serving at the leprosarium and kissing the single leper on the road, which makes the kiss (of Jesus?) the formative mystical experience, contrary to the sense of the Testament, where the lepers are plural. L3C prefaces the leper incident with a vision in which the Testament's reversal of sweet and bitter is put into the mouth of God himself. 2C turns the leper into a Christ figure, who vanishes after getting alms and a kiss. See Miccoli (1964), 784–85, on these theological transformations, and Manselli (1980), 19–21, who contrasts the absence of the poverty theme in the Testament with its dominance in L3C and 2C. See Desbonnets (1972), 93, on the priority of L3C to 2C. The plain, unvarnished version of 1C is free of this kind of supernatural theologizing; it is the most primitive version.

More than anyone else, Raoul Manselli, in his articles and biography, has called our attention to the leper incident, which Francis makes the pivotal event of his spiritual life. Maranesi (2007) contrasts Francis's own conversion narrative (contact with the lepers) with that of the San Damiano cross (identified with Brother Leo and Clare) and argues that they complement each other. The treatment is suggestive, but as I consider the talking cross unhistorical, the conclusions have more to do with later Franciscan self-understanding than with the Historical Francis. In contrast to the spiritual movements of the eleventh century that, as described by Mollat (1967), made poverty their focus, and sound like Franciscans before the name, Manselli sees Francis's conversion as involving something more radical than material poverty. Theologically, Manselli (1975), 269–70, interprets the leper incident as Francis's discovery of "Christ crucified, Christ poor, Christ despised," in the marginalized. Manselli (1995), 192–96, extended this idea to include Francis's identification of his sinful self with the outcast, but he admits that Francis would have to develop this sophisticated understanding over the rest of his life. This sounds basically right to me, as far as it goes.

Other interpreters of the incident strike me as less perceptive. Miccoli (1991), 52–53, sees the leper incident as inverting worldly values, which, while true, seems to domesticate it. Others tend to retroject later Franciscan ideas about poverty into this very early period. For example, Flood (1983), 31, sees the leper incident as Francis's protest against bourgeois society and protocapitalism, especially as exemplified in the institutions of the Assisi church. This would mean that Francis was misunderstood by Church authorities from the beginning. To quote Flood (1983), 47, "Lepers loved Francis, Guido loved Francis but never understood him." This view has much in common with

Trexler (1989), 57, who made the renunciation of property to be Francis's conversion. Desbonnets (1983), 11, links the leper incident with "doing penance," which for him was "adopting voluntary poverty as a life style," a very modern Franciscan way to view it.

Schmucki (1986), 248–49, found in the leper incident a mystical reorientation of Francis's affections by God, and this interpretation is perhaps closest to my view in its cosmic significance. All the other interpretations, even Manselli's, smack of poverty retrojection from Francis's later life or even from debates after his death.

The lepers and "leaving the world" (pp. 16–17)
As Pellegrini (1977), 300, has pointed out, all the "conversion" narratives seem to provide a strict chronological order, which makes the positioning of the leper incident so important. Hagiographers knew that, in his Testament, Francis placed his "leaving the world" (*exire de saeculo*) "a little" after the encounter with the lepers. L3C and 2C make the renunciation of the inheritance into a choice for Franciscan poverty and treat it as, if not the only "conversion," at least the most important one. But Francis could not have considered the renunciation of the dowry as his "leaving the world." After all, he did not himself initiate it, and it involved no real change of state. It was merely the renouncing (albeit dramatic) of inheritance rights.

AP has no lepers, because this experience was private to Francis, and AP focuses on the early brothers as a group. L3C has theological motives for placing the leper incident before the renunciation of the dowry; the renunciation is about Franciscan poverty and refusal to touch money, and thus the central event. 2C mimics L3C for the same reasons. As theologically driven by the assimilation of poverty and conversion, the chronology in L3C and 2C should be rejected.

In contrast, only 1C 16 records any activity by Francis between the renunciation and the encounter with the lepers (recorded in 1C 17, L3C 11, and 2C 9), and only 1C puts the lepers after the renunciation. 1C 17 also puts the lepers before the "Mass of the Apostles" (1C 22) because, in that version, the Mass is the pivotal event in Francis's conversion, the decision to follow the Gospel on poverty. Although 1C's description of the Mass of the Apostles is dubious, as we shall see, that version has no theological motive to put the lepers after the renunciation. All things considered, 1C has the right order: renunciation, then lepers, then "conversion," that is, "leaving the world."

The most comprehensive treatment of what "exire de saeculo" would have meant for Francis is Koper (1959), who thinks it meant merely to abandon worldly concerns and focus on God, which I think ignores the more common medieval usage as entering a particular religious state. In contrast, Esser (1978), 115–17 (Karecki trans., 25–27), argues that "exire de saeculo" in the Testament means "to enter a religious state," and so to enjoy the *privilegium fori*. Thus Francis's "leaving the world" was the reason the inheritance case had to be passed to the bishop. I think that legal linkage is correct, but, as Scivoletto (1977), 115, notes, Francis's use of the phrase in his Testament alludes rather to 1 Cor. 5:10. I find the picture of Francis thinking in canonical terms very unlikely. That Francis placed his conversion before the renunciation, or even during it, is untenable. In the Testament, the "conversion" has to be after the leper incident, not before it.

Although he conflates the renunciation with the conversion, and his definition of "conversion" as "going to serve others" is (at least at this early date) retrojection, Manselli (1995), esp. 184–90, is right that becoming a brother of penance was not what Francis meant by "leaving the world." This was so, even if it had made him an "ecclesiastical person." No medieval source connects Francis's "conversion" with being a brother of penance. If he did become a brother of penance, which I think he did, given the loosely defined nature of a brother of penance at that time, it was before the renunciation, thus the dispute over the proper legal forum. Maranesi (2007), 296–97, suggests the link between Francis's expression of mercy to the lepers and his experience of God's mercy toward himself.

"Leaving the world" can thus only mean entering the form of life Francis took up after the leper incident. 1C describes it: living not merely as a penitent, but as a hermit in the woods, leaving that hermitage only to work among the lepers. For medieval Italians, brothers of penance were "in the world," even though ecclesiastical persons. Hermits have "left the world," even if they are attached to a church. Francis would have agreed. I conclude that for Francis, "leaving the world" was taking up the life of a full-time, freelance hermit.

ON CHAPTER TWO

A N INTRODUCTION, ALBEIT uncritical, to the material in this chapter is offered in Schmucki (1988), which is most useful for tracing Francis's knowledge and use of the Bible. Francis is more broadly considered for this period in Manselli (1982), 62–112. More detailed, especially for background, is Vauchez (2009), 62–102.

Francis at San Damiano

Church repair (pp. 19–20)

Sources for Francis's residence at, and repair of, San Damiano are 1C 18 and L3C 20–23. Lambertini-Tabarroni (1989), 29, discusses the importance of churches as residences for early Franciscans. It is no surprise that Francis returned to Assisi, and to the church where he had first found refuge. *Pace* Flood (1983), 9–10, 44–50, who utilizes Victor Turner's theory of liminality in arguing that Francis "left Assisi" to distance himself from its bourgeois protocapitalism, there is nothing in the sources to suggest that he planned to leave Assisi at this time. His veneration for the physical space of churches and his use of liturgical texts in prayer show Francis to be a typical medieval Italian layman: see Thompson (2005), 343–77. Miccoli (1991), 53–54, correctly sees Francis's choices in this period as an expression of Catholic orthodoxy against contemporary Cathar and Waldensian heretics, but I doubt that Francis was thinking in those theological terms.

The San Damiano cross (p. 21)
Readers will no doubt have noticed that I have omitted the famous "speaking cross" miracle. This miracle is absent from 1C 18, in which Francis simply reconstructs the church. L3C 13 uses this story, which becomes an allegorical prophecy, to explain a perfectly normal medieval penitential practice (church repair). Dalarun (1996), 88, agrees that the miracle is a theological gloss, not a historical event. As Miccoli (1991), 169, notes, 1C 21 speaks of Francis repairing another church after San Damiano, traditionally identified as that of San Pietro della Spina. With the Porziuncula, that gives the symbolic number of three churches. I am inclined to think (cf. L3C 27) that Francis repaired several churches; trying to calculate the number is speculation. As for a place of residence, only San Damiano is mentioned.

Begging (p. 21)
1C 18, L3C 20–24, and 2C 12–14 all present Francis as living by street begging in this period. Given that AP 12 and L3C 30 also describe him as using money to buy stones, the presentation of begging as Francis's means of support is, at best, incomplete. For me, the exclusive focus on begging smacks of retrojection of later Franciscan practice. I doubt Francis did much begging at all during this period. He used money that, if not his own, he earned by day labor. I am also unsure as to the incident where he begs for money to buy oil, but it is not impossible that Francis was out of cash on that occasion. The use of French when begging in Rome fits his known behavior (L3C 10; 2C 8). There is a discrepancy between L3C 22–23 and 2C 12–13 as to whether begging triggered family abuse. I follow L3C as the earlier (and more logical) presentation of the events.

Both Manselli (1982), 70, and Dalarun (1996), 78–79, accept this early begging as genuine. Dalarun (1996), 195, argues that L3C 24 is good on Assisi local events, and that Francis's words can be translated into rhyming French: "Venez m'aider en l'oeuvre ouvert à Saint-Damien, | En ce lieu qui sera monastère de dames | Dans l'Eglise entière et leur vie et leur fame | Viendront glorifier le Père célestien." The position of Manselli and Dalarun is odd, as both reject the Clare prophecy as later retrojection founded on 1C 19–20. I agree that the Clare prophecy is not historical, and that calls into question this French jingle. There seems, as Bertoli (1993), 172, notes, to have been a common source for Francis's prophecy about nuns at San Damiano behind L3C, 2C, and TestCl. Bertoli thinks TestCl is itself the source, but there is debate over the authenticity of Clare's Testament. Scholarly opinion remains mixed, but there seems to be a growing consensus that TestCl is the work of Clare over a number of years.

God Sends Francis Followers

Sources for the two years just before Francis's visit to Rome in 1209 are much better than those for the earlier period, if harder to interpret. Pellegrini (1994), 37–51, outlines the problems in the later sources for this period.

The "Mass of the Apostles" (p. 21)

Readers will also notice that I omit the "Mass of the Apostles" story (1C 22, repeated in L3C 25). This story is a doublet of the Gospel divination story in AP 11, L3C 27–29, and 2C 15. There are so many problems with 1C 22 that is hard to list them all: the quotes are not a single Mass Gospel; Francis had followers when he lived at the Porziuncula; the narrative is obviously modeled on the life of Saint Anthony of the Desert, etc. In contrast, AP 11 is wholly believable, if somewhat embarrassing for its "lay superstition." The event reported in AP must be placed after the arrival of followers. That both versions made it into the conflated L3C is not surprising. 1C has taken an earlier version of the divination story and cleaned it up; tellingly, in 2C, written after the divination story was in circulation, the Mass Gospel story is dropped.

All sources retroject later Franciscan practices into this period, making them divinely inspired norms, and the Mass Gospel becomes "the" revelation to the founder, as Miccoli (1964), 779, long ago noted. Later, Miccoli (1991), 181, decided that the Mass of the Apostles version was crafted to make Francis the sole founder of the order, inspired with the later Franciscan ideal immediately by God, and (ibid., 155) flatly rejected the Mass of the Apostles as unhistorical. Desbonnets (1983), 7–8, does not reject it out of hand but considers the AP 11 story more likely. Two authors did accept it as a historical event. Di Fonzo (1982), 78–82, struggled to find an actual Mass proper that would fit the story and finally opted for a hypothetical "Votive Mass of an Apostle." Manselli (1982), 71–73, simply accepts the event as historical, without resolving any of the problems it presents. Given the powerful arguments against this story, I reject it as unhistorical.

Francis's appearance (p. 22)

Beguin (1979), 16–17, perceptively notes that AP seems to draw on eyewitness testimony for Francis's appearance, probably that of Brother Bernard and Brother Giles: AP 10–14b, 15–16c 20b–22, 31–36d. Dalarun (1996), 109–11, agrees with this detection of the witnesses. With Dalarun (1996), 256–57, I reject the usual skepticism about the description of Francis in 1C 83. Although the text is a reworking of that in the *Vita Sancti Bernardi,* the changes are not flattering, and that gives this report verisimilitude. On the remarkable image in the Sacro Speco at Subiaco, see Brooke (2006), 160–64. She dates the fresco to the same period as the inscription on the dedication fresco (19 March 1228 to 18 March 1229). The lack of a halo, the use of the title "Frater" not "Sanctus," and the absence of the stigmata all suggest Francis had not yet been canonized when the fresco was painted. Gregory IX canonized Francis on 16 July 1228, thus my dating.

The first followers (p. 22)
Miccoli (1991), 168, thinks that the statement in 1C 21 that Francis found his form of life "three years" after his conversion should be taken symbolically. Brown (1965), 374–76, labors over the "three years" problem because he would have the "Mass of the Apostles" on the feast of St. Matthias, 24 February. Like Brown, Di Fonzo (1982), 84–85, dates the first followers to 1208, putting their arrival in the fall because he accepts the Mass of the Apostles story. I reject that story in favor of the divination doublet, but I agree that 1208 is the best year. If we take 1C to mean "in the third year," it fits perfectly.

Among the early followers, the best recorded is Bernard of Quintavalle, whose "surname" seems to be a patronymic: Fortini (1959), 2:273–76. His conversion and dispersal of his goods was placed at San Giorgio by Bonaventure, LMj 15.5. On Bernard, see first Manselli (1971). For a short biography in English, see Brown (1965), 432–33. His arrival is reported in 1C 24, AP 10, L3C 27, and 2C 15. It seems he had a brother, Marzio di Quintavalle, unknown to Franciscan sources, who was moderately well-to-do. I agree with critics, like Trexler (1989), 47, who argue that the Bernard of the sources has been reworked into an antitype of the Rich Young Man of the Gospels and is modeled on Nicodemus, "who came to Jesus at night." The hagiographers intend him as a model for future rich converts to the movement. I follow 1C's lack of emphasis on his wealth and greater reticence about the exact consultation process he went through with Francis. As Francis's "form of life" will not be discovered until they have the priest of San Nicolò do Bible divination, the idea that Francis had a ready-made program for Bernard at his arrival is dubious. Brother Bernard would become a fierce critic of Brother Elias. Salimbene visited him in 1241. He died sometime before 1246.

Given AP's excellent witness on this period, I believe that Bernard was joined by another convert, probably named Peter. Scholars usually identify him as Brother Peter of Cataneo: Brown (1965), 438; De Beer (1963), 143; Fortini (1959), 1:1:344–45; Vauchez (2009), 72. Peter of Cataneo, later Francis's vicar, was (cf. ChJG, pp. 9, 12) a doctor of law. Fortini (1959), 2:276–80, thinks Cataneo was also a canon. As Peter of Cataneo was a highly educated man, he cannot be this Peter. If he were, then AP's statement that none of the men present for the divination incident could read Latin very well would be nonsense. This Peter is, thus, otherwise unknown.

Dating the sortes *(pp. 22–23)*

Di Fonzo (1982), 83, recognizes that the date 16 April in AP 3 relates to an event in Francis's life, not in Bernard's, and thinks it is the date of the Mass of the Apostles. As the Mass of the Apostles is fictitious, the logical conclusion is that 16 April was when Francis learned about his way of life; in AP that happened at the *sortes*. I think that dating very likely and construe accordingly. There has been debate over where the *sortes* happened. Some, like Miccoli (1991), 159, favored L3C's location at San Nicolò; others discussed by Di Fonzo (1972), 366, following the *Vita Fratris Bernardi de Quintavalle,* AF 3:36, put it at Santa Maria del Vescovado. That San Nicolò was Francis's parish church, now certain because of archaeology, confirms again the authenticity of L3C for local Assisi color.

The Bible divination (p. 23)

Sources for the divination incident are AP 11, L3C 27–29, and 2C 15. Such a random opening of the Bible to find God's will is called *sortes biblicae,* that is, "Bible lot-casting." On the practice, see Courcelle (1953). As Miccoli (1991), 161, noted, L3C has turned the simple AP story into a typology of how to become a Franciscan (by giving all to the poor) and made Bernard the model convert (a rich man doing almsgiving). This overlay should be rejected as a later gloss. Francis, in his Testament, says that God gave him a style of life *after* he got followers, as Miccoli (1991), 171–72, and Manselli (1975), 267, both correctly note. In my interpretation, Francis understood the *sortes* as a direct message from God, and that underlies his statement in Test 14 that "nemo" (i.e., no human being) told him what to do.

On the ambiguous status of the *sortes* in canon law, see Gratian, *Decretum,* C. 26, qq. 1–4, where it is tolerated only when not used to predict the future, for money, or for immoral purposes. Although superstitious, perhaps, it was still common in both clerical and lay society of the period. For examples of its use in the history of the Dominican Order, see Petrus Ferrandi, *Legenda Sancti Domini* 42–44 (MOPH 16:240–42); *Vitae Fratrum* 13.6 (Monumenta Ordinis Fratrum Praedicatorum Historica 1:184–86). I thank Simon Tugwell, O.P., for these references, and for use of his unpublished editions of the two works. I agree with Esser (1978), 48—*pace* Sabatier (1894) and now Desbonnets (1983), 14—that this passage does not veil some disappointment with the "institutional Church." Francis got help from his parish priest after all, and there is no evidence he had earlier tried to consult Guido or anyone else. I second the suggestion of Vauchez (2009), 77–78, identifying the *sortes* as the event in which Francis believed God had revealed his will for him.

The San Nicolò altar missal (p. 23)
Further confirmation that the event happened at San Nicolò comes from the identification, in Voorvelt-Van Leeuan (1989), of the actual altar missal in the Walters Art Museum in Baltimore, Maryland. This article (esp. 265 n. 10) corrects errors of Manselli, Desbonnets, and Schmucki about the meaning and use of the *sortes* in the Middle Ages. FA:ED 2:38 n. c follows the corrections in this article. The Walters missal does not include Matt. 19:21 (quoted in AP 11 as the first text found), but it does include the parallel in Mark 10:21 (ibid., 271). The quotation by AP from the better-known Matthew was a natural mistake of memory. A reproduction of the Luke Gospel (fol. 119ᵛ) is found on the second plate following p. 276, and a page-by-page description of the MS on pp. 278–321.

The Penitents Go to Rome

The trip to Rome (p. 24)
Francis's trip to Rome is described in 1C 31–33, AP 32–36, L3C 47–53, and 2C 16–18. AP is probably the report closest to the event, although, as Dalarun (1996), 189, notes, AP has an agenda, to prove that it was not contrary to Francis's intentions that the order developed from this ad hoc group. All of the evidence suggests that the trip to Rome was Francis's idea. Desbonnets (1983), 80, representing the consensus of scholarly opinion, puts the departure for Rome in spring 1209. Debate arises from the problem of making the brothers' return to Assisi mesh with the emperor Otto IV's passage by Assisi. Otto passed Assisi in September 1209 on the way to Rome and, then again, during his return trip on 4 November 1210: *Regesta Imperii,* ed. J. F. Boehmer et al. (Innsbruck, 1881), 5:100–107, 126. On the dating, see Di Fonzo (1982), 97.

Purpose of the visit (p. 24)
1C 32, AP 31, and L3C 46 all describe Francis's decision to write a "rule" and get it approved, making this a result of Francis's prophetic foresight that he would attract followers and that the Franciscan Order would expand throughout the whole world. On the other hand, Francis himself puts the decision after the arrival of followers and says (Test 14–15): "The Most High himself revealed to me that I ought to live according the form of the holy Gospel. And I had it written in a few words and simply, and the Lord Pope confirmed it

for me." Notice that he only speaks of himself, not even of his first followers, much less the future Franciscan Order. That growth in number of followers may have played a role, but Francis's motivations seem personal. Francis did have Bishop Guido as a spiritual adviser, and the bishop was surprised the little group showed up in Rome (cf. 1C 32; L3C 47). Desbonnets (1983), 28, contends that Bishop Guido had not given Francis any approval to found a movement until they met in Rome. This is a likely conclusion. Certainly the idea that Guido was unhappy with the "Franciscan Order" leaving Assisi at this early date is absurd. It did not yet exist.

Ghinato (1973), 42–43, thinks that Francis's 1209 decision to seek approval from the pope was the result of a "Catholic scruple" about the need to distinguish his movement from heretical sects. He contrasts this to the 1223 Rule approbation, when the need was to formalize a set way of life. Miccoli (1991), 73, links the decision to get Roman approval to Francis's desire to subordinate himself to the Catholic clergy who ministered the Eucharist. This is an important insight. I also agree with Miccoli (1991), 58–72, that renunciation of one's own will is the essence of "poverty" for Francis. One can see this in Francis's own writings, e.g., Adm 2. Both scholars are on to something, but I would go a step further.

Francis's decision was about a scruple, but the scruple was a personal, even private one. He wanted an ecclesiastical authority (and who better than the pope?) to certify that the "form of the Gospel" he was to follow was one acceptable to the Church and not the result of an autonomous act of his own will. To obey the Gospel for Francis meant also to obey the Church. Manselli (1995), 193–94, makes the excellent observation that for Francis "poverty" was above all a state without defenses, subordinate to others. That is why he chose to call his followers *minores,* not *pauperes.* Thus the submission of his intentions to the pope. *Pace* Flood (1983), 49, this poverty is really quite different from being "marginal," which is a social state. Francis's concern in 1209 was more spiritual, even psychological, than social, if one wants to use modern language. We have to infer what Francis intended to do in Rome from his own words and known actions, not from retrojection of later Franciscan concerns.

The nature of the "Rule of 1209" (pp. 24–25)

It is premature to call Francis's movement an "order" at this date. Dalarun (1996), 184–85, thinks that only with *Cum Dilecti Filii* (11 June 1219) did the movement get classified as a "religio"; and only with *Pro Dilectis Filiis* (29 May 1220), as an "ordo." I agree with Landini (1968), 138, that Francis, at this early date, probably never intended his group to be more than followers of the

"Evangelical life," according to the biblical texts "revealed" to him. On the relation of this 1209 "forma vitae" to the later Rules, see Esser (1966), 84–87.

I agree with Desbonnets (1983), 17, that all attempts to reconstruct the "proto-rule" from that of 1221 have failed. Desbonnets perceptively notes that Francis called his 1209 document a *vita* (or, I suspect, better *forma vitae*), rather than a *regula*. De Beer (1963), 114, believes he can detect something more like a "rule," and that the discussion of hermitism versus preaching on the way back from Rome shows that issues of common life and ministry had already been raised before the trip to Rome. I doubt it. Innocent III seems the origin of the mission to preach, not Francis.

John of San Paolo Colonna (pp. 25–26)

There is no question that Francis met with the Colonna cardinal, who was essential to the approbation of 1209. Colonna, rather than Hugolino, was for many years the Roman face of the new movement: Di Fonzo (1972), 369. 1C 33, AP 32–33, and L3C 47–48 describe his agency at the Curia. 1C alone reports that he had trouble understanding Francis's intentions. Later sources describe Colonna as so bowled over by Francis's holiness that he spontaneously volunteered to get the brothers an audience with Innocent. I agree with De Beer (1963), 119, that the normally reliable AP, and its parallel in L3C, are glossing over a difficult moment of misunderstanding. For a survey of the many apostolic movements of the 1100s, which all include elements often thought to be distinctively Franciscan, like itinerancy and begging, see Thompson (2011), esp. 3–15.

Innocent III (pp. 26–27)

In comparison to the meeting with Colonna, where 1C seems the most trustworthy version, Dalarun (1996), 184–85, thinks AP superior for the meeting with Innocent. Both AP and L3C emphasize the pope's skepticism over the difficulty of living without property. Francis has to win him over by pleading that God will provide, by telling the famous parable of the king and poor woman (which I, with Dalarun, consider apocryphal here). Retrojection of poverty issues back to the meeting with Innocent smacks of later concerns. 1C never does that. Here the cardinal speaks for Francis. Even AP (and its parallel in L3C) states that Colonna acted as the group's procurator. Speaking for petitioners is what procurators did. Giving him that office is where AP and L3C are surely right. Innocent's decision is recorded in all three sources; he received Francis's profession of obedience, had the brothers profess obedience to Francis, and then told them to preach penance. Although all sources say he "approved the Rule," no explicit legal act is described. The approval was provisional and probably only implicit in the profession of obedience.

Some have doubted that Francis actually met Innocent III at some point. Even Manselli (1982), 104–6, leaves it open to doubt. Dalarun (1996), 91, who can be very critical, rejects such skepticism. I do as well. Direct papal contact appears in 1C and Burchard of Urspeg (FA:ED 1:596), both of which date before 1230 and are independent of each other. Roger of Wendover (FA:ED 1:598–99), who writes before 1235, famously describes the pope telling Francis to go roll in the mud with the pigs, which he does, and so wins the pope over. This is the stuff of legend, but a personal encounter is presupposed. Desbonnets (1983), 26–28, considers the encounter described in L3C 46–53 the best version. I find it highly embroidered with legends.

But both Roger of Wendover (FA:ED 1:598) and L3C 51 (better manuscripts) describe the meeting with the pope as at a *consistorium*, a "consistory." In the time of Innocent III, general consistories with the cardinals happened on Wednesdays and Fridays, with the cardinals free to bring up new business. This would then be discussed among the curalists, and the decision announced at a later consistory. The normal practice was for petitioners to be represented by procurators. Thus Francis would not have been present when his petition was first raised by Colonna. In contrast, Vauchez (2009), 178, thinks Francis was the one who personally convinced the pope to approve his petition when it was proposed. I find that very unlikely. Rather, Francis would have been called in to the second consistory, where the pope gave his decision. It was at this meeting that Innocent would have received Francis's obedience, but even at that consistory, the cardinal, as procurator, did the talking (probably in Latin).

The commission to preach (p. 27)
The commission to preach was the first event that began changing Francis's mission into one of service to the Church. On Francis's lack of technical training in preaching, see Cardini (1983a), 59, on the Bologna sermon of 2C 73. The preaching commission is peculiar for a "contemplative" group, which the Assisi hermits seem to be. Merlo (1991b), 67, contrasts it with Innocent's treatment of the Humiliati, who were not permitted to preach publicly. Penance preaching was, however, something Innocent approved for any number of other lay groups. Desbonnets (1983), 26, counts some twenty papal letters approving lay preaching in the period around 1210. Vauchez (2009), 91–102, treats the parallels between Francis's approbation by Innocent and those of other lay preaching groups.

Innocent's sermon (p. 27)
Cracco (1982), 117, identifies Innocent III's Sermon 17 (*Patrologia Latina* 215:537–38), where the presentation of Saint John the Baptist sounds so much

like Francis. Innocent's reconciliation of heretics and approval of their preaching is treated in Edward Peters, *Heresy and Authority in Medieval Europe* (Philadelphia: University of Pennsylvania Press, 1980), 166–67; the current standard on the early Humiliati is Frances Andrews, *The Early Humiliati* (Cambridge: Cambridge University Press, 1999). On the contrast in approach between Innocent and Colonna, see De Beer (1963), 120.

The tonsure (p. 28)

The tonsuring of the brothers is recorded in AP 36 and L3C 52. Manselli (1982), 11–12, seconded by Rusconi (1994), 82–84, considers this report anachronistic and a retrojection of later practice, perhaps from the time when Francis become a deacon. Manselli is too skeptical here and seems to know only L3C as a source. Robson (1999), 77, is very good on this. There is simply no controversy about it among medieval writers, who were somewhat perplexed that Francis's humility did not prevent the advancement. AP also records the incident and calls the haircut a "clericam," and it is usually very good on what happened to the early friars. 1C never mentions the incident. The witness of AP is enough for me to tilt in favor of the historicity of the event. Much ink has been spilled (from Bonaventure on) in trying to decide what this rite meant. It gave the brothers, in canon law, the "clerical state"; they were already ecclesiastical persons as penitents subject to Bishop Guido. Stanislao da Compagnola (1973), 390 n. 148, citing Esser (1966), Italian ed., 43, 48, argues that "clericus" for the early Franciscans merely meant "able to read"—not tonsured or in holy orders. I do not find this bald assertion convincing.

Landini (1968), 30, notes that Bonaventure, LMj 3.10, says that the brothers received "little tonsures": "Approbavit regulam, dedit de poenitentia praedicanda mandatum et laicis fratribus omnibus, qui servum Dei fuerunt comitati, fecit coronas parvulas, ut verbum Dei libere praedicarent." Landini wants this to mean that this was not a "clerical tonsure." This is peculiar, to say the least. In the early 1200s, no distinction of tonsures by size existed, as there would be in the time of Bonaventure: Trichet (1990), 118. When the term "grandes coronas" appeared in 1238 legislation in France, all it meant was that the tonsure was to be large enough to be distinguished from a lay haircut (ibid., 149). Trichet (1990), 105–07, reviews legislation of the 1190s to Lateran IV (c. 16) and finds nothing on size. As he shows (ibid., 135–38), for tonsure and the clerical state, they are convertible. Vauchez (2009), 101, while accepting Bonaventure's description of the "small tonsure," admits that it makes Francis and his companions clerics. When they were tonsured, the brotherhood became clerics, as well as ecclesiastical persons. That is all there is to it.

Dream visions at Rome (p. 28)

Reports of Francis's visit to the pope are replete with prophetic dreams and parables. With Dalarun (1996), 200, I reject Innocent's dream of Francis holding up the Lateran, as a later theological gloss. I am not sure if Dalarun (ibid., 91) makes his case for a borrowing from Constantino of Orvieto's *Life of St. Dominic* (usually dated 1244–46), which he thinks predates 2C (usually dated 1245–47) and L3C (now usually dated 1241–47). The possible early date of L3C could allow it to be Constantino's source. The parable of the king and the poor woman is surely Francis's, and the most likely original form of it is found in a sermon (dated 1219) by the Englishman Odo of Cheriton (FA:ED 1:591). The versions of the parable reported in AP 35 and L3C 50 reflect a later period, since they imply an exponential growth anachronistic for 1209. As De Beer (1963), 269, notes, 2C 16 has turned it into a poverty parable, another reworking. Even in the primitive form, I find it difficult to place it in 1209. Issues of provisions and poverty seem just too anachronistic at this date.

The one "marvelous" story that might actually have occurred during the Rome visit is Francis's "Dream of the Tree." The Dream of the Tree is in 1C 33, which places it before leaving Rome; and in L3C 33, in which it occurs on the road going home. There is nothing prophetic or anachronistic about it, and it might well reflect Francis's subconscious reaction to his reception by the pope. This is the one allegorical story from the Rome visit that I would consider authentic. It has no prophetic elaboration and no supernatural function. It follows the events at Rome, which Francis uses to interpret it. That he repeated this dream shows that he considered it a ratification of the events in Rome.

The journey back to Assisi (pp. 28–29)

De Beer (1963), 118, suggests that the "monita et praecepta" that the brothers discussed probably concerned the pope's instruction to preach penance. Ghinato (1973), 48, and Desbonnets (1983), 30, perceptively surmise that the group's first issue was to determine how to combine penance preaching and the life of penance, something unclear in the "propositum" presented to Innocent. I agree with De Beer (1963), 114 n. 11, that *Actus Beati Francisci et Sociorum* 16, which I usually consider too late to be trustworthy, accurately describes Francis's spiritual crisis over how to combine preaching and penance: "Fuit Franciscus in magnae dubitationis agone, an scilicet vacaret orationi continue an praedicationi aliquando intenderet." For once, a Spiritualist concern is not an anachronism. 1C 34 alone records the short stay in Orte.

See Lambertini-Tabarroni (1989), 30–31, on the false but common stereotype that only clerics could preach publicly in the twelfth and thirteenth centuries. Conversely, sacerdotalism and evangelical preaching were not in any way exclusive among the early Franciscans: Merlo (1991b), 83. Good on preaching by Francis and his followers, generally considered, is Delcorno (1977), 128–30, who wrongly makes the "Mass of the Apostles," not Innocent's commission, the origin of Franciscan preaching. As Esser (1978), 126–27 (Karecki trans. 35–36), notes, Francis forbade preaching without permission of parish priests in Test 3a, which goes far beyond the requirements of medieval canon law, where the bishop's permission was sufficient.

The Fraternity of Brothers

Rivo Torto (p. 29)

I find the dating for Rivo Torto by Brown (1965), 377–82, convincing. This stay is described in 1C 43 (with much praise for the austerity of the life there) and L3C 55 (very brief). AC provides us with datable anecdotes about Rivo Torto. Events at Rivo Torto are found in AC 50 (LP 1), 92 (LP 55), 97 (LP 62), and perhaps 9 (LP 102) and 51 (LP 2). Manselli (1980), 58–65, has perceptive remarks on Francis's growth as a guide of souls while at Rivo Torto. Work with lepers in this period appears in AC 9 (LP 102) and L3C 55 (where giving the hut to the lepers is mentioned). Francis's desire that the brothers work with their hands is famous: see esp. Test 20–21 and 2C 161 (AC 48). A perhaps anachronistic description of begging, probably set at Rivo Torto, is found in AC 51 and 2C 74.

The Franciscan habit (pp. 29–30)

Francis and his followers may have devised a particular habit before going to Rome, but most likely it appeared later: the group of three did not need a uniform. AP 19 describes people's perplexed reaction to the brothers' "habit," but I am not sure the word here means anything more technical than their miserable clothing. Other historians doubt a special habit at this time. Miccoli (1991), 150, 177, thinks that AP's description of the habit is nothing more than a peasant's smock, and notes that the wearers were called "rustici." Desbonnets (1983), 5, agrees but thinks that the reported dropping of "hermit" garb merely means that Francis had decided to give up his ecclesiastical status as a penitent. I find this kind of legal calculation unlikely.

Are the "hermit garb" and new "habit" of 1C merely a literary device? It is hard to say. The events and intentions behind these early changes of clothing are murky. But it is telling that so many non-Franciscan sources remarked on the oddity of the brothers' attire and place the appearance very early. Esser

(1966), 97, lists non-Franciscan commentators: Thomas of Spoleto, Burchard, the "Passion of San Verecundio," Roger of Wendover, Richer of Sens, the Dominican Breviary, Boncampagno of Signi, and Jacques de Vitry. Readers may find these reports in the "related documents" sections of FA:ED volumes 1 and 2. Esser, however, doubts that Francis intended his poor clothing to be a habit in the canonical sense, at least at this early time. I am inclined to think that some kind of particular clothing came very early, but it was more free-form than the later "habit." Francis puts his comments on it early in the reminiscence part of the Testament.

The trousers under the habit (p. 30)

For the interpretation of the word usually translated "trousers," see Desbonnets (1983), 21. Test 16 and LR 9 use "braca" (which means "ample pants"); other sources use "femoralia" (thigh-covering undershorts). Benedictines wore "femoralia" for travel, but peasants seem not to have worn underwear under their smocks. On the cord, 1C says that Francis replaced his leather belt with a cord. But Francis, in Test 16, uses the word "funiculum," and that word simply means "belt," as Desbonnets (1983), 20–21, notes.

Brother Giles (p. 30)

The conversion of Giles at Rivo Torto is described in AC 92 (LP 55). This surprising report is so specific and sounds so much like an eyewitness that I am convinced that it is correct as to place. *Vita Aegidii,* AS 12 (Apr. III), 318–21, dates Giles's conversion as 23 April. The event happened at Rivo Torto, as AC 92 says, so it happened after Rome. If 16 April was the date of the *sortes,* and 23 April was the conversion of Giles and is after Rome, that leaves one week for Francis to get to Rome and back. This window is very narrow. I suspect the date of Giles's conversion given in the *Vita* has been moved up to match the order in AP 14–15 and L3C 32, which put Giles's conversion after the *sortes* but before Rome. That order is wrong. So both sources have to manufacture a new location: the Porziuncula.

That Giles entered after Rome at Rivo Torto, as AC says, resolves an old and fruitless controversy, and this confirms that it is correct. If Giles had been tonsured in Rome, how can ChTE, pp. 51–52; *Vita Aegidii,* AS 12 (Apr. III), 241; and *Cronica XXIV Generalium Minorum,* AF 3:81, 253, all call him a *laicus conversus?* They can do so because he *was* a lay *conversus:* he was not in Rome to be tonsured. The conversion of Giles seems to lie behind AP 28, L3P 44, AC 91, and 2C 156, which have turned it into an exemplary moral story about willingness to give up things to the poor. The version in AC 91 seems to have drifted to Francis's final illness, when he made a habit of giving away clothing. Giles would be with Francis at Rieti in 1225 and again with him at the saint's death. Giles then retired as a hermit to Cortona and then to Monteripido near Perugia, where he was visited by Gregory IX (1234/5) and Bonaventure (1260). He seems, like Bernard, to have become a critic of changes in the order in his old age. He died 22 April 1262.

Francis as spiritual guide (pp. 30–31)
The story of the hungry brother appears twice: AC 50 (LP 1) and AC 53 (LP 4), which are perhaps a doublet. On Francis's care for the sick brothers: 2C 177, 175 (AC 45). "Brother Fly" appears in AC 97 (LP 62).

Francis at the Porziuncula

Arrival at the Porziuncula (pp. 31–32)
In the scholarship, it is an open question whether the brothers lived at Santa Maria degli Angeli before going to Rome. As Beguin (1979), 117, 174, shows (cf. 1C 21), Francis did not leave San Damiano until after he had followers; any squatting at the Porziuncula would have occurred after other men joined him. The 1C 21 dating of the move to the Porziuncula seems premature. Miccoli (1991), 170–81, notes that 1C, which is fixated on making Francis alone the founder of his movement, has him restore the Porziuncula alone before getting followers for ideological reasons. Miccoli concludes (and I agree) that this report is "molto sospetto." AP has the friars squatting at the Porziuncula; L3C has them go there when they are "house-hunting."

In a believable settlement narrative, AC 56 describes a contract to lease the church for a basket of "small fish" a year, but the dating is unclear. But this AC version has a contract for permanent residence—something that makes sense only after Rome. 2C 18 delays the move until after the trip to Rome, which is correct for final occupation and would be the logical time to start paying rent.

So even if Francis drifted through the Porziuncula before Rome, there was no regularization of residence there until after 1209. On the way home from Rome, the brothers parked first at Orte and then moved to Rivo Torto. Nothing suggests that the Rivo Torto stop was intended to be temporary. After filtering out the theological agendas, the most likely scenario is that Francis and his followers did no more than squat at the abandoned Porziuncula (among other churches) before finally settling there. It is not impossible that residence at the Porziuncula before Rivo Torto is totally mythological, and that is my view.

Manselli (1982), 134, allows for a less transient early use of the church, but he correctly links the move from Rivo Torto to the need for a church. Serious rebuilding was certainly the work of the whole community.

Acquiring the Porziuncula (pp. 31–32)
Desbonnets (1983), 70, correctly links the Porziuncula to papal approbation and the group's first institutionalization. 1C 30, typically retrojecting later aspects of the order, puts the occupation of the Porziuncula before the trip to Rome. L3C 32 repeats this information and links it to the conversion of Giles (which is close to correct, since that happened at Rivo Torto soon before). But L3C 56, supported by AC 56 (LP 8–12) and 2C 18, correctly puts the settlement at the Porziuncula after Rivo Torto. On the contrasting stories here, see Dalarun (1996), 213–14. I agree with Manselli (1980), 66–74, who favors the later dating found in AC 56 and 2C 18–19.

The decision to contract for the Porziuncula was probably the result of the need for a stable place near Assisi for the friars to live. I politely disagree with Dalarun (1996), 109–11, who thinks the donkey incident comes from an eyewitness. It is a retrojected poverty story. L3C provides the more sober explanation that the community moved out so that poor lepers could have a place to live. The long speech by Francis in AC 56, with its prophecies of Franciscan decadence, is a retrojection, as is Francis's supernatural foresight, as both Desbonnets (1983), 70, and Dalarun (1996), 200, note. Also to be rejected is L3C's prophetic dream. AC 56 explicitly links the Porziuncula acquisition to the need to find a place to recite the Office, which makes perfect sense for the now-tonsured group of clerics. But even if they were not tonsured, a desire to celebrate, or at least be present at, the Divine Office would fit the lay piety of the age. See Thompson (2005), 241–45, on sung Office in parish churches and lay attendance at it. The choice of this particular church may also reflect Francis's personal devotion to Mary and the Angels (2C 195–97; SalBVM), as also suggested in AC 56. There is no good evidence for the so-called Porziuncula Indulgence until well after Francis's death: Rusconi (1982).

Francis around Assisi (p. 32)
There is little reliable material on the life of the first followers, save some stories of their journeys and wanderings. The descriptions of their life and Francis's reflections and exhortations in 1C 26–28, AP 13, 18–19, and L3C 31, 34–37, are so full of anachronism, mystical prophecies, and romanticized ideals as to be worthless as historical evidence. All three of the earliest biographies retroject much later matter into the period before Francis went to Rome; this retrojection increases after the return. Even a cursory reading of the reports shows that

the style of life described is too precociously developed for that period. About one thing the reports are certainly right, which is confirmed by the Testament: the brothers lived in churches, they cleaned them, and they repaired them.

The number of early companions (p. 32)

Much time and effort, in both the medieval and modern periods, has been spent trying to identify the original "Twelve" (or was it "Eleven"?) who joined Francis and may (or may not) have gone to Rome with him. And was "Alberto" the beggar one of them? On this problem, see Beguin (1979), 126–28. Hagiographers needed the number twelve (with or without Francis), so that the Christological parallel would be clear. As Desbonnets (1983), 25, notes, taking that number at face value is making something literal out of a symbol. It is not impossible that Francis would have wanted recognition of his group when he had twelve followers (it would fit his symbolic view of the world), but that he did I consider not only unlikely but impossible.

The early sources fudge the numbers. That only two men went to Rome with Francis is revealed by AC 92, which also explicitly says there were only two brothers with Francis at Rivo Torto until Giles joined them there. Perhaps, after Rivo Torto, there was a point when the group numbered more or less a dozen followers. For what it is worth, one may consult Brown (1965), 427–40, for the attempts to show that a historical dozen followers really existed. Little more has been added since that essay.

Names of the early companions (pp. 32–33)

Significantly, AP, our best source for this period, gives no names after the first three. LMj 4–5 names only Giles and Silvester and mentions only "six" as the number of disciples before Rome. Along with Bernard, Peter, and Giles, three other early followers (Sabbatino, John, Morico) are known by name in L3C 35 and AC 17. Perhaps this is the origin of LMj's "six followers." 1C 25 makes Philip the seventh follower. One might even wonder whether the total of seven is not itself as symbolic as the number twelve. Early sources do not give a surname to link this Philip with the later Philip Longo. If the "Philip" of 1C was Philip Longo, then he was visitator of the Clares in 1219/20 and 1228–46. Fortini (1959), 2:283–85, struggles to identify him in archival records; the best he can do is find members of the supposed family. Vauchez (2009), 84–85, accepts the traditional identifications of the "original twelve" without much skepticism.

Morico is otherwise unknown, and later Franciscan writers seem to conflate two individuals of the same name (neither of whom is definitely he): Fortini (1959), 2:282. Attempts to identify L3C's "John" with the "Judas of the

Twelve" in the later legends, John of Cappella, seem gratuitous. Fortini (1959), 2:283, assumes such an identification and tries to find evidence for his life with little result. No early sources give names for the remaining five (or four) brothers to complete the "apostolic band." The most likely identification for one of the unnamed friars is probably the later-mentioned Brother Masseo. Ubertino of Casale, who had met him, identified him as Masseo di Marignano, a knight of Perugia, AFH 1 (1908): 267. He seems to have left some unpublished prayers and reflections when he died at Assisi in 1280. Frankly, this seems as much as we will know about the membership of the first band at the Porziuncula.

Desbonnets (1983), 19, considers the first followers of mixed social rank but generally identifies them as "rich" or "knights." His sample is skewed by easy acceptance of traditional identifications (e.g., Peter as Peter of Cataneo) and by inclusion of many who arrived after 1209, when the chroniclers tended to play up prize catches and ignore the rest. His characterization would fit Bernard (perhaps), and Masseo (if really an early follower) seems to have been a knight, but the rest are hard to pin down.

It seems safest to say that they were probably men like Francis himself, higher than middling rank, but not very rich or noble. I like the suggestion of Cardini (1976), 192–98, that Francis's first followers were mostly "second generation" members of mercantile families, who rejected their parents' values. The assertion of Le Goff (2000), 56, that they were making a "reactionary" choice in favor of the chivalric values of the twelfth century is an example of odd neo-Marxism and certainly does not fit Masseo. De Beer (1963), 147 n. 10, emphasizes legal training for the canon Silvester, the legist Peter of Cataneo, Brother Elias (consul of Assisi according to Fortini [1959], 1:1:154), Peter Parenti, Haymo, Crescentius, and John of Parma. This characterization may be true, but none of these men were of the original band. Manselli (1982), 83–84, mistakenly, I think, puts Silvester's arrival before the trip to Rome. Silvester, first priest member of the movement, was with Francis at Arezzo in 1217 and died at Assisi in 1240. Virtually nothing else is known of him.

The primitive community (p. 33)
Manselli (1982), 112–69, treats the material of this period, although perhaps a bit less critically than I would. As Miccoli (1991), 231, observes, the historian's problem is to filter out all the retrojection found even in good sources like 1C and AP. Descriptions of life at Santa Maria degli Angeli are mostly very generalized and idealized. These include 1C 38–41 (on the brothers' virtues), 1C 45–54 (on Francis's spiritual insight), AP 26–30 (set before the Rome visit), and L3C 36–46 (also set before Rome). More concrete, but no less idealized, are the stories in AC that either are set in this period or seem to be. I would include

here AC 61 (cleaning churches), 64 (service to lepers), 98 (begging), 54 (visit by Bishop Guido), and Francis's series of spiritual crises described in AC 55, 63, and 78. Francis's spiritual crises are also found in 2C 97 and 99.

Merlo (1992), 536–39, accepts the conclusion of Miccoli (1991), 81–82, that the core of Francis's *propositum* was to cultivate an absolute dependence on God. I strongly agree. This means that ideas of strategy, social reform, and organizational "planning" were alien to Francis. I do not follow Merlo in the attempt (shared with Flood) to make Francis's significance his rejection of protocapitalism. This is the very kind of "useful" purpose that is so alien to Francis's exclusive concern with dependence on God alone. I follow Merlo, not Miccoli, that Francis was to a great extent an active collaborator in the ecclesiastical project of turning his private spiritual quest into a religious order. Unlike Merlo, I see nothing "inauthentic" in his cooperation with the "institutional Church." Francis was a thirteenth-century orthodox Catholic, not a modern spiritual individualist, and in his Testament he ordered that heretics be turned over to the authorities for punishment. Cooperation with the hierarchy was natural to him.

ON CHAPTER THREE

MY INTERPRETATION OF Francis as a leader in his new movement is based on my own reading of the sources. But the work of a number of modern scholars has been very suggestive, and I will flag them. This period is covered in Manselli (1982), 95–186, and Vauchez (2009), 102–35.

Francis as a Spiritual Leader

Influences on Francis's spiritual vision (pp. 34–35)

Pazzelli (1990), the principal study of the two exhortations usually called "Letters to the Faithful," is convincing in his argument that the titles "Earlier Exhortation to the Brothers and Sisters of Penance" and "Later Admonition and Exhortation to the Brothers and Sisters of Penance" are to be preferred. A translation of the Earlier Exhortation is found in FA:ED 1:41–44. As background on lay piety, since Francis and his followers were laymen, I recommend Delaruelle (1971) and (1975), 247–75, which avoid polemics. On the penitent movement itself, see Thompson (2005), 69–102. Nonetheless, it is impossible to pass over the acrimonious debates over the influences on Francis, and on the form and structure of early Franciscan life. These debates fall into three groups.

First was the old debate (personified in Sabatier and Esser) as to whether some pure form of Franciscan life was corrupted by involvement with the "institutional Church." This debate is basically defunct outside of popularizing biographies and movies, where Sabatier's antipathy for the medieval Catholic Church still has some traction. The individualist-institutional tension of this model is generally considered anachronistic.

The next debate was over how well the Franciscans fit into the religious movements described by Grundmann (1995), if they did. Flood (1977b) vigorously attacked the idea that the Franciscans fit into the mystical/heretical developments sketched by Grundmann. (That they are not part of Grundmann's third movement, women's piety, is obvious.) If one ignores Flood's assertion that Francis had, at least implicitly, an anticapitalist agenda to create a "new humanity," this is a useful essay. Merlo, the foremost student of medieval dissent in Italy, refutes the commonplace in scholarship that Francis fits into the world of medieval religious dissent; see Merlo (1991b), esp. 45–46. No contemporary mistook him or his followers for heretics, except when their language skills failed (e.g., ChJG 4–6). The brothers' orthodoxy was obvious, even to their critics, and even when these critics denounced the movement's novelty: Buoncompagno (FA:ED 1:590); Chronicle of Lauterberg (FA:ED 1:592); and Burchard of Ursperg (FA:ED 1:593–94).

The third debate questioned how much Francis and his followers drew from earlier forms of religious, especially monastic, life. Flood (1967), 74–75, correctly rejects the idea that the Franciscans are a version of the twelfth-century movements of "Apostolic Life." As Desbonnets (1983), 15–16, notes, there was a natural tendency, even in Franciscan sources, to read Francis as an imitator of the twelfth-century *vita apostolica,* with its emphasis on preaching. The *forma evangelica,* as discovered by Francis, was something very different from this earlier preaching movement. No secure references to Franciscan preaching exist for a long period after their 1209 approval by Innocent III. My belief is that the best place to look for earlier models is among the lay penitents, the *conversi.*

Vauchez (1994), esp. 194, is good on the continuities and contrasts between earlier hermit preachers and Francis's later preaching style. Beyond this, the issue becomes one of source interpretation, since even the earliest reports retroject much anachronism from the later life of the Order. See Desbonnets (1983), 66, and De Beer (1963), 285–86, who flag the inconsistencies of such anachronistic reports. Beguin (1979), 229–30, rightly observes that even AP, which is quite free of ideological slant and anachronism, wants to present the early brothers as models for later friars, with a subtle, perhaps romanticizing effect.

In comparison to the issues of poverty and preaching, which I will take up presently, no issue exercises modern Franciscan scholarship on Francis like that of monastic influences. There is a somewhat antimonastic bias (at least as a model for their own order) among modern Franciscans, but that is a modern concern. In contrast, the thirteenth-century friars were not bothered by admitting a debt to the Desert Fathers and the monks. Merlo (1991b), 74–75, who has no stake in the fight, observes that Brother Leo in *Vita Aegidii* 57, AS 12 (Apr. III), 235, had no problem putting the following statement in the mouth of one of the first followers: "If not for the model of the hermit fathers, we might not have entered the state of penance." The phrase "vivere secundum evangelium," meaning "to be a hermit," goes back to Stephen of Muret in the early 1100s.

Meersseman (1965), 205, emphasizes the deep debt of the early Franciscans to eremitic models. Dalarun (1997), 213, admits it too, much to his chagrin, for their avoidance of women. In the early 1200s, lay pursuit of the eremitic life was common: in Italy one thinks of Saint Giovanni Buono of Mantua or the Servite founders. Merlo (1991b), 69–70, notes the close similarity of Francis and Giovanni Buono, not just in their hermitism, but in their powerful devotion to the sacraments, church buildings, and the Real Presence. None of this was probably direct (Francis the unconverted layman does not seem to read any pious literature), but one can absorb a spirituality unconsciously.

Francis and his fraternity (p. 35)

That Francis showed little interest in being a successful leader is a point made by Miccoli (1991), esp. 81. He suggests that Francis sought to make Christ present in others without concern for the results. That was what total abandonment to God meant for him. Dalarun (1996), 254, argues that Francis's personal holiness led to the "success" of his movement (as opposed to the hagiographic presentation of Francis in L3C and LMj, in which his success proved the holiness). I agree that Francis as a person was, at least at first, the attraction, not some reform vision or religious program. This marks him as different from other heretical (and orthodox) founders and reformers, who often had overt "Church reform" projects.

Francis's understanding of his movement (pp. 35–36)

Francis continued to call his movement a *fraternitas* for most of his life, and sources privilege this word in the early period. Esser (1966), 25, considered Francis's usage of the word loose and "synonymous with Ordo and Religio." This fluidity of usage and, perhaps, preconceptions about what Francis's temperament would have allowed have generated a lively debate over the status of the brotherhood at the Porziuncula. Desbonnets (1983), 22, argues that Francis never intended to found an "order" in the traditional sense. He declared: "None of the known early friars were clerics." A very odd assertion, since it is simply false, and lay status would not have prevented the movement from being an order, even if it were true. Even excluding the priest Silvester, Francis, Bernard, and Peter were tonsured in Rome, and so were clerics. Miccoli (1985) reviewed Desbonnets (1983), and while mostly appreciative, he is not convinced by the argument that Francis never intended to found an order. In contrast, Esser (1966) is basically a long argument that Francis intended to found an order from the start.

Stanislao da Compagnola (1973), 382, citing Esser, describes Francis's movement as a *fraternitas* that was neither lay nor clerical by definition. Even before the first *fratres de poenitentia* in the mid-1100s, loose groups of followers clustered around charismatic holy men and hermit preachers like Robert of Arbrissel: Vauchez (1994), 188. These figures bridged the gap between cleric and lay. Neither ordained nor monastically professed, they drew their spirituality and piety from a monastic and clerical milieu. Like other laypeople, their prayer life focused on the liturgy of their local church, and they prayed using Latin liturgical formulas. On this lay style, see Thompson (2005), 351–63.

I would suggest that scholars generally import into Francis's worldview a level of conceptual clarity and legalistic concern that is very unlikely. He was a layman, not a theologian or lawyer. Nevertheless, it is clear, to me at least, that within a few years of his conversion, Francis's group did have some kind of rule, a habit, and a liturgical life. That does sound like an order. But I doubt that Francis ever worried about defining his movement in terms of canon law. In Test 18, Francis speaks of "we clerics" saying Office "like other clerics," by which he meant something more regular and structured than the casual attendance at services typical of devout laypeople. Recitation of the Office seems a result of being tonsured. When we strip away retrojection, we find a Francis who is reacting to a series of events, not a man with a systematic, coherent plan. Desbonnets is probably right that Francis did not "plan" to found an order, but Esser is right when he says that when this happened, Francis accepted it. Selge (1969), perhaps the most in point, emphasizes the personal role of Francis, rather than formal structure, in the early days, although he tends to read later material (e.g., ER) back into the early period.

Peace and joy (pp. 36–37)
Francis mentions the origin of his peace greeting in Test 23, the reminiscence section of the document. The most systematic treatment of the peace greeting is Schmucki (1976), 215–23, which discusses its novelty and possible biblical and liturgical roots. Schmucki links it theologically to Adm 15 and CtC, both of which are later. See also Desbonnets (1983), 79, on the novelty of "God give you peace" as a greeting, and the perplexity it caused. On the link between

peace and penance, see Thompson (1992), 150–56. Schmucki, although some-what uncritical of sources, emphasizes Francis's lack of a "social" program or ecclesiastical reform agenda, as Clasen (1952), 109–21 and Roggen (1965), esp. 56–62, did earlier. Miccoli (1991), 80, 204–5, reached similar conclu-sions. This attitude is summed up in Adm 5, and in TPJ, which is admittedly late. On the problems with TPJ as a historical source, see Miccoli (1991), 244. Some also see similarities with the greeting in descriptions of Francis given in 2C 125 and 145.

On the Road around Assisi

Travels to Florence and Trevi (pp. 37–38)

Early biographies give extensive reports on "missionary" travels by Francis and the first followers, with the Porziuncula as a base: AP 15–25, paralleled in L3C 33–41. These reports usually place the missions after arrival at the Porziun-cula, and place that occupation before the trip to Rome. This is anachronistic retrojection. There is an important statement in L3C, which is trustworthy here, that Francis, and it is understood the others, did not preach to the people "at this time." This is surely correct, and the descriptions of sermons are ret-rojection. The biographies also include long hortatory spiritual conferences by Francis, full of prophecies of the order's later greatness and consolations for friars when they are persecuted. Whether Francis made any guesses about the future or not, which we cannot know, this material sounds so *ex eventu* that it cannot be used as a source for this period. For this reason, I have set aside Francis's quasi-prophetic utterances and counseling in 1C 26–28, AP 18, and L3C 36. Some of the travel stories have a claim to belief and probably reflect an unsettled style of life.

1C 30 has nothing on local journeys in Italy, but it mentions a trip by "Ber-nard and James" to Spain that may be authentic, perhaps a pilgrimage. Beguin (1979), 119–20, remarks on the "vivacité" of Celano's report on the journey to Florence and suggests it stems from eyewitnesses' reports. The stay of Francis and Pacifico near Trevi is mentioned in AC 65 (LP 23) and 2C 122–23 and is more credible, since no preaching is involved. The Trevi incident, however, includes a prophetic vision by Pacifico. In it, he sees Satan's throne in heaven empty: we are to understand that it is waiting for the humble Francis. I abstain from speculating on the historicity of the vision. Who this Pacifico was is up for grabs. He is not to be identified with the Pacifico of the *Fioretti*. Attempts to identify him in secular sources are not convincing. His conversion at the monastery of the Clares, San Salvatore di Colpersito near San Severino, in 2C 106, is dubious, as he would already have been a friar by 1215, and the Clares are not recorded there until 1223. Perhaps he is the Pacifico who was provincial of France in 1217, acted as visitor for the Clares, and then died in 1230.

Daily life, work, and prayer (pp. 38–39)
In Test 20–21, Francis emphasized manual labor as model behavior. Manual labor was his primary understanding of poverty. The later glossing of reports from this period to emphasize poor buildings, poor clothing, etc., as the meaning of poverty is anachronistic. It would make sense only if more comfortable choices are possible. As one strips away the residue of poverty concerns that later retelling interjected into stories about the early friars, "poverty" looks very subordinate to Francis's desire for absolute dependence on God. The later legalistic concerns about handling money and property are absent. As Esser (1966), 232, remarked, it was the Franciscans' bare feet, not their avoidance of coins, that fascinated non-Franciscan chroniclers.

For an exchange of scholarly opinion on Francis and poverty, see "Tavola rotunda" (1975), esp. 301, where Luigi Pellegrini notes that earlier "poverty" movements went begging because they did not work for a living—thus they looked like a kind of clergy. This was not Francis's intention. Begging for Francis in the Testament is a secondary recourse, when manual labor does not provide for the group's needs. On this, see also Esser (1978), 151 (Karecki trans., 56); Manselli (1975), esp. 264; and Manselli (1995), 32. Manselli (1975), 277–79, is good on Francis's insistence that the brothers help those who are poor not by choice.

Unlike the twelfth-century apostolics, however, no good evidence exists for preaching as a major part of Franciscan life at this early period. Cardini (1983a), 57, is no doubt right that for his whole life Francis considered *operibus praedicare* and *facere poenitentiam* to be very closely related. A similar point is made by De Beer (1963), 135 n. 65.

Reactions to the movement (p. 39)
Much speculation about the "popularity" of Francis and his movement seems to presuppose that the movement was already very well-known at this stage. I am very skeptical of hypotheses that link Francis's popularity to his "lay" piety and spirituality, unless this refers to his movement's acceptance of laymen as members. The Cistercians had a surge of lay brother recruits too. Laypeople were attracted to religious life in the Middle Ages. In addition, the kind of rigid lay-clerical/illiterate-literate/vernacular-Latin divisions sketched by Langeli (1984), 56, following Duby and Grundmann, are rather anachronistic. This casts doubt on Langeli's characterization of the Franciscans as representing an "orgogliosa rivendicazione della propria cultura." Lay and clerical piety are hard to separate. One has only to read AP on the *sortes biblicae* to see priests

and laymen practicing the same religiosity. De Beer (1963), 153, correctly says that when Francis called the early brothers "idiotae" he meant that they were not theologically trained, not that they could not make sense of the Latin Bible and liturgy. There is no evidence that Francis got help drafting his *praepositum* in 1209. And, like the records of his family business, it would have been in simple Latin.

The medieval hagiographers made the expansion of the order the work of Francis himself, but this is deceptive. Nearly all who joined the order after 1215, the period of its real takeoff, never knew Francis intimately. Making Francis responsible for the expansion of his movement leads Langeli (1984), 39–57, to say that it was his "lay style" and contact with popular piety that made him popular. This somewhat anticlerical perspective, that Francis was popular because he was not a priest, is rejected by Cracco (1982), 105, who notes his numerous clerical followers.

In contrast to these rosy images of admiration and rapid growth, not all observers had a positive view of Francis and his movement. Lambertini-Tabarroni (1989), 22–23, discusses Boncompagno's criticisms of gyrovagism, immaturity, and excessive rigorism. Signs of similar criticism are reported in L3C 17, 34–35. The insight of Merlo (1991b), 71, is that what made Francis different from earlier evangelical heretics is not that he was obedient to the pope (even Valdes seems to have tried to be so), but that he gave no impression of being in competition with the clergy, especially with respect to preaching. At least initially, Francis's movement had no pretensions to being an alternative clergy. Nor is there any evidence—Merlo (1991b), 57–58—that antiheretical activity was part of Francis's original plans.

Esser (1966), 138–47, inventories the complaints made about the early Franciscans: no conventual life or proper formation ("gyrovagism"), friars leaving the movement or being away without permission, heresy. Only the last seems patently untrue. Especially criticized was Francis's habit of admitting anyone who asked to join, and then not giving him any systematic formation. Again, see Esser (1966), esp. 54–58, on the oddities of the early movement in comparison to other orders. There seems to have been no real system of superiors until the 1220s, something even the Curia found perplexing; before Francis instituted local superiors, papal communications already came addressed to Francis and "the priors" of the "order." Local superiors remain hard to track until after Francis's death.

The Porziuncula and fixed residences (p. 39)

There is no question that early sources make the Porziuncula into the mother house of a religious order. 1C makes the return to the Porziuncula after the first "mission" a miraculous return in response to Francis's prayers; AP and L3C say they came back at "established" or "appointed" times. The less marvelous story is more primitive. But does this mean that they were using Santa Maria degli Angeli as a permanent home base? Later behavior makes that unlikely. On the "return" to the Porziuncula, see Beguin (1979), 122. Lambertini-Tabarroni (1989), 24, notes the negative reception of Francis and his followers.

Disposal of worldly goods (pp. 39–40)
Francis's rejection of the man who gave his money to his relatives is in AC 62 (LP 20) and 2C 80–81. In both cases, the story has been given a "poverty spin" to make it a model for later friars. 2C is filled with stories, often miraculous, about early brothers getting punished for poverty violations: 2C 65 (= AC 27), 66, 68, 78; AC 98 (LP 63) = 2C 76. Given squalid conditions at Rivo Torto and the early Porziuncula, these stories are hard to take at face value. Manselli (1982), 142–43, warns against trusting the romantic images of poverty as given in the *Sacrum Commercium*. John the Simple appears in AC 60–61 (LP 18–19) and 2C 190 (which omits all but John's conversion). I am not sure the incident is historical, but Francis's behavior, like the treatment of Brother Fly, rings true, so I have included it.

Nevertheless, even if we accept the story of the rejected aspirant to the community, touching money or coin does not seem the shibboleth it later became. De Beer (1963), 249, notes that Francis and the brothers handle money in 2C 12–13, 88, and 109. 2C 12–13 reflects the better information available to Celano when he wrote the later life. 1C toes the later party line and avoids references to handling cash. I do not mean to say that the brothers took wages for their manual labor; that seems excluded. But certain symbolic gestures, like avoiding coins on principle, took time to develop—*pace* Dalarun (1996), 185. Even in Test 22, Francis still puts begging (so central to later Franciscan identity) second to manual labor. Manselli (1975), 272–73, and Desbonnets (1983), 23, are good on this. The word *laboritium* used in the Testament is cognate with the Italian *lavoraccio,* meaning "tedious manual work." Along with wandering about, day labor seems a central marker of Francis's pre-1209 life.

Early Franciscan preaching (pp. 40–41)
For examples of the nonverbal element in the brothers' preaching, see 1C 27, 1C 86, and 2C 157, and of the preference for actions over words, 2C 207. Delcorno (1977) is the best overview of early preaching by Francis and his followers. But he should be read with care because of his very uncritical treatment of sources. He accepts (ibid., 153) the fourteenth-century version of the sermon to the birds, making them birds of prey, rather than the sober account in 1C. He accepts without issue the Mass of the Apostles story (ibid., 128). Especially

good is his discussion of possible refinements of Francis's early rough-and-ready methods (ibid., 146–49). I am skeptical of the text (AC 103), which Delcorno (1977), 142–43, adduces to show that Francis used secular literary examples (here Roland and Oliver) in his sermons. In a less helpful essay, Cardini (1976), 60–62, gives a useful catalog of behavior reported of Francis. Late witnesses to Francis as aggressively seeking opportunities to preach (e.g., from reluctant bishops in 2C 147) do not ring true. Manselli (1975), 260, says rightly: "La vera predicazione di Francesco era la sua vita." Delcorno (1977), 136, discusses Francis's encounter with the Dominican, where the saint explains Ezekiel; see 2C 102–103 = AC 35–36.

Delcorno (1977), 133, argues that Francis and his first followers principally preached repentance and peace. Although 1C uses biblical models, the reports in Jacques de Vitry and others make this credible. Repentance and peacemaking went together in thirteenth-century preaching. See Delcorno (1977), 134–36, again on Francis urging people to praise God. The themes of repentance, peace, and praise are linked in 1LtCus and 2LtCus. The Perugia peace sermon is in AC 75 (LP 35) and 2C 37 and is probably connected with a civil war there in 1222. For comparison, see Thompson (1992), 136–56, which discusses preaching against civic faction.

Francis as a preacher (pp. 42–43)
The doctor's report on Francis's preaching is in 2C 107b. See Manselli (1982), 185, on political harangues (*concinationes*) of the period; Boncompagno of Signi, the contemporary teacher of rhetoric, describes them as involving gesture, costumes, shaking of weapons, etc., as much as spoken words. The Bologna sermon is also described by Thomas of Split (FA:ED 2:808), and in a sermon of Federico Visconti, edited in *Rivista di Storia della Chiesa in Italia* 6 (1952): 236. Both were eyewitnesses. On the Bologna sermon, see also Delcorno (1977), 150–52, who considers it an early version of the "modern style" of thirteenth-century preaching, based on divisions and exempla. For Francis's singing in French when preaching, see 2C 127 (= AC 38). See Dalarun (1997), 144–45, on the wordless sermon to the nuns. The sermon at Terni, and "I could still have sons and daughters," are in AC 10 (LP 103); 2C 133 (no location); 2C 141–42 (with location). Miccoli (1991), 244, considers Francis's self-deprecatory reference to "sons and daughters" certainly authentic.

Francis and miracles (pp. 43–44)
What distinguishes miracles reported of Francis is the theme of compassion. Examples of Francis helping brothers tempted by lust are found in 2C 110 and 118, where the events receive a miraculous flavor from the presence of the

demonic. The depressed brother is in AC 55 (LP 7) and 2C 124. The abbot's encounter is in AC 76 (LP 30) and 2C 101 (which identifies the monastery). The woman with the cruel husband is in AC 69 (LP 27) and 2C 38.

The earliest collection of "life miracles" for Francis, as opposed to those worked after death, is found in 1C 62–70, and the stories I recount are from this source. As miracle collecting (and inventing) is perhaps the most typical aspect of hagiographic fabrication, this least-developed collection is most likely to record actual historical events. There is little to distinguish the 1C miracle stories from the typical life miracles reviewed in Thompson (1992), 111–17; and Thompson (2005), 206–16. Francis's hesitancy to work miracles itself is a hagiographic conceit, but probably authentic.

Francis's temptations (p. 45)
AC 78 (LP 37b), L3P 14, AC 63 (LP 21), and 2C 116 and 97 describe a severe temptation or spiritual crisis soon after the establishment at the Porziuncula. The link with the Porziuncula is explicit in L3P. AC says that the crisis lasted about two years and happened "a few years after his conversion." All reports, including a general one in 2C 99, suggest that prayer was the only remedy.

The attempted voyage to the Middle East (pp. 45–46)
Only one source (1C 55) records Francis's attempt to go to the Holy Land. The dating of his trip in "sexto namque conversionis suae anno" (in the sixth year of his conversion) places it between the summer of 1211 and the summer of 1212. Since Clare's conversion would occupy Francis in the spring of 1212, and the stormy weather encountered suggests the end of the sailing season, summer 1211 seems best. This also fits the end of the two-year period of "temptations." Di Fonzo (1982), 101–2, summarizes arguments for the earlier dating, but this places the arrival at the Porziuncula far too late. 1C puts the best spin possible on this decision to run away: Francis was a bold disciple of Christ, willing to risk all for him. His little band of followers probably took a less sanguine view.

The Conversion of Clare

On Clare and her movement, see Alberzoni (1996) and Bertoli (2002); Vauchez (2009), 104–11, provides a brief overview.

It is interesting that although sources for Francis's life mention Clare and the Poor Ladies, none describe Francis's role in her conversion in any detail. This event must be reconstructed from sources for Clare, particularly PC (CA:ED 139–98) and LCl (CA:ED 272–329), which is often ascribed, probably wrongly, to Thomas of Celano. LCl 5–8 describes Clare's conversion. This version says that she heard of Francis, sought him out on her own initiative, and visited him clandestinely. Nevertheless, PC 12.2, the testimony of her sister Beatrice, says that the first contact was made by Francis. Bona di Gualfuccio in her testimony, recorded in PC 17.3, reports numerous secret meetings with Francis. Her version fits better with the story that it was Rufino who brought Clare to Francis's attention. In any case, all versions indicate that she came to him more often than he went to her.

The writings ascribed to Clare and used in the past as sources for Francis may be derivative and of no independent value, even if Clare was their author. TestCl and the PrPov may rework material from L3C, on which, see Dalarun (1996), 29. Bertoli (1993) also rejects TestCl but suggests that Clare's oral testimony may have helped form the image of Francis for those who compiled material for Crescentius of Iesi. He suggests they got information from a "San Damiano circle" of nuns. It is also possible that, as Dalarun (1997), 194, suggests, some of the reminiscences in PC concerning Francis are authentic.

As to the hagiographic assertion (L3C 24) that Francis foresaw a female branch of his order at San Damiano, I agree with Dalarun (1996), 82, in rejecting this as retrojection. I also agree with his opinion (ibid., 52, where he reports an oral communication to the same effect from Miccoli) that Francis never anticipated recruiting women, an opinion also shared by Manselli (1982), 151.

Clare's family (p. 46)

Fortini (1959), 2:315–17, 327–49, proves that Clare's family were not the Scifi, lords of Sasso Rosso or Coccornano. Her parents were Favarone (alive in 1229) and Ortolana (no dates given). She was niece of Monaldo, lord of Coriano, and her grandfather Offreduccio di Bernardo (1145–77) was a "bonus homo." Perhaps the family was in exile in Perugia at the time of Collestrada, but this has not been proved. I am not willing to speculate, as Di Ciaccia (1982b), 327–35, does, about a supposed clash between Francis's bourgeois family and the aristocratic family of Clare, a conflict not found in any sources.

Clare's "conversion" (p. 46)

The old debates over whether Clare had her hair cut on Palm Sunday 1211 or Palm Sunday 1212 has now been settled in favor of the later date. The work of Cresi (1954) and Hardick (1962) ended this debate. Di Fonzo (1982), 101–2, presents systematic arguments for the later date. See Brown (1965), 382–83, for a brief discussion of this dating. Thus the event occurred on 18 March 1212. We actually know very little with certainty about Rufino, who seems to have collected stories for Crescentius of Iesi; for possible leads, see Fortini (1959),

2:383–87. That Bishop Guido died before 14 September 1212 seems proved by a document of that date for the then Bishop Guido that mentions a lawsuit "predecessori tuo" dated to 1208. That earlier bishop, also named Guido, was the bishop of Francis's conversion and the early years of the movement. On the two bishops named Guido, see D'Acunto (1996), esp. 500. On Francis's cutting of Clare's hair and its significance, see Padovese (1992).

That Francis composed a rule of some sort for Clare and the nuns of San Damiano is reported in 2C 204, FLCl 6.2, and, of course, TestCl 27–29. On the value of these reports, see Bertoli (1993), 174–78. On the other hand, FLCl has such clear parallels with LR that it, rather than some lost original Rule for Clare, would seem to be the source. On the close textual borrowings, see Grau (1953), who thinks that Clare wanted to adopt the LR itself as that of the nuns.

Clare and Francis (p. 48)

Imagination runs wild over the relationship between Clare and Francis. Evidence of intense personal contact is certain only around the time of her conversion, as Flood (1983), 8, notes, citing the PC testimony of Bona di Guelfuccio. Some stretch these reports to mean more than they literally do. For example, Di Ciaccia (1982b), 327–35, constructs a chivalric relationship between Francis and his "Lady Clare." Dalarun (1997), 199, is more guarded: nearly all encounters of Francis and Clare are by writing, not in person. Dalarun admits (ibid., 36) that San Damiano was not a "branch" of the men's "order," and that if Francis had a close relationship with any woman, it was with "Brother Jacoba," not Clare (ibid., 123). Vauchez (2009), 166–67, concurs with Dalarun's analysis.

In 2C 205, the friars themselves notice that Francis avoids contact with women, even the Clares. Perhaps, as Dalarun (1997), 63–64, suggests, the adoption of the title "Poor Ladies" for Clare's followers represents an attempt to distance the friars from penitent women drawn to the movement, but he is loath to ascribe such a move to Francis. Frankly, I don't see why not. There is plenty of conventionally "misogynist" ascetical concern about women in the later biographies, all put into Francis's mouth: AC 69; 2C 38, 53, 59, 60, 86, 92, 95, 132, 155, 157; and especially 2C 113–14 (= AC 37). But I agree with the editors in FA:ED 2:321 n. b, that these passages represent the 1240s, not the 1210s.

In the face of all the wishful thinking about Francis's positive attitudes toward women, I have to agree with Dalarun (1997), 102–3, who, with resignation, concludes that virtually every description of Francis encountering a woman in 1C and 2C rewrites an incident from the Life of St. Martin of Tours, and so seems hagiographic invention. I consider further speculation on Francis's attitudes toward women pointless.

Francis's trip to Spain (pp. 48–49)
The sole source for this journey is 1C 51. Tellingly, the story is introduced and concluded by reports that many men, from all states of life, were entering the fraternity. The rise in numbers and the trip seem linked. The event is not dated, but sometime within the two years after Clare's conversion (1213–14) is most likely. Like Francis's first, failed attempt to reach the Holy Land, this trip was an embarrassment to Celano and disappeared from his second life. The sense that Francis was twice on the run and got nowhere does not fit the image of a divinely guided saint.

Francis Faces New Growth

Manselli (1982), 169–223, covers the material of this section, as does Pellegrini (1982b), who also treats more directly the movement's canonical status in the period.

La Verna (p. 49)
The donation of La Verna to Francis is recorded in a 9 July 1274 act of Orlando, Cungio, Bandino, and Guglielmo, all sons of Count Orlando, ratifying their father's oral transmission of the property. The document was still in the archives of Borgo San Sepulchro in the 1700s. Mencherini (1924), 38–39, presents an edition of the text. The document records that the brothers also gave the friars the tableware that Francis had used when he visited the count. Unfortunately, what motivated the donation—supposedly an especially moving sermon by Francis on the saints at the castle of the Count of Montefeltro, where Orlando was a guest—is found first in the very late *Actus Sancti Francesci et Sociorum* 9 and the derivative *Fioretti*. 1C 94 mentions the gift. On these events, see Lazzeri (1913). By 1215, Brother Giles had already decided to become a full-time hermit, as Esser (1966), 228, notes. This place would serve as a hermitage.

Names for the movement (p. 49)
Francis's use of *vita* in the Testament, and the sources' use of *religio*, rather than *regula* and *ordo*, have led some scholars, including Lambertini-Tabarroni (1989), 28, to emphasize the "formlessness" and "spontaneity" of the early brotherhood. In contrast, Desbonnets (1983), 65, concludes that *religio* and *ordo* were synonyms by the 1200s. But he still wants the *fraternitas* founded by Francis to be more free-form than earlier religious orders. I would emphasize, along with Dalarun (1996), 182, that Francis's followers described themselves as "penitents from Assisi." Unlike Dalarun, but following Desbonnets (1983), I suspect this

means that they associated their way of life with the *fratres de poenitentia,* which was a canonical status and an *ordo* in the medieval sense. The *fratres* were the first lay order, the *conversi* or *penitenti,* and they predate Francis. He did not have to invent the status. This is most likely the canonical category in which Church authorities put the early brothers as well.

Francis, Fourth Lateran, and Saint Dominic Guzman (pp. 49–50)

On the supposed revision of the Rule after Lateran IV, and approval by Honorius III between 1216 and 1219, see Vauchez (2009), 137–38. Fourth Lateran Council, c. 13, required founders of new religious orders to adopt one of the traditional rules. Historians have supposed that Francis was at this assembly, perhaps to argue that his order was exempt because it predated the council. I am very suspicious of this speculation, which does not mesh with Francis's nonlegalistic mind-set. Readers conversant with images from legends and art know that Francis met the founder of the Order of Preachers, Saint Dominic Guzman, at Lateran IV. Sources for this meeting are so late and so politically invested as to be worthless as evidence for the saint's presence in Rome and at this supposed meeting. The earliest report of a meeting of the two founders is 2C 148–50 (repeated by AC 49), which says nothing of the Lateran Council. The background of this story may well be the 1246 letter of the master general of the Dominican Order, Johannes Teutonicus, and the Franciscan minister general, John of Parma, on fostering harmony between the orders. The close match of dates for the 2C report and the letter suggest that the story is an exemplum, not a historical event. The 2C story includes a long diatribe against friars seeking prelacy and ends with Dominic trying to merge his southern French movement into the Franciscans, as yet a small group of penitents around Assisi. The anachronism is painfully obvious.

A meeting of the two saints is not impossible at some date, but no report of such a meeting is trustworthy. Vicaire (1964), 494 n. 41, is very dubious about any meeting between the two founders. On the story of the dinner with Hugolino itself, in all its permutations, see Pásztor (1976), 225–34. She has doubts similar to mine about the historicity. Manselli (1982), 354, believes the story of Francis embarrassing the prelates by going out and begging for his dinner. Such an act seems to me totally out of character for Francis, who always showed an exaggerated respect for clerics. Brooke (2006), 229–39, probably makes the best case for the historicity of the meeting at Hugolino's, but her major argument is that such a meeting was necessary to convince Dominic to change his order of canons regular into "mendicant friars." On the anachronism of such a transformation of the Order of Preachers at this early date, see Thompson (2011).

Jacques de Vitry on the "Lesser Brothers and Sisters" (pp. 50–52)
The only source for the "Lesser Brothers and Sisters" is Jacques de Vitry, on which see De Beer (1977). De Beer's biography of Francis is founded on the idea that de Vitry and Francis's own writings are the only secure primary sources for events during Francis's life. As Lambertini-Tabarroni (1989), 22, notes, Jacques de Vitry was the first non-Franciscan witness to the movement. Dalarun (1996), 84, noting de Vitry's use of the phrase *fratres et sorores minores,* suggests a "true community between men and women" in the movement's early days but denies (ibid., 53) mixed communities of men and women. This would doubtless have produced grounds for much criticism, were it the case. Stanislao da Compagnola (1973), 435 n. 263, wonders if these minor sisters were eventually suppressed. Manselli (1982), 175, thinks "sorores" merely refers to the nuns at San Damiano. Van Asseldonk (1992), esp. 612–24, who uses late and doubtful sources, discusses the state of the question without any conclusive result.

The more recent consensus is represented by the essays of Maria Pia Alberzoni, Marco Bartoli Langeli, and Alfonso Marini in *Chiara* (1998). The scholars favor mixed male and female Franciscan groups, at least at some early point, and tend to include the San Damiano group as among these "Lesser Sisters." These women would be working along with the brothers in hospitals and leprosaria and have nothing like the later cloister. For a summary, see Vauchez (2009), 106–8. This vision of actively apostolic gender equality has proved very attractive to some scholars. But Jacques de Vitry's characterizations remain open to other interpretations. As for Francis himself, it seems that he objected to the use of the term *sorores minores,* when it was used by Cardinal Hugolino for the San Damiano group, and instead preferred Dominae Pauperes, a name that distinguished them from the Friars Minor, but the *sorores minores* themselves do not seem to have been formally suppressed until 1241 by Gregory IX: Vauchez (2009), 251–52. On Clare's relationship to Hugolino, see Vauchez (2009), 167, 256–68. On Clare's relations with the papacy, especially after Francis's death, see Alberzoni (1995).

Observers of Francis's movement (pp. 52–53)
See De Beer (1977), 62–63, on de Vitry's and Chateauroux's reactions to Francis's lax admissions policies. The story of the poor woman and the king is found in a primitive form in a 1219 sermon of Odo of Cheriton (FA:ED 1:591), AP 35, L3C 50, and, in a reworked version, 2C 16–17. The three later versions have Francis telling the story to the pope, where the punch line is about poverty, not gatekeeping. On the incident, see Dalarun (1996), 91, and De Beer (1963), 269–71. The date of 1219 for the exemplum of Odo is somewhat

debatable: Friend (1948). But it does fit well with conditions in 1216–19. The beans incident is in AC 52 (LP 3). Giving the cloak to the beggar woman is in AC 82 (LP 41) and 2C 132. In 1C 52, Francis expresses the same concern about hypocrisy. Merlo (1992), 541–52, is right about the "reformist" appeal of Francis to men of his age, but I cannot follow his suggestion that it entailed a personal frustration with the "institutional Church."

ON CHAPTER FOUR

V AUCHEZ (2009), 135–54, covers the period of this chapter; see ibid., 122, on the dedication inscription in Santa Maria Maggiore, Assisi.

Francis and Nature

Bibliography (pp. 54–58)
A great deal of writing has focused on Francis's relationship to nature, not all of it careful when interpreting sources. The most sober scientific study of Francis and nature is Marini (1989), which is scrupulous about trying to retrieve the historical events behind the legends. Marini divides studies of the topic into four categories: historical, theological, mystical, and ecological. I agree with Marini's approach that writings in the last three categories must be founded on solid work in the first.

Among historical studies, Marini flags three as deserving attention. These are Manselli (1982), whose interpretation of Francis's relationship with nature as "white magic" Marini (1989), 17, rejects; Armstrong (1976), which is marred by an uncritical approach to texts; and, finally, Cardini (1981), which is a literary study of animals in Francis's hagiography, with little on the historical events themselves. Similar to Cardini, in English, is Short (1988).

Nature in Francis's writings (pp. 55–56)
Sorell (1988) attempts to place Francis's relationship to nature within the Christian tradition. On Francis's own use of animal images, see Marini (1989),

33–34. I thank Nathan Jennings for the biblical source of the "Dream of the Black Hen." Francis's legislation is LR 41–42, on horses; and ER 15, on pets. See Marini (1989), 38, for Francis's identification of horses with pride. Feeding animals on Christmas is recorded in AC 14c. Biblical nature imagery appears in ExhP, "Praises to Be Said at All the Hours" 8, "Salutation of the Virtues" (cf. John 19:11), and 2LtF (cf. Rev. 5:13). Animals as models of obedience to God appears uniquely in Adm 5:1–2.

For a table of animal stories in the hagiography, see Marini (1989), 181–82. As Short (1988), 493–95, notes, the usual focus in stories on Francis and animals is, following hagiographic stereotype, his power over them. When stories in 1C do not show this characteristic, they may well be unreworked and historical. Marini (1989), 93, 97, notes that stories in early sources often show a warm familiarity with animals; later stories turn them into opportunities for moral lessons or displays of power (Manselli's "white magic"). Simple 1C animal stories later become, for example in L3C, exemplary anecdotes. Especially in late sources like Bonaventure, "humanized" animal behavior and miracles dominate.

Because of the progressive assimilation of animal stories to hagiographic stereotypes, I restrict my discussion to the animal stories found in 1C and some of the more clearly unreworked stories in AC. The earliest animal stories are 1C 58 (preaching to the birds), 59 (the swallows at Alviano), 60a (the hare at Greccio), 60b (the hare at Trasimeno), 61 (the tench at Pediluca), 77–78 (the lamb of Osimo), 79 (the lambs in the Marche), 80a (the worms on the road), 80b (bees as a model), and 84–85 (the crèche at Greccio). Other animal stories with a claim to authenticity, such as the flight of larks over Francis's cell at his death (L3C 32; AC 14—a *Nos qui cum eo fuimus* report), which are linked to specific incidents in his life, I include later at the proper chronological points in Francis's life. A good number of independent stories in AC, with little glossing or symbolism, are probably historical, but the material listed is sufficient to discuss Francis's relation to nature. See Marini (1989), 121, on the AC witnesses, who focus on Francis's love of animals directly.

Short (1988), 493–95, is good on how Francis's love of animals becomes control over them through hagiographic reworking. He singles out two primitive elements in the stories: Francis's personal relation to animals as his brothers/ sisters, and how they moved him to prayer.

Hagiographic nature stories (pp. 56–57)
Sister Cricket is in AC 110 (which already implies power over nature) and, with more miraculous tone, in 2C 171. The care for worms is in 1C 80 and (perhaps more primitive because of the absence of biblical typology) in 2C 165. On this incident, see Marini (1989), 89, who notes that saints who save

animals, which then refuse to depart, is a hagiographic topos. The animal-release stories in 1C 60–61 are wholly conventional, save in the personal affection Francis expressed for the creatures. See Short (1988), 488–93, on nonstereotyped aspects of these release stories. See Marini (1989), 106–7, on Celano's heavy glossing of such stories. The lamb stories are in 1C 77–79; on them, see Marini (1989), 80–81.

The "Sermon to the Birds" (pp. 57–58)

On the famous incident of Francis preaching to the birds, see Marini (1989), 98–100, who, unlike Manselli, thinks it is probably historical. As Marini notes, there are two versions of this incident: at Bevagna (1C 58), where Francis simply delights in the birds; and at Aviano (1C 59), where he tells them to be silent and listen while he preaches to people. The Aviano story is stereotyped in showing power over animals; the Bevagna incident, which I retell without Celano's glosses, is not about power at all. Its lack of stereotype and its unmediated simplicity convince me that the incident is authentic. See Short (1988), 478–88, on the stereotyped elements present, and how they seem an intrusion.

Finally, we should not romanticize Francis's relationship to nature: he could be tormented by mice and vermin and consider them agents of the devil (AC 83), or even consider a gluttonous bird that drowned as cursed. See Marini (1989), 150–52, on this unexpected side of Francis.

Integration into the Life of the Church

The visit of Bishop Guido (p. 58)

See D'Acunto (1996) on the contrast between "Guido II" and "Guido III." Although this article proves to my satisfaction that a different Guido was bishop after 1212, this position remains controversial. For a summary that assumes the same man was involved, see Canonici (1980). AC 54 (LP 6) and 2C 100 describe the unannounced visit to Francis's cell and the miraculous expulsion of the bishop because he was "indignus" to see Francis. On this story, see Canonici (1980), 490. This divine intervention, like Bishop Guido III's vision of Francis in heaven in 2C 220, is probably hagiographic confection, but that there were unannounced episcopal visits to give rise to the story is certainly possible. See Canonici (1980), 190–92, on these texts. See also Flood (1983), 61, 122, on the ecclesio-political moves of Guido III.

The 1217 Pentecost chapter (p. 58)

That Francis wanted the brothers to meet twice yearly is recorded in AP 36 and L3C 57. The only trustworthy sources on Franciscan chapters before 1217 are AP 37–39 and L3C 58–59. L3C sometimes seems more vivid than

AP, but both sound secondhand and generalized in comparison to the sur-rounding material. For evaluation of these opaque but important sources, see Beguin (1979), 16–17, and Di Fonzo (1972), 369. AC 109 may be a descrip-tion of an early chapter. I have followed AP and L3C for Francis's concerns at these chapters. The exemplum of brothers rejecting his teaching is from AC 109.

Di Fonzo (1972), 370, Desbonnets (1983), 34, and Callebaut (1926), 540–41, date the chapter of ChJG 3, AP 44, and L3C 61 to Pentecost 1217. This is the current consensus. I believe it is correct, even though Jordan of Giano says the date was 1219. Giano's date is too late to fit in another chapter before Francis left for Egypt. The actual dating in Jordan is garbled, with an impossible year of indiction, but the dating of the chapter as on the tenth before the calends of June (23 May) puts it on the Monday after Pentecost Sunday of 1217; no other year has a Pentecost date even close to a match.

On Elias of Assisi, see Barone (1992), esp. 61, on the loconymic "of As-sisi." This essay has extensive bibliography and updates Barone (1974), 89–108, which deals with the period of Francis's lifetime. Since Brooke (1959), histori-ans have tended to present an image of Elias less warped by Spiritual Francis-can propaganda. One thirteenth-century document suggests that he was from Orsaia near Cortona: Fortini (1959) 2:299. Fortini (1959), 2:300, and Di Fonzo (1961) compile information about Elias's family and background. He seems to have worked as a scribe (or a notary, which would mean university training in law), but secure information for before he entered the order is scarce. Fortini would have him as a consul of Assisi in 1198, based on surname identification. He probably entered the order about 1215.

ChJG 7 and 9 tell us that Elias was sent east after the 1216 chapter, which may also have sent the martyrs to Spain, and that Francis appointed him as minister for the group going to Syria. Elias's departure is also recorded in Richer of Sens (FA:ED 2:810), on which, see De Beer (1977), 98.

Supposed division of provinces (p. 58)
There is no evidence in the sources for division of the order into provinces at this date. What ChJG 3 actually says is the following: "It sent brothers to France, Germany, Hungary, Spain, and the other provinces of Italy." AP 44 says the chapter "sent some of the brothers throughout almost all the provinces of the world where the Catholic faith was practiced"; L3C 61 says: "Ministers were chosen and sent with some of the brothers throughout nearly the entire world in which the Catholic faith was practiced and observed."

The modern idea, assumed in Manselli (1982), 200–202, that this meant the creation of geographical divisions is anachronistic and unfounded. On the actual appearance of geographic provinces in the Franciscan and Dominican orders, see Tugwell (2005), 29–45. Esser (1966), 72, repeats a story from Olivi about Saint Dominic being at a Franciscan general chapter, which could only have been be that of 1218. This is a flimsy source for an impossible event (at that date). Dominic left Rome for Spain, by way of Bologna, in early May 1218, a month before the June chapter in Assisi; see Vicaire (1964), 249.

Hugolino at Florence (pp. 59–60)

I agree with Rusconi (1994), 85–86, that the period after 1215 saw escalating interest in the Franciscans by Rome. ChJG 11 describes the Franciscan Rule in 1217 as "non...confirmatam a papa regulam, sed concessam." Callebaut (1926), 549–51, suggests friendly contacts between Jacques de Vitry and Hugolino and notes that Hugolino was witness to an act of arbitration between Guido III and his canons on 8 May 1217. D'Acunto (1996), 513–14, suggests that Bishop Guido III was one of those opposed to the new Franciscans, which seems a stretch, although Franciscan sources are less positive in reference to Guido III than to his predecessor.

Francis's encounter of Cardinal Hugolino in Florence is mentioned briefly in 1C 75, with a very diplomatic description of Hugolino's attitude. AC 108 (LP 79–82) has more detail and is less flattering to the cardinal; 2C 108 and 201 contain parallels but omit the actual encounter of the cardinal. After introducing Hugolino in 1C 73, 1C 75 rehearses the encounter at Florence as a flashback after describing Francis's trip to Egypt, but it is clear that this event is connected with the chapter of 1217.

Pásztor (1976), 209–17, is very useful in disentangling the sources for Francis's encounter of Hugolino at Florence. Beguin (1979), 132, notes that 1C 73 wrongly introduces Hugolino as already cardinal protector, which is corrected in 2C 74–75. Miccoli (1991), 201–3, commenting on 1C 73–75, thinks that Francis committed the Order to him at this time, which is certainly too early. This was an initial brief encounter, into which hagiographers retrojected later realities. The encounter seems casual and unplanned on the part of Hugolino.

There is no need to doubt the report in AP 43 that after Hugolino extended his offer of support, Francis invited him to attend future Franciscan chapters. The number he could have actually attended (cf. AP, which says "all") is rather small. Modern biographers usually introduce Cardinal Hugolino as a participant at early Franciscan chapters, but he was surely not at any meeting before 1217, the year he first met Francis. As he was legate in Lombardy during the chapters of 1220 and 1222–26, the only early chapters he could have attended are those of 1218 and 1219 (when Francis was abroad).

"The Hugolino Problem" (p. 60)
Manselli (1982), 187–213, introduces the "Hugolino Problem" at this point in his narrative, although he says that "the result of most recent research on the role of Ugolino in the history of Franciscanism in its early years is very modest indeed." I am even more skeptical than Manselli of Hugolino's importance before 1219. Even if he came to the chapter of 1218, which I think likely, Hugolino was not regularly involved in Franciscan affairs until after 1220, and not "cardinal protector" until that office was invented in 1223. I do not see Hugolino's early involvement with Francis as an expression of Church policy, as Selge (1971), 192–93, does.

Francis Dispatches Letters and Missions

Francis and the Eucharist (pp. 60–63)
AC 108 explicitly links Francis's teaching on reverence for the Host and written holy words to his inability to go to France. The "First Letter to the Clergy" is Francis's oldest letter, because the "Exhortation to the Brothers and Sisters of Penance" is not a letter. Reverence for the Host and devotion to the Mass (after perhaps Christ on the Cross, to which they are closely related) are the most recurring themes in Francis's writings. In fact, they vastly outnumber references to poverty. The quotations from Francis come from Test 4–5 (churches), 10–11 (Eucharist), and 6, 9 (priests). One can cite not just the long section of the Testament, but also Adm 1, 7, 26; 1LtCl; 2LtCl; 1LtCus; 2LtCus; 1LtF; 2LtF 4–27, 32–36; LtOrd 12–16; LtR 6–8; ER 20. On Francis's wish that friars supply precious pyxes to churches lacking them, see AC 108 (LP 80).

Francis's sacramental and rubrical fixation does not go down well with some modern writers, including Franciscans. It is telling that Flood (1983), 142, can discuss Francis on the Eucharist and priests in a mere four sentences. Schmucki (1986), 256–58, however, is very good on the Eucharistic aspects of Francis's mysticism. For him, Francis is a "sacramental" mystic, not a "nature" mystic. See Miccoli (1991), 56–58, on Adm 1; and Grau (1970), who defends its authenticity effectively. On this admonition generally, see also Freeman (1988) and Esser (1960), which is the most systematic treatment.

Francis's reverence for sacred words (p. 63)
Francis's explanation of why he venerates written words from the scriptures is found in 1C 82 (cf. Adm 17.18). He dwells on this topic in 1LtCl, 2LtCl, 1LtCus, 2LtCus, LtOrd, and Test. Schmucki (1980), 253, links Francis's "fissazione" on parchment scraps to his liturgical sensitivity, which is no doubt

true, at least in part. In contrast, Langeli (1984), 46–50, links his concern for the Host and written sacred words to their "corporeality," which is no doubt also correct. But, less convincingly, Langeli sees this as an example of Francis's "magical" and "popular" piety. Less convincing, because of date, is his attempt to link the development to Jewish and Muslim practice in Egypt. "Magical" is right here, if the word is understood in an anthropological sense, as exemplified by the approach of Douglas (1973), 9–11, but there is nothing particularly lay about this medieval attitude. Medieval clergy and laity both had, to use Langeli's words, a "sacramentalismo magico." On this common medieval attitude, see Thompson (2005), 253–64, 358–63. Delcorno (1977), 131, is good when he connects word and sacrament in Francis's piety.

Francis at Pentecost chapters (pp. 63–64)
As Rusconi (1994), 85–86, remarks, even if the Franciscan movement in the period 1210–16 was canonically more a lay confraternity than an order, the appearance of regular chapters after the Lateran Council is very significant; see Esser (1966), 76–80, and Desbonnets (1983), 31. Lateran IV, c. 12, mandated regular chapters for religious orders and recommended that experts be invited to help conduct them. Cistercians often provided these experts. See Esser (1960), 29–30, on the names given the movement at this date. Burchard of Ursperg (FA:ED 1:593) still calls them "pauperes minores" as late as 1228; in 1216, Jacques de Vitry called them "minores" and "fratres minores." But they will not be the "Ordo Fratrum Minorum" until 1221. I agree with Manselli (1982), 177–78, that if there ever were two chapters a year (as L3C 14 says), this practice was obsolete by 1216, when de Vitry reported only one a year. If de Vitry was wrong, then the number of chapters was at some point reduced. LR 8.3 says that they need to happen at least once in three years, not that they no longer happen twice a year. On the number of chapters a year and their purpose, see Esser (1966), 76–80. I have not been able to find a single reference to a September chapter. The appearance of September chapters in various scholars' chronologies is hypothetical and unjustified. The only datable chapters were at Pentecost. It is telling that 1C, which focuses directly on Francis rather than his order, says nothing about chapters, save one legend about a much later provincial assembly in Provence. Specific activities at chapters are recorded in AP 44 and L3C 61–62; ChJG 3–19 is by far the most informative and thorough.

2C 191–92 contains descriptions of Francis's behavior at chapters, which sound authentic. He urged the learned to act humbly and the simple to recite some scripture so that they have something to contribute. See De Beer (1963), 16, on Odo of Cheriton's sermon. My reading of Francis's difficulty in providing the correction required of a religious superior because of his refusal to place his own will over those of others draws much from Miccoli (1991), 58–72, who cites Adm 2, LtMin (which is later), TPJ (even later), and 2C 152, where martyrdom is better than convincing people to convert. Miccoli (1991), 56, dates the *Admonitions* to the "heroic" period (1209–21). Francis's emphasis on reverence for the clergy and sacraments in this (and later) periods has led Landini (1968), 55, to suggest that Francis himself was a "crypto-clericalizer" of his own order. Maybe it just means he was not an anticlerical.

On the first missions and their poor reception, see ChJG 4–9, AP 44, and L3C 62. AP says that the expulsion was linked to the lack of an approved rule. Both AP and L3C show verbal similarities to ChJG.

Cardinal Hugolino at Pentecost chapters (p. 65)
AP conflates the complaints to Cardinal Hugolino with the approbation of the 1223 Rule, but the complaining must have started on the missionary friars' return, if Hugolino was at the 1218 chapter. In 1218, Hugolino was at Siena on 30 May and Perugia on 31 July, and the chapter was on 3 June—a trip of four days from Siena to Assisi is possible. In 1219, he was in Bologna on 18 May and on 12 June, and the chapter was 26 May—Callebaut (1926), 536. So, in terms of distance, 1219 is less likely than 1218 for the appearance at the chapter mentioned in AP.

Roman protection for missions (p. 66)
I doubt Francis sought out Roman support in this period. Merlo (1991b), 82, notes that the only time Francis ever used the words "Curia Romana" in his writings was when he forbade seeking privileges there. AP is very blunt and says that "the brothers" (not Francis) complained to the cardinal; L3C puts a better face on this by rendering the complaint in the passive voice. Rusconi (1994), 88, links Honorius's *Cum Dilecti Filii* (11 June 1219) with the missions of the 26 May 1219 chapter, which seems a bit quick to me. Francis's negative reaction to a brother's suggestion that recourse be made to Rome for protection is in AC 20 (LP 115). Although this story's references to the Rule are anachronistic, the condemnation of the brothers' avarice certainly expresses Francis's views accurately.

Francis Abroad

The Fifth Crusade (pp. 66–71)
On the Fifth Crusade and the politics of the Orient in the 1210s and 1220s, see Powell (1986), esp. 158–60, 187, on Francis's presence in Egypt. Golubovich (1926), in spite of its age, is very sober and generally convincing, even

if I do not accept all its conclusions. Over the centuries, stories and artifacts purported to relate to Francis's visit to the sultan appeared or were fabricated (including the gifts that Francis refused); those wanting a history of the way the visit has been understood, beginning with the earliest sources, may consult Ghinato (1964).

Sources for Francis in Egypt (pp. 66–71)

Principal sources for Francis's trip to Egypt are 1C 57 (sketchy and celebratory), 2C 30 (Francis predicts disaster for the Crusaders), ChJG 10–15, and Jacques de Vitry (FA:ED 1:582–85). See also the commentary in the Huygens edition of Jacques de Vitry's *Letters,* pp. 21 and 102, on the motivations of Cardinal Pelagius. As De Beer (1977), 27–38, notes, de Vitry's treatment of Francis in Egypt is heavy with biblical allusion (twenty references in sixteen lines) and formulaic at times. See Fortini (1959), 2:137–46, for the possible identifications of Brother Leonard of Assisi as the companion of Francis in Egypt. That Illuminato was with Francis, indeed was his *socius,* is in Bonaventure, LMj 9, n. 8, which is supposed to be the friar's eyewitness report. I prefer the more contemporary report of Jordan of Giano that his *socius* was Peter of Cataneo.

My description of the route to the East is what was "typical"; an exact determination of date or city of departure is impossible. Matanic (1976), 251, gives typical travel dates. I do not trust the commonly given date from Bartholomew of Pisa, whose departure date of 24 June sounds typological, as it makes Francis a new John the Baptist in Egypt.

Francis and the Crusaders (p. 67)

I will not speculate on the perennial topic of whether Francis's activities were "pacifistic" or "opposed to crusading." Francis never mentioned crusades (or war) in any of his writings. Medieval Franciscan and non-Franciscan chronicles give only two reasons for Francis's decision to go to Egypt: conversion of the sultan (and other Muslims by implication), and desire for martyrdom. Those are the only aspects of the trip treated by Francis in ER 16. Celano is candid that Francis was disturbed and emotionally upset, although he never says why. The Francis of 2C 30, a prophecy story, wanders about voicing anxiety about danger, not opposition to the Crusade in general. I take this report as it stands, and refuse to overinterpret it.

A review of scholarship up to the 1970s is found in Matanic (1976), 243–50, which is itself uncritical. It is speculation to suggest that Francis favored the princes and the "peace" party, rather than Cardinal Pelagius and the "war" party, although the sultan probably hoped as much. I take Francis at his word

(ER 16.5–7) that his hope was to convert the sultan, nothing more. That conversion of the Muslims would end (at least in theory) the Crusades does not mean that evangelization and crusade are somehow opposed concepts. On this, see Cardini (1974), esp. 221–34, which, although dated in many ways, is right on that point.

2C 30 is the earliest source to mention Francis's dire prophecy concerning the attack on Damietta. Much as it would be attractive to read Francis's words as advocating pacifism and as criticism of the military projects of the Crusade, I agree with Vauchez (2009), 152, that the point of the passage is Francis's clairvoyance, not opposition to the military. The report is essentially a miracle story to show Francis's supernatural vision of events. It has all the marks of an *ex eventu* prophecy. Its absence in all near-contemporary sources forces me to exclude it. As the prophecy predicts the failed attack of 29 August on Damietta, excluding this story as historical removes that date as a determined *terminus post quem* for arrival in Egypt.

The mission to the sultan (pp. 67–69)

On the mission to the sultan, see Tolan (2009), whose focus is principally on development of the legends surrounding the event. The mission is perhaps the best-documented event in Francis's life, at least in non-Franciscan sources. Moses (2009) is readable and popular but anachronistically reconfigures Francis as an antiwar activist. Lemmens (1926) has conveniently collected nearly all sources, original and derivative, on the visit to Egypt. The visit is described by Jacques de Vitry (FA:ED 1:582–85) and in a number of lay chronicles. The most extensive is the Old French *Chronicle of Ernoul* (FA:ED 1:605–7), around 1226/7, on which, see Morgan (1973). It is interesting that for all his detail, Ernoul does not seem to know Francis's name. Shorter, but different in several ways, is the Old French report in Bernard the Treasurer's *The Death of Coradin, Sultan of Damascus* (FA:ED 1:608), 1229/30, which confuses al-Kamil with his brother Malik al-Mu'azzam (Coradin). Bernard reports Francis's self-identification as an "ambassador of Christ," which sounds more authentic than the complex theological discourse Ernoul puts in Francis's mouth. The Old French *History of the Emperor Eracles* (FA:ED 1:609), 1229/31, has only a brief entry on Francis in Egypt but is very important for the detail that he left for Syria after the capture of Damietta because of the "growth of sin" in the conquering army. I draw on all these chronicles and de Vitry for my version of the event.

See Vauchez (2009), 146, on the Fâkhr ad-Din al-Fârisi inscription reported by a fifteenth-century Arab, Ibn al-Zayyât, who claimed to have seen it in the Cairo cemetery. Louis Massignon, "Mystique musulmane et mystique chrétienne," in *Opera minora* (Beirut, 1972), 2:482–84, first noticed this reference. De Beer (1977), 83, gives Yusuf Ahamd, *Turbal al-Fâkhr al-Fârisi* (Cairo, 1922), 17–18, as the published source. *Pace* Manselli (1982), 219–20, I do not find it surprising that al-Kamil received Francis: the sultan had been frustrated by Pelagius, and Francis gave him hope that negotiations might resume. It helped that Francis did not come with armed soldiers to protect him: he would have seemed a peace emissary to al-Kamil, just as he does to many modern scholars.

Francis's interview with al-Kamil (pp. 68–69)

The best discussion of the interview with the sultan is Powell (1983). See also Kadar (1984), 119–31. Less useful, I think, is De Beer (1977), 166–77, who is concerned to promote Francis's project as a peace emissary implicitly supporting Jean de Brienne and the princes against Cardinal Pelagius. This Francis sounds too politically motivated to me. De Beer's interpretation is very much influenced by his acceptance of Francis's prophecy in 2C 30 as historical. Powell (1986), 159, suggests September as the time of the visit. He is correct in placing it before the fall of the city, as Jordan of Giano reported, rather than after, as fourteenth-century chroniclers had it.

"The Trial by Fire" (p. 69)

I reject this famous incident found in LMj 9.8. Bonaventure is the earliest testimony that Francis offered to prove his faith to the sultan by walking through fire. That story implies a testing of God that seems alien to Francis, and the story is absent in all near-contemporary reports. The dialogue in "De Verbis Fratris Illuminati," Golubovich (1906) 1:36–37, from a fourteenth-century sermon collection, sounds just like a homiletic exemplum. Francis catches out the sultan in a series of Bible-quoting tricks and finally suggests that Muslims are blasphemers unjustly holding Christian lands. This sounds just the opposite of the approach Francis recommended in ER 16. I mention these late stories only because they are well known and I omit them. See Vauchez (2009), 191, on the "cor d'ivoire ainsi que deux baguettes" that the sultan supposedly gave Francis, now relics at the Sacro Convento in Assisi.

Francis on Muslim missions (pp. 69–70)

Jacques de Vitry makes the length of the stay with the sultan "dies aliquot" in his history and "multi dies" in his letter. Exactly how long is impossible to tell. ER 16, "On Those Going among the Saracens and Other Unbelievers," is very suggestive of Francis's own behavior in Egypt and his way of approaching the sultan. Francis proposes two forms of witness to Muslims: the first is simply to live a holy life among them; the second is to announce salvation in Christ. He seems to exclude attacking Islam, but he emphasizes that should persecution or death come, the friars are to accept it as from God. LR 12 cuts these personal reflections on preaching to Muslims.

Defections to the Franciscans (pp. 69–70)

Jacques de Vitry, *Letter* VI (FA:ED 1:581), describes defections from his clergy to the Franciscans. De Vitry wrote within a year of the event. Golubovich (1926), 315–16, publishes the document mentioning the Franciscan church in Damietta. He believes (ibid., 232) that Francis stayed in Egypt six months longer to personally take possession of this church in February. This deduction seems gratuitous and would make a trip to Syria less likely. The view of Manselli (1982), 223, is that Francis stayed until the reconquest of Damietta by the Muslims—that is, over a year. This seems even less likely, unless one puts the arrival of news from Italy in Egypt, not Syria. *History of the Emperor Eracles* (FA:ED 1:609) is the only source with a date, and it is uninvested in it. So I accept it: Francis left Damietta soon after 5 November. The violence of the sack may well have brought on the flashbacks of post-traumatic stress.

Francis in Syria (pp. 70–71)

ChJG 11–12 describes the nonvegetarian lunch. ChJG 14 seems to imply that Francis was in Syria when the lay brother arrived from Italy. Flood (1983), 139, who is often very critical of the sources, accepts Jordan's report. It may be that the presence of Elias, minister in Syria, is the origin of the story that Francis went to Syria. On the other hand, it seems unlikely that the new fasting laws were passed, and the lay brother arrived in the Orient by early November, when the *History of the Emperor Eracles* places Francis's departure from Egypt. So I too accept the trip to Syria.

The return to Italy (p. 71)

In spite of 1C 20's phrase "Syriam perambulans," there is no good evidence that Francis visited Jerusalem. Such a visit is unknown before Angelo Clareno. The Jerusalem visit is probably speculation based mostly on what Francis would have wanted to do, for which there is no evidence either. Basetti-Sani (1972) not only reviews the lack of evidence for a Jerusalem visit but edits Honorius III's bull *Cum Carissimi* (23 July 1217), forbidding Christian visits to Muslim Jerusalem. This alone would probably have prevented Francis from going. Francis, at most, visited the tiny stretch of Crusader-held coast.

See Brown (1965), 384, for the scholarly consensus favoring a late return. I see no reason to draw out Francis's stay in the East. The usual reason to extend the visit till spring is the "closing of the sea" during the winter. Although risky, shipping did not stop during the winter, and pilgrims did travel in winter: witness the Dominican Jordan of Saxony, whose ship back from the Holy Land sank with all hands in February 1237.

ON CHAPTER FIVE

S EE MANSELLI (1982), 223–46, and Vauchez (2009), 155–67, on the period
covered in this chapter.

Francis and the Cardinal

The "Fall from Grace" (p. 72)
Since Sabatier, those seeking a "Fall from Grace" among the early Franciscans
have focused on the events between 1219 and 1223. For a Fall from Grace
narrative, see Flood (1983), esp. 170. The older version of this story was that
poverty was compromised in this period. This is less popular today, and among
Franciscans themselves, "institutionalization" has become the original sin of
the 1220s. Esser (1960), Italian ed., 241; Stanislao da Compagnola (1973), 386;
Manselli (1982), 230–46; and Rusconi (1994), 89–92, all see the year 1220–21
as a period of crucial change in the movement. They are right. Francis tried to
set up structures that would keep the movement on track after he resigned and
withdrew. The changes arose because of Francis's decision; if the movement
fell from grace at this time, then it was the founder's fault. I do not believe in
Garden of Eden periods, so I see no reason to find someone to blame for this
supposed original sin.

Dietary regulations (p. 73)
Lambertini-Tabarroni (1989), 34–36, describes the events at home while Francis was in Egypt, but very generally. ChJG 12 is the most complete and best

source for these events. But, as Esser (1960), 93–94, notes in his useful commentary on the dietary changes, it is unlikely that the "rule" in use in 1219 imposed a fast on Wednesday, since even ER itself mentions only a Friday fast. Desbonnets (1983), 41, suggests that the changes in dietary regimen were "Cistercian inspired"; De Beer (1977), 45, goes further and says this legislation triggered in Francis a personal dislike for Cistercians.

I do not follow the logic of these arguments. The Cistercians, like other religious orders of the time, practiced perpetual abstinence from meat in their communities, except in the infirmary refectory. The rule imposed by the two vicars does not reflect any monastic observance that I know of. Rather, the new rules resemble lay fasting practices: see Thompson (2005), 85–86. There is an interesting incident in 2C 78 in which a skeptic tries to discredit Francis by showing around some meat (capon) Francis had given him from his own plate in alms. The important point was that religious (and penitent laymen) were expected to avoid eating meat. That Francis allowed it seemed scandalous.

John of Cappella and Philip Longo (pp. 73–74)

Although some scholars make the new fasting laws the problem that most bothered Francis, others have detected violations of poverty. They usually cite 2C 58, an undated incident in which Francis ejects the sick friars from the friars' house in Bologna, supposedly because it was too lavish. Aside from this undated incident, there is no evidence that poverty violations were what confronted Francis on his return. Rather, the best source for the events of 1220–21, ChJG 13–14, states that the issues that most upset Francis were the projects of John of Cappella and Philip Longo. Jordan says these events were even foretold to Francis by a Middle Eastern clairvoyant (*pythonissa*). He is very clear that the actions of these two friars, not dietary concerns or poverty issues, made Francis turn to the pope. See Manselli (1995), 224, and Vauchez (2009), 156, on Francis's rejection of John of Cappella's leper project. Vauchez suggests that it was "specialization" in the Franciscan project that offended Francis. This incident is the only real knowledge we have of John, who in fourteenth-century Franciscan legend became the "Judas" of the original twelve followers. The incident of John the Simple and the leper is in AC 64 (LP 22); see Manselli (1980), 148–51, on this event.

The "Dream of the Black Hen" (p. 74)

The dream of the black hen and her chicks is reported in L3C 63. Of the dreams ascribed to Francis in early sources, this one has, I think, the best claim to historicity. It is a "stress dream," and its message is one of inadequacy, not inspiration or prophecy. The allegory fits Francis's predicament in 1220 exactly. The version in L3C makes the dream prophetic of Francis's commitment of the order to the pope and cardinal protector; that part is retrojection. See Rusconi (1994), 99–100, for an interesting commentary on this incident. He suggests that the dream reflects the older Francis's growing pessimism, in contrast to his youthful carefree attitude. Dalarun (1996), 201, rejects the story as later embroidery. His reasoning seems to be to distrust any story that implies that Francis approved introduction of hierarchical control into the order in place of his charismatic leadership. To me this seems like a priori reasoning.

Francis and Honorius III (p. 74)

Francis's encounter with Honorius and the request for Hugolino as his "pope" is recounted in detail by ChJG 14, 1C 74, and AP 45. L3C 65 gives a summary version. On these sources and their relations and divergences, see Pásztor (1976), 216–22, and Selge (1971), 194–204. Jordan of Giano alone gives an approximate date; he puts the meeting with the pope immediately on Francis's return from the East, before Francis called the chapter to deal with the problems. I simply follow his, the best order. Selge (1971), 199–201, places the meeting at Orvieto, where the Curia was from June to September 1220; Manselli (1982), 225, places it at Viterbo, where the Curia was resident from spring 1220 until June. There is no way to identify the place with confidence, since we cannot date the visit precisely. Jordan of Giano asserts that Francis was so upset he could not even speak to his vicars or troublemakers directly. One can hardly imagine him taking time out for trips to Venice or Bologna. So I see no reason to intrude undated material, such as a lengthy stay in Venice, at this point.

Hugolino as troubleshooter (pp. 74–75)

Beguin (1979), 134, in his reading of AP 45a, considers it "historically true" that Hugolino's appointment as "cardinal protector" happened only after the approval of the LR in 1223. Perhaps this is the case for the title, which does not appear until the LR, but Jordan and other sources show him functioning as a "protector" from 1220 on. Brooke (1959), 59–67, is convincing that Hugolino became active in Franciscan affairs after the winter of 1220–21, whatever title he used—if any. I avoid using the title "cardinal protector" until 1223, however, since sources do not record it until then.

The 1220 chapter(s) (p. 76)

ChJG 15 tells us that after Hugolino resolved the problem of the troublemakers, Francis announced "statim" the meeting of a chapter. Scholars distinguish this chapter from that of Pentecost 1221, described in ChJG 16, and have long struggled to date it. It is usually agreed that Francis did not make it back in time for the 17 May 1220 Pentecost chapter. I do not see this as impossible, but there is no good evidence to confirm an arrival after Pentecost. I think that Francis was likely already back by late May 1220, because the new "letter of recommendation," *Pro Dilectis Filiis,* is dated 29 May and seems linked to Hugolino's letter-writing campaign, something that followed Francis's return. I date events accordingly.

Nevertheless, the chronology of events after Francis's return in 1220 remains unclear. Brown (1965), 384–85, summarizes the debates. *Pace* Vauchez (2009), 156, there is no evidence whatsoever that the chapter at which Francis resigned was on the feast of St. Michael, a date repeated in virtually every history: e.g., Fortini (1959), 1:1:2, 130, and Manselli (1982), 230. Scholars assume that Michaelmas chapters were normal. This is gratuitous. ChJG 15 is clear: "Beatus autem Franciscus statim ad sanctam Mariam de Porciuncula indixit capitulum generale." Jordan takes this chapter to be the 1221 Pentecost chapter, which occurred as much as a year later; that is the force of the "ergo" that opens ChJG 16 on the 1221 chapter. Straightforward reading dictates that we should dispense with the hypothetical Michaelmas general chapter of 1220, and with any other general chapter between Francis's return and May 1221.

I do not like to dissent from the virtually unanimous consensus of the scholars, especially Manselli (1982), 230, but a general chapter in fall 1220 is founded solely on the assumption that September general chapters were an annual event, and that is when Jordan says Francis called a general chapter right after his return. Therefore, it would have to happen on that date. There is no evidence for either assumption, and thus no foundation for that conclusion.

Dalarun (1996), 184–85, notes the growing "formality" of the language used in successive papal bulls: *Cum Dilecti Filii* (11 June 1219) still calls the movement a "religio"; *Pro Dilectis Filiis* (29 May 1220) calls it an "ordo"; and then *Cum Secundum* (22 Sept. 1220) does so with even greater formality. Although I would not structure the events as he does, Rusconi (1994), 89–92, is right that 1220 was a crucial year for formation of a Franciscan Order, and that *Cum Secundum* (FA:ED 1:560–61) is a central document, although it still does not use the correct title for superiors, calling them "priores," not "custodes." This last letter initiated the process of drawing up the final version of the Rule.

Letters of Honorius III (pp. 76–77)

Honorius III's letter *Cum Dilecti Filii* (FA:ED 1:558) is dated to 1218 (at Rieti) or to 1219 (at the Lateran) and has been much debated because of the conflicting dates and places in the manuscripts. Callebaut (1926), 549, favored the earlier date. Thompson (1971), 379, argued for the later. I find the earlier date highly unlikely because of Francis's coolness toward papal letters. A date while he was away is more believable. Both AP 45 and L3C 66 say that Hugolino, after appointment by the pope as responsible for the movement, had letters sent to bishops vouching for the Franciscans, and that he urged other cardinals to do so too. *Pro Dilectis* (FA:ED 1:559–60) is probably a product of that campaign—another reason to place the cardinal's appointment in 1220, rather than before the trip to Egypt. See De Beer (1977), 44–46, for his very perceptive remarks on the differences between Franciscan structures in de Vitry's letters of 1216 and his *Historia Occidentalis* of 1220. On this topic, one may also consult Elm (1977), but I have doubts about his dating (e.g., Hugolino as "cardinal protector" in 1217) and some other anachronisms. On *Cum Secundum*, 22 Sept. 1220 (FA:ED 1:560–61), see Desbonnets (1983), 33, concerning Jacques de Vitry's complaints about the lack of a Franciscan novitiate. Examples of friars admitted without testing who proved to be problems are found in 2C 39 and 32–34, both reports admittedly late, but believable. Another example, this of a brother who was a pious fraud, is in AC 116 (LP 93) and 2C 28.

As De Beer (1977), 11–12, notes, Francis seems to have been the personal recipient of only four papal letters: *Cum Dilecti; Cum Secundum; Devotionibus Vestrae,* 29 March 1222, giving permission to celebrate Mass during interdicts; and *Solet Annuere,* 29 Nov. 1223, the Rule (FA:ED 1:99–106). *Cum Secundum* does not, however, address Francis by name. On the other hand, Francis seems to have used the permission for portable altars in *Quia Populares,* 3 Dec. 1224 (FA:ED 1:562–63), although it was not addressed to him personally. Only after Francis's final retirement in 1224 did papal letters for the Franciscans become common. It is probable that Francis was directly involved only in the requests for the three letters in which he is named. Esser (1978), 156–65 (Karecki trans., 61–69), questions whether Francis's rejection of papal privileges in Test 8 can be turned into a hard-and-fast norm: it does not reflect his own practice. Esser is correct that retrojectively making Test 8 a general rule in this period is anachronistic, but I think he overstates his case a bit.

The "dinner with Hugolino" (p. 77)
I agree with Desbonnets (1983), 121–22, that Francis meeting with Saint Dominic at Hugolino's house in 2C 148–50 (= AC 49), often placed at this point, is wholly fictitious. Its punch lines are: first, to castigate friars for wanting to be bishops; and, second, to have Dominic acknowledge Francis's superior holiness. The first is wholly anachronistic at this period—the first Franciscan bishop, Angello of Fez, was not appointed until sometime after Francis's death. The description of Dominic's deference is itself a product of later order rivalry and anachronistic. Equally unconvincing is the story of Francis begging for food and putting it on Hugolino's lavish dinner table in AC 97 (LP 61–62)

and 2C 73, 75. This is a moralizing exemplum against friars too proud to beg. As such, it represents a period after Francis's death, as if the idea that Francis would publicly embarrass a prelate is itself not good enough reason to reject it.

Francis before the Curia (pp. 77–78)

Francis's sermon is in ChJG 14, 1C 72, L3C 64, and 2C 25. 2C transports this event back to the early days of the movement and turns the black hen parable into a prophecy of future growth. 1C and L3C make it the occasion of Francis's request for Hugolino as cardinal protector and imply that the initiative for that appointment came from Hugolino himself. Jordan of Giano's version of the request for a single "pope," done at Francis's initiative and out of desperation at the problems he faced on return, is to be preferred as the least sanitized and theologized. Francis's introduction to the Curia would be a result, not the precursor, of the cardinal's appointment. The story of the Curia sermon appears late, and simultaneously, in LMj 12.7 and Stephen of Bourbon (FA:ED 2:789–90). In Stephen, Francis resists preaching to the dignitaries out of humility, and Hugolino then suggests memorization (an embarrassing anecdote not in Bonaventure). I agree with Delcorno (1977), 148, in accepting this story. It fits with the resistance to public speaking that the saint exhibits in early sources.

Francis's demonic attack (p. 79)

Francis's obsession at Cardinal Brancaleone's palace is described in AC 117 (LP 92) and 2C 119–20. On this distinguished ecclesiastic, see *Dizionario biografico italiano* 13:814–17. This story is not dated and could have happened any time between the fall of 1220 and Francis's retirement in 1223. Brancaleone was cardinal priest of Santa Croce from 1202 to 1230. Winter 1223 is unlikely as too late, so the choice is between winter 1220–21 or winter 1221–22. The earlier year, when he visited Hugolino, seems more likely. In either case, it is a window into Francis's troubled soul as he struggled with the situation of the early 1220s. On Angelo Tancredi, who first appears here, see Brown (1965), 431–32, who summarizes the attempts of Sassetti, Fortini, and Pratesi to identify him in Assisi. The assumption is that he was from there because AC says he was one of the original twelve—although not mentioned as such in 1C, AP, or L3C. Their conclusions are mostly hypothetical. Angelo did, however, become a close companion of Francis during his last illnesses and is buried near him at Assisi.

Both versions of the demonic attack include cautionary moralizing about the dangers of friars living at court. These are a later gloss, as such a living situation was rare, if not nonexistent, in 1223. Manselli (1980), 103–13, has an extended and insightful analysis of this story, which he considers an eyewitness report by Angelo Tancredi—although it is not signed *Nos qui cum eo fuimus*. I am dubious, however, of his interpretation, which makes Francis's problem a guilty conscience because he is being waited on and living in a fine building when other Franciscans are living in the open and in rural hermitages. Manselli takes the moralizing about poverty in the story to be historical. I do not. The story is vivid, colorful, and concrete, while the interpretive section is abstract, cold, and didactic. It has exactly the tone typical of a rigorist retelling the story long after Francis's death. I am inclined to think that the shorter version in 2C, which cuts out nearly all of the moralizing, is closer to the original than AC.

Francis returns home (pp. 79–80)
The trip back from Rome is described in AC 120 (LP 95); the stop to read the Breviary is repeated in 2C 96; the devil's-methods section is repeated in 2C 120. The bulk of this pericope on spiritual joy (also in 2C 128–29) is flagged as not connected to the trip home by its introduction: "And he used to say." The Breviary story is totally believable, given Francis's attitude toward the Office in his writings and later life. As Esser (1960), 109, notes, commenting on Eccleston, the first friars to arrive in England in the 1220s chanted the Office "with notes," even when only three or four were present in choir.

Francis Resigns

Date of the resignation (p. 80)
On the debate on the dating of Francis's resignation, see Schmitt (1977). Francis's resignation is described in AC 11 and 39 (and its parallel 2C 143). Since Francis does not seem to have resigned and appointed Peter of Cataneo at the Pentecost chapter of 1220, and he had already resigned, and Cataneo was dead by the 30 May Pentecost chapter of 1221, the chapter of the resignation was not a Pentecost one. Brooke (1959), 76 and 106, has argued, unconvincingly I think, that the AC 11 resignation took place in 1217 or 1218. It is better to place it after Egypt. Rusconi (1994), 92–94, argues that Francis's resignation was related to changes in the Rule at the 1220 Pentecost chapter. Since we know nothing of what happened at that chapter, this is conjecture. I am mystified by the logic of FA:ED 2:142 n. a, which identifies the resignation chapter as "the Pentecost Chapter held at the Porziuncula in September 1220." Pentecost is in the spring, not in September. I have already expressed my doubts about whether there ever were any "Michaelmas" general chapters at all.

Both AC 11 and 39 place the events "at a chapter at the Porziuncula." They never call this meeting a "general chapter," and it is gratuitous to assume that it was. "Chapters" would have happened regularly at the Porziuncula, as they did in every religious house. There is no reason, then, to make the resignation chapter a "general" chapter. Francis's "resignation" does not sound like a great public event, and this was not the first time that Francis had appointed a vicar. He appointed Gregory of Naples and Matthew of Narni vicars before he went to Egypt. In AC 11 the resignation seems definitive, not temporary. Schmitt (1977) is the place to begin on the role of the vicars during Francis's lifetime. Manselli (1980), 43–53, reads AC 11 (2C 151) as showing that power was slipping from Francis's hands at the time of his resignation. I am not so sure. His role at the 1221 chapter suggests that any real loss of control did not happen until after 1223.

The "Chapter of Mats" and internal politics (p. 80)

The famed "Chapter of Mats" is one of the more disputed events in early Franciscan history. Desbonnets (1983), esp. 42–46, identifies the 1219 Pentecost chapter as the "Chapter of Mats" and asserts that Hugolino was "cardinal protector" by that time. He considers AC 18 (LP 114), the fight among the senior ministers about the nature of the Rule that left Hugolino speechless, unhistorical and concocted. Nevertheless, he does see it—and its doublet in AC 17 (LP 113) set at Monte Colombo—as evidence for a fight over control of the order at that time. He thinks Francis and his inner circle were still in control during the chapter of 1219, but that Francis's grip was slipping. Desbonnets (1983), 39, himself admits that Hugolino seems absent from what he considers the only authentic report of the resignation, AC 11. For him, a power struggle continued from 1219 to 1223 between the senior brothers, who wanted an institutionalized religious order, and Francis, who wanted a more charismatic and unstructured movement. I agree with Miccoli (1985), 628, who rejects this hypothesis.

Jordan of Giano, our best source for internal politics in the movement, says nothing to support a power struggle that early, and every other report (1C 74; AP 45; L3C 65–66) puts Hugolino's appointment as protector after the Egypt trip. On the Desbonnets-Miccoli debate over this chapter, see Merlo (1992), 549. Moves like the appeal to Honorius for help, Peter of Cataneo's appointment as vicar, the eventual naming of Hugolino as cardinal protector, and the revision and approbation of the Rule were all at Francis's initiative. He, not the ministers, was the primary player in the events following his return from Egypt.

Pace Dalarun (1996), 121, I do not see Francis's recourse to Hugolino and Elias as a way to check some move by the brothers to subvert Francis's position, in short, to stop a power grab. Events imply just the opposite: a power vacuum had arisen while Francis was away. John of Cappella and Philip Longo went off on their own tangents; the vicars turned to Cistercians for advice; and everyone else seems to have been panicked, thinking that Francis had died. *Pace* Flood (1983), 132–34, who thinks Francis was a model leader (by the standards of modern "leadership" theory), the saint's defects as a superior are obvious. Alone, Brooke (1959), 105, senses somewhat the logic of choosing Elias as vicar. Francis's defects were central to his choice of assistants. Elias supplied what Francis did not have in leadership skills—organizational ability and a willingness to command. Hugolino supplied something else that Francis lacked—canonical training. Dalarun (*pace* Sabatier) is right: the two were not corruptors of the order or evil subverters of some pure Franciscan vision. They were part of Francis's own "plan." See Lambertini-Tabarroni (1989), 44, on Elias's status as lay brother and the issues that raised for Franciscan clerics after Francis's death.

Francis and Peter of Cataneo (pp. 80–81)

On Peter's title (and that of Elias), see Schmitt (1977), 253–58, who favors "vicarius sancti," Celano's language. AC 64, 80, and 93 all use the anachronistic term "minister general." "Vicar" is probably best, but it is hard to imagine someone "obeying" his own vicar. I doubt there was any formal name for Peter's office. Francis may well have called him his "mother," the title used for the one in charge in RH, and which 1C 98 uses for Elias during Francis's last illness. No head of the order was called "minister general" until John of Parma in 1227.

Peter of Cataneo acted as "vicar" until his death in March 1221. The stories of his vicariate suggest that he held the office for at least a couple of months. His vicariate could begin only after Francis's return from Egypt, since Peter was with him in the Middle East. It would have made no sense to appoint him as vicar and then take him along to Egypt, leaving Gregory and Matthew in charge. Peter, at the lunch with meat incident in the East, told Francis: "You have the power." So Francis has not made him the superior at that point. So, unless Francis resigned at the Pentecost 1220 chapter, which no one believes, Peter must have been appointed at the resignation chapter sometime in the fall of 1220. I have put the resignation and appointment after Francis's visit to Rome, because no story about this visit suggests that the vicariate was already in existence. A late fall date seems likely for the chapter and the appointment.

For an excellent summary of the vicariate of Peter of Cataneo, which corrects many fossilized errors in the scholarship, see Schmitt (1977), 237–46. Unfortunately, all the evidence for Peter's activity datable to the six months or so of his vicariate is found in three stories of AC and one of 2C. These seem heavily reworked to emphasize Proto-Spiritualist views on poverty. There are three other stories datable to this period: AC 64 (LP 22) on James the Simple, a *Nos qui cum eo fuimus* passage; and AC 80 (LP 39) on Francis's penance for eat- ing meat. AC 93 (LP 56; parallel in 2C 91) is the last, another *Nos* story. Here Francis has Peter give a poor woman the Porziuncula's only New Testament, a book essential for performing the Office, "since they did not have Breviaries." This story is so much a poverty parable, and so out of harmony with Francis's concern for the Office in his own writings, that I would be inclined to reject it, at least in the form we have it. Still, it has good suport as a *Nos* text, so I will pass it. An anachronism about holding money taints Francis's rebuke of Peter in 2C 67. Anachronisms aside, the anecdotes certainly give us a good idea of what it was like for Peter to have Francis as a "subject."

Francis's resignation (p. 81)
It would be wonderful to have Francis's own reasons for his resignation. Schmitt (1977), 247–51, summarizes scholarly conjecture as to the reasons: health, hu- mility, difficulty of governing. I think the last was important as a background reason. Francis and the chronicles never mention health. When friars pose the question in 2C 188 (= AC 44), Francis does not answer but rails against bad su- periors who want to follow the model of older rules: obvious retrojection, and not a reason to resign at all! The closest we have to Francis's own expression of his reasons is his black hen dream and allegory: he was not up to the job now that the order had grown so large.

Francis's temptations (p. 82)
Miccoli (1991), 82, calls attention to Francis's temptations after his resignation. Older scholars were also aware of this Dark Night: Englebert (1965), 234, and Schmucki (1991), 149–51. Examples of his temptations and doubts: 2C 115–17, 119–20, 122; AC 63 (LP 21); 2MP 99; examples of diabolical attack: 1C 122, 119; AC 117 (LP 92). 2C 97–99, though late, is probably accurate that prayer alone brought Francis relief. It is telling that this crisis came immediately on the heels of the founder's resignation. The decision to resign came at a cost.

More Letters and a Spiritual Testament

The focus of the letters (p. 82)
It would be hard to overemphasize the importance of Francis's datable writ- ing, and especially his nine letters, for interpretation of the period 1220–21. Biographers of Francis, privileging for this period anecdotes from the "Assisi Compilation," where later poverty debates are polemicized, would have us

think that Francis's major concern in this period was fighting off the onslaught of a group of senior friars, led by Elias and abetted by Cardinal Hugolino, who want to subvert Francis's teaching on poverty. In fact, the word "poverty," as well as anything like the later concept, is virtually absent from Francis's writings of this period. The lone exception is ER, but this document is a composite, not an ad hoc production of 1220–21. Had "poverty" been Francis's burning concern at this time, one would think he would have mentioned it, at least in 1LtCus and 2LtCus. He does not. What he harps on, much to modern readers' annoyance, is Eucharistic devotion, proper vestments, clean altar linens, and suitable chalices for Mass. This has to be taken seriously. If we want to know what concerned Francis, we have to start with his own writings. I am determined to do this.

Francis's literacy (pp. 82–83)
On Francis's precocious literacy and his use of written letters, see Langeli (1994), 151–53. On the role of secretaries in Francis's compositions (not just the letters), see Scivoletto (1977), esp. 121–24 on his Latin style. On the letters' authenticity, doubts about LtCus (which I accept), and the *Forma Vitae* Letter in FLCl 6 (which I doubt), see Pellegrini (1982a), 314–17, and Scivoletto (1977), 104–5; cf. Bertoli (1993), 182. My quotations from the 1220 letters follow FA:ED 1, with minor modifications.

Francis's sacramental piety (pp. 83–84)
De Beer (1977), 98–106, suggests that the increased reverence for the Sacrament found in the 1220 letters reflects Muslim emphasis on divine transcendence, something Francis supposedly had contact with in Egypt. I am skeptical: the themes noted by De Beer are all present in 1LtCus, written before Egypt. On the careful Latin style of the 2LtF, see Schmucki (1986), 247. On this text's authenticity, see Scivoletto (1977), 113–14. For an extended discussion of "popular piety" and Francis's reverence for writing containing the holy names and the Mass's words of institution, see Langeli (1984), 41–50, which removes the need to invoke Muslim origins for this behavior. On the importance of the "Priestly Prayer" from John's Gospel in Francis's writings, see Matura (1982), 113. Francis used it directly three times: 1LtF 13–19, 2LtF 56–60, and esp. ER 22.41–55.

Brother Elias and the 1221 Chapter

The "Chapter of Mats" again (p. 88)
Correctly, Dalarun (1996), 217, rejects the identification of the 1221 chapter as the "Chapter of Mats" in AC 18 (LP 114), with its conflict between Francis

and the senior ministers over the Rule. I agree with his conclusion that the AC story is a retrojection of later poverty debates into the period. But it is not impossible that the 1221 chapter was the historical origin of the legendary "Chapter of Mats." However, all general chapters of the post-Egypt period had so many friars present that the participants would have had to live in makeshift huts. The "Chapter of Mats" is most likely a conflation of all the chapters in this period, dressed up with poverty concerns of the later 1240s and beyond.

The 1221 general chapter (pp. 88–90)

The major source for the 1221 chapter is ChJG 16–17. The dating of the chapter found in ChJG is problematic, but the year given, 1221, is correct. The manuscript and edition read "14" for the year of indiction, which should be 9. This is clearly a copying error. X and V are often confused, and a copyist has read XIIII for VIIII. I thank Fr. Simon Tugwell, O.P., for confirming my observation. The date of chapter is "X Kalendas iunii," which would be 23 May. Pentecost 1221 was 30 May. But it is likely, since Jordan speaks of the chapter lasting a week, that it began on 23 May and ended on Pentecost. So this date can be saved.

As Merlo (1992), 541 n. 49, notes, the number three thousand in ChJG is probably a biblical type alluding to Acts 2:41; as is the number five thousand in Eccleston: Matt. 14:21, Acts 4:4, Matt. 16:9. These numbers probably mean "many"; but if the twenty-three tables mentioned in ChJG had two sittings (as was common in religious houses), and each seated something like fifty, then actual attendance between two thousand and three thousand is probably a good guess and similar to the estimate by Vauchez (2009), 113. *Pace* Merlo (1992), 544 n. 62, who observes that Francis always referred to himself as "frater Franciscus" and thus chose not to take a position of authority, the use of "the Brother" for Francis by Elias and others in Jordan of Giano's description of the chapter of 1221 shows that "Brother," in this case, was a title of authority. As in *A Connecticut Yankee in King Arthur's Court,* only one man was called "the Brother" (the Boss).

The German mission (pp. 89–90)

The mission to Germany, and Jordan's obedience to join it, are in ChJG 18–19. Unfortunately, Jordan tells us nothing about the chapter's other decisions. Merlo (1991b), 49, cites Jordan's own prayers against Lombard heretics and hostile Teutons as evidence that knowledge of heresy and preaching against it were, as yet, minimal among the Franciscans. Perhaps, but 1C 62 speaks of heretics converted by Franciscan sermons, although the report is very generic. The prayers do show that knowledge of Germany was minimal. Rusconi

(1994), 92–94, thinks that the supposed struggle between Francis and the "fratres sapientes" over the writing of the final Rule started with this chapter, climaxing with the description in the "Assisi Compilation" of the conflict at the 1222 chapter and Francis's withdrawal from active life in the order. I find nothing like this supposed conflict, even between the lines, in the sources quoted.

ON CHAPTER SIX

V AUCHEZ (2009), 168–94, covers this period of Francis's life; his perspective is evident in subtitle of the relevant chapter in his 2009 work:
"Le projet franciscain entre utopie et codification: Le temps des régles
(1221–1223)." Manselli (1982), 257–86, deals in particular with the redactions
of the Rule. His treatment is probably the best summary of scholarly opinion.
Reconstruction of the process of composition for any particular section of
ER or LR is possible only if the concrete incidents that triggered the original
legislation can be identified. Otherwise, chapters of each Rule are best considered a revision of undatable previous legislation responding to unknown
earlier events. On the known examples of earlier legislation that lie behind the
Rule(s), see Ghinato (1973), esp. 1–54.

Francis's Working Paper

The "Earlier Rule" (p. 92)
ER is translated in FA:ED 1:63–86; see also "Fragments Connected to the
Rule" in FA:ED 1:87–96. The foundational work on ER is Flood (1967),
which was followed by the edition and commentary of Esser (1974). Also to
be consulted is Flood-Matura (1975), which brings Flood's earlier work up
to date after Esser. Flood (1977a) very critically reviews Esser, principally for
his stemma and use of Italian versions of the Rule. In any case, the variants
preferred by Flood do not, in my opinion, seem to change the meaning of the
text in any significant way. The general consensus is that reconstruction of the

original "Rule of 1209" is impossible. I am skeptical about dating individual parts of ER. On composition of ER and LR as a means to make the friars independent of Francis (and he of them), see Dalarun (1996), 187.

Drafting the Earlier Rule (p. 92)
Francis was aware of criticisms made of his movement, and these informed his redaction of the Rules. Esser (1966), 138–47, gives a summary of criticisms up to the early 1220s. He lists lack of ministerial preparation, especially for missionaries; idleness; unformed "enthusiasm"; and growing anonymity of life. On the absence of poverty violations in this period, see Esser (1966), 185. For dating ER, and its linguistic links with 1LtF, see Pazzelli (1989). He confirms the dating of Schmucki (1986), 249.

On ER as a "working paper" or "draft in process," see Ghinato (1973), 39–41; Pellegrini (1982b), 59; and, especially, Desbonnets (1983), 37, who points out the lack of evidence it was ever reviewed by the brothers or by a chapter.

There has been lively debate about the supposed "monasticization" of the Franciscan movement in the early 1220s, mostly among Franciscans struggling to clarify their modern identity. Much is made of the replacement of manual labor by intellectual work and preaching: Stanislao da Compagnola (1973), 400; Lambertini-Tabarroni (1989), 40; Dalarun (1996), 240. I do not find the characterization of this change as "monastic" convincing. The Rule of Benedict prescribed manual labor, not intellectual work and preaching. There is nothing specifically "monastic" about the choral office (thirteenth-century parish priests, at least in Italy, chanted the Office daily), nor are study and preaching "monastic." On the Office, possession of liturgical books, and the Rule, see Landini (1968), xxiv-xxv. On the whole, the changes of the 1220s that scholars highlight made the friars less like monks, not more so.

Biblical language in the Rule (p. 93)
On the formula in ER 1.1–5, and its conventional elements as reflecting one aspect of Francis's project, see the profound and correct remarks of Manselli (1975), 269. That ER Prologue 2 was not part of the original Rule but an addition, perhaps by Angelo Clareno, see Flood (1983), 69–70. Flood (1983), 72, also considers stylistic formulas (including biblical quotation) as "conventionally acceptable" trappings. See Schmucki (1988) on the biblical roots of Francis's language. For attempts to sort out Francis's role in the authorship of ER in contrast with the contributions of others, see Scivoletto (1977), 109–10, and Desbonnets (1983), 35, who thinks that the biblical allusions are mostly from Cesarius of Speyer.

Obedience (pp. 93–94)
Francis's most direct reflections on religious obedience are ER 4–6 and Adm 3. On ER 5 and Adm 3, see Desbonnets (1983), 52–54. Desbonnets has doubts about the authenticity of Adm 3 because of its "Cistercian" language and use of the word "praelatus." I would see the borrowed language and more undeveloped theory of obedience as evidence that Adm 3 is early: the biblical tags with which it begins are pure Francis. Desbonnets is uncomfortable with a Francis who emphasizes obedience. For a contrasting view, which comes close to saddling Francis with a theory of "absolute" obedience, at least toward ecclesiastics, see Merlo (1991b), 42. Perhaps the best explication on Francis on obedience is still Esser (1952), which places the concept in its Christological context. On the local chapter in Germany, see ChJG 20.

Poverty and preaching (p. 98)
I respectfully disagree with Flood (1983), 20–22, who sees behind ER 8 a refusal to engage in "social welfare" work (even with lepers) so that the brothers might opt out of the injustices of early "capitalism" and not become enablers of the "system." He writes of ER 8: "They are initiating economic action. . . . The whole passage makes an economic point." I cannot square this with the Rule's proviso that, for the sake of lepers and the sick, Franciscans can not only work for pay but also accept monetary alms. On the prehistory of ER on preaching and missions, see Desbonnets (1983), 36.

The "Rule for Hermitages" (pp. 99–100)
Some have considered RH as the first attempt at a rule for the movement as a whole; Manselli (1982), 274–79, who surveys the scholarship and opinions of Esser and Goetz. On eremitism among the early Franciscans, see Pellegrini (1976). On the date of RH, see FA:ED 1:61–62. The usual date for this document is between 1217 and 1221. The earlier date is suggested by the link between hermitism and the martyrs in Spain made by 2C 178–79. There are counterindications. First, the Rule treats minister and *custos* as distinct offices held by different people. No datable document makes this distinction before LR, which also mentions "guardians," an office absent in RH. Furthermore, as Esser (1966), 56, notes, the reference to "hermitages and other places" in ER is omitted in LR, suggesting that it was no longer needed; i.e., RH already existed. So a date between 1221 and 1223 seems likely to me.

For a general discussion of RH, see Van Asseldonk (1979), who compares it to Aelred of Rievaulx's *De Institutione Inclusarum,* which also used the Mary and Martha trope. See also Chiara Augusta Lainati's introduction to the documents on Clare, in *Fonti* (1977), 228–29, which compares RH to the practice of the San Damiano nuns. See Dalarun (1997), esp. 56–58, 152–54, on the mother-son relationship.

Revision and Approval of the Rule

Lay brothers and clerics (p. 100)

The story of the novice and the Psalter is in AC 103–5 (LP 70–74), where the encounters have been turned into three events of increasing intensity. AC reworks the event into a poverty parable that hides Francis's objections to education and learning to read—all too obviously the real point. On this story, see Rusconi (1994), 76–78, who correctly sees that it was originally about clericalization, but fails to see that the problem is not clerics themselves, but a layman who wants to be a cleric. See also Cardini (1983a), 58, whose insightful comments I generally follow. Desbonnets (1983), 37, turns the point of the incident around and thinks the legislation in the Rule is to make sure lay brothers who can read are allowed to say Office—probably a reading back of later issues of the 1250s to this period. *Pace* Desbonnets, in ER, Francis saves his big blast for the illiterate who are not satisfied with saying Paters. Vauchez (2009), 196, accepts without hesitation that the novice and the Breviary story is about poverty.

In the 1250s, the clerics were very much in control, and papal letters (such as *Tamquam Vert* in 1252) had started to call lay brothers "conversi" and make them lay auxiliaries to the clerics. On this development, see Landini (1968), 140–41. The clerical redactors of this story, most of whom had received clerical status after education in the order, and had been trained for ordination, turned the attack on status climbing into a poverty parable.

The "Letter to a Minister" (pp. 100–101)

See Esser (1966), 226, on LtMin. Since the authority of superiors in the letter is less developed than it is in ER 5, and even less developed than in LR 7 and 10, I cannot see how it could be dated after Pentecost 1221, by which date ER was complete in the form we have it.

Francis the "New Fool" (p. 102)

With considerable reservation, I agree with Miccoli (1991), 76–77, and accept AC 18 as historical when it reports that Francis rejected the use of older rules as models and called himself in vulgar idiom a "novus pazzus." Francis's rudeness to ecclesiastics in this story is harder to believe. On the supposed loss (or destruction) of an interim version of the Rule in this passage, see Desbonnets (1983), 84. The narrator makes this lost rule one "written by God's instruction," and its "loss" a ploy to allow Elias and the ministers a chance to put pressure on Francis to "relax" the Rule. Again, this sounds like Proto-Spiritualist propaganda; I am very skeptical of it. For another take on the incident, see Manselli (1982), 257. Francis rejected ownership of goods in common as well as individually, so AC 16 does give Francis's position, but in a form far more rigid than his own directives on money in ER. In the form we have the incident in AC, it reflects later debates. Since the 1200s, writers have pitted Francis against the ministers (and Hugolino) in the writing of the Rule. The three AC passages already discussed provide the only evidence. There is no evidence for such a fight in Francis's own writings.

Francis at Fonte Colombo (p. 102)

1C, AP, L3C, and ChJG have virtually nothing about Francis's redaction work at Fonte Colombo. There are two narrative reports, and both focus on the "ministers" who try to thwart Francis's will. AC 17 (LP 113) reports Francis's retirement to Fonte Colombo and provides a story that pits the "lax" ministers and Elias (stand-ins for the Proto-Conventuals) against Francis and God (who are both Proto-Spirituals). Elias and the minsters may have visited during redaction—they probably did—but the rebuke by a voice from heaven thundering "no gloss" is later propaganda. AC 16 (LP 112) reports a miraculous voice from heaven chastising "the ministers" when they ask Francis to let them have property in common.

Brooke (1959), 260–61, and (1970), 57–66, date the present form of these AC reports to about 1257. That would be in the heat of the controversies over the fall of John of Parma. She is willing to admit some historicity to what seem to me to be anachronistic political elaborations. All three pericopes so much reflect later poverty controversies that it is difficult to identify their historical core. In addition, Conti (1978) demonstrated the conscious remodeling of these stories to make them parallel biblical accounts of Moses on Sinai. This biblicism will become even more exaggerated in later Spiritual Franciscan recountings.

There are two cases where we might be able to reconstruct the context of legislation that made its way into ER—the decision as to which friars can have books, and how superiors are to correct their subjects—and they provide a very different picture from AC in both cases. Francis's adversaries in both cases are human frailty (including his own), not the ministers' violation of poverty. After we discount the AC stories for later quarrels, special pleading, and vilification of stand-ins for the Proto-Conventuals, much of the "conflict" disappears. I am not saying that the conflict stories taken at face value by Ghinato (1973), 34–36, 51, cannot have been real, or that the imagined "violent controversies" supposedly papered over by Celano according to Miccoli (1991), 211–12, could not have happened. But given the tendentious nature of the AC reports, such conclusions seem rather naive. I agree with Esser (1961) that the composition and redaction of the Rule was Francis's response to his internal conflicts (and his own wish to withdraw from leadership), not ministerial manipulation or curial pressure.

Frankly, I despair of finding anything historical in these pericopes, except perhaps that Francis retired to that hermitage to work. Francis's writings at the time, LtMin and the two Rules, show little, if any, evidence of a controversy over poverty or common property. On the other hand, that Francis consulted the ministers and Hugolino seems certain. Hugolino himself, as Pope Gregory IX, in *Quo Elongati* says he was at Francis's side during the drafting. This may be a bit exaggerated, but a legist's hand is clear in the received version of LR. Nevertheless, Francis praised the final product and claimed it as his own: 2C 208 (= AC 46) and 2C 209.

The Role of Hugolino and the Roman Curia (pp. 102–3)

Even more than "the ministers" as adversaries in Francis's redaction of the Rules, scholars have polemicized about the influence of Cardinal Hugolino and the Roman Curia. The agendas of historians from Sabatier to the 1970s when dealing with Hugolino and the Rule are canvassed in Pázstor (1976). For a useful, and mostly fair-handed, summary of the debate into the 1980s, see Zerbi (1982). He is, however, very uncritical of sources; e.g., he accepts the story of Francis and Dominic meeting at Hugolino's house. In the spectrum of opinion, the other extreme is Esser (1961), who sees Francis's attachment to the orthodox Church as the primary optic for interpretation: Francis and the papacy are mutually supportive and worked together without any tension. In his view, there is little space for conflict on any level. Admittedly, Francis's own writings could support such an interpretation. In contrast to Esser was Giovanni Miccoli, who in his various publications saw Hugolino as forcing Francis to abandon his principles to produce an approvable rule. Zerbi tends to Miccoli's view because of his uncritical acceptance of *Nos qui cum eo fuimus* texts in AC, a dangerous approach, since these passages reflect poverty controversies and use Hugolino and the ministers as stand-ins for the Proto-Conventual position.

My position is close to Selge (1970), and even more so to Selge (1971), esp. 204–22. In this view, Francis and Hugolino worked in parallel, each with his own goals, and these did not need to be in conflict. Similar to Selge in his conclusions is Desbonnets (1983), 88–89, who saw the two men as working at cross-purposes, but concludes as to Francis and LR: "It is his handiwork."

Rusconi (1994), 96, takes a similar position. Others will differ. In a throwback to Sabatier, Flood (1983), 161–62, concluded: "Hugolino's work meant the subordination of the Franciscan movement to the cultural forms of its age." He is speaking here about the order's relations with the Clares, but this is also his judgment of LR as a whole—as if Francis were not a product of his age! Most balanced, perhaps, is Vauchez (2009), 193–94, who, while admitting that the Latin of LR is too grammatical and legally technical to be that of Francis, the result preserves "l'essentiel du message de François, mais sans la radicalité evangelique du 'document de base' de 1221."

The Earlier Rule versus the Later Rule (pp. 103–4)

Tied up with the question of influences on the Rules is the relationship between Franciscan life before ER and after LR. Flood (1983), 130, outlines the scholarly groups. Group 1 (e.g., Esser) sees a natural and smooth translation; group 2 (mostly Italian scholars) sees institutionalization as inevitable, thinks that "minoritismo" predates the 1220s, and believes that ER was part of that development; group 3 (Miccoli, Pellegrini) tends to ignore ER as an expression of Francis's will and emphasizes discontinuity. Manselli (1982), 264–71, summarizes the general consensus: LR is authentically Francis and in continuity with ER and before. But LR has been reworked by a trained canonist (Hugolino) whose mental furniture was very different from that of Francis. I am closest to group 2 and Manselli, except that I put Francis himself at the center of the project. This a position similar to that of Vauchez (2009), 160–61, who thinks Francis accepted the shift from charisma to institution by the admission, implicit in his resignation, that he was no longer capable of leadership.

For comparison of ER and LR, see Esser (1965), esp. 22. Scholarly consensus, as summarized by Desbonnets (1983), 81–95, is that in content LR is in continuity with ER but differs in the structure and the routinization required by a large group of men. For a good survey of the increasingly formal legal structures in the movement after 1209, see Rusconi (1994), esp. 89–90. I agree with Vauchez (2009), 179, that the 1221 Rule is less strict on poverty than that of 1223 because of the removal of exceptions.

The word ordo (p. 104)

Rusconi (1994) considers 1220 the crucial date for the transformation of the "religio" into an "ordo." Desbonnets (1983), 81, thinks the use of the word *ordo* in LR was an imposition by the Curia and that "virtually everyone except Francis wanted the group to become an order." I do not think Francis thought in terms of canonical terms and structures, whether positively or negatively. So this distinction is probably not in point. There is no evidence Francis opposed language like "ordo": indeed, he eventually used it. But I think Desbonnets' choice of 1223 as the crucial year is well founded, that is, if we need to find a "turning point" at all.

More measured is Landini (1968), 115–16, who thinks Hugolino and the Roman Curia tried to fit the Franciscans into the apostolic life of the Church (especially preaching), but that they did not force clericalization on the movement; rather, internal dynamics of growth, education, and utility to the Church allowed Franciscans to clericalize themselves. But, *pace* Landini (1968), 45, LR does not forbid lay preaching; rather, superiors were to decide who was suitable, whether lay or cleric. On legislation concerning the nuns, see Desbonnets (1983), 93, and Dalarun (1997), 34–35.

The Roman Office (pp. 104–5)
For liturgical practice before 1223, see Esser (1966), 104. For a diffuse but useful description of the Office of the Roman Curia, which LR adopted for the movement, compared to other uses of the time, see Clop (1926). Schmucki (1988), 26–27, probably exaggerates the effect of this change. The Roman Psalter was used almost exclusively in a couple of Roman basilicas, and not much outside of Rome. The Curia used the Gallican Psalter. Francis did not have to memorize a new Psalter. Exactly when this legislation went into effect is debated, because of ambiguity in the Latin text: see Desbonnets (1983), 89.

Francis's Breviary (p. 105)
On Francis's own Breviary, its history, and contents, see S. Van Dijk (1949). Brother Leo's note about how Francis used the Breviary and the Gospels is on fol. 1ᵛ: "Evangelium beatus Franciscus ex maxima reverentia Domini osculabatur evangelium." Franciscans seem to have made do with secondhand Breviaries until 1230, when the general chapter sent exemplars to the twelve provinces for standardization and copying: see Desbonnets (1983), 109.

The new houses in Bologna and Assisi (pp. 105–6)
The ejection of the sick brothers from the house in Bologna is found in 2C 58, which is tagged as an eyewitness report by one of the sick brothers. The story also appears, with less detail, in the late 2MP 6. On this incident, see Manselli (1980), 157–58, who thinks 2MP is more primitive than 2C, and dates the event to August 1220. Conventionally dated to before 1221, but after Francis's return from Egypt, this event could just as well have happened between 1221 and 1223, when it would be part of the background to the redaction of the Rule. The narrative does not require that Hugolino be in Bologna or in Lombardy at the time. For Selge (1970), 210–11, the Bologna ejection incident

is an example of how two very different projects (absolute poverty and practical service to the Church) can be made to intersect, here by Hugolino's claim of ownership.

The attempt to pull down the house near the Porziuncula is in 2C 57, and in AC 56b (LP 8–12). If it too, like the Bologna incident, lies behind LR 6, the chapter would be that of 1222 or 1223 (a bit late for influencing redaction and so less likely). Manselli (1980), 72, on AC 56, notes the Assisi manuscript breaks off at "His little plant," and that the story about the knights of Assisi has to be supplied to Biglaroni's edition from 1MP. The knights' story is also in 2MP 7–8, separated from the first story. The similarity of AC's description to that of Francis's behavior in the Bologna incident leads me to trust the story, although it still may be a doublet. Miccoli (1991), 227, is correct when he rejects most of the other material in AC 56 as a later assimilation of Francis's role to that of an abbot.

Francis, the Rules, and poverty (pp. 106–7)
The best synthesis of what poverty meant for Francis himself is probably still that in Lambert (1998), which draws on the early lives even more than the Rules. For a variety of older views, see *Povertà* (1975). Rather conventional is Stanislao da Compagnola (1975), which shows, however, how little there is on poverty, as such, in the Rules. I question his view that LR has a "less strict" view of poverty than ER: for example (ibid., 247), he understands the "amici spirituales" of LR in a legalistic way more suited to the period after Francis's death. When all is considered, I agree that when Francis was writing the Rules, there were already questions about how the friars were to observe poverty. Even if the characterization of the differing views by hagiographers reflects a later period when interpretation of the Rule itself had become a central issue, the stories about Francis and poverty are too many in this period to be wholly projection of later concerns. Identifying Francis's own concerns must begin with what he says in his own writings during the this period. These passages are the chapters that treat dwellings, ER 7.13 and LR 6.1–3.

Francis stripping the altar (p. 107)
The incident of the mother asking alms is in AC 93 (LP 56) and 2C 91, which may be the more primitive version. On this text, see especially Manselli (1980), 100–103. There is a similar story in 2C 67, where Francis orders a brother to strip the Altar of the Blessed Virgin to give alms to the poor. I find this text suspect for its implicit devaluation of the cult (cf. Francis's letters) and the lack of anything like it in other sources for Francis. On it see Manselli (1980), 103 n. 163. There were limits to Francis's willingness to help friars' families: see

2C 206, where Francis punishes a lay brother who wants to give a gift to his daughters who are nuns.

Solet Annuere (p. 107)

On the form of this bull, which promulgated LR, see Desbonnets (1983), 97–104, who draws on Langeli's observations in *Francesco* (1982). He suggests that the *Solet Annuere* form of the bull must represent some hidden controversy. Perhaps the form was meant to convince Francis that his order had already been approved fully by Innocent; perhaps Francis never requested approval, because he did not believe he needed it (although Hugolino and "the ministers" did); or, the banal version, the bull is a retaliation, because Francis rejected something in the final product. Again, the pope issued it without Francis's involvement because the founder did not want a papally protected "order." These interpretations all strike me as very preconceived and baroque. Francis and Hugolino wrote LR.

Since Francis was represented at the Curia by Hugolino, as he had been by Colonna in 1209, he did not need to be present for the approbation. Hugolino, as his proctor, would have used standard forms. That a bureaucratic form was used to approve legislation of an already existing order is not a mystery. The bull itself says that Honorius "ratifies" the "Rule of your Order, herein outlined, and approved by our predecessor Pope Innocent." Hugolino undoubtedly described that 1209 event to Honorius as Francis understood it: an approval, albeit tentative, of the movement. On both the continuities and the differences between 1209 and 1223, see Ghinato (1973), 31–43. Merlo (1991b), 43, is exactly right in his emphasis on Francis's desire for Roman confirmation in both approaches to the Curia.

Francis as the "Living Rule" (pp. 107–8)

AC 112 (LP 86) and 2C 158 contain a classical formulations of the concept that Francis should be viewed as a living example of the Rule. Manselli (1982), 271–72, thinks that, after 1223, Francis responded to prevailing laxity by creating a model community at the Porziuncula, which is a version of this idea. There is no question that Francis wanted to live simply; unfortunately, the numerous stories and anecdotes told to this effect sound more like later commentary than contemporary witness. Examples include the following. He wanted simplicity in possessions: 2C 69 (= AC 28–30), 2C 63 (= AC 26), 2C 60 (= AC 24); he praised poverty: 2C 70, 2C 82; he wanted friars to beg: 2C 71, 2C 72; less generically, and closely connected with the Rule, he forbade friars from touching coins: 2C 65 (= AC 27; cf. 2C 66), 2C 66, 2C 68 (an exemplary miracle). The way in which perhaps authentic incidents are turned into "desired legislation" is found in AC 57, 2C 56, and 2C 59, where Francis refuses to live in a cell that is too nice or because they called it "Francis's cell." Perhaps the incidents are true, but the retelling has become a gloss on the Rule and the Testament on poverty, intended to make them more legally binding. Even Manselli (1980), 75–79, who likes these stories, doubts the legal elaborations they contain could have originated with Francis himself.

In addition to exemplary stories, both AC and 2C contain material, some with a claim to come from companions of Francis, that purports to give his teachings on the "true" meaning of the Rule and poverty. The most famous of these is AC 101–6, the *Intentio Regulae.* Although some of this may well go back to Francis, I do not see how it can be used to reconstruct Francis's actual views, because of the heavy editing to address much later debates. Miccoli (1991), 43, is very perceptive, when discussing AC 44, on how later reworking conformed Francis's words to much later concerns.

For now, it is enough to note that this material falls into three groups. First, there are teachings and stories that present Francis as a spiritual guide of a rather conventional monastic type, almost an abbot. From what we can tell, from good sources, the "father abbot" model does not fit Francis, so I discount these logia and stories. The next group of passages focus on poverty, often presenting Francis as very upset over violations of the Rule. This material is generally anachronistic, as is proved by its tracking of poverty debates of the later thirteenth century. Finally, there is a group of stories and logia in which Francis is very upset about disobedient or "lax" brothers. There is no question that some early Franciscans did not live up to Francis's standards, and some of these stories may well be true. Indeed, the harsh and rigid, almost judgmental, Francis presented in these stories may well accurately reflect his personality as his health and patience failed. Francis rebuking, correcting, and even cursing lax friars appears in: 2C 156–57; 2C 182; 2C 29; AC 116 = 2C 28; 2C 154.

Examples of Francis giving "monastic" spiritual counsel may be found in AC 114 (LP 89); 2C 85 (against rash judgment); 2C 152 (three kinds of obedience; cf. John Cassian, *Institutes* 12.32); 2C 163 (qualities of good vocations: hardworking, studious); 2C 155 = AC 41 (importance of charity); 2C 146 = AC 19 (manners with secular clerics); 2C 184–86 = AC 42–43 (qualities of superiors); 2C 187 (responsibilities of superiors). The entire *Intentio Regulae* (AC 101–6) seems to me like a canonical consultation on minutiae in the Rule—the kind of glossing that other sources claim Francis condemned. Sometimes the anachronism is obvious. Examples of Francis rebuking the friars for failures in poverty include 2C 56, 59 = AC 23 (they should not own land!); 2C 162 (against lavish table!); 2C 194 (clerics cannot keep private property!); AC 98 (LP 63); 2C 76 (Francis praises a friar who begs, which seems exceptional); AC 113 (LP 88) = 2C 84 (poor people are poorer than Franciscans). On the other hand, 2C 153 = AC 1, in which Francis warns against superiors giving formal precepts, does seem very much in character. And the concern that begging might harm the poor, and his preference that friars should support themselves by manual labor (AC 15 [LP 111]) sound quite authentic.

Francis Prepares to Retire

Francis at Greccio (pp. 108–9)

Francis and the deed for the Clares is discussed in Oliger (1912), 200, and De Beer (1977). On Francis's diminishing leadership after 1222, see Manselli (1980), 43–53, who puts Francis's decline earlier—citing AC 11 (2C 151)—than I would. On Honorius's letter concerning excommunication, see Landini (1968), 56. 1C 84 ("3. anno ante mortem") tells us that Francis spent from Christmas 1223 to Easter 1224 at Greccio. The dating of the departure from Greccio in the spring of 1224 is based on the information given at the beginning of 1C 88. The crossing of the lake to Greccio is in 2C 167.

Creation of the crèche (pp. 108–9)

Sources for the Greccio Christmas are 1C 84–87; 2C 199–200 (which presents the crèche as an annual event). There is no reason to doubt the historicity of the crèche, which matches Francis's piety so well. That it was an annual affair is possible, but probably retrojection. The story attracted animal marvels (2C 35–36; AC 74), in particular the taming of wolves (the origin for the late "Wolf of Gubbio"?), which fit the hagiographical stereotype of "power over animals" as proof of sanctity.

Francis and Christmas (pp. 108–9)

Francis wanting the emperor to pass a law to feed animals on Christmas is in AC 12; the Christmas on Friday incident is in 2C 199. There is a long poverty-themed story placed during the sojourn at Greccio: AC 74 (LP 32–34) and 2C 61. It very much resembles the story of Hugolino's dinner for Francis and Dominic, which I have rejected as unhistorical. The anecdote has Francis rounding on the brothers for having too nice a Christmas dinner. This hardly matches Francis's famous attitude about humans, animals, and even houses feasting at Christmas (AC 12). AC then introduces Hugolino, during "a chapter at the Porziuncula," admiring the friars for eating on the ground, not at tables. As the eyewitness Jordan of Giano tells us that the friars eat at tables during the general chapter, this too sounds like editorializing from the 1250s. I omit both stories from my narrative as of dubious historicity.

On Chapter Seven

FRANCIS'S PERIOD OF withdrawal, sickness, and death is treated in Manselli (1982), 246–55, 326–43; and, very briefly, in Vauchez (2009), 194–202. Chronology of Francis's last two years is very difficult because of the random nature of the reports in AC and the lack of chronological indicators in 1C.

Central to the reconstruction of this period is the witness of the "Assisi Compilation" reports. In spite of its lack of order, AC is a very good, even eyewitness, source for the last two years: Manselli (1980), 53. The later poverty controversies, however, have skewed the reporting. I agree with Schmucki (1981), who takes Manselli to task for not recognizing the Proto-Spiritualist reworking of the *Nos qui cum eo fuimus* passages. But even Manselli (1980), 132–41 (on AC 106), admits that stories like that of the friar who asked Francis why he resigned and allowed laxity to infect the order are later editorializing.

Pace Manselli (1982), 37, who asserts that we must either accept the AC stories as they are or reject them entirely, the stories can be evaluated individually and controlled for later concerns. Although some reports may come from Brother Leo himself, it is best to consider AC as the product of a group of companions. These friars will probably remain unidentifiable, as Manselli (1975), 274 n. 31, came to believe. Matanic (1981) criticizes Manselli for overprivileging the *Nos* texts. Matanic would have them be the remains of lost canonization *acta,* not a response to Crescentius of Iesi's request for stories. Lazzeri (1920) notes that the phrase *Nos qui cum eo fuimus* parallels "Perché furono presenti" and "Perché furono con lei" in PC. Even if the texts are from lost canonization *acta,* this does not mean that they could not have been reworked before the creation of the AC manuscript in 1310. AP and L3C do not provide independent witnesses for this period.

Older biographers, such as Terzi and Fortini, tried to harmonize the material in early sources (1C, 2C, AC), as well as very late material, sometimes of nearly worthless historicity (e.g., 2MP 104, *Legenda Antiqua* 25, *Actus Sancti Francisci* 21, *Fioretti* 19). Manselli wisely restricted himself to the more trustworthy earlier sources and did not try to construct a strict chronology. I follow him in this, although I do think some chronological reordering is possible. Perhaps the best "timetable" for the period is Brown (1965), 385–90.

The Francis of AC is a conflicted and difficult personality. Desbonnets (1983), 108, thinks that his snappishness and bad temper were the result of his growing alienation from the now "institutionalized" order. Dalarun (1996), 209–10, is more measured. He considers the Francis of AC to be the real Francis and blames his bad temper on the saint's misguided attempt to impose "monastic asceticism" on himself. He dismisses Francis's harshness to others in AC as interjection by the "monasticized" reporters. To me, both scholars seem overly concerned to distance their order's founder from things they do not like in contemporary Franciscanism: close links to ecclesiastical authorities and conventional monastic spirituality.

Francis was never a "conventional monk," but an honest reading of AC reveals not a "free spirit," but rather a tortured man who occasionally lashed out at those around him. The best analysis of this "complex" Francis is probably Manselli (1980), 174–88, who notes that the AC reports have virtually no hagiographic stereotyping. Manselli (1980), 177, is certainly right that Francis had not only strong and inflexible views about his mission, but also a grave problem correcting others who misunderstood it, because correction violated his understanding that a "lesser brother" should not be above others in any way. Merlo (1991b), 42, and others have suggested that Francis wanted to rule by example in his later years, in parallel to, and perhaps in competition with, the official leadership. While this may be what happened, I am not sure it was intentional. Spiritualist hagiographers probably exaggerated the contrast between the "two hierarchies" so as to accent their own exemplarity as a criticism of the order's leadership.

Francis Withdraws from Leadership

At Rieti (pp. 110–11)
The crossing of the lake of Rieti is recorded in 2C 167 and given a hagiographic miraculous gloss. The Lent at Greccio is recorded in AC 73 (LP 31) and 2C 45, both of which make the pillow incident into a miraculous event.

2C includes the two brothers' visit. The pillow incident itself is presented as a poverty issue in AC 119 (LP 94) and, even more so, in 2C 64.

Events in the order (pp. 111–12)
The ordination of the first Franciscan priests is recorded in ChJG 30; for *Quia Populares,* see FA:ED 1:561–63. On the 1224 general chapter and the decision to allow provincial superiors to admit novices, see L3C 66, AC 70 (LP 28), and 2C 40. ChTE 1 intimates that Francis was present by naming him as the one who selected the deacon Agnello of Pisa as leader of the mission to England.

Anthony of Padua and studies (p. 112)
The text of LtAnt (FA:ED 1:107) is known only in the 1300s, when it was cited in the *Chronica XXIV Generalium Ordinis Minorum* (Quaracchi: Collegium S. Bonaventurae, 1897), 132, but no serious questions as to authenticity have been raised. Francis's respect for theologians is emphasized in 2C 172–74; his use of "bishop" for theologians is also in Test 13. 2C 195 (AC 47) puts into Francis's mouth some very negative comments about study and scholarship, which have prophetic glossing that suggests anachronism. The tone of that anecdote is hard to square with the LtAnt. On LtAnt and its interpretation, see Manselli (1982), 280–86, who correctly notes that academic study among the Franciscans became common only in the 1230s, after the conversion of Alexander of Hales.

The "difficult" Francis (p. 113)
Manselli (1980), 25, describes the Francis of AC as sick and middle-aged. AC 81 (LP 49) and 2C 130–31 describe his behavior when sick. On his attitude toward medical treatments, see 2C 210–11. Both Dalarun (1996), 211, and Merlo (1991b), 40, agree that the outbursts of authoritarianism that mark Francis's last years in AC are genuine and not the creation of reporters. On Francis's difficult relations with his caregivers, see AC 11 (LP 105–6); 2C 151. On his refusal of assigned helpers, see 2C 144 (= AC 40).

The dream prediction of Francis's death (p. 114)
Elias's prophetic dream is in 1C 109, with the dating "eighteen years" after his conversion; it is dated "two years" before his death in 1C 108. For the chronological issues here, see Brown (1965), 390–91. The event fits more logically before La Verna.

On Mount La Verna

An introduction to the sources and events of the La Verna retreat may be found in Schmucki (1988), 29–39, which emphasizes Francis's mystical experiences.

Miccoli (2000) traces the growing importance of the La Verna events in Franciscan identity during the 1200s and thoughtfully relates the stigmata to Francis's Christocentric piety.

Up the mountain (p. 114)

What seems to be the story of Francis's trip to La Verna on horseback is found in 1C 63. That ride is sometimes interpreted to be from La Verna to Siena, but that is unlikely, because there was no hermitage in Siena, and the story involves a trip to a hermitage: see Schmucki (1991), 164. Brother Leo was on La Verna, but evidence for the other companions is less certain. ChTE 13 and LMj 13.4 mention Illuminato and Rufino as present. The late and unreliable Bartholomew of Pisa adds Angelo Tancredi and Masseo of Marignano. Esser (1978), 86–87, takes the anecdotes in AC about Francis's last days at face value and concludes that Francis had around him a group of disillusioned reactionaries nostalgic for the early days of the order. I think we have to discount the tone of the AC reports as a result of conditions in the order during the later 1250s.

Demonic and fraternal torments (p. 114)

It is clear from AC 118 (LP 93), which records the "sign of the birds," that Francis was very troubled during his stay on La Verna and complained about temptations by demons. 1C 103–4 (cf. 2C 188) reports Francis's concerns in the later years and mentions not violations of poverty, but the unseemly rush for advancement to ordination as priests and for positions of authority. Even AC 21 (LP 116), which records a revelation of Christ's complaints to Brother Leo about the brothers, mentions backbiting and lack of gratitude, not violations of poverty, as the typical fault in this period. On Francis's use of Bible divination on La Verna in 1C 91–93, see Schmucki (1991), 169–70. See Schmucki (1991), 174 n. 39, for Mass on La Verna. AC 87 (LP 50) records the daily reading of the Gospel and the fire incident. The fire incident is, in the opinion of Brooke (2006), 112–13, perhaps one of the best-attested anecdotes we have about Francis. Schmucki (1991), 229, labors over Francis's "forty days" on La Verna. This number is so obviously symbolic that it is impossible to read it literally. The best guess is that Francis was on La Verna about a month or a little more.

Francis and the Lord's Passion (pp. 115–16)

For an example of Francis's meditation on the Passion during illness, see AC 77 (LP 37). Much has been written on the role of Christ's Passion in Francis's prayer and mysticism. Schmucki (1986), 254–55, is a good place to start. More comprehensive and sensitive is Nguyên-Van-Khanh (1989). Authors often try to show that Francis's devotion to the Passion was "not typically medieval" because of the balancing focus on the Resurrection. I am not convinced. One might compare it to the thirteenth-century liturgy of Holy Week and Easter and find just such a balance there too, and that liturgy is certainly "medieval." The best edition of the Office of the Passion (FA:ED 1:139–53), which replaces that of Esser, is Gallant (1978). On Gallant's edition, see Pellegrini (1982a), 319–20. Gallant thinks the selection of Psalm verses is "theatrical" and influenced by the *jongleur* repertoire. I do not think one has to look beyond the standard liturgical use of the Psalms to find the work's inspiration. Another interpretation is von Rieden (1960), esp. 5–17, which positions the work within Francis's other writings on the Passion. Schmucki (1986), 253, discusses the Marian title "Spouse of the Holy Spirit" in SalBVM; for more on Francis's devotion to Mary, see Di Ciaccia (1982a).

The seraph apparition (p. 116)

I follow the description in 1C. AC 118 (LP 93) describes the apparition of the seraph but curiously says nothing of the stigmata. LCh 11 is the first source to speak of the seraph as "causing" the stigmata, which seems a logical deduction. It is taken for granted to be the case by Frugoni (1993) in her interesting treatment of the iconography. ChTE 92, admittedly late, adds interesting information about the vision, supposedly firsthand from Leo and Rufino. We can discount the seraph's promises of rewards and punishments for friends and enemies of the Franciscan Order, but Francis's supposed report to Rufino that the seraph "eum dure tractavit," and that Rufino should wash and anoint the rock where Francis was praying with oil, seem likely to be authentic. On Eccleston, see Schmucki (1991), 186–87, 219–20, who also accepts the story about washing and anointing the rock.

The stigmata (pp. 117–18)

The most comprehensive work on the stigmata is still Schmucki (1991), which, although less than critical on sources, is solid in its basic conclusions. Schmucki (1991), 7–69, has an invaluable and exhaustive bibliographical essay on scholarship on the stigmata. The two more or less independent sources for the stigmata are 1C 94–96 and the much-debated "Letter of Elias." Francis's warning not to speak of mystical experiences is in Adm 21. A document in the Assisi archives (FA:ED 2:770–71), dated to 1237–50, gives the names of those who claimed to have seen the stigmata after Francis's death. L3C 68–73, which is lacking in the earliest manuscripts, is almost certainly based on LMj, as Beguin (1979), 182, and Desbonnets (1972) conclude. The report in Matthew of Paris's Chronicle is fantastic and worthless.

The older general consensus of scholarship—summarized in FA:ED 1:485–87—was that the Elias letter is a reconstruction of a lost circular letter and dates to some twenty to sixty years after Francis's death. It seems modeled on the report of such a circular in ChJG, pp. 45–46. Now Accrocca (1999) has effectively demonstrated that the Elias letter is a late forgery, at least to my satisfaction. It is dependent on 1C and contains striking anachronisms. Nevertheless, the letter has defenders: Vauchez (1968), 62, who accepts the Elias letter without hesitation; Schmucki (1991), 321, who concludes that the letter is authentic but not as trustworthy as 1C; and Barone (1974), 106–8, and Vauchez (2009), 204–5, both of whom consider it authentic. Given the dubious status of the letter, I rely on 1C as the "harder" and so more genuine version as the stigmata event, making the marks in the hands "nail-heads." The more conventional form (holes in hands and feet) would be the "easier" version, and less likely authentic. In this I follow Dalarun (1996), 130, and Schmucki (1991), 322–23. Gregory IX did not mention the stigmata in his bull of canonization, but he did vouch for their reality in 1237.

Vauchez (1968), 61, accepts without question the feast of the Exaltation of the Cross (14 Sept.) as the date of the stigmata, an idea going back to Bonaventure, LMj 13.3–4. This seems to me like liturgical symbolism. The best we can do is to date the event during the retreat on La Verna: Schmucki (1991), 166.

Controversy over the stigmata (p. 117)

On those who questioned the stigmata, including some Franciscans, see Vauchez (1968), 61–89, esp. 63–64. He notes that the first example of the phenomenon was a 1222 fraud in Oxford, England. Other known examples were often heretical in tone. In contrast, Schmucki (1991), 81–89, canvasses the testimonies as to the marks after Francis's death, which are numerous and trustworthy. Schmucki (1991), 105–10, also discusses possible natural causes. For the Petrarch letter, see Vauchez (1968), 88.

The Leo parchment (p. 118)

The parchment includes PrsG and LtL. This parchment is edited in Lapsanski (1974), which differs from the older edition of Esser only in punctuation. Langeli (1994), has produced another edition, which includes a diplomatic version that refuses to supplement lacunae and unreadable sections from later copies and editions. For English translations of both editions, see FA:ED 1:109–12. Leo's inscription on the parchment and 2C 49 describe the circumstances of the composition. Langeli (1984), 50–55, notes the relic's talismanic nature. On BlL, see Van Dijk (1954), who identifies the liturgical variant in the Numbers 6 text as that found in a pontifical of Pope Innocent III. On the human context of both compositions, esp. Brother Leo's personality, see Manselli (1983), 334, which also shows why the parchment should be dated to this period and not earlier.

The "Praises of God" (p. 118)

Miccoli (1991), 83, notes that PrsG contains the only commentary Francis ever made on the stigmata. For comparison, see Thompson (2005), 364–71, on extant lay compositions from thirteenth-century Italy. See Langeli (1994), 116, on Francis's handwriting, which is typical of the lay mercantile hands of rural towns of Umbria of the period, especially those with "scarsa o nulla tradizione culturale." The style is usually called "minusola comune." See Langeli (1994), 108–9, on the afterlife of the parchment. The attempt in De Beer (1977), 108–10, to relate the Tau and the doodles on the blessing to Islam is not convincing. AC 107 (LP 78) and 2C 160 suggest that Francis required delinquent brothers to recite the PrsG as a penance, but the legalism of the passages does not sound like Francis.

Francis and mysticism (pp. 118–19)

See, as an introduction to this topic, Schmucki (1986), esp. 263, on Francis's "sacramental" approach to nature. Authors before Schmucki usually conformed Francis to current theories of mystical experience or to Bonaventure's system, rather than focusing on the saint's own writings. On Francis's understanding of God, see Matura (1982), 113, who especially emphasizes Francis's use of Christ's so-called Priestly Prayer (John 17:1–26), with its links to the Passion. Examples are found in 1LtF 13–19, 2LtF 56–60, and especially ER 22.41–55. As suggested in the discussion of OfP, Francis's language about God is always strongly biblical. Otherwise, his language is mostly Trinitarian rather than Christocentric: Matura (1982), 124–27. Dalarun (1997), 230, observes that Francis, unlike Saint Bernard, never used the Song of Songs in his writings. Manselli (1995) is a sensitive analysis of Francis's views on suffering and the Cross.

Francis Descends the Mountain

The return from La Verna (p. 119)

AC 83 (LP 42) dates the departure from La Verna and mirrors the duration of Francis's final illnesses in 1C 102: "nearly two years." LMj 13.7 is the first source to describe the actual trip down La Verna, and it is late. Schmucki (1991), 230, reasonably suggests that the motive for the move was medical. For *Quia Populares Tumultus,* see FA:ED 1:562–63. For the letter to the bishop of Paris, *Non Deberent Ecclesiarum Praelati,* see BF 1:22–23, no. 21.

The "Letter to the Entire Order" (pp. 119–20)
On LtOrd (FA:ED 1:116–21), see Schmucki (1986), 247, esp. on its Latinity. Flood (1983), 119, citing Assisi, Biblioteca Comunale, MS 338, thinks this letter was written to a chapter, which the direct injunctions to Elias and the ministers contained in it make likely. Flood takes the whole letter to be a prohibition of private Masses, and Francis's unexpressed judgment to be that they are "clericalizing." Desbonnets (1983), 120, repeats the same hypothesis. I would say that while clericalization certainly represents a problem in the modern Franciscan Order and became an issue soon after Francis's death, there is no evidence in the letter for reading it any differently than Francis's earlier letters on the Eucharist. Francis's sole explicit concern about liturgical practice was always that it be reverent and noble.

On the peremptory tone of LtOrd, and its effective excommunication of delinquents, see Merlo (1991b), 36–40, who correctly balances this with the counsel of forgiveness in charity found in LtMin. See Schmucki (1986), 247, on the implicit mystical theology of the prayer that "inwardly cleansed, inwardly enlightened, inflamed by the Holy Spirit, we may be able to follow the footprints of Christ." This prayer is the most polished Latin in the letter, and Francis may have had help composing it. That would show its importance to him.

The "Letter to Brother Leo" (pp. 121–22)
The commentary on the translation of LtL in FA:ED 1:122 suggests that Francis's crabbed writing on the parchment may show that he was in pain from the stigmata when he wrote it. On the letter, see Pratesi (1984), which is, with Lapsanski (1974), the best introduction to the document. Dalarun (2007) is good on the "maternal" quality of the letter. See also Langeli (1994) for what is actually in Francis's hand and for a diplomatic edition. Langeli concludes that the document was composed in two parts and the Tau then added. 3C 153 and LtMin 2.9 also mention the Tau. I follow the corrected translation for the second part of LtL, found in Dalarun (1997), 58. Desbonnets (1983), 49–50, considers the letter Francis's final statement on the spiritual autonomy implied by his understanding of obedience. See Langeli (1984), 50–58, on the talismanic nature of the parchment.

The "Canticle of Brother Sun"

Conditions at San Damiano (p. 122)
On Francis's rapidly declining health, see 1C 97–98. AC 83 (LP 42) describes the miserable conditions in the hut attached to San Damiano, including the torment by mice and vermin. See Marini (1989), 150–52, on this passage. The

vermin story, contrary to hagiographic convention, presents Francis as tormented by animals and powerless over them; it is certainly authentic.

"Cantico di Frate Sole" (pp. 122–24)

The oldest manuscript of this poem (with blank staves for music) is Assisi, Biblioteca Comunale, MS 338, fol. 22^r. The best introduction to the poem, in English, is still probably Leclerc (1977). Paolazzi (1992) is also good. A good textual analysis of CtC is Baldelli (1971). Manselli (1980), 83–92, however, criticizes Baldelli's failure to use AC witnesses to the composition. Baldelli places the poem in the context of earlier vernacular works (outside of Sardinia, it is among the oldest vernacular *laude*), localizes the dialect (Assisi), and emphasizes the biblical parallels. The origin of CtC is first witnessed directly in AC 83 (LP 42), on which depends 2C, Bonaventure, and all other reports. AC 83 places the event "two years before Francis's death," a phrase mirrored in 1C 102, which says the period from the Rieti medical intervention to the saint's death was "nearly two years."

Brown (1965), 385, remarks that the two most fruitlessly debated issues in Francis studies during the second half of the twentieth century were the location of the family home (now solved) and the place of composition for CtC. Both Benedetto (1941), esp. 150–56, and Terzi (1959) argued that CtC was composed while Francis was with the parish priest at San Fabiano near Rieti. I find Brown's contention that the CtC was composed in its traditional place, San Damiano, convincing, if not conclusive.

"Mother Earth" (p. 123)

Dalarun (1997), 41, remarks, citing an unpublished University of Ottawa thesis by Cristiana Garzena, that Francis's characterization of "Mother Earth" is revolutionary. I am not convinced; the image of Earth as Mother, whose womb gives birth to living things, is found in the early twelfth-century Bernardis Silvestris, *Cosmographia* (New York: Columbia University Press, 1973), 80–82.

Personal influences on the Canticle (pp. 123–24)

See Cardini (1983b), 297–308, on Francis's treatment of fire in CtC and its possible reference to the seraph. See Dalarun (1996), 212–13, on the demonology and negative view of animals in AC 83. That both seem so unlike the stereotypical Francis shows their authenticity, at least for me.

The translation of "per" (p. 124)

On the "causal" and "agent" use of *per*, see Schmucki (1986), 260, who supports the consensus of modern scholars that "per" in the Canticle shows cause ("for"), not agent ("through"). Manselli (1980), 91–95, strongly argues for the causal reading. It is telling that Francis's companions also understood "per" as causal. The context of the composition also suggests this and excludes the agent sense. In contrast, Benedetto, in numerous articles cited by Manselli, has argued for the "agent" interpretation, which is reflected in the translation I have taken from FA:ED 1:113–14. See Benedetto (1941), 33–34, 41, and Schmucki (1986), 261, on the liturgical sources for CtC.

Additions to the Canticle (pp. 124–25)
On the addition of the peace strophe, see AC 84 (LP 44). I have no trouble following AC 7 (LP 100), where the strophe on death is added later, just before Francis's death. Thus I follow Schmucki (1986), 261, not Benedetto (1941), 186–89, who would have Sister Death present in CtC from the beginning. I do not find the view that AC 7 is apocryphal, a mere elaboration of AC 100 (LP 65), convincing.

The "Canticle of Exhortation for the Ladies of San Damiano" (p. 125)
On CtExh (FA:ED 1:115), see Boccali (1978), where it is edited. This poem is not in Esser's edition. Its composition is described in AC 85 (LP 45), on which, see Boccali (1977). On interpretations of the Italian, see FA:ED 1:115 n. d.

ON CHAPTER EIGHT

V AUCHEZ (2009), 202–22, focuses on the Testament and Francis's death, and ibid., 222–40, on the canonization and new tomb. Manselli (1982), 343–63, covers this period more narratively, albeit in a sketchy and hurried form.

Failed Medical Treatments

Francis the patient (pp. 126–27)
A description of Francis as a patient is given in 1C 97–98, 102, where, after discounting the spiritual elaborations, Francis's difficulty in accepting his illnesses is very evident. His refusal to hear readings from scripture is in AC 79 (LP 38) and in 2C 105, where Francis seems even more abrupt (and so it is probably authentic). On this incident, see Miccoli (1991), 243. Manselli (1980), 80, considers Francis's need for special food, but refusal of it—AC 50 (LP 1) and AC 111 (LP 85)—an example of Francis's self-presentation as a model friar, a very generous interpretation. See Manselli (1980), 141–43, on Francis's patched tunic.

At Rieti (pp. 127–28)
1C 99 records the move from Assisi to the Rieti area; AC 111, which seems to fit this period, has Francis at the hermitage of Sant'Eleuterio. For Francis at Rieti itself, see 1C 99. Schmucki (1991), 235, thinks that this was when Rainald of Segni (later Pope Alexander IV) saw the stigmata: LMj 13.8. See AC 68 (LP 26) and 2C 44 for the woman bringing food to Fonte Colombo. AC 71

(LP 29) records the shark and crab dinner. The lute music incident is in AC 66 (LP 24) and 2C 126. Francis refusing to put out his burning drawers is in AC 86 (LP 46–48) and 2C 166; see Manselli (1980), 88–90, on this incident. That God would have to repay Francis's caregivers is in AC 86 and 2C 166; on which, see Manselli (1980), 83–92. The "Basabove" incident is in AC 94 (LP 57); on which, see Schmucki (1991), 244. Francis's medical operation is in AC 86 (LP 46–48) and 2C 166.

Francis's actions while sick (p. 128)
AC 89 and 2C 92 (which places the incident in the bishop's palace) report Francis giving away clothing to the woman with eye problems; on which, see Manselli (1980), 95–99. For other examples of Francis giving away clothing, see 2C 89 (= AC 34); 2C 86 (= AC 31); 2C 90; 1C 76. The healing of Gedeone is in AC 95 (LP 58); 2C 41; cf. 1C 99. The San Fabiano incident is in AC 67 (LP 25); on this event, see Manselli (1980), 114–16, in which he detects an anticurial tone, perhaps typical of the later Proto-Spiritual Franciscan environment of the *Nos qui cum eo fuimus* texts.

At Siena (pp. 129–30)
1C 105 gives the date "six months before his death" for the move to Siena. The trip past Rocca Campiglia is in 2C 93, where it has been theologized into a divine confirmation of Franciscan poverty. On Francis's illnesses at Siena and during the last years of his life, see Schmucki (1999). Schatzlein-Sulmasy (1987) attempted to diagnose Francis scientifically and is useful for medieval understandings of illness. The conclusion that "borderline leprosy" underlies Francis's symptoms (and was the cause of the stigmata) is unconvincing; I see no reason to detect hidden causes of afflictions that clearly present as malaria and dropsy. The residence on land provided by Lord Bonaventura is referred to in AC 58 (LP 14–16).

Proto-testaments (p. 130)
Reporters relate this discourse to Francis's stomach sickness and the "Siena Testament" mentioned in AC 59 (LP 17). 1C 105 also reports this new stomach condition and the arrival of Elias. See Esser (1978), 45–55, on possible "proto-testaments." See Miccoli (1991), 42, on the Siena Testament, which he sees as paralleling the final Testament in its three parts: (1) Love one another. (2) Keep poverty. (3) Be obedient to the hierarchy and clergy. Manselli (1976), 91–99, while admitting that Test 24 speaks of poor residences, has trouble squaring the elaborate detailed legislation in AC 58 with Francis's known writings of the period. We can safely consider it retrojection from later poverty controversies.

Nothing like it appears in the Siena Testament story. Nevertheless, Manselli (1982), 350–52, opts for the authenticity of AC 58. The cloak giveaway at Celle is in 2C 88 (= AC 33); 1C 105 summarizes his illness there and the departure for Assisi.

The Return to Assisi

Francis's return home (p. 131)
The stay at Begnara and the begging there is in AC 96 (LP 59–60) and 2C 77, where, unsurprisingly, considering the date of the source and its intended audience, these reporters turn this wholly believable incident into a "miracle" story, confirming the divine nature of poverty and begging. On the reworking of this story by later retellers, see Manselli (1980), 152–57. The friar's prediction that Francis would soon have a cult is in AC 4 (LP 98), which turns the story into an example of Francis's prophetic powers. The "Bongiovanni" story is in AC 100 (LP 65) and makes sense for this period; on this name, see Menestò (1993), 263–64. On the proper way of making a "Holy Death" in communal Italy, see Thompson (2005), 383–98.

Sister Death (pp. 132–33)
AC 99 (LP 64) records the singing of CtC and Elias's negative reaction; AC 7 (LP 100b) recounts the composition of the strophe on Sister Death. I have modified the FA:ED 1:114 translation of the CtC to make it causal. Benedetto (1941), 67, notes the parallel of ER 21.7–9 and the CtC on mortal sin and death, almost a perfect parallel. Compare also Rev. 21:8.

Francis's Testament

In the Assisi episcopal palace (p. 133)
The gift of the Breviary is known from Leo's autograph note in it, reproduced in Esser (1978), 73: "The blessed Francis left this book for his fellows, Brother Angelo and Brother Leo. When he was well, he prayed his office from it; and when he was ill and could not pray it, he wanted to hear it. He kept this up as long as he lived."

The best introduction to the Testament is now Miccoli (1996). Although popular tradition places this document at the Porziuncula, there is no direct evidence for this. On dating the Testament, see Miccoli (1991), 44, who merely concludes it is after Siena. Any dating other than the summer of 1226 is wholly speculative. As composition of a testament was a part of the rites of holy dying, it belongs with the singing of the CtC and the gift of the Breviary, both of which occurred at the episcopal palace. If it was composed at the Porziuncula, it would have been during one of the stop offs there when Francis was being moved around, which I think unlikely. AC 106, where Francis is made to give a long discourse on just how poor the friars' houses were, seems like a later gloss on the short passage on this topic in the Testament. It appears that the reporters want to make these longer instructions the actual Testament. See Miccoli (1991), 45, who dismisses the historicity of AC 106, arguing that it is elaboration, as does Esser (1978), 46–50. Nevertheless, that the instruction on houses in AC 106 is placed in the palace is significant and indirectly confirms my suspicion that this was the place of composition.

Nature and structure of the Testament (pp. 133–36)

The literature on the Testament is vast. Esser (1978), who follows the traditional placing of the composition at the Porziuncula, remains the best overall introduction. Oddly, none of the early narrative sources ever mention the document, although I think that AC 106 presupposes it. No serious scholar today doubts its authenticity or places it in opposition to LR: see Esser (1978), 33–55. Linguistic evidence, marshaled by Esser (1978), 81–83, suggests that although it was dictated in Italian and translated on the fly by the friar taking down Francis's words, Francis intended it to be a written text. Francis speaks of "haec verba" and "hoc scriptum." There are no biblical citations or embellishments. Esser (1978), 94–97, reads the Testament as in three parts (1–3, 4–8, 9–11) loosely centered on a series of catch ideas and parallel to the Siena Testament. Aubert Stroit, quoted by Esser, thought it was structured as a commentary on LR. I am, however, inclined to agree with Miccoli (1991), 51, that the document lacks a rigid structure. Rather, it consists of the reminiscences (the "autobiographical section"), then a series of ad hoc "commands" in reaction to contemporary events, and finally the "Penal Section." This guides my discussion of the document.

What does "testament" mean? Van Corstanje (1964), 23–25, calls it an "alliance et loi" in the biblical sense of "testament"—not a legal instrument as in "last will and testament." Esser (1978), 67–68, holds a similar position. Miccoli (1991), 42, who considers the Testament a document for the internal use of the order, is more down-to-earth in his analysis. I agree with him, especially in his emphasis on its concrete nature. Francis did not create an abstract theological "testament" or a kind of "program" for the order. Nor is it a "weapon" solicited from the dying Francis for internecine war by some reformist faction. It expresses what was on Francis's mind when he composed it: it is an occasional document. Dalarun (1997), 96, is surely right that the autobiographical section was meant to set the dying man's life in order and provide a model for the brothers. On the centrality of the autobiographical section, see Miccoli (1991), 49.

Poverty and privileges in the Testament (pp. 134–35)

Dalarun (1996), 123, rightly stresses that, at the time of Francis's death, "delinquent" brothers were not guilty of high living. Rather, they wanted prestige or power. Esser (1978), 154–55 (Karecki trans., 59–61), observes that later sources, e.g., 2MP 68 (and I would add AC 106), have to elaborate on the poverty material to make it more impressive than it really is. On the papal letters, see Landini (1968), 56, Esser (1978), 156–65 (Karecki trans., 61–69), and Rusconi (1994), 97–98. These are *In Eo quo Audivimus,* 4 Oct. 1225; *Vineae Domini,* 7 Oct. 1225; *Urgente Officii,* 2 Jan. 1226; and *Ex Parte Vesta,* 17 Mar. 1226.

The "Penal Section" of the Testament (pp. 135–36)

Esser (1978), 172 (Karecki trans., 76), remarks on the Testament's "inquisition-like strictness." In a remarkable example of evasion, Flood (1983), 127, avoids Francis's "inquisition-like strictness" with the offhand comment that "the Rule handles it better." Merlo (1991b), 11, rightly criticizes attempts by Franciscans like Balducci in *Francesco* (1982), 150, who, influenced by Leonardo Boff, try to sanitize this aspect of Francis. On "no glossing of the Rule," see Esser (1978), 185 (Karecki trans., 88). The Testament passage is probably the origin of later miraculous voice stories with the same message. Vauchez (2009), 211–12, suggests the link between this section and the preaching of Brother Paul and comments on its harshness.

Last Days with the Brothers

The move to the Porziuncula (pp. 136–37)

1C 106 alludes to the move to the Porziuncula and records Francis's charge to the brothers to keep and revere the place. The section of AC 56 (LP 8b–9a) that contains the "Porziuncula Testament" elaborates on Francis's affection for the place and has him setting up a strict way of life there as a model for later friars. The detailed legalism of this legislation is not Francis, and the idea of a "model community" reflects a later period. Nonetheless, these later developments are rooted in Francis's love of the place. AC 5 (LP 99) supplies details for the trip to the Porziuncula and presents a longer blessing prayer that is most likely a later reconstruction. AC 12 (LP 108) reports the presence of the priest and physician brothers. On the parsley incident in 2C 51 and 1MP 26, see Manselli (1980), 144–47, who remarks that the version in 1MP is probably more authentic, as Francis is more demanding, and there is less pious elaboration. I agree.

Bertoli (1993), 181, believes that the written blessing for Clare in AC 13 is authentic. That narrative, however, turns the letter into a prophecy that she will see Francis before she dies (fulfilled at his funeral). This I find suspect, but I see no reason to doubt a farewell message. TestCl includes a quotation supposedly from Francis that has itself been called the "Testament for Clare." Much debated, this text is probably authentic: see Robinson (1910) and Lainati (1984). Whether the actual words recorded are authentic or not, making them part of this communication is conjectural, but cf. Manselli (1982), 349–51. The emphasis on poverty reflects Clare's concerns when she revised the document in the 1250s.

Francis, Jacoba, and Pressede (pp. 137–38)

Jacoba de' Settesoli's visit is in AC 8 (LP 101); on which, see Dalarun (1997), 66, 145, who considers it historical, as I do. Dalarun (1997), 258, wistfully admits that there is no good evidence for a close relation between Francis and any woman (including Clare) other than Jacoba. Di Ciaccia (1982b), 327–41, reaches a similar conclusion. 3C 181 includes a report not only that Sister Pressede was close to Francis, but that the saint "received her into obedience" and gave her a habit consisting of a tunic and cord. This action would violate ER 12.4, but it does sound like one of Francis's typical impulsive acts. Unfortunately, 3C only elaborates on the relationship by recounting a posthumous miracle worked for the recluse.

Francis's final blessings (p. 138)

In my opinion, AC 22 (LP 117) and 2C 216–17, which recount the "Last Supper" incident, seem the most primitive and undeveloped form of the blessings event, and so I follow them. On their historicity, see Schmucki (1991), 251–52. 1C 110–11 and 2C 214–17 describe Francis's death and the reading of John's Gospel. On these typical medieval deathbed rituals, see Thompson (2005), 392–98. AC 14 (LP 110) records the flock of larks; on which, see Manselli (1980), 53–57. Francis's death is dated in 1C 88, 108, and 109, and less exactly in 119.

Much ink has been spilled on these blessings. 1C 108 describes Francis giving a blessing with his arms crossed like the patriarch Jacob (Gen. 49). This text has him put his right hand on Elias as his favored son. The brother under the left hand is not named. The dubious Encyclical Letter of Elias used the same image. The famous story in AC 12 (LP 107–8) turns this event into a blessing of Brothers Giles and Bernard, with the right hand on Bernard, Francis's first follower. In this version, Francis also makes a series of prophecies about Bernard's holy life and death, repeated in 1C 24 and 2C 48. It is not surprising that Elias has vanished from texts composed after his fall. 2C 50 recounts that Francis gave his cloak to Bernard while sick in the bishop's palace.

Brooke (2006), 126–27, prefers the AC version of the blessing. The political implication—Leo and his friends are the true sons of Francis—is so overt that I cannot follow her here. But I am not willing to dogmatize that Francis blessed Elias either. Manselli (1967) and Dalarun (1988), 329–66, try to harmonize the blessing stories, suggesting a blessing of Elias as head of the order and of Bernard as an exemplary friar. Dalarun (1996), 63–69, concludes that the 1C and AC blessings are later constructions to honor Elias (1C) and to give a special status to Bernard (AC), and that a general blessing of the brothers is the historical core. Miccoli (1991), 44, is not dogmatic but likes the idea that Francis envisioned a special exemplary role for Bernard. Esser (1978), 52, is more skeptical about the privileging of Bernard. Manselli (1982), 358, categorically rejects the blessing of Elias reported in 1C.

Barone (1992), 77–80, 99–101, in my opinion the best analysis, suggests that the blessing of the friars was historical and suggests that Elias was blessed first as the vicar. Bernard would have been in with the brothers and not singled out. The one aspect of the AC 12 version that I am willing to trust is the timing, just after Jacoba's visit. This timing connection has no propaganda value and so may well be a morsel of historical truth in the propagandist fog.

From Death to the Altar

Discovery of the stigmata (p. 139)
On the lack of rigor mortis, see 1C 112 and AC 12 (LP 108); cf. Schmucki (1991), 256. See Beguin (1979), 182, on L3C 68–73, the report of the stigmata and canonization. Unfortunately, the testimony that communal officials were present at the first showing of the stigmata is the late LMj 15.4, which identifies the judge Jerome as an eyewitness. 1C 113 is the earliest report of the postmortem viewing of the stigmata; cf. Dalarun (1997), 227. For a summary of skepticism and a defense of the authenticity of the stigmata witnesses, see Frugoni (1998), 123–25.

Funeral rites (p. 139)
The San Damiano veneration is in 1C 116–17 and AC 13 (LP 107). The reports are somewhat different. In 1C the body remains in the coffin, and the sisters view it through the communion grille; in AC it is lifted up to the window with the grille removed. 1C sounds a bit sanitized, so I follow AC here. On the funeral itself, see 1C 117–18; and on the entombment at San Giorgio, see 1C 127. For visions of Francis in heaven, see 1C 110, 112, 113; 2C 217–20. For

my narrative of Francis's funeral and the translation of his relics, I rely very much on Brooke (2006), 464–71, who takes into consideration archaeological evidence and presents a good summary of current scholarly conclusions. On the practice of raised tombs for medieval Italian saints, see Thompson (2005), 208–11.

The canonization (p. 140)

On the canonization, see 1C 88, 119–26; 2C 220; and *Mira circa Nos* (FA:ED 1:565–69). The study of the canonization of Francis is not properly part of this biography; those who want to pursue this topic may consult the standard studies by Bihl (1928) and Paciocco (1996). On the canonization bull's use of biblical images and its portrayal of Francis—especially in comparison to Gregory IX's portrayal of Saint Dominic—see Armstrong (1990). See Dalarun (1996), 126, on the delayed promotion of Francis's cult and Hugolino's role in it. On the privileges granted by Gregory IX in 1226–28, see Landini (1968), 61. On the objections to Francis's cult by Spanish peasants, see 2C 102 and remarks on these objections by Vauchez (1968), 78.

[BIBLIOGRAPHY]

Writings of the Saint

The standard edition for most works of Francis:

Opuscula Sancti Patris Francisci Assisiensis: Denuo Edidit iuxta Codices Mss, edited by Kajetan Esser. Bibliotheca Francescana Ascetica Medii Aevi 12. Grottaferrata: Collegium S. Bonaventurae, 1978. Translations in FA:ED 1:40–169.

Two of Francis's compositions to be consulted in editions other than that of Esser:

"Canto di esoratzione di san Francesco per le 'poverelle' di San Damiano." Edition: Giovanni Boccali. *Collectanea Franciscana* 48 (1978): 17–18. This poem's authenticity was in doubt when Esser was published.

Officium Passionis. Edition: Laurent Gallant. *"Dominus Regnavit a Ligno:* L'Office de la Passion de saint François d'Assisi; Édition critique et étude." 3 vols. Ph.D. dissertation, Institut Catholique de Paris, U.E.R. de Théologie et Sciences religieuses du Troisième cycle, 1978. This edition is considered superior to that of Esser.

Medieval Sources for Francis

"The Anonymous of Perugia." Edition: "L'Anonimo Perugino tra le fonti francescane del sec. XIII: Rapporti letterari e testo critico," edited by Lorenzo Di Fonzo. *Miscellanea Francescana* 72 (1972): 117–483. Translation: FA:ED 2:34–58.

"The Assisi Compilation." Edition: *Compilatio Assisiensis dagli scritti di fr. Leone e compagni su s. Francesco d'Assisi dal Ms. 1046 di Perugia,* edited by Marino Bagarini. Assisi: Biblioteca Francescana Chiesa Nuova, 1992. Translation: FA:ED 2:118–230.

Bonaventure. *The Major Legend.* Edition: "Legenda Maior S. Francisci." *Legendae S. Francisci Assisiensis Saeculis XIII et XIV Conscriptae,* 555–652. Analecta Franciscana 10. Quaracchi: Collegium S. Bonaventurae, 1926–41. Translation: FA:ED 2:525–683.

Jacques de Vitry. *Historia Occidentalis.* Edition: *The "Historia Occidentalis" of Jacques de Vitry: A Critical Edition,* edited by John F. Hinnebusch. Spicilegium Friburgense 17. Fribourg: Pressses Universitaires, 1972. Translation of pertinent passages: FA:ED 1:581–88.

Jacques de Vitry. *Letters.* Edition: *Lettres de Jacques de Vitry,* edited by R. B. C. Huygens. Leiden: Brill, 1960. Translation of Letters 1 and 6: FA:ED 1:578–81.

Jordan of Giano. *Chronicle*. Edition: *Chronica Fratris Iordani*, edited by H. Boehmer. Paris, 1909. Cf. recension ed. Bihl, *Archivum Franciscanum Historicum* 2 (1909): 647–50. Translation: *XIIIth Century Chronicles (Jordan of Giano: Chronicle and Letters; Thomas of Eccleston: The Coming of the Friars Minor to England; Salimbene degli Adami: Two Journeys through France)*, translated by Placid Hermann. Chicago: Franciscan Herald, 1961.

Julian of Speyer. *The Life of St. Francis*. Edition: "Vita S. Francisci." *Legendae S. Francisci Assisiensis Saeculis XIII et XIV Conscriptae*, 333–71. Analecta Franciscana 10. Quaracchi: Collegium S. Bonaventurae, 1926–41. Translation: FA:ED 1:368–420.

"The Legend of Perugia." Best edition: Rosalind Brooke, *Scripta Leonis, Rufini, et Angeli, Sociorum Sancti Francisci*. Oxford: Oxford University Press, 1970. Translation (from French translation): *St. Francis of Assisi: Writings and Early Biographies, English Omnibus of the Sources for the Life of St. Francis*, edited by Marion A. Habig, 957–1101. Chicago: Franciscan Herald, 1973. I do not use this hypothetical document as an independent source, but for texts considered part of it I include references.

The Legend of the Three Companions. Edition: "Legenda Trium Sociorum: Édition critique," edited by Théophile Desbonnets. *Archivum Franciscanum Historicum* 67 (1974): 38–144. Translation: FA:ED 2:66–110.

Lemmens, Leonard. *Testimonia Minora Saeculi XIII de S. Francisco Assisiensi*. Quaracchi: Collegium S. Bonaventurae, 1936. Translations of most of these texts are found in FA:ED 1:558–611, "Related Documents"; and 2: 770–821, "Related Documents (1237–1272)."

The Mirror of Perfection, Shorter Version. Editions: *Speculum Perfectionis*, edited by Leonard Lemmens, in *Documenta Antiqua Franciscana*, 1731–1825. Quaracchi: Collegium S. Bonaventurae, 1901. *Speculum Perfectionis Minus*, edited by Mario Bigaroni. Assisi: Edizioni Porziuncula, 1985. Translation: FA:ED 3:214–52.

The Mirror of Perfection, Longer Version. Edition: *Le Speculum Perfectionis; ou, Mémoires de frère Léon sur la seconde partie de la vie de Saint François d'Assise*, edited by Paul Sabatier and Andrew George Little. Manchester: British Society of Franciscan Studies, 1928. Translation: FA:ED 3:253-372.

Thomas of Celano, "The Legend for Use in the Choir." Edition: *Fontes Franciscani*, 427–39, edited by Enrico Menestò and Stefano Brufani. Assisi: Edizioni Porziuncula, 1995. Translation: FA:ED 1:319–26.

Thomas of Celano. *The Life of St. Francis*. Edition: "Vita Prima S. Francisci," edited by Michael Bihl. *Legendae S. Francisci Assisiensis Saeculis XIII et XIV Conscriptae*, 1–117. Analecta Franciscana 10. Quaracchi: Collegium S. Bonaventurae, 1926–41. Translation: FA:ED 1:180–308.

Thomas of Celano. *The Remembrance of the Desire of a Soul*. Edition: "Vita Secunda S. Francisci." *Legendae S. Francisci Assisiensis Saeculis XIII et XIV Conscriptae*, 127–268. Analecta Franciscana 10. Quaracchi: Collegium S. Bonaventurae, 1926–41. Translation: FA:ED 2:235–393.

Thomas of Celano. *The Treatise on the Miracles*. Edition: "Tractatus de Miraculis S. Francisci." *Legendae S. Francisci Assisiensis Saeculis XIII et XIV Conscriptae*, 269–330. Analecta Franciscana 10. Quaracchi: Collegium S. Bonaventurae, 1926–41. Translation: FA:ED 2:397–469.

Thomas of Eccleston. *Chronicle*. Edition: *Tractatus de Adventu Fratrum Minorum in Angliam Fratris Thomae Vulgo Dicti de Eccleston*, edited by A. G. Little and J. Moorman. Manchester: Manchester University Press, 1951. Translation: *XIIIth Century Chronicles (Jordan of Giano: Chronicle and Letters; Thomas of Eccleston: The Coming of the Friars Minor to England; Salimbene degli Adami: Two Journeys through France)*, translated by Placid Hermann. Chicago: Franciscan Herald, 1961.

Sources for Saint Clare

Clare of Assisi: Early Documents: The Lady, edited by Regis Armstrong. New York: New City, 2006.

Clare's "Form of Life." Edition: *Novus Ordo, Nova Vita: Regula di santa Chiara d'Assisi del 9 agosto 1253*, edited by Chiara Augusta Lineati. Matelica: Monastero Clarisse Santa Maria Maddalena, 2001. Translation: CA:ED 108-26.

The Legend of Saint Clare. Edition: *La vita di santa Chiara,* edited by Zefferino Lazzeri. Quaracchi: Collegium S. Bonaventurae, 1920. Translation: CA:ED 277–329.

The Process of Canonization of Clare. Edition: *Santa Chiara di Assisi: I primi documenti ufficiali; Lettera di annunzio della sua morte; Processo e bolla di canonizatione,* edited by Giovanni Boccali. Assisi: Porziuncola, 2002. Translation: CA:ED 141–96.

"The Privilege of Poverty." Edition: Clare of Assisi. *Claire d'Assise: Écrits,* edited by Marie-France Becker et al., 200. Paris: Cerf, 1985. Translation: CA:ED 87–88.

Testament of Clare. Edition: Clare of Assisi. *Claire d'Assise: Écrits,* edited by Marie-France Becker et al., 21–27. Paris: Cerf, 1985. Translation: CA:ED 60–65.

Modern Scholarship

Acta Sanctorum Quotquot Toto Orbe Coluntur, vel a Catholicis Scriptoribus Celebrantur. 69 vols. Paris: Palme et al., 1863–1940.

Abate (1949), Giuseppe. "Storia e leggenda intorno alla nascita di S. Francesco d'Assisi." *Miscellanea Francescana* 49 (1949): 350–75.

Accrocca (1999), F. "Is the 'Encyclical Letter of Brother Elias on the Transitus of St. Francis' Apocryphal?" *Greyfriars Review* 13, Supplement (1999): 19–64.

Alberzoni (1995), Maria Pia. *Chiara e il papato.* Milan: Biblioteca Francescana, 1995.

Alberzoni (1996), Maria Pia. *Clare and the Poor Clares in the Thirteenth Century.* St. Bonaventure, NY: Franciscan Institute, 2004. Translation of *La nascita di un'istituzine: L'ordine di S. Damiano nel XIII secolo.* Milan: CUSL, 1996.

Analecta Franciscana; sive, Chronica Aliaque Varia Documenta ad Historiam Fratrum Minorum Spectantia. 10 vols. Quaracchi: Collegium S. Bonaventurae, 1885–1951.

Armstrong (1976), Edward A. *Saint Francis Nature Mystic: The Derivation and Significance of the Nature Stories in the Franciscan Legend.* Berkeley: University of California Press, 1976.

Armstrong (1990), Regis J. "*Mira circa Nos:* Gregory IX's View of the Saint, Francis of Assisi." *Greyfriars Review* 4:1 (1990): 75–100.

Baldelli (1971), Ignazio. "Il 'Cantico': Problemi di lingua e di stile." In *Francesco d'Assisi e Francescanesimo dal 1216 al 1226,* 77–99. Atti del IV Convegno Internazionale, Assisi, 16–17 ottobre 1976. Assisi: Società Internazionale di Studi Francescani, 1977. Reprint of article in *San Francesco nella ricerca storica degli ultimi ottanta anni.* Todi: Accademia Tubertina, 1971.

Barbero (1990), Alessandro. "La rinuncia di Francesco all'eredità paterna." *Studi Medievali* 3:31 (1990): 837–51.

Barone (1974), Giulia. "Frate Elia." *Bulletino dell'Istituto Storico Italiano per il Medio Evo e Archivio Muratoriano* 84 (1974–75): 88–144.

Barone (1992), Giulia. "Frate Elia: Suggestioni da una rilettura." In *I compagni di Francesco e la prima generazione minoritica,* 59–80. Spoleto: Centro Italiano di Studi sull'Alto Medioevo, 1992.

Basetti-Sani (1972), Giulio. "San Francisco è incorso nella scomunica? Una bolla di Onorio III ed il supposto pellegrinaggio del santo a Gerusalemme." *Archivum Franciscanum Historicum* 65 (1972): 3–19.

Beguin (1979) Pierre-B. *L'Anonyme de Pérouse: Un témoin de la fraternité franciscaine primitive confronté aux autres sources contemporaines.* Paris: Éditions Franciscaines, 1979.

Benedetto (1941), Luigi Foscolo. *Il Cantico di Frate Sole.* Biblioteca Sansoniana Critica 2. Florence: Sansoni, 1941.

Bertoli (1993), Marco. "*Novitas Clariana:* Chiara, testimone di Francesco." In *Chiara di Assisi,* 157–85. Atti del XX Convegno Internazionale, Assisi, 15–17 ottobre 1992. Spoleto: Centro Italiano di Studi sull'Alto Medioevo, 1993.

Bertoli (2002), Marco. *Claire d'Assise.* Paris: Cerf, 2002.

Bigaroni (1992), Marco. "*Compilatio Assisiensis*" dagli scritti di fr. Leone e compagni su s. Francesco d'Assisi dal Ms. 1046 di Perugia, edited by Marino Bagarini. Assisi: Biblioteca Francescana Chiesa Nuova, 1992.

Bihl (1919), Michael. "De Nomine S. Francisci." *Archivum Franciscanum Historicum* 19 (1919): 469–529.

Bihl (1928), Michael. "De Canonizatione S. Francisci." *Archivum Franciscanum Historicum* 21 (1928): 468–514.

Bihl (1929), Michael. "Sancti Francisci Paradola in Sermonibus Odonis de Ceritonia an. 1219 Conscriptis." *Archivum Franciscanum Historicum* 22 (1929): 584–86.

Boccali (1977), G. "Parole di esortazione alle 'Poverelle' di San Damiano." *Forma Sororum* 14 (1977): 54–70.

Boccali (1978), G. "Canto di esoratzione di san Francesco per le 'poverelle' di San Damiano." *Collectanea Franciscana* 48 (1978): 5–29.

Bracaloni (1914), Leone. "Assisi medioevale: Studio storico-topografico." *Archivum Franciscanum Historicum* 7 (1914): 3–19.

Bracaloni (1932), Leone. "Casa, casato e stemma di s. Francsco." *Collectanea Francescana* 2 (1932): 520–34; 3 (1933): 81–101.

Bracaloni (1943), Leone. *La chiesa nuovo di s. Francesco converso: Casa paterna del santo in Assisi.* Todi: Tuderte, 1943.

Brooke (1959), Rosalind B. *Early Franciscan Government.* Cambridge Studies in Medieval Life and Thought, New Series, 7. Cambridge: Cambridge University Press, 1959.

Brooke (1970), Rosalind B. *Scripta Leonis, Rufini, et Angeli, Sociorum Sancti Francisci* (Oxford: Oxford University Press, 1970).

Brooke (2006), Rosalind B. *The Image of St. Francis: Responses to Sainthood in the Thirteenth Century.* Cambridge: Cambridge University Press, 2006.

Brown (1965), Raphael. "Appendices I–VII." In Omer Englebert, *Saint Francis of Assisi: A Biography,* 356–433. Translated by Eve Marie Cooper. 2nd ed., rev. Ignatius Brady and Raphael Brown. Chicago: Franciscan Herald, 1965.

Brown (1981), Raphael. *The Roots of St. Francis: A Popular History of the Church in Assisi and Umbria before St. Francis as Related to His Life and Spirituality.* Chicago: Franciscan Herald Press, 1981.

Bullarium Franciscanum 1: Ab Honorio III. ad Innocentium IV. 1759. Reprint, Assisi: Porziuncola, 1983.

Burr (2003), David. *The Spiritual Franciscans: From Protest to Persecution in the Century after Saint Francis.* University Park, PA: Penn State University Press, 2003.

Callebaut (1926), André. "Autour de la rencontre à Florence de s. François et du cardinal Hugolin (en été 1217)." *Archivum Franciscanum Historicum* 19 (1926): 530–58.

Campbell (1967), Jacques. *I fiori dei tre compagni: Testi francescani latini ordinati con introduzione e note.* Milan: Vita e Pensiero, 1967.

Canonici (1980), L. "Guido II d'Assisi: Il vescovo di san Francesco." *Studi Francescani* 77 (1980): 187–206.

Capitani (1991), Ovidio. "Verso una nuova antropologia e una nuova religiosità." *La conversione alla povertà nell'Italia dei secoli XII-XIV (Todi, 14–17 ottobre 1990).* Todi: Academia Tudertina, 1991.

Capitani (1993), Ovidio. "Dalla *Fraternitas* all'ordine: Impressioni di lettura di un non-francescanista." In *Gli studi francescani dal dopoguerra ad oggi,* edited by Francesco Santi, 113–42. Atti del Convegno di Studio, Firenze 5–7 novembre 1990. Spoleto: Centro Italiano di Studi sull'Alto Medioevo, 1993.

Cardini (1974), Franco. "Nella presenza del Soldan superba: Bernardo, Francesco, Bonventura e il superamento dell'idea di crociata." *Studi Francescani* 71 (1974): 199–250.

Cardini (1976), Franco. "L'avventura di un cavaliere di Cristo: Appunti per uno studio sulla cavaleria nella spiritualità di s. Francesco." *Studi Francescani* 73 (1976): 127–298.

Cardini (1980), Franco. "San Francesco e il sogno delle armi." *Studi Francescani* 77 (1980): 15–28.

Cardini (1981), Franco. "Francesco d'Assisi e gli animali." *Studi Francescani* 78 (1981): 7–45.

Cardini (1983a), Franco. "Aspetti ludici, scenici e spettacolari della predicazione francescana." *Storia della Città* 26–27 (1983): 53–64.

Cardini (1983b), Franco. "Francesco e il fuoco: Dalla 'Creatura Ignis' al serafino fiammeggiante." *Studi Francescani* 80 (1983): 297–308.

Cavallin (1954), Sam. "La Question Franciscaine comme problème philologique." *Eranos* 52 (1954): 239–70.

Chiara (1998). *Chiara e la diffusione delle clarisse nel secolo XIII,* edited by Giancarlo Andenna and Benedetto Vetere. Atti del Convegno di Studi in Occasione dell'8. Centenario della Nascita di Santa Chiara, Manduria, 14–15 dicembre 1994. Galatina: Congedo, 1998.

Clasen (1952), Sophronius. "Franziskus von Assisi und die soziale Frage." *Wissenschaft und Weisheit* 15 (1952): 109–21.

Clasen (1966), Sophronius. "Von Franziskus der Legende zum Franziskus der Geschichte." *Wissenschaft und Weisheit* 29 (1966): 15–29.

Clasen (1967), Sophronius. *Legenda Antiqua S. Francisci: Untersuchung über die nachbonaventurianischen Franziskusquellen, Legenda Trium Sociorum, Speculum Perfectionis, Actus B. Francisci et Sociorum Eius und verwandtes Schriftum.* Leiden: Brill, 1967.

Clop (1926), Eusèbe. "Saint François et la liturgie de la chapelle papale." *Archivum Franciscanum Historicum* 19 (1926): 753–802.

Conti (1978), Martino. "Sinai—Fonte Colombo: Il peso di un'analogia nell'interpretazione della regula francescana." *Antonianum* 53 (1978): 23–55.

Courcelle (1953), P. "L'Enfant et les 'sorts bibliques.'" *Vigiliae Christianae* 7 (1953): 194–220.

Cracco (1982), Giorgio. "Francesco e i laici: Il desiderio di Dio nella 'Civitas' medievale." In *Francesco d'Assisi nell'ottavo centenario della nascita,* edited by G. Lazzati, 104–26. Milan: Vita e Pensiero, 1982.

Cresi (1954), Domenico. "Cronologia di s. Chiara." *Studi Francescani* 50 (1953): 260–67.

D'Acunto (1996), Nicolangelo. "Il vescovo Guido oppure i vescovi Guido? Cronotassi episcopale assisanna e fonti francescane." *Moyen Age* 108 (1996): 479–524.

Dalarun (1988), Jacques. "La dernière volonté de saint François: Hommage à Raoul Manselli." *Bullettino dell'Istituto Storico Italiano per il Medio Evo e Archivio Muratoriano* 94 (1988): 329–66.

Dalarun (1996), Jacques. *The Misadventure of Francis of Assisi: Toward a Historical Use of the Franciscan Legends.* Trans. Edward Hagman. St. Bonaventure, NY: Franciscan Institute, 2002. Translation of *La malavventura di Francesco: Per uno storico dell leggende fracescane.* Milan: Editione Francescana, 1996.

Dalarun (1997), Jacques. *Francis of Assisi and the Feminine.* Trans. Edward Hagman. St. Bonaventure, NY: Franciscan Institute, 2006. Translation of *François d'Assise: Un passage, femmes et féminité dans les écrits et les légendes franciscaines.* Arles: Actes Sud, 1997.

Dalarun (2007), Jacques. "*Sicut Mater:* Une relecture du billet de François d'Assise à frère Léon." *Le Moyen Âge* 113 (2007): 639–68.

De Beer (1963), François. *La conversion de saint François d'Assise selon Thomas de Celano: Étude comparative des textes relatifs à la conversion en Vita I et Vita II.* Paris: Éditions Franciscaines, 1963.

De Beer (1977), François. *We Saw Brother Francis.* Trans. Maggi Despot and Paul Lachance. Chicago: Franciscan Herald, 1983. Translation of *François, que disait-on de toi?* Paris: Éditions Franciscaines, 1977.

Delaruelle (1971), Étienne. "Saint François d'Assise et la piété populaire." In *San Francesco nella ricerca storica degli ultima ottanta anni,* 125–55. Todi: Accademia Tubertina, 1971.

Delaruelle (1975), Étienne. *La piété populaire au Moyen Âge.* Turin: Bottega d'Erasmo, 1975.

Delcorno (1977), Carlo. "Origini della predicazione francescana." In *Francesco d'Assisi e Francescanesimo dal 1216 al 1226,* 125–60. Atti del IV Convegno Internazionale, Assisi, 16–17 ottobre 1976. Assisi: Società Internazionale di Studi Francescani, 1977.

Desbonnets (1967), Théophile. "Recherches sur la généalogie des biographies primitives de Saint François." *Archivum Franciscanum Historicum* 60 (1967): 273–316.

Desbonnets (1972), Théophile. "La légende des trois compagnons: Nouvelles recherches sur la généalogie des biographies primitives de saint François." *Archivum Franciscanum Historicum* 65 (1972): 66–106.

Desbonnets (1974), Théophile. "Legenda Trium Sociorum: Édition critique." *Archivum Franciscanum Historicum* 67 (1974): 38–144.

Desbonnets (1983), Théophile. *From Intuition to Institution: The Franciscans.* Trans. Paul Duggan and Jerry DuCharme. Chicago: Franciscan Herald, 1988. Translation of *De l'intuition à l'institution: Les Franciscains.* Paris: Éditions Franciscaines, 1983.

Desbonnets (1999), Théophile. "Application de la statistique à l'étude des sources franciscaines." In *Bonaventuriana: Miscellanea in onore di Jacques Guy Bougerol ofm,* edited by Chavero Blanco, 577–95. Rome: Antonianum, 1988.

Di Ciaccia (1982a), Francesco. "Il 'Saluto alla Vergine' e la pietà mariana di Francesco d'Assisi." *Studi Francescani* 79 (1982): 55–64.

Di Ciaccia (1982b), Francesco. "S. Chiara 'domina' e Jacopa dei Settesoli 'fratello' di s. Francesco d'Assisi." *Studi Francescani* 79 (1982): 327–41.

Di Fonzo (1961), Lorenzo. "Elie d'Assisi." *Dictionnaire d'histoire et de géographie ecclésiastiques* 15:167–83.

Di Fonzo (1972), Lorenzo. *L'Anonimo perugino tra le fonti francescane del sec. XIII: Rapporti letterari e testo critico.* Rome: Miscellanea Francescana, 1972.

Di Fonzo (1982), Lorenzo. *Per la cronologia di S. Francesco gli anni 1182–1212.* Quaderni Francescani 1. Rome: Edizone Miscellanea Francescana, 1982.

Dolcini (1994), Carlo. "Francesco d'Assisi e la storiografia degli ultimi vent'anni: Problemi di metodo." In *Frate Francesco d'Assisi,* 5–35. Atti del XXI Convegno Internazionale, Assisi, 14–16 ottobre 1993. Spoleto: Centro Italiano di Studi sull'Alto Medioevo, 1994.

Douglas (1973), Mary. *Natural Symbols: Explorations in Cosmology.* New York: Vintage, 1973.

Elm (1977), Karl. "Die Entwicklung des Franziskanerordens zwischen dem ersten und letzten Zeugnis des Jakob von Vitry." In *Francesco d'Assisi e Francescanesimo dal 1216 al 1226,* 195–233. Atti del IV Convegno Internazionale, Assisi, 16–17 ottobre 1976. Assisi: Società Internazionale di Studi Franciscani, 1977.

Englebert (1965), Omer. *Saint Francis of Assisi: A Biography.* Trans. Eve Marie Cooper. 2nd ed., rev. Ignatius Brady and Raphael Brown. Chicago: Franciscan Herald, 1965.

Esser (1952), Kajetan. "Bindung zur Freiheit: Die Gehorsamauffassung des hl. Franziskus von Assisi." *Wissenschaft und Weisheit* 15 (1952): 161–73.

Esser (1960), Kajetan. "Missarum Sacramenta: Die Eucharistielehre des hl. Franziskus von Assisi." *Wissenschaft und Weisheit* 23 (1960): 81–108.

Esser (1961), Kajetan. "Sancta Mater Ecclesia Romana: Die Kirchen Frömmigkeit des hl. Franziskus von Assisi." In *Sentire Ecclesiam: Das Bewusstsein von der Kirche als gestaltende Kraft der Frömmigkeit,* edited by J. Danielou and H. Vorgimler, 218–50. Freiburg: Herder, 1961.

Esser (1965), Kajetan. *Die endgültige Regel der Minderen Brüder im Licht der neueren Forschung.* Werl/Westfallen: Dietrich-Coelde-Verlag, 1965. Translation: *The Definitive Rule of the Friars Minor in the Light of the Latest Research.* Trans. Bruce Malina. Werl/Westfallen: Dietrich-Coelde-Verlag, 1965.

Esser (1966), Kajetan. *Origins of the Franciscan Order.* Chicago: Franciscan Herald, 1970. Translation of *Anfänge und ursprüngliche Zielsetzungen des Ordens der Minderbrüder.* Leiden: Brill, 1966.

Esser (1974), Kajetan. *Textkritische Unterschungen zur Regula non Bullata der Minderbrüder.* Spicilegium Bonaventurianum 9. Grottaferrata: Collegium S. Bonaventurae, 1974.

Esser (1978), Kajetan. *Il Testamento di san Francesco d'Assisi.* Trans. Alessandro Gerna and Luigi Padovese. Milan: Edizioni Francescane "Cammino," 1978. Translation: *Das Testament des heiligen Franziskus von Assisi: Eine Untersuchung über seine Echtheit und seine Bedeutung.* Vorreforatinsgeschichtliche Forschungen 15. Munster: Aschendorffsche Verlagsbuchhandlung, 1949. Translation of chapters 5, 6, and the conclusion: *The Testament of St. Francis: A Commentary.* Trans. Madge Karecki. Pulaski, WI: Franciscan Publishers, 1982.

Esser-Oliger (1974). Esser, Kajetan, and Rémy Oliger. *La tradition manuscrite des opuscules du Saint François d'Assisi: Préliminaires de l'édition critique.* Rome: Institut historique O.F.M.Cap., 1974.

Flood (1967), David E. *Die Regula non Bullata der Minderbrüder.* Franziskanische Forschungen 19. Werl: N.p., 1967.

Flood (1977a), David E. Review of *Textkritische,* by Kajetan Esser. *Archivum Franciscanum Historicum* 70 (1977): 163–68.

Flood (1977b), David E. "The Grundmann Approach to Early Franciscan History." *Franziskanische Studien* 59 (1977): 311–19.

Flood (1983), David E. *Francis of Assisi and the Franciscan Movement.* Quezon City: Franciscan Institute of Asia, 1983.

Flood-Matura (1975). Flood, David E., and Thadée Matura. *Birth of a Movement: A Study of the First Rule of St. Francis.* Trans. Paul Schwartz and Paul Lachance. Chicago: Franciscan Herald, 1975.

Fonti (1977). *Fonti francescane.* Biblioteca Francescana di Milano. Assisi: Movimento francescano, 1977.

Fortini (1959), Arnoldo. *Nuova Vita di san Francesco.* 4 vols. in 5. Assisi: Porziuncula, 1959. Translation: *Francis of Assisi.* Abridged and trans. Helen Moak. New York: Crossroad, 1981.

Francesco (1982). *Francesco d'Assisi: Documenti e archivi, codici e biblioteche, miniature.* Milan: Electa, 1982.

"Francesco storico" (1993). Il 'Francesco storico": Discussione sulla relazione di Ovidio Capitani." In *Gli studi francescani dal dopoguerra ad oggi,* edited by F. Santi, 362–69. Atti del Convegno di Studio, Firenze 5–7 novembre 1990. Spoleto: Centro Italiano di Studi sull'Alto Medioevo, 1993.

Frate Francesco (1994). *Frate Francesco d'Assisi.* Atti del XXI Convegno Internazionale, Assisi, 14–16 ottobre 1993. Spoleto: Centro Italiano di Studi sull'Alto Medioevo, 1994.

Freeman (1988), Gerard Pieter. "'Usquequo Gravi Corde? Zur Deutung der 1. Ermahnung des Franziskus." *Laurentianum* 29 (1988): 386–415.

Friend (1948), Albert. "Master Odo of Cheriton." *Speculum* 23 (1948): 641–58.

Frugoni (1984), Chiara. "La giovanezza di Francesco nelle fonti (testi e immagine). *Studi Medievali* 3:25 (1984): 115–43.

Frugoni (1993), Chiara. *Francesco e l'invenzione delle stimmate: Una storia per immagine fina Bonaventura e Giotto.* Turin: Einaudi, 1993.

Frugoni (1998), Chiara. *Francis of Assisi: A Life.* New York: Continuum, 1998.

Gallant (1978), Laurent. "*Dominus Regnavit a Ligno:* L'Office de la Passion de saint François d'Assisi; Édition critique et étude." 3 vols. Ph.D. dissertation, Institut Catholique de Paris, U.E.R. de Théologie et Sciences religieuses du Troisième cycle, 1978.

Gattucci (1979), Adriano. "Dalla 'Legenda Antiqua s. Francisci' alla 'Compilatio Assisiensis': Storia di un testo più prezioso che fortunato." *Studi Medievali* 20 (1979): 789–870.

Ghinato (1964), Alberto. "S. Franciscus in Oriente Missionarius ac Peregrinus." *Acta Ordinis Fratrum Minorum vel ad Ordinem Quoquomodo Pertinentia* 83 (1964): 164–81.

Ghinato (1973), Alberto. *Una regola in camino: Il dinamismo della Regola nella evoluzione storica dei Frati Minori.* 3rd ed. Rome: L.I.E.F., 1973.

Gilson (1940), Étienne. *The Philosophy of St. Bonaventure.* Trans. Illtyd Trethowan and F. J. Sheed. London: Sheed and Ward, 1940.

Golubovich (1906), Girolamo. *Biblioteca bio-bibliografica della Terra Santa e dell'Oriente Francescano.* Quaracchi: Collegio di S. Bonaventura, 1906.

Golubovich (1926), Girolamo. "San Francesco e i Francescani in Dalmiata (5 nov. 1219–2 febb. 1220)." *Studi Francescani* 3–4 (1926): 307–30.

Grau (1953), Engelbert. "Die Regel der hl. Klara in ihrer Abhängigkeit von der Regel der Minderbrüder." *Franziskanische Studien* 35 (1953): 211–74.

Grau (1970), Engelbert. "Zur Authentizität der ersten Admonitio des heiligen Franziskus." *Franzikanische Studien* 52 (1970): 120–36.

Grundmann (1995), Herbert. *Religious Movements in the Middle Ages: The Historical Links between Heresy, the Mendicant Orders, and the Women's Religious Movement in the Twelfth and Thirteenth Century, with the Historical Foundations of German Mysticism.* Notre Dame: University of Notre Dame Press, 1995.

Hardick (1962), Lothar. "Zur Chronologie im Leben der hl. Klara." *Franziskanische Studien* 35 (1953): 174–210.

Hyde (1973), John Kenneth. *Society and Politics in Medieval Italy: The Evolution of the Civil Life, 1000–1350.* New York: St. Martin's Press, 1973.

Jørgensen (1907), Johannes. *St. Francis of Assisi: A Biography.* Trans. T. O'Conor Sloane. London: Longmans, Green, 1912. Translation of *Den hellige Frans af Assisi: En Levnedsskildring.* Køb: Gyldendal, 1907.

Kadar (1984), Benjamin. *Crusade and Mission: European Approaches towards the Muslims.* Princeton, NJ: Princeton University Press, 1984.

Koper (1959), R. *Das Weltverständnis des hl. Franziskus von Assisi: Eine Untersuchung über das "Exivi de Saeculo".* Franziskanische Forschungen 14. Werl: N.p., 1959.

Lainati (1984), Chiara Augusta. "Testamento." In *Dizionario Francescano,* 1827–46. Padua: Edizioni Messaggero, 1984.

Lambert (1998), Malcolm. *Franciscan Poverty: The Doctrine of the Absolute Poverty of Christ in the Franciscan Order, 1210–1323.* Rev. ed. St. Bonaventure, NY: Franciscan Institute, 1998.

Lambertini-Tabarroni (1989). Lambertini, Roberto, and Andrea Tabarroni. *Dopo Francesco: L'eredità difficile.* Altri Saggi 12. Turin: Gruppo Abele, 1989.

Landini (1968), Lawrence C. *The Causes of the Clericalization of the Order of Friars Minor: 1209–1260 in the Light of Early Franciscan Sources.* Chicago: Pontificia Universitas Gregoriana, 1968.

Langeli (1977), Attilio Bartoli. "Francesco d'Assisi e ricerca storica: Un discorso aperto." *Laurentianum* 18 (1977): 338–60.

Langeli (1978), Attilio Bartoli. "La realtà sociale assisiana e il patto del 1210." In *Assisi al tempo di san Francesco,* 272–336. Atti del V Convegno della Società Internazionale di Studi Francescani, Assisi, 1977. Assisi: Università degli Studi, 1978.

Langeli (1982), Attilio Bartoli. *S. Francesco d'Assisi: Documenti e archivi—Codici e biblioteche—Miniature.* Milan: Electa, 1982.

Langeli (1984), Attilio Bartoli. "Le radici culturali della 'popolarità' francescana." In *Il Francescanesimo e il teatro medievale,* 41–58. Atti del Convegno Nazionale di Studi (San Miniato, 8–10 ottobre 1982). Castelfiorentino: Società Storica della Valdelsa, 1984.

Langeli (1994), Attilio Bartoli. "Gli scritti di Francesco: L'autografia di un *illiteratus.*" In *Frate Francesco d'Assisi,* 101–59. Atti del XXI Convegno Internazionale, Assisi, 14–16 ottobre 1993. Spoleto: Centro Italiano di Studi sull'Alto Medioevo, 1994.

Lapsanski (1974), D. V. "The Autographs on the 'Cartula' of St. Francis of Assisi." *Archivum Franciscanum Historicum* 67 (1974): 18–33.

Lazzeri (1913), Zepherinus. "L'atto di conferma della donazione della Verna." *La Verna* 11 (1913): 101–5.

Lazzeri (1920), Zepherinus. "Il processo di canonizzazione di s. Chiara d'Asssi." *Archivum Franciscanum Historicum* 13 (1920): 403–507.

Leclerc (1977), Éloi. *The Canticle of Creatures: Symbols of Union; An Analysis of St. Francis of Assisi.* Trans. Matthew J. O'Connell. Chicago: Franciscan Herald Press, 1977. Translation of *Le Cantique des créatures ou les symboles de l'union: Une analyse de saint François d'Assise.* Paris: Fayard, 1970.

Le Goff (2000), Jacques. *San Francesco d'Assisi.* Rome: Laterza, 2000.

Lemmens (1926), Leonard. "De Sancto Francisco Christum Praedicante coram Sultano Aegypti." *Archivum Franciscanum Historicum* 19 (1926): 559–78.

Manselli (1965), Raoul. "Rassegna di storia francescana." *Rivista di Storia e Letteratura Religiosa* 1 (1965): 123–37.

Manselli (1967), Raoul. "L'ultima decisione di s. Francesco: Bernardo di Quintavalle e la benedizione di s. Francesco morente." *Bullettino dell'Istituto Storico Italiano per il Medioevo e Archivio Muratoriano* 78 (1967): 137–53.

Manselli (1969), Raoul. "San Francesco d'Assisi: Orientamenti della ricerca storica." In *Francesco e i suoi compagni,* 21–34. Biblioteca Seraphico-Capuccina 46. Rome: Isituto Storico dei Cappuccini, 1995. Originally published in *Frate Francesco* 36 (1969): 19–24, 160–69.

Manselli (1971), Raoul. "Bernardo di Quintavalle." *Dizionario biografico degli Italiani.* (Sub voce.) Rome: Encyclopedia Italiana, 1971.

Manselli (1975), Raoul. "La povertà nella vita di Francesco d'Assisi." In *La povertà del secolo XII e Francesco d'Assisi,* 255–82. Atti del II Convegno Internazionale, Assisi, 17–19 ottobre 1974. Assisi: Società Internazionale di Studi Francescani, 1975.

Manselli (1976), Raoul. "From the Testament to the Testaments of St. Francis." *Greyfriars Review* 2 (1988): 91–99. Translation of "Dal Testamento ai testamenti di san Francesco." *Collectanea Franciscana* 46 (1976): 121–29.

Manselli (1980), Raoul. *We Who Were with Him: A Contribution to the Franciscan Question.* St. Bonaventure, NY: Greyfriars Review; Franciscan Institute, 2000. Translation of *Nos Qui cum Eo Fuimus: Contributo alla Questione francescana.* Rome: Bibliotheca Seraphico-Capuccina, 1980.

Manselli (1982), Raoul. *St. Francis of Assisi.* Trans. Paul Duggan. Chicago: Franciscan Herald, 1988. Translation of *San Francesco d'Assisi.* 3rd ed. Rome: Biblioteca di Cultura, 1982.

Manselli (1983), Raoul. "Un giorno sulla Verna: San Francesco e frate Leone." *Frate Francesco* 50 (1983): 161–71.

Manselli (1995), Raoul. *Francesco e i suoi compagni.* Bibliotheca Seraphico-Capuccina 46. Rome: Istituto Storico dei Cappuccini, 1995.

Maranesi (2007), Pietro. *Facere Misericordiam: La conversione di Francesco d'Assisi: Confronto critico tra il Testamento e le biografie.* Assisi: Porziuncula, 2007.

Marini (1989), Alfonso. *Sorores Alaudae: Francesco d'Assisi, il creato, gli animali.* Assisi: Edizioni Porziuncola, 1989.

Matanic (1976), Atanasio. "Del viaggio di san Francesco in Oriente." *Studi e Ricerche Francescane* 5 (1976): 243–58.

Matanic (1981), Atanasio. Review of *Nos Qui cum Eo Fuimus,* by Raoul Manselli. *Antonianum* 58 (1981): 496–98.

Matura (1982), Thaddée. " 'Mi Pater Sancte': Dieu comme Père dans les écrits de François." *Laurentianum* 23 (1982): 102–32.

Meersseman (1965), Giles-Gérard. "Eremitismo e predicazione itinerante dei secoli XI e XII." In *L'eremitismo in occidente nei secoli XI e XII,* 164–79. Atti della Seconda Settimana Internazionale di Studio, Mendola, 30 agosto–6 settembre 1962. Milan: Vita e Pensiero, 1965.

Mencherini (1924), Gaudenzio. *Codice diplomatico della Verna e delle ss. stimate di s. Francesco di'Assisi nel VII centenario del gran prodigo.* Documenti Francescani 3. Florence: Gualandi, 1924.

Menestò (1993), Enrico. "Per un'edizione critica delle biografie e leggende francescane." In *Gli studi francescani dal dopoguerra ad oggi,* edited by Francesco Santi, 246–68. Atti del Convegno di Studio, Firenze 5–7 novembre 1990. Spoleto: Centro Italiano di Studi sull'Alto Medioevo, 1993.

Merlo (1991a), Grado G. "A proposito di G. Miccoli." In *Francesco d'Assisi: Realtà e memoria di un'esperienza cristiana,* 39–97. Turin: Einaudi, 1991.

Merlo (1991b), Grado G. "Tensioni religiose agli inizi del Duecento." In *Tra eremo e città: Studi su Francesco d'Assisi e sul Francescanesimo,* 33–92. Assisi: Edizioni Porziuncola, 1991.

Merlo (1992), Grado G. "Su e oltre frate Francesco." *Nuova Rivista Storica* 76 (1992): 531–52.

Merlo (1993a), Grado G. *Intorno a frate Francesco: Quattro studi.* Milan: Biblioteca Francescana, 1993.

Merlo (1993b), Grado G. "La storiografia francescana dal dopoguerra ad oggi." In *Gli studi francescani dal dopoguerra ad oggi,* edited by F. Santi, 3–32. Atti del Convegno di Studio, Firenze 5–7 novembre 1990. Spoleto: Centro Italiano di Studi sull'Alto Medioevo, 1993.

Miccoli (1964), Giovanni. "La 'conversione' di san Francesco secondo Tommaso da Celano." *Studi Medievali* 3:5 (1964): 775–92.

Miccoli (1974), Giovanni. "La storia religiosa." In *Storia d'Italia 2.1: Dalla caduta dell'impero romano al secolo XVIII*, edited by R. Romano and C. Vivanti, 431–1079. Turin: G. Einaudi, 1974.

Miccoli (1985), Giovanni. Review of *De l'Intuition à l'institution*, by Th. Desbonnets. *Cristianesimo nella Storia* 6 (1985): 628.

Miccoli (1991), Giovanni. *Francesco d'Assisi: Realtà e memoria di un'esperienza cristiana.* Turin: Einaudi, 1991.

Miccoli (1996), Giovanni. *Le Testament de saint François.* Paris: Brepols, 1996.

Miccoli (2000), Giovanni. "Francesco e La Verna." *Studi Francescani* 97 (2000): 225–59.

Mockler (1980), Anthony. "Pietro Bernardone: An Unorthodox Character." In *The Francis Book*, edited by Roy M. Gasnick, 39–31. New York: Collier Books, 1980.

Mollat (1967), M. "Le problème de la pauverté au XIIe siècle." In *Vaudois languedociens et pauvres catholiques*, 23–47. Toulouse: Cahiers de Fanjeaux, 1967.

Moorman (1976), John. *St. Francis of Assisi.* New ed. London: S.P.C.K., 1976.

Morgan (1973), Margaret R. *The Chronicle of Ernoul and the Continuation of William of Tyre.* London: Oxford University Press, 1973.

Moses (2009), Paul. *The Saint and the Sultan: The Crusades, Islam, and Francis of Assisi's Mission of Peace.* New York: Doubleday, 2009.

Muscat (2005), Noel. "The Birthplace of St. Francis." In *The Franciscan Experience: Living the Gospel through the Centuries.* Created 2005. http://198.62.75.1/www1/ofm/fra/FRAsan02.html.

National Center for PTSD (2010). National Center for Post-Traumatic Stress Disorder. *Fact Sheet: What Is PTSD?* Created 2010. http://www.ptsd.va.gov/public/pages/what-is-ptsd.asp.

Newman (1985), Matthias. "The Holiness of Saint Francis: Spiritual Vision and Lived Suffering." *Review for Religious* 44 (1985): 679–90.

Nguyên-Van-Khanh (1989), N. *The Teacher of His Heart: Jesus Christ in the Thought and Writings of Saint Francis.* St. Bonaventure, NY: Franciscan Institute, 1994. Translation of *Le Christ dans la pensée de saint François d'Assise d'après ses écrits.* Paris: Éditions Franciscaines, 1989.

Oliger (1912), Livarius. "De Origine Regularum Ordinis Sanctae Clarae." *Archivum Franciscanum Historicum* 5 (1912): 181–209, 413–47, 644–54.

Paciocco (1986), Roberto. "La proposta cristiana di Francesco d'Assisi e la Chiesa." *Rivista di Storia della Chiesa in Italia* 40 (1986): 138–40.

Paciocco (1996), Roberto. *Sublimia Negotia: La canonizzazione dei santi nella curia papale e il nuovo Ordine dei frati Minori.* Centro Studi Antoniani 22. Padua: Centro Studi Antoniani, 1996.

Padovese (1992), L. "La 'tonsura' di Chiara: Gesto di consecrazione o segno di penitenza?" In *Chiara: Francescanesimo al femminile*, 393–406. Rome: Dhoniane, 1992.

Paolazzi (1992), Carlo. *Il Cantico di Frate Sole.* Genoa: Marietti, 1992.

Pásztor (1973), Edith. "Gli scritti leonini." In *La "Questione francescana" dal Sabatier ad oggi*, 201–12. Atti del I Convegno Internazionale, Assisi, 18–20 ottobre 1973. Assisi: Società Internazionale di Studi Francescani, 1974.

Pásztor (1976), Edith. "San Francesco e il cardinale Ugolino nella 'Questione francescana.'" *Collectanea Franciscana* 46 (1976): 206–39.

Pásztor (1985), Edith. "Tommaso da Celano e la Vita Prima: Problemi chiusi, problemi aperti." In *Tommaso da Celano e la sua opera di biografo di s. Francesco*, 50–73. Celano: Presso il Comitato del Centenario, 1985.

Pazzelli (1989), Raffaele. "Le somiglianze di idee e di fraseologia tra la 'Lettera ai fedeli' e la 'Regola non Bollata' come ipotesi di datazione." *Analecta Tertii Ordinis Regularis Sancti Francisci* 21 (1989): 213–34.

Pazzelli (1990), Raffaele. "The Title of the 'Recensio Prior of the Letter to the Faithful': Clarifications reguarding Codex 225 of Volterra (cod. Vo)." Trans. Nancy Celaschi. *Greyfriars Review* 4:3 (1990): 1–6.

Pellegrini (1976), Luigi. "L'esperienza eremitica di Francesco e dei primi franescani." In *Francesco d'Assisi e Francescanesimo dal 1216 al 1226*, 281–313. Atti del IV Convegno Internazionale, Assisi, 16–17 ottobre 1976. Assisi: Società Internazionale di Studi Franciscani, 1977.

Pellegrini (1977), Luigi. "Considerazioni metologiche per una analisi delle fonti francescani." *Laurentianum* 3 (1977): 292–313.

Pellegrini (1982a), Luigi. "Francesco e i suoi scritti: Problemi e orientamenti di lettura in alcuni recenti studi." *Rivista di Storia della Chiesa in Italia* 36 (1982): 311–31.

Pellegrini (1982b), Luigi. "Studi recenti sulle fonti biografiche di Francesco d'Assisi." *Quaderni Medievali* 14 (1982): 236–51.

Pellegrini (1988), Luigi. "A Century of Reading the Sources for the Life of Francis of Assisi." Trans. Edward Hagman. *Greyfriars Review* 7:3 (1993): 323–46. Translation of "Un secolo di 'lettura delle fonti' biografiche di Francesco d'Assisi." *Laurentianum* 29 (1988): 223–50.

Pellegrini (1994), Luigi. "La prima *Fraternitas* francescana: Una rilettura delle fonti." In *Frate Francesco d'Assisi*, 37–70. Atti del XXI Convegno Internazionale, Assisi, 14–16 ottobre 1993. Spoleto: Centro Italiano di Studi sull'Alto Medioevo, 1994.

Povertà (1969). *Povertà e ricchezza nella spiritualita dei secoli XI e XII*. Convegni del Centro di Studi sulla Spiritualità Medievale 8. Todi: Accademia Tudertina, 1969.

Povertà (1975). *La povertà del secolo XII e Francesco d'Assisi*. Atti del II Convegno Internazionale, Assisi, 17–19 ottobre 1974. Assisi: Società Internazionale di Studi Francescani, 1975.

Powell (1983), James. "Francesco d'Assisi a la Quinta Crociata: Una missione di pace." *Schede Medievali* 4 (1983): 68–77.

Powell (1986), James. *Anatomy of a Crusade, 1213–1221*. Philadelphia: University of Pennsylvania Press, 1986.

Pratesi (1984), A. "Autografo di san Francesco nel Duomo di Spoleto." In *San Francesco e i Francescani a Spoleto*, 17–26. Spoleto: Accademia Spoletina, 1984.

Questione francescana (1974). *La "Questione francescana" dal Sabatier ad oggi*. Atti del I Convegno Internazionale, Assisi, 18–20 ottobre 1973. Assisi: Società Internazionale di Studi Francescani, 1974.

Robinson (1910), P. "The Writings of St. Clare of Assisi." *Archivum Franciscanum Historicum* 3 (1910): 442–47.

Robson (1999), Michael. *St. Francis of Assisi: The Legend and the Life*. London: Continuum, 1999.

Roggen (1965), H. *Die Lebensform des heiligen Franziskus von Assisi in ihrem Verhältnis zur feudalen und bürgerlichen Gesellschaft Italiens*. Mechelen: St-Franciskus-Uitgeverij, 1965.

Rohr (1981), Richard. "A Life Pure and Simple." *Sojourners* 10:12 (December 1981): 12–24.

Roncaglis (1953), Martiniano. "Fonte arabo-musulmana su san Francesco in Oriente." *Studi Francescani* 25 (1953): 258–59.

Rusconi (1982), Roberto. "Dal sepolcro di Francesco all'indulgenza della Porziuncula." In *Francesco d'Assisi: Storia e Arte*, 159–64. Milan: Electa, 1982.

Rusconi (1994), Roberto. "Clerici Secundum Alios Clericos: Francesco d'Assisi e l'istituzione ecclesiastica." In *Frate Francesco d'Assisi*, 71–100. Atti del XXI Convegno Internazionale, Assisi, 14–16 ottobre 1993. Spoleto: Centro Italiano di Studi sull'Alto Medioevo, 1994.

Sabatier (1894), Paul. *Vie de Saint François d'Assise*. Paris: Libraire Fischbacher, 1894.

San Francesco (1971). *San Francesco nella ricerca storica degli ultimi ottanta anni*. Convegni del Centro di Studi sulla Spiritualità Medievale, 13–16 ottobre 1968. Todi: Accademia Tudertina, 1971.

Schatzlein-Sulmasy (1987). Schatzlein, Joanne, and Daniel P. Sulmasy. "The Diagnosis of St. Francis: Evidence for Leprosy." *Franciscan Studies* 47 (1987): 181–217.

Schmitt (1977), Clément. "I vicari dell'Ordine francescano da Pietro Cattani a Frate Elia." In *Francesco d'Assisi e Francescanesimo dal 1216 al 1226*, 237–63. Atti del IV Convegno Internazionale. Assisi: Società Internazionale di Studi Francescani, 1977.

Schmucki (1976), Octavian. "San Francesco messaggero di pace nel suo tempo." *Studi e Ricerche Francescane* 5 (1976): 215–32.

Schmucki (1980), Octavian. "La Lettera a tutto l'Ordine di San Francesco." *L'Italia Francescana* 55 (1980): 245–86.

Schmucki (1981), Octavian. "Opera Intuitu VIII Centenarii Edita." Review of *Nos qui cum eo fuimus*, by R. Manselli. *Collectanea Franciscana* 51 (1981): 31–37.

Schmucki (1986), Octavian. "The Mysticism of St. Francis in the Light of His Writings." Trans. Ignatius McCormick. *Greyfriars Review* 3.3 (1989): 241–66. Translation of "Zur Mystik des hl. Franziskus von Assisi in Lichte seiner Schriften." In *Abendlandische Mystik im Mittelalter: Symposion Kloster Engelberg 1984*, edited by Kurt Ruh, 241–68. Stuttgart: Metzlersche, 1986.

Schmucki (1988), Octavian. "The Way of Life according to the Gospel as It Was Discovered by St. Francis of Assisi." *Greyfriars Review* 2:3 (1988): 1–56.

Schmucki (1991), Octavian. *The Stigmata of St. Francis of Assisi: A Critical Investigation in the Light of Thirteenth-Century Sources*. Trans. Canisius F. Connors. St. Bonaventure, NY: The Franciscan Institute, 1991. Translation of "De Sancti Francisci Assisiensis Stigmatum Susceptione: Disquisitio Historico-Critica Luce Testimoniorum Saeculi XIII." *Collectanea Franciscana* 33 (1963): 210–66, 392–422; 34 (1964): 5–62, 241–338.

Schmucki (1999), Octavian. "The Illnesses of Francis during the Last Years of His Life." *Greyfriars Review* 13 (1999): 42–46.

Scivoletto (1977), Nino. "Problemi di lingua e di stile degli scritti di san Francesco." In *Francesco d'Assisi e Francescanesimo dal 1216 al 1226*, 101–24. Atti del IV Convegno Internazionale, Assisi, 16–17 ottobre 1976. Assisi: Società Internazionale di Studi Francescani, 1977.

Selge (1969), Kurt-Victor. "Reichsgestalt und Idee der frühen Gemeinschaft des Franz von Assisi." In *Erneuerung der Einen Kirche: Arbeiten aus Kirchengeschichte und Konfessionskunde; Heinrich Bornkamm zum 65. Geburtstag gewidmit*, edited by J. Lell, 1–31. Göttingen: Vandenhoeck & Ruprecht, 1969.

Selge (1970), Kurt-Victor. "Franz von Assisi und die römische Kurie." *Zeitschrift für Theologie und Kirche* 67 (1970): 129–61.

Selge (1971), Kurt-Victor. "Franz von Assisi und Hugolino von Ostia." In *San Francesco nella ricerca storica degli ultimi ottanta anni*, 157–222. Todi: Accademia Tubertina, 1971.

Short (1988), William J. "Hagiographical Method in Reading Franciscan Sources: Stories of Francis and Creatures in Thomas of Celano's 'Vita Prima' (21:58–61)." *Laurentianum* 29 (1988): 462–95.

Sorell (1988), R. D. *St. Francis of Assisi and Nature: Tradition and Innovation in Western Christian Attitudes toward the Environment*. New York: Oxford University Press, 1988.

Stanislao da Compagnola (1973). *Le origini francescane come problema storiografico*. Perugia: Palazzo della Spienza, 1973.

Stanislao da Campagnola (1975). "La povertà nelle 'Regulae' di Francesco d'Assisi." In *La povertà del secolo XII e Francesco d'Assisi*, 217–53. Atti del II Convegno Internazionale, Assisi, 17–19 ottobre 1974. Assisi: Società Internazionale di Studi Francescani, 1975.

St. Francis of Assisi (1981). *Sojourners* 10:12 (December 1981): 12–24.

Studi francescani (1993). *Gli studi francescani dal dopoguerra ad oggi*, edited by Francesco Santi. Atti del Convegno di Studio, Firenze 5–7 novembre 1990. Spoleto: Centro Italiano di Studi sull'Alto Medioevo, 1993.

Tamassia (1909), Nino. *San Francesco d'Assisi e la sua leggenda*. Padua: Drucker, 1906.

"Tavola rotunda" (1975). "Tavola rotunda: La povertà del secolo XII e Francesco d'Assisi." In *La povertà del secolo XII e Francesco d'Assisi*, 283–306. Atti del II Convegno Internazionale, Assisi, 17–19 ottobre 1974. Assisi: Società Internazionale di Studi Francescani, 1975.

Terzi (1959), Arduino. *Il Poverello di Assisi nella valle reatina*. Rieti: Operaia Romana, 1959.

Thompson (1992), Augustine. *Revival Preachers and Politics in Thirteenth-Century Italy: The Great Devotion of 1233*. Oxford: Oxford University Press, 1992.

Thompson (2005), Augustine. *Cities of God: The Religion of the Italian Communes, 1125–1325*. University Park, PA: Penn State University Press, 2005.

Thompson (2011), Augustine. "The Origins of Religious Mendicancy in the Middle Ages." In *The Origin, Development, and Refinement of Medieval Religious Mendicancies,* edited by Donald Prudlo, 3–30. Leiden: Brill, 2011.

Thompson (1971), Williel. "Checklist of Papal Letters relating to the Three Orders of St. Francis: Innocent III—Alexander IV." *Archivum Franciscanum Historicum* 64 (1971): 367–580.

Tolan (2009), John V. *St. Francis and the Sultan: The Curious History of a Christian-Muslim Encounter.* Oxford: Oxford University Press, 2009.

Trexler (1989), Richard C. *Naked before the Father: The Renunciation of Francis of Assisi.* New York: Peter Lang, 1989.

Trichet (1990), Louis. *La tonsure.* Paris: Cerf, 1990.

Tugwell (2005), Simon. "The Evolution of Dominican Structures of Government: Terminology, Nomenclature, and *Ordo* of Dominican Provinces." *Archivum Fratrum Praedicatorum* 75 (2005): 29–94.

Unvergleichliche Heilige (1958). *Der unvergleichliche Heilige: Gedanken um Franzikus von Assisi,* edited by J. Lortz. Düsseldorf: Patmos-Verlag, 1952. Italian translation: *Un santo unico: Pensieri su Francesco d'Assisi.* Alba: Paoline, 1958.

Van Asseldonk (1979), Optatus. "La Regola 'pro Eremitoriis Data.'" *Studi e Ricerche Francescane* 8 (1979): 3–18.

Van Asseldonk (1992), Optatus. "Sorores Minores: Una nuovo impostazione del problema." *Collectanea Franciscana* 62 (1992): 595–634.

Van Corstanje (1964), Auspicius. *Une peuple de pélerins: Essai d'interprétation biblique duTestament de saint François.* Présence de Saint François 16. Paris: Éditions Franciscaines, 1964.

Van Dijk (1949), Stephen. "The Breviary of St. Francis." *Franciscan Studies* 9 (1949): 13–40.

Van Dijk (1954), Stephen. "Saint Francis' Blessing of Brother Leo." *Archivum Franciscanum Historicum* 47 (1954): 199–201.

Vauchez (1968), André. "The Stigmata of St. Francis and Its Medieval Detractors." *Greyfriars Review* 13 (1999): 61–89. Translation of "Les Stigmates de saint François et leurs détracteurs dans les derniers siècles du moyen âge." *Mélanges d'Archéologie et d'Histoire* 80 (1968): 595–625.

Vauchez (1994), André. "François d'Assise entre littéralisme évangélique et renouveâu spirituel." In *Frate Francesco d'Assisi,* 185–98. Atti del XXI Convegno Internazionale, Assisi, 14–16 ottobre 1993. Spoleto: Centro Italiano di Studi sull'Alto Medioevo, 1994.

Vauchez (2009), André. *François d'Assise: Entre histoire et mémoire.* Paris: Fayard, 2009.

Vicaire (1964), M.-H. *Saint Dominic and His Times.* New York: McGraw-Hill, 1964.

Von Rieden (1960), Oktavian. "Das Leiden Christi im Leben des hl. Franziskus von Assisi: Eine quellenvergleichende Untersuchung im Lichte der zeitgenössischen Passionsfrömmigkeit." *Collectanea Franciscana* 30 (1960): 129–45.

Voorvelt-Van Leeuan (1989). Gerhard C. P. Voorvelt and Bertulf P. van Leeuwen. "L'Évangéliare de Baltimore: Étude critique sur le missel que saint François aurait consulté." *Collectanea Franciscana* 59 (1989): 261–321.

Zerbi (1971), Pietro. "Discorso conclusivo." In *San Francesco nella ricerca storica degli ultimi ottanta anni,* 241–54. Todi: Accademia Tudertina, 1971.

Zerbi (1982), Pietro. "San Francesco d'Assisi e la Chiesa romana." In *Francesco d'Assisi nell'ottavo centenario della nascita,* edited by Stanislao da Compagnola, 75–103. Milan: Vita e Pensiero, 1982.

[INDEX]